*About the Author*

Catharina Day was born in 1957 in Kenya and moved to Ireland
at the age of three. She was educated at the predominantly
Protestant Londonderry High School and at St. Mary's Convent,
Ascot, then she studied History, English and Philosophy at
Exeter University.

She now lives in the Republic of Ireland.

Connie and Bob McClelland

May, 1992

# AROUND IRELAND

A Handbook for the Independent Traveller

## CATHARINA DAY

HIPPOCRENE BOOKS, INC.
171 Madison Avenue
New York, NY 10016

# Contents

## Part IV
## THE PROVINCE OF LEINSTER
**Republic of Ireland:**

## Part V
## THE PROVINCE OF MUNSTER
**Republic of Ireland:**

**Part VI**
**THE PROVINCE OF ULSTER**
**Republic of Ireland:**
**Northern Ireland:**

# LIST OF MAPS

All maps drawn by Clare Henshall

# PART I

# GENERAL

# INFORMATION

## Introduction

the layout of the book p.10    language p.11    the meaning of Irish place names and other expressions p.12    religion p.14

---

Ireland is a magical country. It is a land of water, whether in the form of a little ribbon of blue amongst the turflands or a huge lough studded with secret islands. The curling waves of the Atlantic and the Irish Sea surround it and the grey waters of the sea loughs curve round the browns and greens of the farms. Uncrowded roads wind their way past fairy raths, pre-historical graves, villages full of friendly bars, woods and bogs dancing with bog cotton and heather, and green gently rounded fields. It is a marvellous place for fishing, boating and swimming, or just walking along the river banks listening for birds and looking at all the wild flowers.

Ireland is famous for its rainfall, and the high level of water vapour in the air gives it a sleepy quality and softens the colours of the landscape; for the winds from the East increase the haziness and mute the colours, but these are nearly always followed by winds from the North-West which bring clearer air and sunshine. So the clouds begin to drift and shafts of changing light touch the land. Nearly every drizzly day has this gleam of sunshine which is why the Irish are always very optimistic about the weather.

Imagine for a moment that Ireland is shaped rather like a saucer, with mountains around the rim and flat land in the middle. Most of the coast line is dramatic; ancient rock cliffs alternate with sandy bays, whilst the large central plain of limestone is dotted with low hills called drumlins. Blanket bog has covered a good deal of the lowland so that the surface water has collected and been prevented from draining to the sea by the mountains. But where the surface rises above the water table the land is covered in a rich, light soil, which grows the grass that ultimately produces all that delicious Irish butter. The Gulf stream in the Atlantic means that there are never extremes of cold or hot.

The people you meet on your travels will mostly work either on the land or at some agricultural industry. Ireland has no industrial stretches like the Black Country of England. The Irish character has prompted endless comments, not least by the Irish themselves. If you are a tourist the first thing you notice is the friendliness and the chat which accompanies almost every encounter you have with the Irish people. If you rush through Ireland a lot of the Irish charm will pass you by, for you have to give time to everything. Conversations will be started as you are filling up your car with petrol or buying a pint of milk which can touch on every subject and you will probably end up with a lot of local knowledge that a guide book could never tell you. Asking the way is never cut and dried for with old-fashioned courtesy you will be given all possible routes to a place. One characteristic is that they hate to offend you or disappoint you to your face and say only what they think you want to hear. This can sometimes lead to very colourful stories, for the Irish have powerful imaginations and will supply any story where the historical guide is silent.

---

**THE LAYOUT OF THE BOOK:** Ireland can be most conveniently divided into **Ulster, Connacht, Leinster** and **Munster**. These are the ancient provinces of Ireland and each used to have its King who jostled and fought to increase their lands.

Ulster covers 26.3% of Ireland and consists of the Counties of Londonderry (Derry in the Republic), Antrim, Tyrone, Armagh, Fermanagh and Down, which are in N. Ireland, and Cavan, Donegal and Monaghan which are in the Republic.

Connacht covers 21% of Ireland and consists of the Counties of Sligo, Galway, Leitrim, Mayo and Roscommon.

Leinster covers 23.4% of Ireland and consists of the Counties of Louth, Dublin, Kildare, Carlow, Kilkenny, Leix, (formally Queen's County) Offaly (formally King's County), Meath, West Meath, Wicklow, Wexford, Longford.

Munster covers 29.3% of Ireland and consists of the Counties of Cork, Kerry, Clare, Limerick, Tipperary and Waterford.

The two major cities, Dublin and Belfast, are treated separately. Eating places are included under the town or place you will find them in. Accommodation is listed for each county at the end of the description, but you should check the introduction for general information.

## Introduction

The four modern provinces of Ireland correspond roughly to very ancient divisions of Ireland derived from the Fir Bolg invaders. They are used as general geographical indicators – thus Ulster for North, Munster for South, Connaught for West and Leinster for East. The provincial boundaries have administrative uses for matters such as the Irish Language, but more important is the 'cultural' character of the division, as one ancient authority has it: Ulster represents Battle (Cath); Munster, Music (Seis); Connaught, Learning (Fis); Leinster, Prosperity (Blath). Perhaps this is too much of a generalization but you may find it an interesting pastime to recognise the subtle characteristics that set off the different quarters of Ireland.

---

**LANGUAGE:** The Irish language is the purest of all the Celtic languages and Ireland is one of the last homes of the oral traditions of pre-historic and medieval Europe. Preserved by the isolated farming communities there are also many expressions from the dialects of early English settlers. Irish was spoken by the Norman earls and they patronised the Gaelic poets and bards. But with the establishment of an English system of land tenure and an English speaking nobility Gaelic became scarce, except in the poorer farming areas. The potato famine hit the people who lived in such areas, thousands died and emigrated and Gaelic speaking was severely reduced.

The Gaelic League, founded in 1870, initiated a new interest and pride in the language and it became identified with the rise of nationalism. In 1921, its survival became part of the new State's policy. It was decided that the only way to preserve it was to protect and stimulate it where it was still a living language. The areas where it is spoken are mostly in the West and around the mountainous coast and islands: they form the Gaeltacht. Here everything is done to promote Irish speaking in industry and at home. Centres have been set up for students to learn amongst these native speakers. The carrying over of the Irish idiom into English is very attractive and expressive. J. M. Synge captured this in his play 'Riders to the Sea'. There are special grants for people living in Irish speaking areas but the boundaries are rather arbitrary. For instance in Galway, there's a boundary line through a built up area so there's a certain amount of animosity towards those living on one side of the line, Irish speakers or no! There is also the problem of standardising Irish, for the different dialects are quite distinct, but modern media tends to iron out these with the adoption of one in preference to others. Ulster seems to get the worst deal being so much further from the centre of administration, although it has the largest number of native speakers. You can appreciate all the reasons for promoting Irish, but it is only in this generation that the language has become popular; before it was left to Douglas Hyde and Lady Gregory to demonstrate the richness of Irish language and myth. They did have the advantage of being far away from

11

the grim realities of hunger and poverty that the Irish speakers knew. Gaelic like certain foods, usually vegetables, had associations with hunger and poverty, and belonged to a hard past. Even now people prefer to use English rather than stay in the Gaeltacht existing on grants and other government handouts. Gaelic is a compulsory subject in schools, and there is a certain amount in the newspapers, on television, sign posts and street names (with English translations!). But on the whole it is only just a living language.

---

**THE MEANING OF IRISH PLACE NAMES:** The original Gaelic has been complicated by attempts to give them English spelling. In the following examples the Gaelic spellings of the prefixes come first with the English following last.

agh, augh, achadh, a field
aglish, eaglais, a church
ah, atha, áth, a ford
all, ail, aill, a cliff
anna, canna, éanach, a marsh
ard, ar, árd, a height
as, ess, eas, a waterfall
aw, ow, atha, a river
bal, bel, béal, the mouth (of a river or valley)
bal, balli, bally, baile, a town
ballagh, balla bealach, a way or path
bawn, bane, bán, white
barn, bearna, a gap
beg, beag, small
boola, booley, buaile, booleying, the movement of cattle from lowland to high pastures.
boy, buidhe, yellow
bun, the foot (of a valley or the mouth of a river)
caher, cahir, cathair, a fort or a city
carrick, carrig, corrig, carraig, a rock
cashel, caiseal, a castle
clogh, cloich, a stone
clon, clun, cluain, a meadow
derg, dearg, red
doo, du, duv, duf, dubh, black
dun, dún, a fort
glan, glen, gleann, a valley
illaun, oileán, an island
inch, inish, inis, an island
knock, cnoc, a hill
ken, kin, can, ceann, a headland
kil, kill, cill, a church

12

lis, liss, lios, a fort
lough, loch, a lake, or sea inlet
ma, may, moy, magh, a plain
mone, mona, móna, turf or bog
monaster, mainistir, a monastery
more, mor, mór, big or great
owen, avon, abhainn, a river
rath, a ring fort
rinn, reen, a point
roe, ruadh, red
ross, ros, a peninsula, a wood
see, suidhe, a seat, i.e. Ossain's seat
shan, shane, sean, old
slieve, sliabh, a mountain
tir, tyr, tír, country
tubber, tobrid, tubbrid, tobar, a well
tra, traw, tráigh or trá, a strand or beach

---

## SOME ULSTER AND OTHER EXPRESSIONS YOU MIGHT COME ACROSS WHILE IN IRELAND

| | |
|---|---|
| assay | calling attention, as in Hi. |
| brave | commendable, worthy, i.e. she's a brave wee sort of a girl |
| bravely | doing well, could be worse, i.e. business is doing bravely |
| boreen | country lane |
| clever | neat, tightfitting usually ref. to a garment |
| cleg | horsefly |
| coul | wintry, cold |
| crack | fun, lively chat |
| cut | insulted, hurt |
| dead on | exactly right |
| deed | passed away, dead |
| dither | slow |
| dingle | dent, mark with an impression |
| dip | bread fried in a pan |
| dulse | edible seaweed |
| fairly | excellent, i.e. that wee lad can fairly sing |
| fern | foreign |
| fog feed | lavish meal |
| feed | meal |
| guff | impertinence, cheek |
| harp six | tumble |
| jar | a couple of drinks |
| neb | nose |

13

| | |
|---|---|
| ni | now, this moment |
| mended | improved in health |
| mizzlin | raining gently |
| oul | not young, but can be used about something useful<br>– my oul car |
| owlip | verbal abuse |
| parletic | intoxicated |
| rare | to bring up, educate |
| rightly | prospering: he's doing rightly now |
| scalded | bothered, vexed, badly burned |
| themins | those persons |
| sex | the hour before seven in Ballymena |
| skiff | slight shower or rain |
| spittin' | starting to rain |
| quare | memorable, unusual |
| thundergub | loud voiced person |
| wee | little, also in the North means with, i.e. did I<br>see you wee that man? |
| wain | child |
| fierce | unacceptable, extreme, i.e. it's fierce dear (expensive) |
| soft | rainy, i.e. it's a grand soft day |
| terrible | same use as 'fierce' |

The Irish are very good at expressing themselves, it's the way they put the words together, rather than any difference in the English language itself. Gaelic is a beautifully expressive, but rather gutteral sounding language, however an Irishman speaking English brings a softness and elegance to the most down to earth expressions.

---

**RELIGION:** The Irish are obsessed with religion, especially those who live in the North where extreme Presbyterian and Catholic attitudes are reminiscent of 17th century Europe. Unfortunately, despite efforts by the clergy of both sides who organise ecumenical meetings, their congregations ignore such moves. In the Republic, the Catholic majority is obviously the controlling force in political and social life and the Protestant minority has bowed out gracefully. The Protestants used to represent almost ten per cent of the population, this figure has declined to under five per cent through mixed marriages. The atmosphere of the Catholic Church is heavy on the land, you can not fail to notice the huge neo-Gothic cathedrals which on Sundays overflow with people.

The Catholic priest is a very powerful man in Irish society, he is also very approachable, you might easily meet him in the village bar having a drink and a chat. Catholic taboos are as strong as ever and are reflected in the laws of the land. Schooling is still mostly in the hands of the Church; if you look through an Irish 'Who's Who' you will find that most of the politicians and local officials went to Christian Brothers schools – the old boy network is very strong. Until 1973 it was still a mortal sin for a Catholic to go to Trinity College, Dublin, even though it had been opened up to everybody in 1783. In the North the Catholic population is rising and this has fanned the Protestant fear that the Catholics eventually hope to outvote them by having endles baby booms. In the Republic it is against the law to use contraception and to get a divorce, so the Irish have to go to the North or to England to take advantage of a more liberal society.

The Irish have been religious for 5,000 years, there are plenty of chambered cairns to prove it. The Celts who arrived in about BC 500 believed that the human head was the centre of man's powers and thoughts. Their stone masons carved two-headed gods and the style in which they worked has a continuity which can be traced right up to the 19th century. There are heads in the Lough Erne district which are difficult to date, they could be pagan, early Christian or comparatively modern. The origins of the Tuatha de Danann are lost in legend, they may have been pre-Celtic gods or a race of invaders, themselves vanquished by the Celts. They were supposed to have magical powers and today they are thought of as the wee folk who live in the raths and stone forts. Here they make fairy music which is so beautiful that it bewitches any human that hears it. The wee folk play all kinds of tricks on country people, from souring their milk to stealing their children and so a multitude of charms have been devised to guard against these fairy pranks. I can remember being told about the fairies who used to dance in magic rings in the fields; the trouble was that if you tried to go up to them they would turn into yellow ragwort dancing in the wind. The leprechaun is the most famous Irish fairy. He is a surly little cobbler who has buried his crock of gold at the end of a rainbow. If you look around you in Ireland there seem to be leprechauns with tweed caps on them everywhere – only they are not tapping at a fairy shoe, they are herding red cows along the road!

An example of the assimilation of the Druidic religion by the Christians is the continuing religious significance of the Holy Wells. Ash and rowan trees, both sacred to the druids, are frequently found near the Holy Wells and Christian pilgrims leave offerings of rags on the trees as a sign to the devil that he has no more power over them. Patterns and games used to be held at the wells although they often shocked the priest who would put the well out of bounds and declare that the healing powers of the well had been destroyed. In cottages and farmhouses you might see a strange swastika sign made out of rushes. These are St. Brigid's crosses and are hung above the door or window to keep the evil spirits away. Fairy or sacred trees are still left standing in the fields even though it is uneconomic to plough round them; but bad luck invariably follows the person who cuts one down.

St. Patrick is a symbol of Irish Christianity, he used the shamrock to symbolize the Holy Trinity to a sceptical king. St Patrick's Day has become a remembrance day for the Irish living all over the world, when they produce bedraggled bits of shamrock sent from home. The Ireland of

'Saints and Scholars' reached its peak in the 7th century. The monks sought an ascetic and holy way of life although this was pursued in a fierce and warlike manner. The ultimate self-sacrifice was self-imposed exile, and so they founded monasteries in France, Italy and Germany.

Religious discrimination is long established in Ireland. At different times both Catholics and Protestants have suffered by not conforming to the established church. The Huguenots arrived when Louis XIV revoked the Edict of Nantes in 1685, they were Calvinists and inter-married easily with the other Protestant groups. The Huguenots were very skilled and established the important linen industry, as well as weaving and lace making. The Presbysterians were the biggest group of dissenters and most of them were Scots who had settled in Ulster during the 17th century. They had been persecuted in Scotland because of their religious beliefs and now they found that Ireland was no better; they were as poor as the native Irish and many found life so hard that they emigrated to America. Quakers, Palatines (German Protestants), Baptists and Methodists also settled in Ireland, but their numbers have declined through emigration and inter-marriage.

Death and weddings are always an occasion for a bit of crack, and there is also a party whenever the priest blesses a new house. Irish couples spend more on their engagement rings and their weddings than their English counterparts, it's a really big occasion. An Irish wake has lost many of its pagan rituals: mourning with keening and games involving disguise, mock weddings, jokes and singing. Nowadays, the dead person is laid out in another room and people come in to pay their last respects and then spend the rest of the evening drinking, eating and reminiscing.

# Getting To and Around Ireland

---

## BY AIR TO THE REPUBLIC

**From Europe,** British Airways, British Midlands, Air UK, Dan Air, KLM, TAT, Sabena, Swiss Air, SAS, Air Italia, Lufthansa, and Iberia run regular, scheduled flights from European capitals and major cities. Aer Lingus handles an enormous number of flights from European destinations, and if you are going to immerse yourself in all things Irish you might as well start with this airline with its air hostesses all dressed in green; prices are always in a state of flux and expensive unless you book a Super Apex ticket, buy a student fare, go between November and March or get a bargain fare. Aer Lingus student fares must be booked at least two weeks in advance with definite dates given for entry and departure. The Student Air Travel Association, SATA, operate charter flights during the summer months between Dublin, Amsterdam, London, Paris and Zurich. Reservations can be made through student travel bureaux in Europe, or through USIT, the travel company of the Union of Students in Ireland, based at 7 Anglesea St. Dublin 2.

**From USA and Canada**

Prices are in a constant state of flux and there are so many different deals going, so the first thing to do is find yourself a travel agent who is going to tell you about the cheap and reliable options. The time of year you chose can make a great difference to the price and availability of tickets. Expect to pay more and book earlier if you want to travel between June and August. Apex and Super Apex are the most reliable and flexible of the cheap fares, a typical fare going Super Apex on Aer Lingus would be New York-Dublin $565.00 between 15th June and 31st August, $498 between September and March. You have to book 21 days in advance and the ticket is valid for 6 months; if you want to change the date of your return, it will cost around $100. Freddie Laker's Skytrain, budget and standby are all approximately the same price. Budget is the most secure of these but you do not known exactly what day and what flight you are booked on until 7 days before take-off. Charter flights are numerous – look in the Sunday travel section of the New York Times. Remember to read all the small print, there are often catches: big cancellation fees, or difficulty if you want to change the date, sometimes charter contracts include provisions that allow charter companies to cancel your flight, change the dates and add fuel surcharges after you have paid your fare. Sometimes it pays Canadians to travel from the USA as there are few cheap flights going in Canada. Check with the Canadian - University Travel Service, 44 St Georges St., Toronto, Ontario, Tel: (416) 979 2406, open to non-students. Freddie Laker's Skytrain does not actually go to Dublin, despite frequent rumours that it will soon. Nevertheless, it is well worth getting as far as London and then combining it with a train/ferry deal to Ireland. Your travel agent should give you all the details. North West Orient airlines operates a standby fare to Shannon. Ask about the various deals which include a return airfare with a hired car thrown in for your stay in Ireland.

Aer Lingus operates flights

| From | To | Telephone |
|---|---|---|
| Amsterdam | Cork,Dublin,Shannon | (020) 239589 |
| Barcelona | Cork,Dublin,Shannon | (93) 3256000 |
| Birmingham | Cork,Dublin | (021) 236 6211 |
| Boston | Dublin,Shannon | (800) 223 6537 |
| Bristol | Dublin | (0272) 290046 |
| Brussels | Cork,Dublin,Shannon | (02) 219 45 73 |
| Chicago | Dublin,Shannon | (800) 223 6537 |
| Copenhagen | Cork,Dublin,Shannon | (01) 126055 |
| Dusseldorf | Cork,Dublin,Shannon | (0211) 8 02 32 |
| Edinburgh | Dublin | (031) 225 7392 |
| Frankfurt | Cork,Dublin,Shannon | (0611) 29 20 54/6 |
| Geneva | Cork,Dublin,Shannon | (022) 321656 |
| Glasgow | Dublin | (041) 248 4121 |
| Jersey | Dublin | (0534) 22201 |
| Liverpool | Dublin | (051) 236 6135/6 |
| London | Cork,Dublin,Shannon | (01) 734 1212 |
| Lourdes | Cork,Dublin,Shannon | (62) 345985 |
| Madrid | Cork,Dublin,Shannon | (91) 2414216 |
| Malaga | Dublin,Shannon | (952) 213731 |
| Manchester | Cork,Dublin | (061) 832 8611 |
| Milan | Cork,Dublin,Shannon | (02) 700080/783565 |
| Montreal | Dublin,Shannon | |
| Munich | Cork,Dublin,Shannon | (089) 287033/4 |
| New York | Dublin,Shannon | (212) 557 1110 |
| Paris | Cork,Dublin,Shannon | (01) 742 12 50 |
| Rome | Cork,Dublin,Shannon | (06) 4758518 |
| Toronto | Dublin,Shannon | (416) 362 6565 |
| Zurich | Cork,Dublin,Shannon | (01) 211 28 50 |

Frequent air services connect Cork, Shannon and Dublin. There is also an air service between Dublin and Londonderry run by Avair, Tel: Dublin 686695 or Londonderry 810628. Buses and trains run between Cork Airport and Cork City, Shannon Airport and Limerick City and from Dublin Airport to Busaras (the main provincial bus station in Dublin in Store Street). Shannon Airport is a freeport with a huge variety of duty free goods plus a selection of Irish specialties: cut crystal glass, Connemara rugs and marble, Donegal tweed, etc. If you do not want to get burdened with lots of paper parcels you can get everything here at the last minute. Packages bought in the duty free area just before take off will be taken on the plane without any extra weight charges.

**Telephone numbers and addresses for airlines in Dublin** (01 is the code for Dublin)
Aer Lingus: Dublin Airport, Tel: 370011
40 Upper O'Connell Street and 42 Grafton St., Tel: 377747 for all trans-atlantic, continental and Jersey bookings. For all other routes Tel: 377777.
Air Canada: 4 Westmoreland St., Tel: 771488
Alitalia: 60/63 Dawson St., Tel: 775171
British Airways: 112 Grafton St., Tel: 686666
British Midlands: Link Buildings, Dublin Airport, Tel: 373235
Dan Air Airport Handling: Cork Airport, Tel: (020) 961277
Iberia Airways: 3 Grafton Arcade, Tel: 774368
KLM: Hawkins Hs. Hawkins St., Tel: 778241
Lufthansa: Gratton Hs. 68 Lower Mount St., Tel: 761595
North West Orient Airlines: Suite 206/207 Gresham Hotel, O'Connell St., Tel: 787081
Sabena: 7 Dawson St., Tel: 716677
Swiss Air: 54 Dawson St., Tel: 778173
Scandinavian Airlines: Room 112, Link Building, Dublin Airport, Tel: 421922
Transamerica Airlines: 5 Lyon Hs. O'Connell St., Tel: 720925
TAT Airport Handling: Cork Airport, Tel: (021) 961277

American Express Travel specialises in flights to and from North America, 116 Grafton St., Dublin 2, Tel: 772874
Club Travel: 30 Abbey St., Tel: 681477 specialises in charter flights.
USIT Student Travel: Cecil St. Upper, Limerick, tel: (061) 4 50 64, and 7 Anglesea St., Dublin 2, Tel: 778117

Information on transport and accommodation are available at the tourist offices at all the airports, open all the year round.

# BY AIR TO NORTHERN IRELAND

Air UK have recently introduced cut price rates on Blackpool, **Exeter,** Leeds/Bradford and Southampton to Aldergrove routes e.g. an instant purchase (if within 24 hours of flying) ticket from Exeter to Belfast costs £72 return.

You can buy cheap tickets on scheduled flights from Heathrow to Aldergrove. These are either standby at about £25 single or guaranteed standby which will get you away within three flights, about £30 single. There are also cheap returns if you stay in Ireland over a Saturday or Sunday. Student discount rates at 25% off are available on British Airways, flights on Saturday and Sunday only. For full details ask at any travel agency.

These are the direct air services from Great Britain, Europe and the Republic of Ireland.

| Departure | To | Airline | Telephone |
|---|---|---|---|
| London Heathrow | Belfast | British Airways | (01) 370 5411 |
| London Gatwick | Belfast | British Midland | (01) 581 0864 |
| Amsterdam | Belfast | K.L.M. | Amsterdam (020)434242 |
| Birmingham | Belfast | British Airways | (021) 236 7000 |
| Bristol | Belfast | Dan Air | Rhoose (0446) 710053 |
| Cardiff | Belfast | Dan Air | Rhoose (0446) 710053 |
| East Midlands | Belfast | British Midland | Derby 810552 |
| Edinburgh | Belfast | Loganair | (041) 889 3181 |
| Exeter | Belfast | Air UK | Freefone 3586 |
| Glasgow | Belfast | British Airways | (041) 332 9666 |
| Glasgow | Londonderry and Enniskillen | Loganair | (041) 889 3181 |
| Isle of Man | Belfast | British Midland | Douglas 24419 |
| Jersey | Belfast | British Midland | Jersey 44350 |
| Leeds/ Bradford | Belfast | Air UK | Freefone 3586 |
| Liverpool | Belfast | British Midland | (051) 494 0200 |
| Manchester | Belfast | British Airways | (061) 228 6311 |
| Newcastle- upon-Tyne | Belfast | Dan Air | Newcastle 611395 |
| Dublin/ Shannon | Belfast | Aer Lingus | Limerick 45556 |
| Dublin | L'derry | Avair | Londonderry 810628 |
| Southampton | Belfast | Air UK | Freefone 3586 |

Major airlines operate regular, standby or reduced fares from the USA to Belfast via London, Heathrow and Gatwick. Freddie Laker's skytrain operates with no seasonal differences in the fares to London and you could then get a standby flight to Belfast. The only snag would be that you have to buy the standby ticket outside the airport, so just hop on the tube and buy it at any travel agent and then get back to Heathrow. Budget and standby tickets on other airlines are approximately the same price.

The telephone number to ring in New York to find out about the Laker skytrain is: (212) 459 7323 and outside New York it is (800) 221 0374. The main Laker office in New York is at 95-25 Queens Blvd. in Queens. There are plenty of connections from Dublin and Shannon to Belfast if you do not want to go via London. Charter flights fly into Belfast Aldergrove in the summer.

Transport from the airport: there are infrequent buses to Belfast and Londonderry. If you want to go to Antrim railway station, try and share a taxi to the station as they are expensive.

---

## BY BOAT TO THE REPUBLIC

### Car and passenger services

Le Havre-Rosslare direct from the Continent on the Irish Continental Line. Five departures per week in each direction; the journey takes approximately 21 hours.

| | | |
|---|---|---|
| Cherbourg-Rosslare Irish Continental | Two departures per week in each direction approx. 17 hours | Tel: Dublin (01) 774331 or Le Havre 26 57 26 |
| Roscoff-Cork Brittany Ferries | One departure per week in each direction approx. 16 hours. | Tel: Cork 57666 or Roscoff (98) 69 07 20 |

*From England*
B&I
| | | |
|---|---|---|
| Liverpool-Dublin | Daily sailings approx. 8 hours | Tel: Dublin (01) 72 4711 |
| Jetfoil Service | Approx. 3 hours. | |

B&I
| | |
|---|---|
| Pembroke-Rosslare | Daily approx. 5 hours |
| Pembroke-Cork | Nightly approx. 9 hours |

| | | |
|---|---|---|
| Fishguard-<br>Rosslare<br>Sealink | Daily approx.<br>4 hours | Tel: London (01)<br>834 2345 |
| Holyhead-Dun<br>Laoghaire<br>Sealink | Daily approx.<br>3½ hours | Tel: Dublin (01)<br>714455 or<br>801905 or<br>London (01)<br>834 2345 |
| Isle of Man<br>Douglas to Dun<br>Laoghaire<br>Sealink | | Tel: Douglas<br>3824 or<br>Dublin (01)<br>778271 |

If you can produce an International Student Card all these companies will give 25% off the standard passenger rate. Remember that some peak dates require a sailing ticket as well as a travel ticket, check when you book; if you have a Eurorail pass any travel by Irish Continental Line Ferries is included. All the ferry ports are linked to the main city, whether Cork, Wexford or Dublin by bus or train.

---

## BY BOAT TO NORTHERN IRELAND

### Car and passenger services

**Ports and** | **Frequencies**

*Scotland*

| Stranraer-<br>Larne<br>Sealink, Tel:<br>Stranraer 2262 | Several daily<br>sailings takes<br>approx. 2¼ hours<br>student-rail<br>ticket holders<br>get a cheaper<br>ticket. | Car + 4<br>passengers from<br>£58 return. |
|---|---|---|
| Cairnryan-Larne<br>Townsend Thoresen<br>Car ferries<br>Tel: Larne 4321 | Several daily<br>sailings takes<br>approx. 2 hours | |

*England*

| | | |
|---|---|---|
| Liverpool-Belfast | Liverpool | Car + 2 |
| P&O Ferries | nightly dept. | passengers from |
| Tel: Belfast 23636 | 2100 hrs. Belfast | £100 return |
| or Liverpool (051) | nightly dept. | |
| 236 5464 | 2030 hrs, about | |
| | $10\frac{1}{2}$ hours. $12\frac{1}{2}\%$ | |
| | off fare for | |
| | students. | |

*Isle of Man*

| | |
|---|---|
| Douglas-Belfast | June & September |
| Isle of Man | weekly sailings. |
| Steam Packet | Tuesday & Friday |
| Company Tel: | (July and August) |
| Douglas 3824 | Douglas depart |
| | 0830 hrs. |
| | Belfast depart |
| | 1500 hrs. |

It is always better to book your journey both ways especially if you have a car. Foot passengers can buy their tickets just before they get on the boat but on some peak dates a 'sailing' ticket is required as well as a travel ticket. Check when booking. The Scottish ports are by far the nearest and the cheapest but if you are travelling from London, it takes a lot of time, effort and petrol getting up there.

---

## BY TRAIN

All the car ferries plying their way between England and Ireland are scheduled to link up with the British Rail trains which go frequently and speedily from London to Pembroke, Liverpool, Holyhead and Stranraer. You can get couchettes on the night trains, but when it is not crowded it is possible to have a comfortable snooze by just stretching out along the seats. Transalpino, Eurotrain and Sealink all have inexpensive train-boat arrangements from London. With a Eurorail pass you can go from France to Ireland free on the ferry, but not through Britain. Check with British Rail at Victoria Station, Tel: 01 834 2345 or any of the youth travel offices in London for details on Sealink.

B&I lines give a 25% discount if you buy your ticket at USIT, Victoria Student Travel Centre, 52 Grosvenor Gdns., London SW7, Tel: 01-730 8111 or from the B&I line office at 155 Regent St., London NW1, Tel: 01 734 4681. The B&I office in the US is at Suite IE, 180 West End Ave., New York, NY 10023, Tel: 212 580 9011. See 'By Boat' section for details on the ferries.

Ireland is now part of the Eurorail pass network which allows unlimited rail travel on European Railways including Ireland but excluding British Rail, you must buy your pass outside Europe. Prices in US dollars are 7 days $180, 15 days $230, 21 days $290, one month $360, two months $330. A Eurorail youth pass is available for those up to twenty six years old: one month costs $260, two months $330. Transalpino also operates cheap rail and boat transport. You have to be under 26 to be eligible.

Transalpino addresses: in London, 71-75 Buckingham Palace Road, SW1 01 834 9656; in Dublin, 24 Talbot St., Tel: 01 742382; in Belfast, 24 Lombard St., Tel: 48823. British Rail in Dublin, Tel: 01 801905; in Belfast, Tel: Belfast 27520.

---

## BY BUS

Travelling by bus/ferry to Ireland is quite an endurance test because the journey seems so endless with lots of stops through England and Ireland to pick up other travellers. Its main advantage is that it is cheap and gets you straight to destinations in the provinces, so that you do not have to get other buses, trains, and taxis once you get to the capital. The small coaches toing and froing are very flourishing private enterprises in the hands of local individuals. They leave all parts of Ireland for the chief cities of England and Scotland, full to the brim with Irish returning to work and vice versa. You will not find the details at your travel agent, look instead at the back of Irish newspapers which you can buy fairly easily in Britain. Here are some telephone numbers to ring if you are trying to get to Ulster and are starting from Scotland: J.J. Boyce, Tel: 041 647 0603. He operates a service from Ramelton in Co. Donegal to Glasgow but will drop you off anywhere on the way, his price at the moment, £28 return. Anthony McGinley plies between Glasgow and Letterkenny and The Rosses in Co. Donegal, Tel: 041 637 9958, and in the summer does some trips to London, Tel: 01 801 7780.

Ulster Bus Express via Larne (London-Birmingham-Belfast) costs about £39 return and £31 if you travel midweek. Details from National Travel Ltd., Victoria Coach Station, 164 Buckingham Palace Rd., London SW1, Tel: 01 730 0202, or Ulsterbus, Great Victoria St., Bus Station, 10 Glengall St., Belfast, Tel: 20011 (or 21746 on Saturdays). CIE operate between London and Dublin, Tel: Dublin (01) 300777.

---

**GETTING AROUND IRELAND BY TRAIN AND BUS:** Domestic train routes are operated by CIE, the national transport company which also runs a bus network to most parts of the Republic. The train routes radiate out from Dublin and take you through sleepy little country stations and green countryside. The trains and the stations are rather like English stations of forty years ago with the old signal boxes which still need humans to operate them and keep an eye on things. People are always friendly on trains and the ticket inspectors are far from officious. The bus service is efficient and will take you to the most remote places in Ireland, but be warned both the train and the bus are expensive, unless you get a Rambler's Ticket, a Student Travelsave Stamp, or an Overlander Pass (valid on NIR and Ulsterbus services as well). **THE RAMBLER TICKET**gives you unlimited travel on provincial rail and bus services for an 8-day period. It costs IR£20 rail only, IR£36 for rail and bus. 15 day IR£42 rail only; IR£52 rail and bus. (Ramblers tickets can be bought at CIE offices throughout Ireland and from any travel agent.) **A YOUTH RAMBLER TICKET** can be bought only in the United States and only prior to departure from travel agents or CIE Tours International, Ireland House, 590 Fifth Ave., New York, N.Y. 10036. An 8 day rail and bus costs $67. 15 day rail and bus $91. 30 day rail and bus $118. **EDUCATION TRAVEL CONCESSION TICKET:** this entitles a student to greatly reduced travel on all buses listed in the Dublin District bus and train timetable, and for all the suburban train services between Balbriggan and Greystones. You must be able to produce a passport or identity card and the name of the school or college you are attending. Apply to the Group and Educational Dep., Dublin Tourism, 14 Upper O'Connell Street, Dublin 1, Tel: 01 747733.

If you have an International Student Identity Card, you can buy a **TRAVELSAVE STAMP** for IR£3 which gets you some big savings: 50% off all single adult tickets on mainline rail fares costing over IR£1, 50% off all single adult CIE provincial bus journeys costing over IR£1 and 50% off the return fare to the Aran Islands by boat. The travel stamp is available at USIT Head Office, 7 Anglesea Street (off Dame St.), Dublin. Tel: (01) 778117, or in Limerick at 31 Upper Cecil St. Tel: Limerick 45064, or at any student travel offices at Irish Universities, and at the Group and Educational Department, 14 Upper O'Connell St., Dublin. **AN OVERLANDER TICKET** available from CIE and travel agents is the same as a Rambler except that it is valid in the North as well.

CIE operates a variety of chatty 1 day and ½ day tours throughout Ireland from various city depots. For details get in touch with CIE at the following telephone numbers: (01) 300777 for details on coach tours, French and German speaking holidays in Ireland, self-drive cars, chauffeur driven limousines, school education tours.
(01) 746301 for Dublin City Bus Services.
(01) 742941 Busaras (Store St.) Expressway Bus services to all parts of Ireland.
(01) 742941 for party travel and concession rail fares.
(01) 787777 for general bus and train service information.

There is a talking Timetable Service, ring (01) 724222 for details of trains between Dublin and Cork (01) 724666, for those between Dublin and Limerick, and (01) 724777 for those between Dublin and Galway.
The Lough Swilly Bus Service, Tel: Londonderry 62224.
Suirway Bus Service Tel: Waterford 82209.
Princess Bus Service, Tel: Clonmel 21389.
These services run where CIE do not operate.

Remember to pick up a provincial Bus and Expressway Timetable from CIE, or tourist offices and some newspaper stands. It costs 30 pence to reserve a seat on a train.

---

**BY BUS AND TRAIN IN NORTHERN IRELAND:** A **Eurorailpass** is not valid on Northern Ireland Railways, nor is a **Rambler Ticket.** NIR have their own **Rail Runabout Ticket** and do the **Travelsave Stamp** scheme which are available from USIT offices in London, Belfast and Dublin. For information on fares and timetables get in touch with Northern Ireland Railways, Belfast Central station, Tel: 30310 or 30671. Ulsterbus runs frequent services to all parts of Northern Ireland, you can pick up timetables at any Ulster bus station, or the Tourist Office in Belfast. The Ulsterbus head office is at the Great Victoria Bus Station, Tel: Belfast 20011 or 20574, or write to 10 Glengall St., Belfast. Here you can get details on their **7 day Runabout Ticket.** The USIT (youth travel office) will provide you with Travelsave stamps and also book ferry and plane tickets, you will find it at 68 Donegall St., Tel: Belfast 24073. There is also a student travel office in Queen's University at the Travel Shop, Student's Union Building, University Road, Belfast, Tel: 24803.

---

**INLAND WATERWAYS:** This is an unforgettable and exciting way to travel around Ireland. The main areas are: the Shannon which is navigable from Lough Key to Killaloe; the Erne which is the second largest river in Ireland and navigable for more than fifty miles from Belturbet to the little village of Belleek (which makes exquisite china); the Grand Canal and the River Barrow (the canal links Dublin with the Shannon and the Barrow). Along the waterways you pass tumbledown castles, abbeys, beautiful flowers, birds and peaceful lush scenery. In the evening you can moor up your boat for a meal and a jar and listen to some good traditional music. There are festivals and boat rallies, but they only happen for a couple of days a year, so if its peace and quiet you want do not worry. The Erne waterway is beautifully wooded with nature reserves and little islands amongst which to meander. In all, the Erne covers 300 square miles of water.

There are twelve companies offering 560 luxury cabin cruisers for self-drive hire, from two to eight berths, on the Shannon; one of them offers inclusive cruises by river barge. You get an hour of tuition, or more if you need it, and you have to be over twenty-one to be skipper, but no licence of any sort is needed. Ask for details from your travel agent or the nearest Irish Tourist office. Useful reading: *The Shell Guide to the Shannon, The Guide to the Grand Canal* and *The Guide to the River Barrow.* Good pubs along the Shannon: Hough's pub and Killeen's in Shannonbridge, The Sail Inn in Scarriff, the Jolly Mariner, Sean's Bar and the Green

Olive in Athlone. The Crew's Inn in Roosky.

The River Erne and The Grand Canal have one cruiser company each.

---

**BY YACHT:** To bring your own yacht to sail round the coastline and the islands is no problem. Boats may be brought into Ireland for a temporary (holiday) period without tax or duty. A special sticker is issued by a customs official on arrival. Owners of large sea going yachts must apply to the harbour master of all the ports in which they wish to anchor. On arrival at the first point of entry, the flag Q should be shown. Contact should then be made with the local customs officer or with a Garda (civil guard). It is illegal to land any animals without a special licence from the Department of Agriculture, this does not apply to animals which come from Great Britain. Gas cylinders for cooking are available only in 11lb click-on calor Kosangas, so you might have to bring some spare ones.

There are several companies which charter cruisers:

In Co. Cork details and reservations can be got from: Kilbrack Boats Ltd., Kilbrack House, Doneraile, Tel: 022 24146.

From Irish Atlantic Yacht Charters, Ballylickey, Bantry. Tel: Bantry 352.

From Andrew Stott Yacht Charters, Rossbriagh, Glengariff, Tel: Glengariff 188.

From Bantry Bay Yacht Charters, Bocarnagh, Glengariff, Tel: Glengariff 188.

In Co. Dublin from Dun Laoghaire, Sailing School, 115 Lower Georges St., Dun Laoghaire. Tel: 01 806654.

Useful addresses: The Irish Yachting Assoc., 87 Upper George's St., Dun Laoghaire, Tel: 01 800239. The west coast can be quite rough, exposed as it is to the North Atlantic, but the beauty of the coastline is unsurpassable. The east and south coast is better equipped with sheltered harbours and marinas. Useful publications: *Irish Cruising Club Sailing Directions,* two volumes, one for the west and south and the other for the north and east. Available from most book sellers or from Mrs. J. Guinness, Ceanchor Hs., Baily, Co. Dublin. Good reading is *Sailing Round Ireland* by Wallace Clark, Batsford and the *Islands of Ireland* by D. McCormick, Osprey 1977. The radio issues gale warnings on BBC3 and BBC4.

---

**CANOEING:** This is an exciting and compelling way to tour Ireland via the Liffey and the Barrow Rivers with their smooth flowing stretches, rapids and weirs. The other principle rivers are the Nore, Boyne, Slaney, Lee, Shannon, Suir and Blackwater. You can always camp by the waterside as long as you get permission from the owner. For details of the many rivers, and waterways, sea canoeing and tuition, write to: The Hon.

Secretary, Mr. Joe Cassidy, The Irish Canoe Union, c/o Cospoir, The National Sports Council, Floor 11, Hawkins House, Dublin 2. Nearly everything a canoeist could require can be bought at Venture Sports, Blackrock, or the Great Outdoors, Chatham St., Dublin 2.

---

**CAR HIRE OPERATORS:** These are only some of the big ones who will meet you at the airports and the ferry ports in the Republic:
Archers Car Rentals, Sandwich Street, Dublin 2. Tel: 01 764131
Avis Rent A Car Ltd., 1 Hanover Street, East Dublin 2. Tel: 01 776971
Bolands Car Hire, 38 Pearse Street, Dublin 2. Tel: 01 770704
Brendan's Self Drive, 29 Lower Abbey Street, Dublin 1. Tel: 01 787894
Budget Rent A Car, 5 Lyon House, O'Connell Street, Dublin 1. Tel: 01 720777
Dan Ryan Rent A Car, 2 Fitzwilliam Place, Dublin 2. Tel: 01 765594
Flynn Brothers Self Drive, Ballygar, Co. Galway. Tel: 0903 4571
Hertz Rent A Car, 20 George's Quay, Dublin 2. Tel: 01 772971
Murray's Europcar, Baggot Street Bridge, Dublin 4. Tel: 01 681777
T.M. Nationwide Ltd., 617, St Patrick's Quay, Cork. Tel: Cork 51291
Tipperary Self Drive, Limerick Rd., Tipperary. Tel: Tipperary 51213
Renting a car can be an expensive business, you might be able to bargain slightly if business is slack, but it is difficult to get one if you are under 23 and impossible if you are under 21.

In Northern Ireland, Budget Rent A Car is the best with centres all over the province, 96 Great Victoria Street, Belfast. Tel: Belfast 41061 or Belfast Airport, Tel: 94 53319.

---

**BY CAR:** To explore Ireland with the minimum of effort and the maximum freedom bring a car. If you fill it up with people who share the ferry and petrol costs, it wont be too expensive. Petrol in Ireland is around IR£2.20 per gallon and in the North £1.80 per gallon. Buy a detailed road map and if you have time choose a minor road and just meander; it is along these little lanes that the secret life of Ireland continues undisturbed. The black and red cows still chew by the wayside whilst the herdsman, usually an old man or a child, salutes you with an upward nod. Nearby is the farmstead cluttered with bits of old machinery and a cheerful sense of makeshift; everthing is kept to be used again, an old front door will stop a gap in the hedge, old baths serve as cattle troughs. Clucking hens roost on the old haycart; next year it might be bought by the tinkers who will varnish it up to adorn some suburban garden. You will come upon castles, ruined clochans still breathing with memories, tumbled even further by the local farmer in search of stone, and there are views of the hills around, which have never been described in any guidebook.

One of the best things about driving in Ireland is the lack of other cars and the absence of efficient but ugly motorways with their obligatory motor inns and petrol stations. There are some big roads with all that sort of thing, but very few; in Northern Ireland the roads manage to be very good but still countrified and you feel as though you are gliding along after the bumps and wavey roads of the Republic. One thing you will have to get used to is the Irish idea of driving, which can make you very annoyed until you just accept it. An Irish driver tends to drive right in the middle of the road, never looks in his mirror to see if anyone is behind and is unlikely to indicate if he suddenly decides to turn left or right. Beware of the driver who wears an old tweed cap they are usually the worst offenders. Cars frequently pull out of a side road in front of you and just as you are getting up enough steam to pass suddenly decide to turn off down another side road again. Do not expect many cars to dip their lights at night. Petrol stations stay open until around 8 in the evenings, and the village ones are open after mass on Sundays. If you are desperate for petrol and every station seems closed, you can usually knock somebody up who will start the pumps for you. The general speed limit in the Republic is 60 mph and 30 mph through the villages and towns. In the North the speed limit is 70 mph., 40 mph in built-up areas and 30 mph in towns. The ideal is left hand drive but it's usually middle of the road, and you must always wear your seat belt, it is illegal not to.

Ignore the sheepdog which appears from every cottage door to chase your car – they are well skilled at avoiding you.

Residents of the Republic of Ireland, Northern Ireland and Great Britain using private cars, motorcycles and bicycles may cross the border with very little formality, a full up to date licence is all you need, there is inter-availability of driving licences for motorists on a temporary stay. Under EEC regulations private motor insurers will provide the minimum legal cover required in all EEC countries, although they may need to be told before you travel. It is a good idea always to carry the vehicle registration book. If you have hired a car all the insurance headaches should have been dealt with by the hire company. AA offices will usually give you all the details if you are not clear about anything. Their main office in the Republic is at 23 Suffolk Street, Dublin, Tel: 01 779481 and in Belfast, Fanum House, 108-110 Great Victoria Street, Belfast, Tel: 26242.

There are some excellent motoring maps: Bartholomew's quarter inch gives good details of minor roads obtainable from the AA and Bord Fáilte. The road marking system is in transition – some are marked T for trunk and L for secondary , but the plan is to renumber them all N for national routes. Scenic routes are sign-posted and marked on the Bord Fáilte map. If you cross the frontier on an unapproved road you are liable to very severe penalties, including confiscation of your car. These are the frontier posts on the approved roads:

| Northern Ireland | Republic of Ireland |
| --- | --- |
| Culmore | Muff |
| Buncrana Road | Bridgend |
| Killea | Kildrum |

| | |
|---|---|
| Mullenan | Carrigans |
| Strabane Bridge | Lifford-Strabane Bridge |
| Kilclean | Kilclean |
| Tullyhommon Bridge | Pettigo |
| Belleek | Cloghore |
| Belcoo | Blacklion |
| Mullan | Swanlinbar |
| Clontivrim Bridge | Clones |
| Rosslea | Inishammon |
| Aughnacloy | Moy Bridge |
| Middletown | Tyholland |
| Carnagh | Tullynagrow |
| Tullydonnell | Drumbilla |
| Killee | Carrickcarnan |
| Upper Fathom | Ferryhill |

Just before the border on the Northern Ireland side you will have to pass through an army check-point, all you need is your licence or some means of identification.

Parking meters are used to control car parking in the central zones of Dublin. The meters are in operation during specific hours from Mondays to Fridays, when street parking other than at meters is prohibited. Yellowlines along the kerbside or edge of the roadway indicate waiting restrictions. In Cork a disc system is used to control parking in the centre. Parking discs can be bought usually in books of ten costing 50p. Unexpired time on a parking disc can be used at another parking place. You buy the books at shops and garages, near the car parks. In Belfast parking is limited to car parks and the central shopping area is shut off to cars.

Breakdown service is available, 7 days a week to 11 pm; they are much easier to find in Northern Ireland but there is usually one open from 8 am to 6 pm in every town.

**Belfast:**
WH Alexander Ltd., 62-64 Gt. Victoria Street, Tel: Belfast 28424
Connsbrook Filling Station, 125 Connsbrook Av., Tel: 653000
McLean and Bryce Ltd., Prince Regent St., Tel: 51111
Maguires, 534 Falls Rd., Tel: Belfast 613141

If your car breaks down in any part of Ireland you will always be able to find a mechanic to give you a hand, whether its late at night or on a Sunday, just ask someone. They will sweep you up in a wave of sympathy and send messengers off in all directions to find your man who has the reputation of a mechanical genius. If it is some small and common part that has let you down he will either have it, or do something that will get you by until you come to a proper Renault garage or whatever. One thing you will notice is that the Irish have a completely different attitude to machinery than most nationalities. In England if you break down, it is occasion for embarrassment, everybody rushes by hardly noticing you or pretending not to. In Ireland if your car has broken down, the next passing car will probably stop and the problem will be readily taken on and discussed with great enjoyment. The Irish can laugh at the occasional failure of material affairs, sure it's God's will!

**BY MOTORBIKE OR BICYCLE:** Ireland is one of the pleasantest places to bike around. The roads are uncrowded, there are still lots of birds and animals that live around the hedgerows, and there is no pollution to spoil the illusion of rural Ireland. In between the delicious whiffs of gorse or honeysuckle will come strong manure smells! It is impossible to hire motorbikes or scooters, but if you have one they cost very little on the ferry; remember to wear a helmet as it's illegal not to wear one. You can bring your bicycle free on the ferry or rent one. There is a Rent A Bike Raleigh network, with centres through the whole of Ireland. Tandems, racing bikes, and ordinary touring bikes are available and cost approximately IR£2.60 a day or IR£14.60 a week. For full details pick up a leaflet at the nearest Bord Fáilte or Northern Irish Tourist Office, or write to Irish Raleigh Industries, 8 Hanover Quay, Dublin 2. Transporting your bike by train costs approximately IR£3 for a major three hour journey.

**HITCH-HIKING:** From all accounts this seems to be a very safe but rather slow method of transport round the south. You will see more cows and sheep wandering along the minor roads than cars. In the North, you might find that people will not pick you up because years of the troubles have made them cautious. It would be unwise to hitch round border areas, there are plenty of buses that will take you through. On major roads write your destination on a bit of cardboard and hold it up, you will find you have to compete with local people who hitch regularly from town to town.

**HORSE DRAWN CARAVANS** may be rented for around IR£150 a week, less in off peak periods. You get a trustworthy horse and a colourful barrel shaped caravan which sleeps four. There are several places in Cork, Kerry, Limerick, Leitrim, Mayo and Wicklow. Write to Bord Fáilte in Dublin and ask for the relevant fact sheet which will give you all the details and addresses. (You travel at the rate of 16 miles a day).

# Where to Stay, Drinking, Eating Out

hotels p.32   guesthouses p.33   farmhouses, town and country
houses p.34   youth hostels p.35   camping and caravanning p.35
renting a house or cottage p.36   drinking p.36   eating out p.38

---

**HOTELS:** Bord Fáilte and the Northern Ireland Tourist Board register and grade hotels into five categories: A* stands for luxuriously equipped with night service, a very high standard of food and plenty of choice. Most bedrooms have their own bath and suites are available — the sort of place where delicious snacks are automatically served with your cocktails. This grading includes baronial mansions set in exquisite grounds or the rather plush anonymity of some Dublin hotels. A grade stands for a luxury hotel which doesn't have quite so many items on the table d'hôte, nor does it have night service; but the food is just as good and the atmosphere less restrained. B* grade stands for well-furnished and comfortable; some rooms have bath, cooking is good and plain. B and C grade are clean, comfortable but limited, B offering more in the line of bathrooms and food. All graded hotels have heating and hot and cold water in the bedrooms. If you come across a hotel that is ungraded, it is because its grading is under review or because it has just opened. The prices of each hotel vary enormously, no matter what grade they are. This will give you an idea:

Price of bed and full breakfast

| | A* | A | B* | B | C |
|---|---|---|---|---|---|
| Single bedroom between | £23.50 & £34 | £10.50 & £16.50 | £9 & £17.50 | £8 & £11 | £7.50 & £9.50 |
| Double between | £27 & £56 | £18 & £28 | £14 & £24 | £12 & £19 | £12 & £18 |

A room with a private bathroom in grade B or C hotel ranges from £1.50 to £3 extra.

Prices in Northern Ireland seem similar to those in the Republic but the difference in value between the sterling pound and the Irish pound is considerable and must be taken into account. Bord Fáilte and the Northern Ireland Tourist Board will give full details on prices, facilities, telephone numbers etc. Their publications come in neat booklets which are easy to carry around. Bord Fáilte will make your reservations for you for the price of the telephone call to the hotel. Make sure that you book early in the peak months June, July and August. You can pick up information on accommodation at any of the county offices, or in the Irish Tourist offices in the U.K, America and the Continent. Bord Fáilte operates a Central Reservation Service in Dublin for hotels, guesthouses, farm and home accommodation. Write or ring the Irish Tourist Board, Central Reservation Service, P.O. Box 273, Stephen St. Dublin 8 Tel: 01 781200. The main Northern Ireland Tourist Office is in River House, 48 High Street, Belfast BT1 2DS Tel: 46609.

---

**GUEST HOUSES:** These are usually houses which have become too large and expensive to maintain as private homes. The grade A houses are just as good as their hotel equivalent and so on down the scale, although the atmosphere is completely different. If you decide to vary your accommodation from guesthouse, to town and country house or farmhouse you will discover one of the principles of Irish life: that everything in Ireland works on a personal basis. If you are on holiday to avoid people, a guest house is the last place you should book into. It is impossible not to be drawn into a friendly conversation whether about fishing or politics. You will get a large, thoroughly uncontinental, breakfast and delicious evening meals with a choice within a set meal. Dinner is always very punctual, at eight, after everyone has sat around by the fire over very large drinks. Lunch or a packed lunch can be arranged. All grades of guesthouse have hot and cold water, and heating in the bedrooms. Grade A guesthouses have some rooms with private bathrooms, but their reputation is based on scrumptious food and comfortable surroundings. This will give you an idea of the price for bed and a full breakfast:

|  | A | B | C |
|---|---|---|---|
| Single | £13-£15 (private bathroom included) | £6-£7 | £5-£6 |
| Double | £26-£29 | £13-£14 | £10-£12 |

You can get full details of guesthouses in the Bord Fáilte and Northern Ireland Tourist Board booklets, which you can pick up in their offices for a small cost. I have mentioned 'binge' places in my accommodation list. (Between £9-£14 for a luxurious night's sleep and £7 for a delicious meal.)

---

**FARMHOUSES, TOWN AND COUNTRY HOUSES:** Often these family homes make your stay in Ireland, for you meet Irish people who are kind, generous and intelligent and who are not putting on a 'paddy' act for your benefit. It is also the most economical way to stay in Ireland if you don't want to stay in a tent or in a Youth Hostel. It is largely a matter of luck whether you hit an attractive or a mediocre set–up but always watch out for the shamrock sign, the Bord Fáilte sign of approval. You get a comfortable bed (if you are tall, make sure it is long enough, as sometimes Irish beds can be on the small side) and an enormous breakfast: orange juice, cereal, two eggs, bacon, sausages, toast and marmalade and a huge pot of tea or coffee. You might find yourself getting rather tired of this fry–up, if so, ask your hostess the night before for something different and she will be happy to oblige. Another thing, the coffee is invariably weak and rather disgusting, it's much safer to stick to tea! After being so critical, it is still a very satisfying meal, and means you don't feel hungry again until the evening.

Bed and breakfast per person ranges from £4.50 to £6.50 and very often you can eat your evening meal there. Again, masses to eat and piping hot, so much better than most of the restaurants and cafes. You should give notice before 12 noon that you want to eat.

Some houses serve dinner which costs between £4.50 — £6 and some serve high tea which costs between £2.50 — £4.50. 'High Tea' is a very sensible meal, which has evolved for the working man who begins to feel hungry at about six pm. You get a plate of something hot, perhaps chicken and chips, followed by fresh soda bread, jam and cakes and a pot of tea. Sometimes you get a salad. This leaves you with plenty of time to go out and explore in the evenings — whether the pubs or the countryside! Some houses provide tea and biscuits as a nightcap for nibblers at around 10 pm.

You will be charged about 60p extra for a bath, such a thing as a private bathroom does not exist unless you want to pay luxury prices. Ask the woman of the house for a towel and take your bath when ever you want, she will ask you how many you had at the end of your stay. The bathroom(s) is shared by everybody, family and guests and it is always immaculately clean. Don't have your bath when it is obvious that everyone else is trying to use the bathroom.

There is great flexibility about breakfast and other meals, they happen when it suits you. For people hitching or using public transport the town houses are the easiest to get to and find, but my favourite are farmhouses, followed closely by country houses. Tucked away in lovely countryside you may find yourself staying in a traditional or modern farm house. The farms concentrate on dairy, sheep, crop farming or beef cattle and often a mixture of everything. The farmer's wife, helped by her children, makes life very comfortable and is always ready to have a chat, advise you on the local beauty spots, and good places to hear traditional music or go for a ceili.

Some of the town and country houses are on fairly main roads, but it is not too noisy as there is so little traffic about. The type of house you might stay in, ranges from the Georgian to the Alpine style bungalow, from a semi–detached to a 1950s dolls house. There are a bewildering amount of architectural styles in the new houses beginning to radiate out from small villages. It is wise to book during July and August, though in my experience you do not have to, except perhaps a night or two ahead. This means that you do not have to be tied and can dawdle in a place as much as you want. If you happen to be there during a festival, it is essential to book.

Full details of Irish Homes can be obtained from the Northern Ireland Tourist Board, and a booklet on farmhouses, town and country houses from any Bord Fáilte office. For an illustrated list of farmhouses write to: Irish Farmhouse Holidays, Libra House Ltd. 7 Clare St. Dublin 2 (60p including postage). For an illustrated Town and Country Homes list write to: The Sec. Town and Country Homes Assoc. St Brendan's, Derrymore West, Tralee, Kerry.

---

**YOUTH HOSTELS:** The Irish YHA is called An Oige and has forty nine hostels. These are distributed all over Ireland, often in wild and remote places so that they are doubly attractive to the enterprising traveller. Members of the International Youth Hostel Federation can use any of these and the hostels in Northern Ireland. If you haven't got a card, you can join for IR£5.50, there is no age limit! All enquiries, essential handbook and an excellent map can be got from the An Oige Office, 39 Mountjoy Square, Dublin 1 Tel: 01 745734 and in Northern Ireland from YHA, 56 Bradbury Place, Belfast. Tel: Belfast 24733. The Youth Hostels are often the most superb old houses but they range from cottages to castles, old coast guard stations to old military barracks. They are great centres for climbers, walkers and fishers and not too spartan; many have a comfortable laxity when it comes to the rules. You must provide your own sheet, and sleeping bag, a flap or pocket covering the pillows, these you can buy at the An Oige office, the hostel provides blankets. Bring your own knives, forks, spoons, tea towels, bath towel and soap and FOOD — meals are not provided but a kitchen and cooking utensils are.

Charges go according to age, month and location; during July and August it is slightly more expensive and it is vital to book. This applies also to weekends. Hostels in Dublin, Cork, Limerick and Killarney are always about 40p more expensive than in other parts where the average is IR£1.30 a night. It's quite a good idea to combine hostelling with staying at B&B's — see under Farmhouses, Town and Country homes.

---

**CAMPING AND CARAVANNING:** There are many official sites with places for washing clothes, drying and ironing rooms, showers, TV, everything that will make camping easy and more civilised, especially if you have children. A complete list of sites is available from any Bord áilte office. Farmers are very tolerant of people turning up and asking if they can camp or park their caravan in a field. You must ask their permission first. Be polite, do not get in the way, and you will find that they will give you drinking water, lots of chat and even vegetables from their garden. You can hire tents and camping equipment in Ireland, the camping and caravanning list tells you where. Prices at official campsites range from £IR1.50-£IR4.

---

**RENTING A HOUSE OR COTTAGE:** This is very easy, every regional office of Bord Fáilte has a list of houses and apartments to let; for the North,look in the back of the accommodation booklet and in newspapers. The Republic has a very popular Rent–an–Irish cottage scheme with centres in Co. Limerick, Galway, Mayo, Tipperary and Clare. On the outside the cottages are thatched, whitewashed and traditional; inside they are well designed with electric cooker, fridge and kettle, all the mod–cons you could want. The bathroom has built–in cupboards, comfy beds, and linen. Simple, comfortable Irish made furniture and fittings make it a happy blend of tradition and modern convenience. The cottages vary in size, some take eight, others five. Easter and the months May and June are the most expensive, but in October, sometimes the nicest month in Ireland weather–wise, a cottage for eight only costs £IR60 a week. The local people take a great interest in you because they are all share–holders in the scheme and so do their best to make you content! Write to Bord Fáilte for details of the scheme and other self catering cottages.

---

**DRINKING:** You are bound to have been lured into trying Guinness by the persuasive advertisements you see all over Europe for the export trade is thriving; but the place to get a real taste of the creamy dark liquor is in Ireland. It's at its most delicious when it is draught and drunk in a bar around Dublin where it is made. Guinness does not travel well, especially on Irish roads. It is said to get its special flavour from the murky waters of the River Liffey and you can go and find out for yourself by visiting the Brewery at St James Gate; there you can see a film of it being made and drink some free into the bargain. It is open Mon–Friday, 10 am to 3 pm. The quality of taste once it has left the brewery depends on how well the publican looks after it and cleans the pipe from the barrel, so it varies greatly from bar to bar. If it's obvious that you are a tourist, your Guinness will be decorated with a shamrock drawn on its frothy head. Bottled draught is a new phenomenon and just coming onto the market. If you are feeling adventurous try something called black velvet — a mixture of Guinness and champagne.

Guinness cake is a delicious invention for those who like really gooey cakes, the ingredients are: 8 ozs of butter, 8 ozs of brown sugar, 4 eggs 10 ozs of flour and two level teaspoons of mixed spice sieved together. 8 ozs sultanas, 4 ozs candied peel. 4 ozs walnuts chopped, 8–12 tablespoons of Guinness. Cream the butter and sugar. Beat in the eggs and fold in the flour and spices. Add the fruit and nuts and mix well. Add 4 tablespoons of Guinness to produce a soft dropping consistency. Put the mixture into a seven inch round cake tin which has been prepared. Bake for an hour at 325°F, regulo 3 and for a further 1½ hours at 300°F, regulo 2. When the cake is cold remove from tin and prick the base with a skewer, spoon over the remaining 4-8 tablespoons of Guinness. Allow to soak overnight, then wrap in foil and keep for a week before cutting.

The old–fashioned serious drinking bar with high counter, engraved glass window, frosted so that the outside world couldn't intrude, is gradually disappearing. It is usually a male preserve, for until a short time ago, it was considered that decent girls didn't drink. Farmers on a trip into town can be heard bewailing the weather or recounting the latest in cattle or land prices. The newest phenomenon is the lounge/cabaret/restaurant inn where husbands happily take their wives for an evening out. What the inns have lost in character they compensate, to a degree, with comfort. The bar of the local hotel is the place to find the priest when he is off–duty, and if you see any member of the clergy eating in the restaurant of a hotel, or any where for that matter, the food is guaranteed to be good. My favourite is the grocery shop which is also a bar, where you ask for a taxi/plumber/undertaker, only to find that the publican or his brother combine all these talents with great panache!

Whiskey has been drunk in Ireland for more than five hundred years and the word itself is derived from 'unisce beatha', the Irish for water of life. It is made from malted barley with a small proportion of wheat, oats and occasionally a pinch of rye. They are several brands but Jameson's and Paddy are the best made in the South and Old Bushmills in the North.

Irish coffee is a wonderful combination of contrasts: hot and cold, black and white and very intoxicating. It's made with a double measure of Irish whiskey, one tablespoon of double cream, one cup of strong, hot black coffee and a heaped tablespoon of sugar. First of all warm a stemmed whiskey glass. Put in the sugar and enough hot coffee to dissolve the sugar. Stir well. Add the Irish whiskey and fill the glass and pour the cream slowly over the spoon. Do not stir the cream into the coffee. It should float on top and the hot whiskey laced–coffee is drunk through the cold cream.

Smithwicks ale and Harp lager are two very good legal brews made in Ireland, but Poteen is illicit whiskey, usually, but not always, made from potatoes. Tucked away in the countryside are stills which no longer bubble away over a turf fire, but on a calor gas stove. Poteen is pretty disgusting stuff unless you get a very good brew and probably kills off a lot of braincells, so it's much better to stick to the legal liquid.

Licensing hours in the Republic: public houses are open Monday to Saturday 10 am to 11.30 pm (unofficially they may stay open into the early hours of the morning) in winter they close half an hour earlier. On Sundays and St Patrick's Day they open from 12.30 pm to 2 pm, and 4 pm to 10 pm. There is no service on Christmas Day or Good Friday. In Northern Ireland public houses are open Monday to Saturday 11.30 am- 11 pm, they are closed on Sundays. You can always get a drink on Sundays at a hotel, though you are supposed to justify it by having a meal as well if you are not staying there. In the Republic, children are often allowed to sit in the lounge bar with packets of crisps and fizzy orange to keep them happy. If you do get into a conversation in a bar, a certain etiquette must be kept to: men always buy everybody in your group a drink when it is your round, women will find they are not allowed to! Both sexes offer their cigarettes around when having one. If there are ten in your group, you will find yourself drunk from social necessity and out of pocket as well!

---

**EATING OUT:** The basis of Irish cooking is excellent beef, lamb, seafood, ham, eggs and butter. Many of the restaurants have international menus, but unless you know that it is really good, it's much safer to stick to plain cooking such as steaks, lamb cutlets or poached salmon. Sometimes, vegetables can be a disaster, overcooked and watery, the Irish do not take vegetables very seriously, they sit being kept warm for far too long. Irish cooking has been influenced greatly by the English, but look out for: home made and crumbly brown soda bread, it has a lovely nutty flavour, Irish stew, which is made from best end of mutton neck, onions and potatoes, and barm brack which is traditionally eaten at Hallowe'en and is a rich fruity bread. For supper in an Irish home you might get bacon and cabbage casserole or potato cakes. Restaurants which specialise in seafood have the pick of the catches, so oysters, scallops, mussels, salmon trout, prawns etc tend to be superb. But if you order fish in restaurants that do not highlight it on their menu – beware, it will turn out to be Bird's Eye frozen whatever!

Your best bet is to tour Ireland armed with Bord Fáilte's booklet 'Dining in Ireland' which gives you an idea of the sort of food served and the price. Eating out can be a very expensive experience, especially in Dublin, for as soon as a restaurant becomes successful, it ups its prices. The Northern Ireland Tourist Board have a booklet entitled 'let's eat out in Northern Ireland' which lists every eating place but does not give such a good idea of the menu or price. If you cannot afford to eat out twice a day, buy yourself a picnic and eat it in some wonderfully scenic place that more than compensates for foregoing the Dublin Bay prawns. If it's drizzling and cold have some pub-grub and a glass of Guinness. Galway is famous for its oysters and the Blackwater River in Cork for smoked salmon.

Amazingly enough, although nowhere in Ireland is more than seventy miles from the sea and every seaweed fringed lough is full of delicious moules and other seafood, it is very difficult to buy fish, lobster or crab.

The fishermen send them straight to France or England where they appear on the starched linen tablecloths of the best restaurants. The reason for this is that the Irish are enthusiastic meat eaters, you cannot fail to notice the number of butchers or fleshers in every town. Any fish that stays at home goes straight to the hotels, but if you would like to buy some salmon straight from the river or lough, it is possible after a lot of enquiry, remember everything in Ireland works on a personal basis. The best place to start your enquiries is at the local newsagent, grocers or butcher, they should at least be able to put you on the right track.

To get round the serious problem of eating cheaply in Ireland, always eat as much as you can of the huge breakfasts provided by bed and breakfast places. If the lady of the house also cooks 'high tea' or supper for guests, take advantage of that as well, the food she produces is inevitably delicious and very good value. Bakeries usually sell tea, coffee and soft drinks along with fresh apple pie, doughnuts, cakes and sausage rolls. Roadside cafes serve the usual menu of hamburgers, chicken'n chips etc. In the North they do a roaring trade in take away foods which have the advantage of being quick and cheap, all the big towns have Chinese and family run restaurants with set all-in menus — filling, cheap and often better than the hotel next door.

The Irish Country Houses and Restaurants Association issue a booklet every year which includes some of the best restaurants in Ireland and they are not necessarily all that expensive. You can often stay at them as well, definitely only for a binge if you are travelling on a tight budget. Service is usually included in the bill at all restaurants. If there is no liquor licence of any sort, the manager is usually quite happy to let you bring in your own wine or beer if you ask.

# Leisure Activities

---

**ANGLING:** The salmon season opens on New Year's Day on some Irish
rivers and continues through to the end of August. Brown trout angling
begins in mid-February and ends in September. Sea trout fishing from
May to 12 October (Kerry) and June to 12 October in some other areas.
There is no closed season for pike and coarse fishing and sea angling is
possible all the year round a day's boat fishing will cost you about £IR9.
Permits are required for salmon fishing, they cost from £IR3 to £IR20
daily. Ask your travel agent about fishing holidays in Ireland run by the
B&I Line.

**NORTHERN IRELAND:** Rod Licences are available from tackle shops
and hotels. If you want to get yours in advance drop a line to the Fisheries
Conservancy Board for Northern Ireland, 21 Church St. Portadown, Co.
Armagh. Some fishing centres are controlled by the Dept. of Agriculture,
if you want to know more about them write to The Fisheries Division,
Hut 5, Castle Grounds, Stormont, Belfast.

**IN THE REPUBLIC:** A state licence is required for salmon, and sea
trout angling. You can get one from the clerks to the Boards of Con-
servators for the various districts and also from various tackle shops, and
hoteliers. A full season licence is £IR10 for all districts, for 21 days it is
£IR5. Bord Fáilte publish guides to game fishing for salmon, sea trout,
brown trout, and rainbow trout, also for sea angling and coarse angling.
The customs are very fussy that you do not bring in worms or maggots for
bait that are packed in soil or vegetable material. Worms and maggots,
flies and other lures can be bought easily in Ireland, or pre-ordered from
Irish Angling Services, Ardlougher, Co. Cavan.

---

**BOARD SAILING (WIND-SURFING):** Ireland has three thousand miles of coastline and plenty of lakes. If you wear a wet suit it is one of the most ideal places to wind-surf. The vital address for all enthusiasts is The Irish Sailing Board Assoc., 63 Grange Park, Baldoyle, Dublin 13 Tel: 01 325535 or Mr. Chris Flemming, Irish Wind Surfer Class Assoc. 98 Bushy Park, Dublin 6. Tel: 01 907710 (home) 01 696584 (office).There are five board sailing centres on the east coast and one on the west.

---

**GOLF:** This sport has really taken off in Ireland and there are many championship courses, as well as fairly rough ones which are good for a fun game. Some hotels offer a special deal for golfing week-ends. You can get details from your travel agent or the Irish Tourist Boards throughout the country. They have a list of golf courses and all the details at a cost of 20p. Write to J.P. Murray, Golf Promotion Advisor, Bord Fáilte, Dublin 2. All golf clubs are very friendly places and charge very little for temporary membership. Altogether there are around 230 courses in Ireland, including the North.

---

**POLO:** You can go to the only residential polo school in Europe: contact Major Hugh Dawnay, MFH, Whitfield Court Polo School, Waterford or watch it (much cheaper) in Phoenix Park, Dublin. Dates and times of play can be checked at the pavilion Tel: 01 776248. A list of *equitation, pony trekking centres* and *riding holidays* can be had from Bord Fáilte offices.

---

**HORSE RACING:** Irish people are wild about horses, and they breed very good ones, you can go and watch them being exercised on The Curragh, a nursery of some of the finest racehorses in the world. The Irish Grand National is run at Fairyhouse in Meath; the Irish Sweeps Derby, St. Leger, The Guineas and other classic races at the Curragh, Kildare. The flat racing season begins in March and ends in November. Steeplechase meetings are held all year round, and point to point meetings in the Spring months, the most fashionable one to be seen at is the Punchestown Races, near Naas, Co. Kildare. Irish point to points are usually freezing cold but great fun with lots of refreshing going on in the tent; the background and form of each horse is known by all, and discussed with great enthusiasm. This is also your chance to glimpse the Anglo-Irish, a dying breed and excellent judges of horseflesh. The greatest fun of all are the horse races held on the Strands during a local festival or regatta.

---

**HUNTING:** This is another popular sport in Ireland, any visitors are welcomed by the various hunts and it's not very expensive. Ask the Irish Tourist Board for a list or local Riding Centre for details. Altogether there are 85 recognised hunting packs, usually on the trail of foxes, although some are stag hunts and harriers. The famous Galway Blazers hunt over stone walls in the west, then there are double banks in the south and ditches and streams in the east. The hire of a horse for a day's hunting costs approximately £IR30 and there is a cap fee which varies a lot.

---

**BEAGLING** is a very, exciting, athletic and challenging sport, you follow the hounds on foot until they pick up the scent of a hare, then you usually have to start running. The hare is always a good match for the hounds when it is on home ground and the baying of the hounds when they have caught the scent is almost musical. You do not need any special clothes or skill and visitors are welcome. The majority of hunts are in the winter and on Sundays. The Irish Tourist Board have a list of Beagle hunt clubs or you can write to The Hon. Secretary, Irish Masters of Beagles Assoc. Bellview, Douglas West, Cork. Tel: 021 293162.

---

**SHOOTING** facilities for visiting sportsmen are strictly controlled. Firearm certificates and hunting licences are granted only to visitors who go to a shoot reserved for them. Before you come to Ireland you need to write to the Forest and Wildlife Service, Upper Merrion Sq. Dublin 2 for details on how to obtain a current Irish firearms certificate and an Irish hunting licence, both necessary if you want to shoot game or birds in Ireland.

---

**ORIENTEERING:** This sport is all the rage in Scandinavia and has only recently come to Ireland. Briefly it is a mixture of cross-country running and map-reading. You need a map case, a red biro, a whistle and a complete change of old clothes. If you are an orienteer and want to pursue this highly competitive sport contact: The Irish Orienteering Assoc. c/o COSPOIR, Hawkins House, Dublin 2. The Association for Adventure Sports, Tiglin, Ashford, Co. Wicklow run weekend courses in it.

---

**SUB-AQUA:** Ireland's oceans are surprisingly warm because they are right in the path of the Gulf Stream, so it would be very difficult to find a better place for underwater swimming or diving. The underwater flora and fauna is vast and varied and you are always bumping into shoals of fish. There are several centres for experienced divers and equipment for hire. Subsea is the official journal of the Irish Underwater Council which publishes information about the affiliated clubs, articles on diving etc. Write to the Editor, Hugh Hennessy, 9 Antrim Rd. Newtownabbey, Belfast, or to Mr. John Geraghty who is the secretary of the Irish Underwater Council, 98 Glendale, Leixlip. Co. Kildare. Tel: 01 789211 ext. 222. By the way, it is against the law to take shell fish from the sea. The centres are in Westport, Co. Mayo, Co. Donegal, Co. Galway,Co. Kerry and Co. Dublin. Ask for the relevant fact sheet in any tourist office.

**MOUNTAINEERING AND HILL WALKING:** Contact the Federation of Mountaineering Clubs of Ireland for a full list of hill walking and rock climbing guide books: 3 Gortnamona Drive, Foxrock, Co. Dublin. The ordnance survey $\frac{1}{2}$ inch to 1 mile maps, and a compass are essentials for serious walkers.

**HURLING** is to the Irish what Cricket is to the English, 15 men with hurleys thrash away at a leather ball and combine neat footwork in perfect combination with the stickwork. Hurling and Gaelic football are promoted by the Gaelic Athletic Association and played strictly for the glory. Money earned is put back into national programmes; the GAA is still closely connected with nationalist objectives. Look in local newspapers for details of matches.

# Irish Traditions and Miscellanea

---

**HISTORIC CASTLES, HOUSES AND GARDENS OPEN TO THE PUBLIC:** If you want to try and understand the Anglo-Irish, who have a very muddled status amongst most shades of opinion, the best thing would be to go and look round one of their houses. The expression 'Anglo-Irish' is said by some to be incorrect, but these big houses were built by families who would probably brain you if you called them English, although as far as the Gaelic Irish are concerned that is what they are!

The buildings are completely different in atmosphere here to their counterparts in England. They have not undergone Victorian 'improvements' or gradually assumed an air of comfortable mellowness over the centuries. It was an act of bravado on the part of the Anglo-Irish to build them at all, for remember they had always to be on the alert against the Whiteboys or some sort of conspiracy. They never had enough money to add on layer after layer in the newest architectural fashion; their houses remained palladian splendours or gothic fantasies built during the Georgian age, when the fortified house could at last be exchanged for something a good deal more comfortable.

The ones that remain are full of beautiful furniture, pictures, objets d'art and the paraphernalia of generations who appreciated beauty, good horses, hard drinking and eating and were generous and slap-dash by nature. It is against this background of grey stately houses looking onto sylvan scenes and cosseted by sweeping trees that one should read Maria Edgeworth, perhaps supplying some details yourself on the penal laws, the famine, the foreigness of the landlords and their loyalties. The big house, the courthouse, the goal and the military barracks were all symbols of oppression and not surprisingly many of them got burnt out in

44

the 1920's. But these houses echo with the voices of talented and liberal people, many of Ireland's patriots were Anglo-Irish and Protestant. The wit of Sheridan, Wilde, the conversations of Mrs Delany, the gleeful humour of Somerville and Ross, drift through the rooms as you wander around. Ask for a list of the houses, castles and gardens which are open, from Bord Fáilte. Many of them are still lived in by the descendants of those who built them. The Irish Georgian Society has done much, with very little money and no government support (except verbal) to save historic houses from ruin (the National Trust has several properties in Northern Ireland). My absolute favourite is Springhill in Co. Tyrone, because it still has the atmosphere of a gracious home, whose owners were never wickedly rich just thrifty in a typically Northern way. Entrance fees vary from 50p to £1.50.

---

**MUSIC:** Traditional Irish music is played everywhere in Ireland, in the cities and the country. Government sponsorship helped to revive it, especially through Radio na Gaeltachta in the west. Now there is great enthusiasm for it amongst everyone, a nine year old will sing a lover's lament about seduction and desertion, without batting an eyelid, to grandfather whose generation scarcely sung at all. The 1845-8 famine silenced the music and dancing for a while, but today Ireland has one of the most vigorous music traditions in Europe. Irish ballads are sung the world over; each emigrant considers himself an exile still and the commercial record industry churns out ballads; most record covers tend to be decorated with the grinning features of a leprechaun and a few shamrocks for good measure. Serious traditional music is not in this sweet folksey style. Listening to it can induce a state of exultant melancholy, or infectious merriment; whatever way, it goes straight to your heart. The lyrics deal with the ups and downs of love, failed rebellions, especially the '98, soldiering, dead heroes, religion; comparatively few deal with occupations or work!

The bard in pre-Christian society was held in honour and a great deal of awe for his learning and the mischievous satire in his poetry and music. After the Cromwellian and Williamite wars, he lost his status all together; music and poety were kept alive by the country people who cheered themselves up during the dark winter evenings with stories and and music. The harp is sadly scarcely used nowadays, except when it is dragged out for the benefit of tourists at medieval banquets in Bunratty Castle, etc. The main instruments used are the uillean pipes, which are more sophisticated than the Scottish bagpipes, the fiddle (violin) and the tin whistle. In West Cork and Kerry, they used the Bodhran, which is a type of drum, and recently, the accordian, the flute and the piano are used by some groups. These are played singly or together. The airs, laments, slip jigs, reels and songs all vary enormously from region to region, and you might easily hear a Cork man and a Leitrim fiddler

45

discussing with heated emotion the interpretation of a certain piece. Pieces are constantly improvised on, and seldom written down; inevitably some of the traditional content gets changed from generation to generation. A form of singing that almost died out by the 1940s is the Sean-Nós, fully adorned, sung in gaelic and unaccompanied by instruments. Now the Sean-Nós section in music festivals is overflowing with entrants.

You will have no difficulty in hearing traditonal ballads or folk music in the local bars or hotels; they usually advertise in the local newspaper, or by sticking up a notice in the window. The group of players seem only too happy to let you join in, and as the atmosphere gets smokier the music really takes off. In 1951, Comhaltas Ceoltoírí Éireann was set up for the promotion of traditional music, song and dance. It now has 200 branches all over the country and their members have regular sessions (seisiún) which are open to all. If you ask at the local tourist office or write to Comhaltas Ceoltoírí Eireann, 32 Belgrave Sq., Monkstown, Co. Dublin, Tel: Dublin 800296. There is bound to be a Fleadh going on somewhere near you, the All-Ireland Fleadh is held at the end of August in a different town every year. There are thirty smaller festivals around the country each year; at these you can hear music of an incredible standard brimming over the street from every hall, bar, hotel and private house. It takes a great deal of stamina and a lot of jars to see the whole thing through.

In Kerry, Father Pat Ahern has got together a National Folk Theatre, which has performances in song, mime, and the dance of life set in rural Ireland years ago. They are based in two thatched cottages in Finuge and the other at Carraig on the west tip of the Dingle Peninsular. Each cottage is known as Teach Siamsa, house of musical entertainment. A Pan Celtic Festival is held in Killarney every May, when players and singers from Scotland, Brittany, the Isle of Man, Cornwall, Wales and Ireland compete with each other and exchange ideas and folklore.

If you get a chance to watch the Orangemen marching with their flute bands (practising ground for the celebrated James Galway when he was a youngster) you will see how important music is to every Irishman. Boys beat the great Lambeg drums till their knuckles bleed, the skilful throwing of the batons makes a great performance, well worth seeing, despite what you read about its sectarian associations. Perhaps the successful new music from Belfast played by Stiff Little Fingers owes much to this background.

Ireland is producing some good musicians of a completely different type to the folk groups; look in the local newspaper of any big town or ask in a record shop, they will know what gigs are on and probably be able to sell you a ticket as well. The local bands that play in the bars and, around the halls may turn out to be as big as the Boomtown Rats, for there is certainly a lot of talent around.

## HOLIDAYS AND FESTIVALS

| | |
|---|---|
| January 1: | holiday in the Republic and the North |
| March 17th: | St. Patrick's Day |
| | holiday in the Republic |
| Good Friday: | holiday in the Republic and the North |
| Easter Monday: | holiday in the Republic and the North |
| May 31st: | Spring holiday in the North |
| June 7th: | holiday in the Republic |
| July 12th: | holiday in the North |
| August 2nd: | holiday in Republic |
| August 30th: | holiday in the North |
| October 25th: | holiday in the Republic |
| December 25th: | Christmas Day |
| | holiday in the Republic and the North |
| December 26th: | St Stephen's Day |
| | holiday in the Republic and the North |

On all holidays the banks are shut, but you will always find a shop that is open which sells practically every sort of grocery, plus newspapers. There is one of these in every village in the Republic which stays open until about 10 pm everyday, regardless of whether it's Sunday, unlike the North where they take the Sabbath very seriously.

The 1982 Calendar of Events, available from Tourist Offices, presents you with a dazzling array of International Festivals and small town extravaganza's, where everyone has a ball: jolly music pours into the street, farmers and tradesmen parade their goods and machinery, and there are endless bouncing baby competitions, discos and drinking bouts. These are the fifteen major festivals, if you want to plan your holiday round one, the following dates are for 1981, check with the tourist office for changes.

**ST. PATRICK'S WEEK** 12th-19th March; events centre round Dublin, Cork, Galway, and Limerick with parades, music, dance and theatre.

**CORK INTERNATIONAL CHORAL AND FOLK DANCE FESTIVAL** 29th April to 3rd May: Further information from Professor Aloys Fleischmann, Festival Director., 15 Bridge St., Cork. Tel: 021 52221.

**PAN CELTIC WEEK** 10th-17th May: music, hurling and chess. Further information from The Pan Celtic Office, Town Hall, Killarney, Co. Kerry. Tel: (064) 31622.

**AN FLEADH NUA**, Ennis, Co. Clare, 29th-31st May: traditional music, song and dance. Further information, Comhaltas Ceoltoiri Eireann, Belgrave Sq., Monkstown, Co. Dublin.

**FESTIVAL OF MUSIC IN GREAT IRISH HOUSES** 5th-18th June: international soloists and orchestras perform. Further information Mr.

D. Laing, Russborough, Blessington, Co. Wicklow or Castletown House, Celbride, Co. Kildare.

**INTERNATIONAL FOUR DAYS' WALKS CASTLEBAR** 25th-28th June: walks and music in the evening, pop, traditional and classical. Information from the Courthouse, The Mall, Castlebar, Co. Mayo.

**FLEADH CHEOIL NAH EIREANN BUNCRANA, CO. DONEGAL** 21st-23rd August: sometimes up to 5,000 traditional musicians congregate to play impromptu sessions. While you are there take to the hills and explore the Inishowen Peninsula. Further information from Comhaltas Ceoltoırı Eireann, Belgrave Sq., Monkstown.

**KILKENNY ARTS WEEK** 22nd-30th August: recitals, poetry, art exhibitions. Further information from Kilkenny Arts Week. Kilkenny Design Theatre, The Parade.

**ROSE OF TRALEE INTERNATIONAL FESTIVAL** 29th August-3rd September: girls of Irish birth and parentage come from all over the world to compete for the title. There are carnival parades, street dancing, fireworks, music, and the Tralee races. Further information from Rose of Tralee Office, 5 Lower Castle St., Tralee, Co. Kerry.

**INTERNATIONAL FESTIVAL OF LIGHT OPERA** 19th September-4th October: a dozen light operas succeed each other, performed in the lovely old Theatre Royal. Further information from the Hon. Executive Secretary, Waterford Light Opera Festival Office, 7 Barker St., Waterford.

**DUBLIN THEATRE FESTIVAL** 28th September-17th October: Dublin has produced so many brilliant writers: Sheridan, Goldsmith, Shaw, Wilde, Yeats, Synge, O'Casey, Beckett and Behan – to name only the most famous – so it is not surprising that this festival holds a special place in the world theatre scene. You can see work by Irish writers, interspersed with productions by well known companies from America and Europe. Further information: Festival Director, 47 Nassau St., Dublin 2. Tel: 01 778439.

**CORK FILM FESTIVAL** 2nd-9th October: films, discussions, workshops, parties, where lots of beautiful people suddenly appear. Further information, 38 Mac Curtain St., Cork. Tel: 021 502221.

**CASTLEBAR INTERNATIONAL SONG CONTEST**: 6th-11th October.

**WEXFORD FESTIVAL OPERA** 21 October-1st November: rare operatic masterpieces are performed in the Theatre Royal, with supporting events of orchestral concerts, chamber music, recitals, films, fringe shows. Further information, The Administrator, Wexford Festival Opera, Theatre Royal, Wexford. Tel: 053 22240.

**BELFAST FESTIVAL** in early November, Concerts, Films, Opera, Theatre, it is said to be a close second to the Edinburgh Festival. Festival Office Tel: (0232) 665577.

**THE DUBLIN INDOOR INTERNATIONAL HORSE SHOW** in November and the **DUBLIN HORSE SHOW** in August are of course world famous. Other fun events are the Connemara Pony Show, the Galway Oyster Festival and the Lisdoonvara Folk Festival; for this last one prepare for a lot of drinking, noise and crowds. The Letterkenny Folk Festival in August is another, but especially memorable because of the countryside around.

---

**IRISH SPECIALITIES TO BUY AND TAKE HOME:** Shopping in Ireland is the most relaxing pastime because nobody ever makes you feel that you have to buy anything, so you can browse to your heart's content. **Irish Lace** is one of the lightest and most precious of all the goodies you can pack into your suitcase and you find it in Carrickmacross, Co. Monaghan, and in Limerick City. Some smart shops, such as Brown & Thomas in Dublin, also stock it, but it is fun if you are there to go around the convents where the lace is made. In Carrickmacross the nuns design lawn appliqué applied to a background of net. In Limerick the lace is worked completely in thread on the finest Brussels net.

**DONEGAL TWEED:** handwoven in the speckled, natural colours of the countryside, you can buy lengths, well designed jackets, coats or skirts and tweed caps very reasonably. Magees in Donegal Town and McNutts in Carrigart have a very good selection and if you explore around Ardara you will still find naturally dyed and extra strong tweed. When in Dublin go to the Kilkenny design shop.

**CONNEMARA MARBLE:** this is a natural green stone found in the west which ranges from bright field green, through to jade and oak leaf colour, sometimes with stripes of brown in it. Many of the craft shops in the area work the marble jewellery fashioned into Celtic designs, and sell it with other locally made things such as paperweights or chess sets. Look out for the attractive striped wool rugs sold in these parts.

**HAND KNITTED SWEATERS:** make sure you buy one which has the hand knitted label on it for it makes the whole difference when you are buying an Aran. These are made out of tough wool lightly coated in animal oils so they are water resistant and keep you as warm as toast. You can get them in the natural white or different colours and the pattern differs quite a bit. In the past the wives of the fishermen used to have a family pattern so that they could identify any one who had drowned. You can get them in a variety of styles and the best place to shop for them is all round the west coast. They stretch after being worn awhile

49

and last for years.

**WATERFORD CRYSTAL:** this is world famous for its quality and design. You can tour the factory to see it being hand blown and hand engraved. Remember you can always buy it later at Shannon or Dublin Airport or have it mailed home, thus escaping 15% VAT. Kilkenny, Cavan, Tyrone and Cork also produce beautiful cut glass. Simon Pearce at Bennettsbridge has made a name for himself producing hand blown goblets, but rumour has it that he is emigrating to America.

**LINEN** and **BELLEEK** pottery are still going strong in the North, so is **BUSHMILLS** whiskey. All over Ireland you can buy baskets made of willow or rush in different shapes and sizes: breadbaskets, turfholders, place mats and St Brigid Crosses, a charm against evil. Amongst all the other trinkets and souvenirs available claddagh rings still remain the nicest of all love tokens and very evocative of the west of Ireland. Ireland has some very good potters, enamel workers and jewellry designers. Your best bet for seeing their imaginative work is to go around the **Kilkenny Design Centre** in Dublin or Kilkenny.

---

**POST OFFICES:** Letter boxes are green in the Republic and red in the North; you have to put British postal stamps on letters posted in the North. If you do not have a fixed address in Ireland, letters can be sent Poste Restante to any Post Office and picked up when you produce proof of your identity. If after three months they are gathering dust in the corner of the post office, they will be sent back to the sender. There is a post office in every village which is usually the telephone exchange as well and a hive of activity. You can send telegrams from the post office. The post office should be open from 9 am to 5.30 pm on weekdays. Closed on Sundays and Public holidays. Sub-post offices close on one day a week at 1 pm. The GPO in O'Connell St., Dublin, is open from 8 am to 11 pm and in the mornings on Sundays and Bank Holidays.

---

**TELEPHONES:** Someone wrote a play fairly recently about a very cosmopolitan Irish family living in Co. Donegal; all the daughters were try to conduct passionate love affairs with men in far away places, but as the drama mounted these poor swains could never get past the Letterkenny exchange with resulting confusion and tragi-comedy. The phones in private houses in parts of Ireland are still wind-up ones and the whole telephone system is in a state of transition, some are on the STD system, some not. It is very difficult trying to be efficient because you spend so much time hanging on as the operator takes you all around Ireland before she gets hold of Cork City. Still, if you are on holiday that doesn't really matter and there is a lot to be said for the old operator system, they will always take a message if you are out and it's important.

Telephone boxes are green and inside are clear instructions on how to use them. Bars and hotels are also a useful source when all the boxes are filled or they have disappeared into thin air. There is no general rule about when it is best to ring far away places, the line is usually clearer in the morning, but that is when calls are at their most expensive, unless you get up before 8 am when it's still cheap rate. Cheap rate is from 6 pm to 8 am every day. The coin boxes take 5 pence and 10 pence pieces. For telegrams dial 116 (non coinbox) or 10 (coinbox). U.S. Bell System Telephone Credit Cards are accepted for charging calls to the US and Canada; you wil find that you have to go through an operator for any long distance calls – dial 10 for the operator. In Northern Ireland telephone boxes are bright red and all towns and villages are on the STD system. 5 and 10 pence pieces are used and you dial 100 for the operator.

---

**WEATHER:** Ireland's temperature is never extreme. Average air temperatures in January and February: the coldest months are between 4°C (39°F) and 7°C (45°F). In July and August, the two warmest months have average temperatures between 14°C (57°F) and 16°C (61°F) but they can reach as high as 24°C (75°F) at times.

There is no best time to visit Ireland, the weather is incredibly fickle which is why Irish people talk about it so much, for whether it rains or shines could mean the difference between a good harvest or a bad one. You may find yourself huddling over a fire on an icy June day or picnicking in the sultry sunshine during February or November. The weather reflects the whole feeling of contrast in Ireland, changing the landscape from dreary dampness to limpid detailed beauty. For those who like to avoid the crowds April/May and September/October are surprisingly sunny, although you do not have such long, light evenings.

---

**SUMMER SCHOOLS AND CAMPS:** Some US and Canadian universities offer summer programmes in Ireland. The Irish Tourist Board will send you (free) an up to date list of programmes and expenses. Ireland's own universities offer summer courses on literature, politics, history and Gaelic. Other organisations offer courses that range from archaeology, arts and crafts, music, theatre, English as a Foreign Language to The Experiment in International Living. One of the most enjoyable is the Yeats International Summer School because it is well run and set in such wonderful countryside. It costs about £100 if you stay for the full two weeks of it in August. Write to The Yeats Memorial Building, Douglas Hyde Bridge, Sligo. Tel: 071 2693. For full details write to the Group and Education Department of the Irish Tourist Board (Bord Fáilte), PO Box 273, Dublin 8, or ask at a regional Tourist office.

USIT organise adventure sports, cycling and water sports holidays, enquiries to: 7 Anglesea St., Dublin 2, Tel: 01 778117. There are several centres for Adventure Holidays, but one of the latest and the best is Creeslough Adventure Sports Ltd., Creeslough, Co. Donegal. Tel: Creeslough 43.

---

**TRACING YOUR ANCESTORS:** If you have any Irish blood in you at all, you will have a passion for genealogy, it seems to go together with the characteristic of looking backwards. When the Irish had nothing left, no land, no Brehon laws, no religious freedom, they managed to hold on to their pride and their genealogy. Waving these before the eyes of French and Spanish rulers ensured that they got posts at Court or commissions in the army. There is no such thing as class envy in Ireland; the next man is as good as you, everybody is descended from some prince or hero from the Irish past. It is the descendants of the Cromwellian parvenus who had to bolster up their images with portraits, and fine furniture. Now the planter families have the Irish obsession too!

The best way to go about finding where your family came from is to write to the Public Record Office in Dublin and the Public Record Office of Northern Ireland in Belfast. First you must have found out as much as possible from family papers, old relatives, records of church and state in your own country; your local historical or genealogical society might be able to help. Find out the full name of your emigrant ancestor, the background of his family, whether rich, poor, merchants or farmers, catholic or protestant. The family tradition of remembering the name of the parish or townland is a great help. An important source of information is the General Civil Registration of births marriages and deaths, which began in 1864. These are kept at the office of The Registrar General, The Customs House, Dublin 1. Marriages of non catholics were recorded from 1845. The Registry of Deeds Henrietta St. Dublin 1 records land matters from 1708 onwards, you may make your research in person for a small fee. The National Library, Kildare St. has many sources in its books, newspapers and manuscripts. The Genealogical Library in Dublin Castle can arrange to make searches for you. Church records are an essential primary source, the parochial registers are in the keep of parish priests all over Ireland, whilst records in urban areas, date back two hundred years in some cases. Unfortunately, the Public Record Office in Dublin was burnt in 1922, and with it many of the Church of Ireland registrars, but not all. If your ancestors were presbyterian, the Presbyterian Historical Society, Church House, Fisherwick Place, Belfast may be able to help. The Ulster Historical Foundation, which is attached to the Northern Irish Public Record office will undertake searches. There is a registration fee of £10 and the average search costs £80. The address to write to is: The Secretary, U.H.S. 66 Balmoral Avenue, Belfast. BT9 6NY Tel: Belfast 66 16 21. Hibernian Researchers, Windsor House, 22 Windsor Rd. Rathmines, Dublin 6, employ a bunch of full-time professional genealogists with plenty of experience; they will undertake searches for you, a five hour search plus a full report costs about IR£30.

---

**WOMEN:** Irish men have an attitude towards women which is as infuriating as it is attractive. They are a grand old muddle of male chauvinism, with a dash of admiration and fear for their mothers, sisters and wives. Irish women tend to stay at home, rear large and happy families and cook their husbands delicious meals. They have a sharpness and wit which makes them more than a match for 'your man' in an argument, but at the same time they work their hearts out cooking and washing. Very few Irish housewives will get a washing machine until her husband has exhausted the list of what he needs on the farm. If you are a lone female travelling through Ireland you will find an Irishman will always help you with your luggage, your flat tyre and stand you a meal or a drink, without any question of you buying him a round. If one tries to chat you up in a bar, or at a dance, it is always a bit of crack, not to be taken seriously, and the game is abandoned at once if you get tired of it. They probably think that you ought to be travelling with somebody else, but it's only the women who will say so, saying, with a smile, that it must be a bit lonesome. If you walk into an obviously male preserve such as a serious drinking pub, don't expect to feel welcomed, because you won't be unless everybody is drunk and by that time you would need to scarper. A bit of advice, which does not apply just to women, was pithily put by an Irish politician 'The great difference between England and Ireland is that in England you can say what you like, so long as you do the right thing, in Ireland you can do what you like so long as you say the right thing'. If you are hitch-hiking on your own, or with another girl, you will get plenty of lifts, and offers to take you out dancing that night; your driver will never believe that you have to get on and be somewhere by a certain date, so the journey is passed in pleasant banter. Whatever happens you are 99.9% safe from attacks and can walk safely down any street late at night.

---

**WHAT TO BRING TO IRELAND:** Whatever you do, come to Ireland expecting rain – wellies, umbrellas, raincoats, etc. are essential, unless you want to stay inside reading a book all day. Once you get out into the rain it is never as bad as it looks and the clouds begin to clear as you appear. Warm jerseys, trousers, woollen socks, and gloves for autumn, winter and early spring. The best thing to do is to expect the cold and wet and then get a pleasant surprise when it's sunny and hot, so do not forget to sneak in a few T shirts just in case. Sometimes the sun shines furiously in March and April and you end up with a very convincing tan.

If you like walking bring a pair of fairly tough shoes, tennis shoes end up very bedraggled and let the water in too easily, fishing rods and swimsuits are worth packing, depending on what you are planning to do. Bring a sleeping bag if you plan to stay at youth hostels. The chemists are well stocked so that headache pills, camera films etc. are easily obtainable. You will be amazed at what the village shops sell, anything from pots and pans to the finest french wines, and maybe some fresh salmon trout if you are lucky. In the Republic you can be sure to of finding a shop open until 10 in the evening and on Sundays as well.

---

**BANKS AND MONEY:** All small towns have at least one bank which is open Monday to Fridays from 10am-3pm (in some towns there is late afternoon banking once a week). The bank usually occupies the grandest house in town, the various banking groups seem to have some sort of conscience about historical buildings which is very rare in Ireland. The moving of money is accompanied by massive security, which looks very out of keeping with the happy-go-lucky attitude in Ireland but is necessary because bank raids have become so common. In Northern Ireland the banks are open from 10 am to 3.30 pm Monday to Friday. On both sides of the border they close for lunch. In many big places in the South, banks have a late opening on Thursdays until 5 pm.

Since the Republic joined the European Monetary System, the Irish and the English pound are no longer worth the same, the difference fluctuates usually to the detriment of the Irish pound or punt which is worth about 25 pence less. The optimists say that when Ireland exploits her vast oil resources things will even up! A great fiddle goes on with change machines and the London underground, because the machines gobble up the coins regardless of whether they have a harp or a crowned head on them. Shopkeepers in the Republic avidly accept sterling but in the North they will not touch your punt, except perhaps in a border town. Both currencies use a pound as currency which divides into 100 pence. There are coins for the pence, notes for the pounds. Traveller's cheques and leading credit cards are accepted throughout Ireland. If the bank is closed hotels and many large shops will take Traveller's cheques. You may bring in any amount of foreign currency to Ireland but you must not leave with more than £IR100 notes, although any Traveller's Cheques letters of credit etc. not cashed which were brought into Ireland may be taken out.

**The main banks in Dublin are:**
American Express International 16 Grafton St. Tel: 772874/772879
The Bank of America 26 Grafton St. Tel: 775404
The first Bank of Chicago 44 St Stephen's Green. Tel: 681522
Bank of Nova Scotia 68 St Stephen's Green. Tel: 781388
Bank of Ireland Lr. Baggot St. Tel: 687155

Banque Nationale de Paris 111 Grafton St. Tel: 712811
Barclays International 47 St. Stephen's Green Tel: 600688
Ulster Bank 31 College Green Tel: 777623 (part of Nat. Westminster group)
Northern Bank 112 Grafton St. Tel: 771571 (part of Midlands Bank group)
Allied Irish Bank 5 College St. Tel: 775461

**In Belfast**
Bank of Novia Scotia, 11 Donegall Sq. Belfast 45801 (Chase and Bank of Ireland).
Northern Bank, Donegall Sq. West 1 Tel: Belfast 45277
Ulster Bank, 47 Donegall Place. Tel: Belfast 20222
Eurocheques are accepted in the North and the Republic.

---

**WORK OPPORTUNITIES:** If you are in need of some cash or have run out of money, it is just possible to get a job in a pub or restaurant in Dublin or Cork. In country areas any jobs that are going will be offered to local people first. You could get a job as an au pair, the following agencies make arrangements: Dublin School of English and Foreign Languages Ltd. 11 Westmoreland St. Dublin 2 Tel: 01 773322/773221 The Language Centre of Ireland, 9-11 Grafton Street, Dublin 2 Tel: 01 716266/716891. If you do get a job while in Ireland, USIT at 7 Anglesea St. Dublin. Tel: (01) 770535, and (01) 778117 can sometimes get you a summer work permit on the spot. The Council on International Educational Exchange (CIEE) in the United States operates a Summer Work Programme with the co-operation of the Irish Union of Students. You have to be a full time student in the U.S. and a U.S. citizen. Contact CIEE, 809 U.N. Plaza, New York NY 10017 Tel: (212) 883 8200 for details.

---

**HAZARDS:** Toads and adders are said to have fled from Ireland at the sound of St. Patrick's bell tollling from the top of Croagh Patrick mountain; unfortunately, the voracious midges of the west coast did not take their cue. They are very persistent on warm summer evenings, so remember to arm youself with insect repellent of some sort. There is plenty of choice in the Irish chemists if you forget. Wasps, hornets and horseflys also emerge in summer to irritate.

If you decide to have a picnic in some inviting green field, just check that there is not a bull in it first. High spirited bullocks can be just as alarming, they come rushing up to have a good look and playfully knock you over in the process!

A major hazard can be strong currents in the sea, one beach may be perfectly safe for bathing and the one beside it not. Always check with locals before you swim, there are lifeguards on most of the resort beaches.

Walkers who intend to go through bog and mountainous country be warned that even though it looks dry enough on the road, once into the heather and moss you will soon sink into water logged ground. Wear stout boots (brogues) and bring at least one jersey extra. Sudden mists and rain can descend and you can get very cold. The experienced mountain rescue teams, which exist in the Lake District, are non-existant here, so if you do disappear into a mountain range leave word locally as to where you plan to go or a note in your car. If you do get stuck in the mountains in the dark, apparently a very efficient way to keep warm is to cover yourself with heather.

During the shooting season: grouse and snipe from August to the last day of January, duck from September to the last day of January and pheasant from the first of November to the first of January, be careful of wandering into a stray bullet on the hilly slopes or in marshy places.

There is just one last possible hazard which you might only have dreamt about: the mischievous fairies might put a spell on you so that you never want to return to your own country; it's not a joke for Ireland is an enchanting country and difficult to leave. As a rule it is no use enquiring about charms against this enchantment or for any other, the answer is always the same. 'There used to be a lot of them in the old days but the priests put them down'. You get that answer about poteen too! Underneath, there is a sort of sneaking belief in fairies, for why, in a perfectly modern housing estate outside Sligo is there a ragged mound which escaped the bulldozer and cement? Perhaps because it is a fairy rath? One last word on fairies, have you ever heard how they came about? Padraic Colum found out from a blind man whom he met in the west who believed in them as firmly as the gospels. When the Angel Lucifer rebelled against God, hell was made in a minute and down to it God swept Lucifer and thousands of his followers, until Angel Gabriel said 'O God Almighty, Heaven will be swept clean'. God agreed and compromised saying 'Them that are in heaven let them remain so, them that are in hell, let them remain in hell; and them that are betweeen Heaven and Hell, let them remain in the air.' And the angels that remained between Heaven and Hell are the fairies.

---

## GENERAL

**Loos** – public ones are usually in a pretty bad way, labelled in Irish Fir (men) and Mna (woman). Nobody minds if you slip into a lounge bar or hotel to go to the loo, though it's a good excuse to stop for a drink as well.

**Electricity** is 220 volts AC, so bring a converter if you have any American appliances.

The best **newspaper** to read whilst in Ireland is the *Irish Times*, followed closely by the *Irish Independent* and the *Cork Examiner*. In Northern

Ireland you either buy a 'protestant' or a 'catholic' newspaper, some are more extreme than others, perhaps the *Belfast Telegraph* and the *Newsletter* are nearer middle of the road. The *Irish Times* on Saturdays lists 'What is on' – exhibitions, festivals, concerts, etc. around the country.
**V.A.T.** 15% on the luxury items such as cameras, watches, electrical domestic appliances and 10% on other items, there is no tax on clothing, food and transport.
**Clochan** - a small stone, circular building, with its roof corbelled inwards rather like a beehive in shape. Nowadays used for storing things, in the past as dwelling places. There are many of them in Kerry and the west.
**Round Towers** – a lot of theories and speculation, it has been agreed that these slender stone towers, which are often crowned with a conical cap, were built between the 9th-12th centuries as belfries and refuges from the Vikings.

**EMBASSIES AND CONSULATES IN DUBLIN:** Tel: code 01

American Embassy 42 Elgin Rd. D4 Tel: 688777
Australian Embassy Fitzwilliam House Wilton Terrace D2 Tel: 761517
Austrian Embassy 5 Ailesbury Rd. D4 Tel: 694577
British Embassy 33 Merrion Rd. D4 Tel: 695211
Canadian Embassy 65 St. Stephen's Green D2 Tel: 781988
French Embassy 36 Ailesbury Rd. D4 Tel: 694777
German Embassy 43 Ailesbury Rd. D4 Tel: 693011
Italian Embassy 12 Fitzwilliam Sq. D2 Tel: 762401
Swiss Embassy 6 Ailesbury Rd. D4 Tel: 692515
Spanish Embassy Ailesbury House, Ailesbury Rd. D4 Tel: 691640
Japanese Embassy 22 Ailesbury Rd. D4 Tel: 694244
Swedish Embassy 31 Merrion Rd. D4 Tel: 694544

**HEALTH:** Visitors from EEC countries to Ireland are entitled to medical treatment in Ireland under a reciprocal agreement. All EEC visitors (except those from the UK) should fill in a E111 form from their own National Social Security offices, before they travel to get free treatment. If you are ill you should produce this form, there is a doctor available from each of the regional Health Boards. Enquire at a Health Board for a list of them. If you have to go into hospital you will be treated free when you show your E111 card. UK visitors should pick up a Leaflet SA 28/July 1978 from their local social security offices before travelling to Ireland to benefit from the EEC reciprocal arrangement.

---

## BORD FÁILTE (ALSO KNOWN AS THE IRISH TOURIST BOARD)

The people who work for Bord Fáilte would get you the moon if they could – should you ask for it. They will do literally anything to help and organise anything that is practical, and if they do not know the answer to something, they can always refer you to someone who does. They are like this in the Northern Irish Tourist Board too. They will load you with free literature, book your hotel or B&B searching around first for one which is in your price range.

The Head Office in Dublin is in Baggot St. Bridge. D2 Tel: 01 765871
For General Postal enquiries write to Bord Fáilte PO Box 273 D8
The other offices in Dublin are 14 O'Connell St. Upr. and 51 Dawson Street, Tel: 01 747733

Other all year round tourist offices are:
Athlone Tel: 2866
Cashel Tel: 61333
Cork City Tel: 23251
Dublin Airport (01) 376387/8
Dun Laoghaire Tel: (01) 806984/5/6, 01 805760 from May to September and 01 807048 from October to April
Ennis Tel: 21366
Galway Tel: 63081
Kilkenny Tel: 21755
Killarney Tel: 31633
Letterkenny Tel: 21160
Limerick City Tel: 47522
Mullingar Tel: 8650
Nenagh Tel: 31610
Shannon Airport Tel: 61664
Skibbereen Tel: 21766
Sligo Tel: 5336/7/8
Tralee Tel: 21288
Waterford Tel: 75788
Westport Tel: 269
Wexford Tel: (053) 23111

In Northern Island:
Belfast Tel: 27888
Derry Tel: 69501

**Offices in Great Britain:**
London 150 New Bond St. W1Y 0AQ Tel: 01 493 3201
Manchester 28 Cross St. M2 3NH Tel: 061 832 5981
Birmingham 6/8 Temple Row B2 5HG Tel: 021 236 9724

Glasgow 19 Dixon St. G1 4AJ Tel: 041 221 2311

**Europe:**
Paris: 9 Boulevard de la Madeleine, 75001 Paris. Tel: 261 84 26
Milan: c/o Aer Lingus-Irish, Via Galleria Passarella, 20122 Milan Tel: 700080/783565
Frankfurt: An der Hauptwache 7/8, 6000 Frankfurt am Main Tel: 0611 287775
Amsterdam: Leidsestraat 32, 1017PB Amsterdam Tel: (020) 223101
Brussels: Rue de Loxum 6-10/te 3 B-1000 Bruxelles Tel: (02) 5137874
Copenhagen c/o Competance Special Service, Store Strandstraede 19 1255 Copenhagen K Tel: 111619

**USA and Canada:**
New York: 590 Fifth Avenue, NY 10036 Tel: 212 2467400
Chicago: 230 North Michigan Av. Chicago. Illinois 60601 Tel: 312 7269356
San Francisco: 681 Market St. San Francisco California 94105 Tel: 415 7815 688
Los Angeles: 1880 Century Park East Suite 314 L.A. California 90067 Tel: 213 557 0722
Toronto: 69 Yonge St. Toronto M5E 1K3 Tel: 416 364 1301

**New Zealand**
Auckland: 2nd Floor, Dingwall Building, 87 Queen St. PO Box 279 Auckland 1 Tel: 793708 and 770374

**Australia**
Sydney: MLC Centre, 37th Level, Martin Place, Sydney 2000 Tel: 232 7460

**Argentina**
Buenos Aires: Av. Santa Fe 1589, 3rd Floor, B.A. 1060, Tel: 42 4004
The Tourist offices in Northern Ireland and Great Britain besides being a fund of free information will also make all types of accommodation reservations on your behalf for a fee of £1. Offices in the other countries do not.

---

**THE NORTHERN IRELAND TOURIST OFFICES:** the people who work in them like their counterpart in Bord Fáilte are friendly, helpful and humourous and very proud of their bit of Ireland.
Head Office in Northern Ireland: River House, 48 High Street, Belfast BT1 2DS. For information Tel: 46609

*Around Ireland*

There are also branches at:
Belfast Airport, Aldergrove,
  Co. Antrim, Tel: Crumlin 52103
Ballycastle Tel: 62024
Banbridge Tel: 22143
Bangor Tel: 2092
Bushmills Tel: 31343
Carnlough Tel: 328
Carrickfergus Tel: 63604
Castlerock Tel: 258
Cushendall Tel: 4215
Enniskillen Tel: 3110

Kilkeel Tel: 63092
Larne Tel: 2313
Londonderry Tel: 67273
(Larne Harbour Tel: 62024)
Newcastle Tel: 22222
Newry Tel: 61748
Portballintrae tel: Bushmills 31672
Portrush Tel: 2286
Portstewart Tel: 2286
Strabane Tel: 883735
Warrenpoint Tel: 2256

Some of these are open only in the Summer months. All of them will give you details of what is on in Northern Ireland, sports, festivals, Arts, bus tours, accommodation etc.

Abroad there are offices in:
London, The Ulster Office, 11 Berkeley St, Tel: 01 493 0601
The Midlands: Sean Taaffe, PO Box 26, Sutton Coldfield, W. Midlands Tel: 021-493 0601
Scotland: Betty Michie, Olympic House, 142 Queen St, Glasgow, Tel: 041 221 5115
North America: Eddie Friel, c/o British Tourist Authority, 680 Fifth Avenue, New York, NY 10019, Tel: 212 581 4708
Europe: Jim Paul, c/o British Tourist Authority, 6000 Frankfurt-AM-Main, Neue Mainzerstrasse 22, West Germany, Tel: 23 45 04

# PART II
# LANDMARKS IN IRISH
# HISTORY

---

If you happen to fall into conversation with an Irishman in any bar the subjects of religion and politics are bound to come up. With any luck you will have a cool glass of Guinness in front of you, for discussions on Ireland are inevitably rather emotional. The Irish are good talkers and have very long memories, so when you are in Ireland it's a good idea to have some idea of their history. Many of Ireland's troubles have stemmed from her geographical situation – too far from Britain to be assimilated, too near to be allowed to be separate; Queen Elizabeth poured troops into Ireland because she appreciated the strategic importance of Ireland to her enemies. Throughout the centuries Ireland has been offered help in her fight for independence, but it was never disinterested help; whoever paid for arms and fighting men in Ireland wanted to further some military, political, religious or idealogical cause of their own. Today in Northern Ireland many of the guns are supplied by Eastern Bloc countries to the IRA; France in the late 18th century supplied arms to Ireland to distract England from other policies. Things have not changed much.

**PRE-CELTIC IRELAND:** The hills and river valleys are scattered with ancient monuments dating from the Stone, the Bronze and the Iron Age. Most of them suggest some religious significance, though the myths and legends of Ireland have swathed them in romance and heroic stories. These were recounted by the Celtic storytellers or shanachies in the cottages and castles, unfortunately only a few survive today as 'memory men'. The earliest record of man in Ireland is dated between 8,700 and 8,600 years ago, as deduced from fragments found at a camp in Mount Sandel near **Coleraine**. These people lived a nomadic life of hunting and

61

trapping; they could not move around very easily as the countryside was covered in endless forests, interrupted only by lakes and river channels. They used curragh boats, similar to the ones used today by fishermen in the west of Ireland. They also built lake dwellings or crannogs, many of which were used until a couple of centuries ago. No one is sure where these people came from but they had the island to themselves for 3,000 years.

Then came the Neolithic man who perhaps is the Fir Bolg in Celtic mythology, but at this stage everything is very vague. These people were farmers and gradually spread over the whole of Ireland, clearing the forest as best they could with their stone tools. They were very concerned with burial rites for they built chambered tombs of a very sophisticated quality, decorated with spirals and lozenge shapes. The Great Burial Chamber at **New Grange** in the Boyne Valley is a superb piece of construction with a tremendous variety of building stone used. The chamber is large enough to contain thousands of cremated bodies. These people must have been very well organized with the energy and wealth to spare for such an ambitious project similar in its way to the pyramids and a thousand years older!

Around 2,000 BC yet another race appeared who were skilled miners and metal workers. They are called the Beaker people and they opened up copper mines and started to trade with Brittany, the Baltic and the Iberian Peninsula. They had different beliefs about burial, their dead were buried singly in graves lined with stone slabs and covered with a capstone. There are a thousand chambered graves, ring shaped cairns, standing stones, rows and circles of stones left from these, and the Boyne Valley culture; they hint at various rituals and it has been suggested at astronomical observations. You will glimpse them from the road, a solitary form in a ploughed field or used as scratching posts for cattle. They are often called fairy stones, and the chambered graves have been nicknamed 'Dermot and Grania's bed'.


**THE CELTS:** The next invaders arrived about 500 BC. These people had iron weapons and defeated the Beakers or the Tuatha de Danaan as they are called in the legends of Ireland. Their magical powers were no defense against the new metal, iron. Known as the Celts or Gaels the new invaders had spread from south Germany, across France and as far south as Spain. They brought to Ireland a highly organised social structure, and the La Tene style of decoration (its predominant motif is a spiral or a whorl). Today everybody in Ireland has pride in the 'Celtic' past; epic tales sing the praises of men and women who were capable of heroic and superhuman deeds, and the beautiful gold jewellery is carefully preserved as proof of their achievements. Ireland was divided into different clans with three classes of people: the free who were warriors, owned land and cattle; the professionals such as the jurists, druids, musicians, storytellers, and poets, who could move freely between the petty kingdoms and finally the slaves. Every clan had a petty king who in his turn was ruled over by the High King at Tara.

The Gaels made use of many of the customs and mythology that had existed before their arrival, so their 'Celtic civilisation' is unique. They were also very fortunate, for although they were probably displaced themselves by the expanding Roman Empire, once they got to Ireland they were isolated and protected to some extent by England who acted as a buffer state. The Romans never got around to conquering Ireland so she escaped their laws and organisation and the Gaels were able to develop their traditions, unlike Asterix and his friends in Brittany. They spent most of their time raiding their neighbours for cattle and women, who were used as live currency. They also had their religion. The stone images and pillars which have survived from those days have a strange and powerful aura, most are head idols. The human head was all important as a symbol of divinity and supernatural power even when it was severed from the body it still retained its powers. The warriors used to take the heads of their slain enemies and display them in front of their houses. The Gaels believed firmly in an after life of the soul, they would lend each other money to be repaid in the next world!

**ARRIVAL OF CHRISTIANITY:** When Christianity arrived in Ireland it quickly became accepted by the kings. One of them Cormac Mac Art who ruled in Tara about a century and a half before Saint Patrick came to Ireland saw the light and told his court of Druids and nobles that the gods they worshipped were only craven wood! The Druids in revenge put a curse on him and very soon afterwards he choked to death on a salmon bone; but before he died he ordered that he was not to be buried in the tomb of Brugh (Newgrange) but on the sunny east point by the River Rosnaree. When St. Patrick lit a fire which signalled the end of Druid worship, legend has it that he was looking down from the Hill of Slane onto Rosnaree.

The Christians displayed great skill in reconciling the pagan practices and beliefs; a famous saying of St. Columba was 'Christ is my Druid'. The early Christians seem to have been a very ascetic lot, they preferred to build their monasteries in the most wild and inaccessible places. Today, you can still see their hive shaped dwellings on Skellig Michael, a wind-swept rocky island off the Kerry coast. Wherever they went these early saints attracted followers and their monasteries expanded without much planning. The monasteries became universities renowned throughout Europe, which was in the throes of the Dark Ages. They produced beautiful manuscripts like the Book of Kells. The abbots held great power as spiritual and land lords; many of the petty kings were relations and left all their precious goods in the monasteries, using them as a sort of bank. From the 6th century onwards, much of the missionary spirit of the Irish monks was directed outwards to the Continent. They founded Boibbio in Italy and other religious houses and the interchange of ideas between the Continent and Ireland was far greater than has recently been thought.

**VIKING INVASION:** The tranquility of Ireland 'land of Saints and Scholars' was brutally interrupted by the arrival of the Vikings or Norsemen. They were able to penetrate right into Ireland through their skilful use of the rivers and lakes. They struck for the first time in 795 but this was only the start of a three hundred year struggle. Much treasure from the palaces and monasteries was plundered, for the buildings had no defences; so the monks built round towers in which to store their precious things at the first sign of trouble. Never had the Gaels been threatened like this before. Eventually the Norsemen began to settle down and they founded the first port/cities: Dublin, Wexford and Waterford and started to trade with the Gaels. Military alliances were made between them when it helped a particular king in the continuous struggle for the High Kingship. Another wave of Norsemen invaded and the plundering began again, but Brian Boru, who had usurped the High Kingship from the O'Connor's, defeated the Vikings at Clontarf in 1014 and broke their power permanently. Unfortunately, for the Gaelic people, Brian Boru was murdered by some Vikings in his tent just after the victory at Clontarf. Now havoc and in-fighting became a familar pattern, as the High Kingship was fought for by the O'Briens, the O'Loughlins and the O'Connors. The Gaelic warriors wasted themselves and their people for no one leader seemed strong enough to rule without opposition. When the Normans invaded they saw their opportunity lay in the disunity of the Irish.

**THE NORMAN INVASION AND CONSOLIDATION:** The Pope gave his blessing to the expedition of Anglo-Normans sent by Henry II to Ireland. The Normans were actually invited over by the King of Leinster, Dermot MacMurrough, who had made a bitter enemy of Tiernan O'Rourke of Breffni by running off with his wife, Devorgilla. He also backed the wrong horse in the High Kingship stakes and soon found that the united efforts of the High King Rory O'Connor and O'Rourke brought about a huge reduction in his kingdom. Dermot approached Henry II, offering his oath of fealty in exchange for an invasion force of men with names like Fitzhenry, Carew, Fitzgerald, Barry– names you still see in Irish villages. The Normans were adventurers and good warriors. In 1066, William, Duke of Normandy had taken the crown of England by force, with only 5,000 men. Now in 1169, several Norman nobles decided to try their luck in Ireland and they found it easy to grab huge tracts of land for themselves. The Gaels had faced so few attacks from outside their country that they were unprepared to do battle. Their weapons were very inferior to those of the Normans and their main advantage was their knowledge of the bogs, mountains and forest, and their numbers. The Normans had a well equipped cavalry who rode protected by a screen of archers. Once they had launched a successful attack they consolidated their position by building motes, castles, and walled towns. Strongbow, one of the most powerful of the Norman invaders, married MacMurrough's daughter and became his heir, but his successes and those of the other Norman barons worried Henry II. In 1171 he arrived in Ireland with about 4,000 troops and two objectives: to secure the submission of the Irish leaders and to impose his authority on his own barons, he achieved both aims. The Gaelic lords still went on fighting, in fact the coming of the

Normans began a military struggle which was to continue over four centuries.

**THE BRUCE INVASION:** In 1314, Robert Bruce of Scotland decisively defeated English forces at Bannockburn, and was in a position to try and fulfil his dream of a United Celtic Kingdom, by putting his brother Edward on the throne in Ireland. At first his invasion was successful, but he left a trail of destruction behind him. 1316 was a year of famine and disease exacerbated by the war. His dream brought economic and social disaster to Ireland, and when Edward Bruce was defeated and killed at Dundalk few of his allies mourned his death. The Normans' control fluctuated within an area known as the Pale and they became rather independent of their English over-lord; in some cases they became more Irish than the Irish, like the de Burgos (Burkes). The Gaelic lords in the north and west continued to hold their territories. However to do so they imported Scottish mercenary soldiers, called gallowglas, who prolonged the life of the independent Gaelic kingdoms for more than two centuries after the defeat of Edward Bruce.

**THE NINE YEARS WAR – ELIZABETHAN CONQUEST AND SETTLEMENT:** Since the Norman invasion, Ireland had been ruined by continual fighting. The country was in the doldrums and it is little wonder that Queen Elizabeth preached a crusade type war to bring civilization to Ireland. Many of the Irish nobles had been educated at her court and she endowed and founded Trinity College, Dublin. However the basic reason for Queen Elizabeth's preoccupation with Ireland was security. She was determined to bring the Irish more firmly under English control, especially the Ulster lords who had so far maintained almost total independence. Her government decided that all the Gaelic lords must surrender their lands to the Crown, whereupon they would be regranted immediately. At this time Ulster, today the stronghold of Protestantism, was the most Gaelic and Catholic part of Ireland, and it was from here that the great Hugh O'Neill and Red Hugh O'Donnell launched a last-ditch struggle against Elizabeth. Initial successes bolstered the rebels' morale. Elizabeth recognising the gravity of the situation sent over her talented favourite soldier, Essex. Most of his troops died from disease and guerilla attacks, and with no reinforcements he had little alternative than to make a truce with O'Neill. Disgrace and execution was his reward. In February 1600 Lord Mountjoy arrived in Ireland with 20,000 troops. The Munster Risings were crushed and with them the aspirations of Connacht and Leinster. The Gaelic chiefs seem to have been ruthless in their allegiances. They had hailed O'Neill as Prince of Ireland but, anticipating defeat they deserted him. O'Neill's hopes were raised by the arrival of the long promised Spanish troops at Kinsale in 1601; but they only numbered 4,000. When they did do battle against Mountjoy the Irish were left confused when the Spaniards failed to sally out as arranged.

**THE FLIGHT OF THE EARLS:** O'Neill returned to Ulster on the 23rd March 1603 and made his submission to Mountjoy, only to learn in Dublin later that Queen Elizabeth had died the very next day. He is said to have wept with rage. Amongst all the nobles only he might have been able to unite the Irish and beat Elizabeth. O'Neill had his titles and lands returned to him, but the Dublin government, greedy for his property, began to bait him. The government took his land at the slightest excuse and forbade him to practise Catholicism; so abandoning hope he sailed to Europe in 1607. This 'Flight of the Earls' took place on the 14th September 1607, from the wild and beautiful shores of the Swilly. It symbolised the end of Gaelic leadership and a new period of complete domination by the English. The Irish lords took themselves off to the courts of France and Spain or into the foreign armies. If you glance through the lists of famous generals, and politicians in Europe, a few Irish names will leap up at you from the pages: in Spain, Wall and O'Donnell; in Austria, the minister Taafe; in France, Admiral Macnamara and General Lally Tullindaly. The 'Flight of the Earls' became glorified in stories and later in the Irish version of history taught in Catholic schools. But on the whole, the nobles were vicious and uncultured, contributing nothing to the mainstream of European thought. They had spent most of their energies warring on themselves and at the last moment deserted their country and left the Irish peasants with no leadership at all.

**1640's – THE CONFEDERATION, CROMWELL AND THE STUARTS:** By the 1640's, Ireland was ready for rebellion again – they had plenty of grievances. James I, a staunch protestant dispossessed many Gaelic and old English families in Ireland because they would not give up Catholicism, and he began the plantation of the most vehemently Catholic province, Ulster with Protestants. Previous plantations had not worked because of inclement weather, but James knew that the Scots would be able to skip about the bogs as well as the Irish! When Charles Stuart came to the throne, many Catholic families hoped that they might be given some religious freedom and retain their estates, but nothing was legally confirmed. In 1633, Black Tom, the Earl of Stafford arrived with the intention of making Ireland a source of profit rather than loss to the king. In his zeal to do so he succeeded in alienating every element in Irish society. His enemies amongst the Puritans in Ireland and England put pressure on the king to recall him and he was eventually executed. English politics became dominated by the dissension between the Round Heads and the Cavaliers and the hopeless Irish took note. Their maxim was *England's difficulty is Ireland's opportunity.*

Charles tried to deal with the growing unrest in Ireland by giving everybody what they wanted, but he no longer had enough power to see that his laws were carried out. The Gaelic Irish decided to take a chance and rebel; many of them came back from the Continental armies with the hope that they might win back their old lands. In October 1641, a small Gaelic force took over the whole of Ulster and there were widespread uprisings in Leinster. In Ulster, the Gaelic people had been burning for revenge and the new colonists suffered terribly, this cruel treatment has not been forgotten by Ulster Protestants.

The Dublin government was worse than useless and the rebels continued to be successful. While the government waited for reinforcements from England, they managed to antagonise the old English, for they made the mistake of presuming that they would be disloyal to the Crown, and so viewed them with suspicion. The old English families decided to throw in their lot with the rebels since they were already considered traitors, but on one condition: a declaration of loyalty to the Crown by the Gaelic leaders.

**THE CONFEDERATION OF KILKENNY:** By February 1642 most of Ireland was in rebel hands. The rebels established a Provisional Government at Kilkenny, and Charles began to negotiate with them hoping to gain their support against the Puritans. Things were too good to last. The usual destructive factors, that had ruined many Irish uprisings before and since, came into play: personal jealousy and religion. The old English were loyal to the King and wanted a swift end to the war; the Gaelic Irish were only interested in retrieving their long lost lands and were ready to fight to the bitter end. This disunity was exacerbated by the rivalry between the Gaelic commander, Owen Roe O'Neill and the commander of the old English army, Thomas Preston. In October 1645, the Papal Nuncio arrived and the unity of the Confederates was further split. He and O'Neill took an intransigent stand over the position of the Catholic Church which Charles I could not agree to.

The rebels won a magnificent victory over the Puritan General Munroe at Benburb but O'Neill did not follow it up. The Confederates torn by disunity and rivalry let opportunities slip past and they lost the initiative. Eventually, they did decide to support the King and end their Kilkenny government, but by this time Charles I had been beheaded and his son had fled into exile. The Royalists were defeated at Rathmines in 1649 and the way was left clear for Cromwell, who landed in Dublin soon after. Cromwell came to Ireland determined to break the Royalists, break the Gaelic nationalists, and to avenge the events of 1641 in Ulster. He shared the puritan hatred for the Catholic Church, it is easy to forget how extreme both religious view-points were then. (In fact Ian Paisley, if you think about it, is just like a 17th century preacher.) Cromwell thought that the priests had engineered the rising, of the Irish character and their grievances he knew little and cared less.

He started his campaign with the Siege of Drogheda and there are the most gruesome accounts of his methods. When his troops burst into the town they put Royalists, women, children and priests to the sword; in all 3,552 were counted dead whilst Cromwell only lost 64 men. Catholics curse Cromwell to this day. The same butchery distinguished the taking of Wexford. Not surprisingly, he managed to break the spirit of resistance by such methods and there were widespread defections from the Royalists' side. Owen O'Neill might have been able to rally the Irish but he suddenly died. Cromwell's campaign only lasted seven months and he took all the towns except Galway and Waterford. These he left to his

Lieutenants.

By 1652, the whole country was subdued, and Cromwell encouraged all the fighting men to leave by granting them amnesty if they fled overseas. The alternative to exile was, for many families, something that turned out to be even worse: compulsory removal to Connacht and County Clare. Some had been neutral during all the years of fighting but that was never taken into account. Cromwell was determined that any one suspect should go to hell or Connacht! If you want to be really snobbish about old Irish families, find out if they came from Connacht, that is where the really ancient ones were banished to. The government had lots of land to play around with after that. First of all they paid off 'the adventurers', men who had lent them money back in 1642. Next, the Round Head soldiers who had not been paid their salaries for a while, got Irish land instead. Thus the Cromwellian Settlement parcelled out even more land to land speculators and rogues.

**STUART AND ORANGE:** After the Restoration of the Monarchy in 1660, the Catholics in Ireland hoped for toleration and rewards for their loyalty to the Stuart cause. They felt threatened by the fast expanding Protestant community, mostly dissenters, who had been given religious freedom under Cromwell. Charles did not restore many Catholic estates because he had to keep in with the ex-Cromwellian supporters, but Catholics were given a limited amount of toleration. However, with the succession of Charles' brother, James, who was a Catholic, things began to brighten up. In Ireland, the Catholic Earl of Tyrconnell became commander of the army in 1658 and later chief governor. By 1688 Roman Catholics were dominant in the army, the administration, the Judiciary, and the town corporations and by the end of the year Protestant power in Ireland was seriously weakened.

James frightened all those Protestants in England who had benefitted from Catholic estates. They began to panic when James II introduced sweeping acts of toleration for all religions. His attempts to re-establish the Catholic church alienated the country to such an extent that the Protestant aristocracy invited William of Orange over in November 1668 to relieve his father-in-law of his throne. James fled to France, but soon left for Ireland which was a natural base from which to launch his counter attack. By the date of his arrival in March 1689, only Enniskillen and Londonderry were in Protestant hands.

**SIEGE OF LONDONDERRY AND BATTLE OF THE BOYNE:** In Derry a group of apprentice boys, in a famous incident celebrated in Orange songs, shut the city gates to the Jacobite army. The subjugation of the city was James' first aim and so began the famous siege of Londonderry. The townspeople proved unbreakable, food was very low and they were reduced to eating rats and mice and chewing old bits of leather. Many did die of starvation during the fifteen weeks of the siege, but just as they were about to give in, the foodship *Mountjoy* forced its way through the great boom built across the Foyle. This military and psychological victory was of enormous significance in the campaign. When

William himself arrived at Carrickfergus in June of 1690, James decided to confront him at the Boyne. William of Orange had an army of about 36,000 comprised of English, Scots, Dutch, Danes, Germans, and Huguenots against James's army of about 25,000 made up of Irish and French. William's triumph in this battle was the result of his numerical and strategic superiority. James deserted the battlefield and Ireland with haste.

In the Battle of the Boyne James seemed to have completely lost his nerve. The Jacobite forces had to retreat west of the Shannon to Limerick, and William promptly laid siege to it. So weak were its walls that it is said they could be breached with roasted apples. The defence of Limerick was as heroic as that of Londonderry. Patrick Sarsfield slipped out with a few followers and intercepted William's siege train and destroyed it. William then gave up and left for England leaving Ginkel in charge. The next year the French King Louis XIV sent over supplies and men as he hoped to divert William in Ireland for a little longer. The Jacobite leader St Ruth who landed with them proved a disaster for the Irish, Sarsfield would have been a better choice. Ginkel took Athlone and Aughrim in June and July of 1691, after two battles in which stories of courage on the Jacobite side have provided inspiration to patriot poets and musicians. The last hope of the Irish cause was now Limerick.

**THE TREATY OF LIMERICK:** Sarsfield skilfully gathered together what Jacobite troops were left and got them back there. St Ruth had been killed by a cannonball, and rather typically appointed no second in command. Ginkel tried to storm the town from both sides, but still Limerick held out and he began to treaty with Sarsfield. Honourable terms were made for the Jacobites, and Sarsfield signed the famous Treaty of Limerick in August 1691. The next day a French fleet arrived and anchored off the Shannon estuary; but Sarsfield stood by the treaty. The treaty seemed to guarantee quite a lot. Catholics were to have the same rights as they had had under Charles II and any Catholic estates which had been registered in 1662 were to be handed back. Catholics were to be allowed free access to the Bar, Bench, Army and Parliament; Sarsfield was to be given a safe passage to the Continent with his troops. But the treaty was not honoured, except for the last clause which got all the fighting men out of the country. This was one of the dirtiest tricks the English played, and to be fair to William of Orange he wanted the treaty to be enforced, but being new and unsure of his support he complied with the treachery. Eleven thousand Irish Jacobites sailed away to join the French army, forming the Irish Brigade. Over the years many came to join them from Ireland, and were remembered in their native land as the Wild Geese.

The Orange/Stuart war still lives vividly in the imagination of the people today. The siege of Londonderry has become a sign of Protestant determination, *no surrender 1690* is scrawled, usually in bright red paint on the walls and street corners of loyalist areas in Northern Ireland; The Battle of the Boyne is remembered in a similar way. Here is an old, old anecdote. An old man is asked by a youth (or a foreigner), *Who is King*

*Billy?*

His reply is *Away man, and read your bible.*

**THE PENAL LAWS:** The defeat of the Catholic cause was followed by more confiscation of land and the penal laws. What had happened was that a bargain had been struck with the Protestant planters. They would be allowed to keep a complete monopoly of political power and most of the land. In return they would act as a British garrison to keep the peace and prevent the Catholics from gaining any power. To do this they passed a series of degrading laws. Briefly they were this: No Catholic could purchase freehold land. Any son of a Catholic, turning Protestant, could turn his parents off their estate. Families who stayed Catholic had their property equally parcelled out amongst all the children, so that any large estates soon became uneconomic holdings. All the Catholics were made to pay a tithe towards the upkeep of the Anglican Church. All priests were banished. No Catholic schools were allowed and spies were set amongst the peasants to report on hedge schools, a form of quite sophisticated schooling that had sprung up; priests that were on the run taught at these schools and celebrated mass. These anti–religious laws had the opposite effect to that intended; Catholicism took on a new lease of life in Ireland. A Catholic could not hold a commission in the army, enter a profession or even own a horse worth more than £5. Economic laws were introduced that put heavy taxes on anything that Ireland produced: cloth, wool, glass and cattle, so that she would not compete with England. The trading regulations were very disadvantageous to the conformist Protestants and many of them left.

The worst thing about these penal laws was the moral effect. It was heroic to break the law, necessary to smuggle and steal; the country turned itself into a huge secret society using every means to outwit the authorities. To be a Catholic meant you had to lie to protect your priest, and if you were a farmer there was no point in making a profit — any Protestant was allowed to come and claim it. It was not always as bad as that, the harshness of the laws did not reach to every part of Ireland, if an official closed his eyes. Sometimes a great family, part of which became Protestant would come to an agreement. The Protestant end held onto the Catholic property in trust and then handed it back when the laws were relaxed or repealed.

The Protestant landlords were a little nervous at first and grabbed as much as they could while the going was good, until this became a habit. They felt under no obligation to their Irish tenants, who they tended to despise and could not understand. Many of them never bothered to learn more than a few words of Gaelic. Not all of them were bad, but they were resented anyway for being alien in religion, race and customs. Gradually things began to relax, the Catholics had been well and truly squashed. The Protestants began to build themselves grand and beautiful houses, the draughty, damp tower houses could be left to decay. Irish squires were famous for their hard–drinking; the expression 'plastered' comes from the story of a guest who was so well wined and dined at a neighbour's housewarming party, that he fell asleep against a newly plastered wall. He woke up next morning to find that his scalp and hair had hardened with the plaster into the wall!

As the 18th century progressed however, there were signs of aggression amongst the peasantry; agrarian secret societies were formed with names like The White Boys, Hearts of Oak and the Molly Maguires. They were very brutal and meted out rough justice to tenants and landlords alike. If any peasant paid his rent to an unfair landlord, he was likely to be intimidated or have his farm burnt down. In Ulster, peasant movements were dominated by sectarian land disputes. In 1782 the penal laws were relaxed a little and Catholics were allowed to bid for land and they incensed Protestants by bidding higher. The Catholics were called the Defenders and the Protestant groups the Peep–O–Day boys. After a particularly bad fight between the two sides which the Protestant boys won, the Orange Order was founded. A typical oath of one of the early clubs was *'To the glorious, pious and immortal memory of the great and good King William, not forgetting Oliver Cromwell, who assisted in redeeming us from popery, slavery, arbitrary power, brass–money and wooden shoes'*.

The American War of Independence broke out and Ireland was left undefended. There were fears of an invasion by France or Spain and a general feeling that there ought to be some sort of defence force. The Volunteers were organised with officers from the Protestant landowning class, but as the fears of invasion receded they turned their considerable muscle to the cause of political reform, and Britain began to fear that they might follow the example of the American Colonies. The land–owners had their own parliament in Dublin, but all important matters were dealt with by London. All colonies were thought to have inexhaustible supplies of raw materials, so they were not allowed to compete in any way through trade or politics. When America sought independence from the British Government, Irish Protestants and Catholics alike watched with approval, particularly since many of the rebel Americans were of Ulster/Scots blood. A group of influential landowners began to think that Ireland would be much better off with an independent Irish parliament. In 1783, the British Government, influenced by the eloquence of the great speaker Henry Gratton, acknowledged the right of Ireland to be bound only by laws made by the King and the Irish Parliament.

**GRATTON'S PARLIAMENT:** Gratton's Parliament was really an oligarchy of landowners, but at least they understood the problems of the economy and tried to bring a more liberal spirit into dealings with Catholics and dissenters. Gratton wanted complete Catholic emancipation, but for that the Irish had to wait, yet Trinity College was made accessible to those of all religious persuasions, although Catholics were forbidden by their Bishops to go there. The great Catholic Seminary at Maynooth was founded, and endowed with money and land from the Protestant aristocrats, who were frightened that the priests educated at Douai might bring back with them some of those frightening ideas of liberty and equality floating around France. Dissenters were given equal rights with the Established Church at this time.

Dublin was now a handsome Georgian City, a centre for the arts, science and society — duelling was the national pastime! All this pleasure was expensive so landowners began to sub-let their estates to the land-hungry tenants. All the dirty work was done by an agent who also pocketed most of the profits, but the system enabled landlords to live in idleness and keep up large houses in Dublin. After the Union, in 1801, the situation became worse and sub-letting became uncontrolled, the landowners left Dublin to take up their aristocratic life in London. Their Irish estates were sub-let at inflated prices and they knew nothing of what went on and often didn't care; tenants who couldn't pay the rents were evicted. More often than not, the absentee landlord amassed such debts in London that he had to sell off his property to the dreaded land agent, who had no scruples at all.

In the early 1790's, fear and anger swept through Europe in the form of the French revolution and the governments of Europe, whether Catholic or Protestant drew nearer together in mutual fear. Many, who at first were delighted with the revolution in France, became disgusted with the brutality of its methods.The Irish Government disbanded the Volunteers and got together a militia and part time force of Yeomanry. It was nervous of a French invasion and increasingly of a middle-class organization 'The United Irishmen' who were sick of a government which only spoke for a tiny proportion of the population.

**WOLFE TONE AND UNITED IRISHMEN:** The aim of United Irishmen was to throw open the Irish Parliament to all Irishmen, irrespective of their rank or religion. Initially the movement was to be non-violent, but when war broke out between England and France, all radical societies were forced to go underground. No liberal ideas could be tolerated during the war effort. Wolfe Tone was a Dublin lawyer and a prominent member of United Irishmen; he crossed over to France to try to persuade the French Directory to help them.

**THE PROTESTANT WIND:** Wolfe Tone succeeded brilliantly in arguing a case for French intervention and on the night of December 16th 1796, the last great French invasionary force to set sail for the British Isles slipped past the British squadron blockading the port of Brest. Five days later 35 ships with 12,000 men aboard arrived and anchored off Bantry Bay. Unfortunately, the frigate carrying the Commander-in-Chief, General Hoche, had become separated from the rest of the fleet during the journey and so it was decided not to land until he arrived. But their good fortune deserted them, after waiting through one clear calm day the wind changed and blew from the east, remembered in all the songs as a 'Protestant Wind'. The fleet endured the rain and storm for three days, then the ships cut cable and headed back for France. Only Wolfe Tone and his ship, *'The Indomitable'*, remained and as Tone put it, *'England had not such an escape since the Armada'*.

Meanwhile, in the Irish countryside increasingly brutal attempts were made by the militia and the yeomanry to stamp out sedition. In Ulster, where the United Irishmen were strong, efforts were made to set the United Irishmen against the Orangemen, many of whom had joined the Yeomanry. This continual pressure forced the Society to plan rebellion. However, government spies had infiltrated the Society and two months before the proposed date many of the leaders were arrested. The Irish peasants had joined the United Irishmen, inspired by the heady doctrine of Tom Paine's *'Rights of Man'*. The increased power of the Irish Parliament had not meant more freedom for them, on the contrary the heretics and alien landlords now seemed to have more power to persecute them in the forms of tithes and taxes. The Gaelic speaking peasants had little in common with the middle–class agitators, and their anger was even more explosive.

**1798 REBELLION:** In May 1798, the rebellion broke out. The United Irish leaders had planned a rebellion believing that they could count on an army of over 250,000 men. However, the absence of leadership and careful, efficient planning resulted in local uprisings with no central support; even those which achieved some success were quickly crushed. In Wexford, the United Irishmen led by Father Murphy, succeeded in capturing Enniscorthy and all the county except New Ross. It took a general, a month of warfare and a pitched battle lasting twelve hours to defeat the rebels. The sad battle of Vinegar Hill, with its grisly and indiscriminate reprisals against Protestants ended in the rebels' defeat, and the usual brutal consequences. In Ulster there were two main risings under McCracken and Monroe. The risings both enjoyed brief success during which time the rebels treated any loyalist prisoners well, a marked contrast to what had happened in other counties. The sectarian battles between the Peep–O–Boys had already soured the trust of the Catholics, and many of them did not turn up to help the mixed bunch of United Irishmen. Poor Wolfe Tone and others who had started the society with such hopes for affectionate brotherhood, saw their ideals drowned in a sea of blood. Nugent, the Commander of the Government Forces in Ulster decided to appeal to the rebels who had property to lose, especially those in the rich eastern counties, and he proclaimed a general amnesty if the Antrim rebels gave up their arms. The rebels of Down did not get off so humanely; when they had been routed and shot down they were left unburied in the streets for the pigs to eat. McCracken and Munroe were executed.

**THE RACES OF CASTLEBAR:** Whilst the war between France and England became more embittered, Wolfe Tone had succeeded in raising another invasionary force. On August 22nd 1798, General Humbert arrived in Killala Bay with a 1,000 men and more arms for the rebels, although most of them had dispersed. Humbert captured Ballina and routed 6,000 loyalist troops in a charge called 'the Races of Castlebar'. But there were not enough rebels and Humbert had to accept honourable terms of surrender in September. Only a few weeks later, another unsuccessful French Expedition arrived with Tone on board and entered Lough Swilly, it was overcome by some British frigates and Wolfe Tone was captured. He appeared before a court martial wearing a French uniform and carrying a cockade. The only favour he asked was the right to be shot which was refused, whereupon he cut his own throat with a penknife and lingered in agony for seven days.

The rebellion of 1798 was one of the most tragic and violent events in Irish History. It had the effect of making people try to bring about change in a non-violent way. In the space of three weeks, 30,000 people, peasants armed with pitchforks and pikes, women and children, were cut down and shot. The results of the rebellion were just as disastrous. The ideas of political and religious equality were discredited, because of the deaths and destruction of property. The British Government found that an independent parliament was an embarrassment to them, especially since the 'Protestant garrison' had not been able to put down the peasant risings without their help.

**THE UNION:** Pitt decided that Union between Great Britain and Ireland was the only answer. First he had to bribe the Protestants to give up their power and many earldoms date from this time. Then the Union Act was passed with promises of Catholic emancipation for the majority. Pitt really did want to give them equality for he saw that it was a necessary move if he wished to make Ireland relatively content. Unfortunately Pitt was pushed out of government, and George III lent his considerable influence to those opposed to Catholic emancipation, he claimed with perfect truth, that the idea of it drove him mad. The Union did not solve any problems: the Catholics felt bitterly let down and the temporary Home Rule of Gratton's Parliament was looked back to as an example. Irreconcilable nationalism was still alive and kicking. Union with England was disadvantagous to Ireland in the areas of industry and trade and many poorer Protestants were discontented. The terms of the 1801 Act were never thought of as final in Ireland, although the English failed to understand this.

**THE LIBERATOR — DANIEL O'CONNELL:** Catholics still could not sit in Parliament, or hold important state offices or get to the senior, judicial, military or civil service posts. Between the Union and 1823 many efforts to have something done about this came to nothing. Then the Catholics found a champion among themselves: a Catholic lawyer called Daniel O'Connell. Daniel O'Connell came from an old Catholic Irish family; he had been sent to school in France where his uncle was a general in the French army. His glimpses of the French revolutionary army had left him completely against violence whatever the political end. The rising of 1798 confirmed him in the belief 'that no political change is worth the shedding of a single drop of human blood'. O'Connell founded the Catholic Association which, amongst other things, represented the interests of the tenant farmers. Association membership was a penny a month and brought in a huge fighting fund. Most important of all, the Catholic priests supported him and soon there were branches of the association everywhere.

**CATHOLIC EMANCIPATION:** A turning point for Irish history and the fortunes of Daniel O'Connell came with the Clare election in 1828, when the association showed its strength. O'Connell had an over-whelming victory against the government candidate when all the forty shilling free–holders voted for him. The whole country was aflame, they wanted to see Daniel at Westminster. Wellington,the PM of the day was forced to give in, and the Emancipation Bill was passed in April 1829. But this was not a gesture of conciliation, for at the same time he raised the voting qualification from forty shillings to a massive £10. Protestant fears had been raised by the power of such a mass movement, for tenant farmers had dared to vote in opposition to their landlords, even though voting was public. To English Catholics Daniel was also a 'Liberator'.

For twelve years O'Connell supported the Whig Government and built up a well disciplined Irish party whose co–operation was essential to any government majority. He was then able to press for some very necessary reforms, and when the Viceroy and his secretary were sympathetic much was achieved. But with the return of the conservatives in 1840 O'Connell decided it was time to launch another popular agitation campaign, this time for the Repeal of the Union. His mass meetings became 'monster meetings', each attended by well over 100,000 people. The Government refused to listen on this issue, British public opinion was firmly against it and in Ulster there was a distinct lack of enthusiasm. Daniel O'Connell arranged to have one of his biggest meetings yet, at Clontarf, where Brien Boru had defeated the Vikings. The Government banned it and O'Connell unwilling to risk violence called it off. He himself was arrested for conspiracy and sentenced with just the sort of packed jury he had been trying to abolish. Luckily for him, the House of Lords was less frightened and more just; they set aside his sentence. But by then O'Connell's influence had begun to fade, and some Irish began to look to violence to achieve their aims.

**THE YOUNG IRELANDERS:** Within the Repeal Association were a group of young men who called themselves the Young Irelanders. They had founded *'The Nation'* newspaper to help O'Connell, but they soon began to move in a different direction. They believed that culturally and historically Ireland was independent of England. They fed their enthusiasm on the painful memories of 1798 and composed heroic poetry which they set to old ballad tunes. They were useless at practical politics and did not have the support of the clergy. In 1848 they responded to the spontaneous and Romantic uprisings in Europe with one of their own. It was a dismal failure and alienated many people who had been in favour of the Repeal of the Union. The movement was not to become respectable again until 1870.

**THE GREAT HUNGER:** The diet of an ordinary Irishman was six pounds of potatoes and a pint of milk a day, and he lived in miserable conditions. The Cromwellian and Williamite plantations, together with the effect of the Penal Laws left the Catholics with only 5% of the land.

Except in the North, where a thriving linen industry had grown up, the people had to make their living from farming. Absentee landlords became more of a problem after the Union, their agents greedier and their rent demands even higher. It was the farmer at the bottom of the pyramid who paid heavily for what he got. From 1845—1848 the potato blight struck, with tragic results.

The population of Ireland, as in the rest of Europe, began to rise quickly in the late 18th century. Perhaps this was because the potato could feed large families on small plots of land; anyway the marriage age, which had previously been very high, dropped right down and more babies were born. The most deprived and populated area of Ireland was the west where the potato was the only crop that would grow. The scene was set for agricultural and social catastrophe. As the potato rotted in the ground, people ate turnips, cabbage, wild vegetables and even grass, but these could not supply more than a few meals. Gradually, thousands of people began to die of starvation, the plague and dysentery. You may ask yourselves what was done to help them? Very little by the government, quite a lot by individuals and private charities. Every day corn and cattle were leaving the country, nothing was done that might interfere with the principle of free trade and private enterprise. The government's attitude was rigid, though they did allow maize in, a crop which nobody had any vested interest. Food distribution centres were set up and some relief work was paid for by the government. But this was not very sensible sort of work; mostly digging holes only to fill them in again. Something constructive like laying a network of railway lines might have interfered with private enterprise! Out of a population of eight and a half million, about one million died and another million emigrated.

**EMIGRATION:** The Irish had been emigrating for years; first to escape persecution by fleeing to the Continent and then as seasonal labour for the English harvests. The Ulster Scots had set the first pattern of emigration to America. They had found that Ireland was not the promised land after being lured over there by grants of land and low rents. Bad harvests, religious discrimination and high rents sent them off at the rate of 4,000 a year. Not many Catholics followed for there were still restrictions on Catholic emigration. After the Napoleonic wars and the agricultural slump, 20,000 of the brighter and wealthier Catholics went to America, by then America was more liberal in its attitude toward Catholics. Many Irish went to Australia as convicts. Boat fares over were very cheap and the opportunities in the New World seemed less biased in favour of the rich upper classes. But the heaviest years of emigration were just after the famine, especially to the United States. The people travelled under appalling conditions, and boats were called 'coffin ships'.

It took six to eight weeks to get to America in these overcrowded and disease–ridden conditions. Irish priests followed their flocks out to America and Australia and founded churches wherever they were needed, so a distinct Irish/Catholic church grew up. Such an influx of starving, diseased Irish Catholics was quite another thing to the steady flow of a few thousand Ulster Scots, and initially a lot of people were prejudiced against them. Most of the emigrants left Ireland loathing the British in Ireland. Their children grew up with the same hatred, and in a way became more anti–British than the Irish left in Ireland. This bitterness was soon transformed into political activity, aided by the Young Irelanders who had fled to America. Many of the emigrants had come from the west where the Gaelic language and culture had existed undisturbed. The rest of Ireland, especially the east, was quite anglicised and became more so with the development of education and transport.

**AMERICA AND IRISH POLITICS:** By 1858, the Catholics in America had reorganised themselves as the Fenian Brotherhood. James Stevens founded a sister movement in Ireland called the Irish Republican Brotherhood (IRB). The Fenians called themselves the legendary Fianna Warriors and were dedicated to the principal of Republicanism. In Ireland, aided with money from America, the Fenians started up the newspaper *The Irish People* which was aimed at the urban worker. When the American Civil War was over many Irish American soldiers came over to help the Fenians in Ireland. But their military operations were always dismal failures. In 1867, the government quickly crushed their uprising and felt confident enough to give the leaders long prison sentences. The clergy opposed any revolutionary secret societies and supported action only when it was through constitutional channels. But Fenianism remained a potent force. John Devoy in America and Michael Davitt of the Irish Land League, were imaginative enough to see that violence was not the only way to fight high rents. They made a loose alliance with Parnell, the leader of the Irish Party in the House of Commons.

John Devoy was head of the Clan-na-Gael, an organisation which cloaked Fenianism. In America, through the Fenians, Parnell was able to collect money for the land agitators and Douglas Hyde found money for the Gaelic League. John Devoy gave money and moral support to the revolutionaries in their fight for independence. The Clan created good propaganda for the nationalists and between the death of Parnell and the rise of Sinn Fein, did everything it could to drive a wedge between the USA and England, and to keep the States neutral during the First World War. It even acted as an intermediary between the Germans and the IRB who were negotiating for guns.

De Valera came to America with high hopes during the War of Independence in Ireland. He wanted two things: political recognition from the government for the Dail Eireann set up in 1919, and money. He failed in his first aim; he was rebuffed by President Wilson, himself of Ulster Scots blood, and very proud of it too. But the President belonged to the strain of Presbyterian emigrants who had flung themselves wholeheartedly into the making of America, and helped draw up the constitution. They had forgotten the hardships they suffered in Ireland and did not continue to bear grudges. However De Valera got plenty of money, six million dollars in the form of a loan, but he fell out with Devoy. He founded a rival organisation called the American Association for the recognition of the Irish Republic (AARIA). When Ireland split over the solution of partition and there was a civil war, the Republicans, who rejected the partition, were supported by the AARIA, whilst the Free Staters had Devoy and Clan-na-Gael behind them. The leading spirit of the AARIA was Joseph McGarrity, who later broke with De Valera when he began to act against the IRA. His group and their successors have continued to give financial support to the IRA during the present troubles in Northern Ireland.

The Irish Americans played such an important part in Irish politics that I have jumped in time from the Great Famine. Now to return to the efforts of the British Government to forestall the repeal of the Union and the efforts of various organisations to bring it about.

**REPEAL OF THE UNION:** The Union Government was blamed by many in Ireland for the tragic extent of the famine, but the government was blind to the lessons it should have taught them. The famine had only intensified the land war and the 1859 Act simply enabled the impoverished landlords to sell their estates, which the peasants had no money to buy. So the speculators moved in, seized the opportunities for further evictions and increased the rents. They cleared the land for cattle rearing and were more brutal towards the peasants than the old landlord. Tenant resistance smouldered stimulated by the horrors of the famine. Michael Davitt organised the resistance into the National Land League, with the support of Parnell. In the ensuing land war, a new word was added to the English language; the peasants decided not to help an evicting landlord with his crops and he had to import some loyal Orangemen from Ulster to gather in the harvest. The offending landlord was a Captain Boycott. The tenants wanted the same rights tenants had in Ulster and fair rent, fixity of tenure and freedom to sell at the market value. They also wanted a more even distribution of the land. At that time 3% of the population owned 95% of the land.

But one of the greatest barriers to reconciliation was the mental block the English had about Ireland. Behind all the agitation at this time and all the obstruction the Irish party caused in Parliament was a desire for the repeal of the Union. But the politicians saw the problem as religion, over-population, famine, anything but nationalism. It did not enter English heads that the Irish might not want to be part of Britain; the Union, in their eyes, was surrounded by a sort of aura. Irishmen were on an equal footing with the rest of Great Britain, they were part of the Empire. The Union was also a security against foreign attack and must stay. Only one man said anything sensible on the subject and he was not listened to, J.S.Mill said that England was the worst qualified to govern the Irish because English traditions were not applicable in Ireland. England was firmly laissez-faire in her economic policies but Ireland needed economic interference from the Government. This they had resolutely refused to do during and after the famine. Parnell, a Protestant landlord, Gladstone and other liberals were soon aware of the discontent. They tried to take the sting out of Irish nationalism by dealing with the individual problems one by one, believing that then the nationalist grievance would disappear.

**KILLING HOME RULE WITH KINDNESS:** One of the first things to be dealt with was religion, for it could not be kept out of politics. The Protestant ascendancy by virtue of education, contacts, etc., still monopolised powerful positions, despite Catholic emancipation. This frustrated the middle classes and created an Irish Catholic national distinctiveness. There may have been no legal barriers anymore but there were unofficial ones. The Anglican Church of Ireland still remained the Established Church until 1869, and until then the Irish peasant had to pay tithes to it. The Catholic hierarchy wanted a State supported Catholic education, but the Government tried to have interdenominational schools and universities. This never satisfied the Catholic Church and consequently, much later on it supported the illegal nationalist organisations. Unfortunately the Government were unwilling to establish the Catholic church in Ireland as they would have had problems with the Protestants in Ulster so although the Catholic church had consolidated its position, it was not conciliated.

The distress of the peasant farmers had, by this time, become identified with nationalism. So the Government set out to solve the economic problems thinking that this would shatter the nationalists. But they acted too late. Only in 1881 were the demands of the tenants met and large amounts of money were made available to tenants to buy up their holdings and by 1916 64% of the population owned land. Many of these new owners had the same surnames as those dispossessed back in the 17th century. But Britain was remembered not for these Land Acts, generous as they were, but for the Coercion and Crime Acts which Balfour brought in to try and control the unrest, and anarchy which existed in some parts of the country. The Land Purchase Acts took away the individual oppressor and left only the Government against whom to focus discontent. The peasants had been given more independence and the landlords were virtually destroyed, so the Union became even more precarious. The nationalists could not be bought off.

**HOME RULE FOR IRELAND?:** Parnell had forced the Government to listen, and for a while he managed to rally the whole nationalist movement behind his aggressive leadership. The bait of universal suffrage was bait enough for the Fenians to try and overthrow the Union from within the system. The Secret Ballot Act in 1872 made this even more attractive than abortive rebellions. But the Home Rule League did not succeed, even though Gladstone and the Liberals had promised to support it. First of all, Parnell was a weakness as well as a strength. His aggressive tactics alienated many Englishmen and his Protestant origins upset some of the Catholic hierarchy, they thought he should have concentrated a little more on pushing the Catholic university they wanted. His affair with Kitty O'Shea and involvement in a divorce case shocked many Victorians and non-Conformists in the Liberal Party. They demanded that he should be dropped from the leadership of the Irish Party, and when the Catholic hierarchy heard this they also began to scold 'the named adulterer' and turned their congregations against him. Another reason for the failure of the Home Rule Bill was that the predominantly Protestant and industrial North of Ireland had no wish to join the South. The North thought that it would be overtaxed to subsidize the relatively backward agrarian South, and the Protestants were frightened of being swamped by the Catholics. Their fear gave them a besieged like mentality; Parnell's divorce case was like a gift from heaven and gave them a reprieve. English opinion was still against Home Rule and it was only because the Irish party had made a deal with the Liberals that there was any hope of them succeeding. With the fall of Parnell, the Irish party split and lost most of its importance.

Parnell's fall in 1891 and the failure of the 1893 Home Rule Bill initiated a resurgence of revolutionary nationalism. The younger generation were shocked by the way in which the Catholic Church condemned Parnell within Ireland over the O'Shea case. As the moral authority of the Church was cast aside, so was one of the barriers to violence. Parnell's failure to work things through Parliament seemed to indicate that only violence would work. Young people began to join the IRB and even the Church began to show more sympathy because at least nationalism was preferable to the aesthetic socialism that was creeping into Dublin. Many of the priests had brothers and sisters in illegal organizations and it was inevitable that they would become emotionally involved.

**GAELIC CULTURAL RENAISSANCE:** There was a new mood in Ireland. The people were proud of being Irish and of their cultural achievements. Sadly, only 14% of the population spoke the Gaelic language, the famine and immigration that followed had seriously weakened its hold. English was taught in schools and knowledge of it led to better jobs and opportunities, and Irish music and poetry were neglected except by a few intellectuals. However, it was in the stories of Ireland's past greatness, her legends and customs that many diverse groups found a common ground. In 1884, the Gaelic Athletic Association started to revive the national game – hurling. Everybody knows how important cricket is to the English village green, now Irishmen were actively and publicly participating in something very Irish. In 1893, the Gaelic League was formed, its President was Douglas Hyde who campaigned successfully for the return of Gaelic lessons to schools and as a qualification for entry to the new universities. He never wanted it to be a sectarian or political force, but it did provide a link between the conservative Catholic Church and the Fenians and Irish Nationalists. 'The Holy Island of St Patrick' developed an ideal: the Catholic, devout, temperate, clean-living Irishman. (England was seen as the source of corruption, whilst Patrick Pearse and De Valera made revolution seem respectable.) The Gaelic League and the Gaelic Athletic Assocation were used by the IRB as sounding boards or recruiting grounds for membership.

The Liberals returned to power in 1906 and things began to look brighter for Home Rule. In 1910, John Redmond led the Irish Party and held the balance of power between the Liberals and the Conservatives. In

1912 Asquith's Home Rule Bill was passed, although it was suspended for the duration of the First World War. But six years later Ireland was in the middle of a war of independence and the initiative had passed from the British into the hands of the revolutionary nationalists. Why did this happen? The British Government had left Home Rule too late; the time lag between when it was passed and when it actually might be implemented gave the Irish public time to criticise it and see its limitations. The nationalists began to despair of ever finding a parliamentary solution, for the British could not force the North into Home Rule and were shutting their eyes to the gun running which had been going on since the formation of the Ulster Volunteers. The Irish people were rather luke warm about organisations like the IRB and the new Sinn Fein Party, founded by Arthur Griffith, but an event on Easter Monday changed all that.

**EASTER REBELLION 1916:** It happened very quickly, suddenly the tri-colour of a new Irish Republic was flying from the General Post Office in Dublin. Two thousand Irish Nationalists volunteers, led by Patrick Pearse of the IRB, stood against the reinforcements sent from England and then surrendered about a week later. People were horrified at first by the waste of life for many civilians got caught up in the gun battles; but then the British played into the hands of Patrick Pearse. All fourteen leaders were executed after secret trials. The timing of the uprising was no coincidence, Pearse and the others wanted it to be a blood sacrifice to the Cause. To him their sacrifice was comparable to the sacrifice of Christ, and the resurgence of the nationalist spirit which followed after such a sacrifice was comparable to the resurrection of Christ.

The executions happened before there could be any back-biting as to why the whole thing had been a muddle. Suddenly they were dead, pity for them grew into open sympathy for what they had been trying to obtain. The Catholic Church was trapped in the emotional wave which advocated revolution. The party which gained from this swing was the Sinn Fein; it was pledged to non-violent nationalism and was the public front of the IRB. John Redmond, the leader of the Irish party at Westminster, had urged everybody to forget their differences with England and fight the common enemy which was Germany, but the Irish nationalists, who were at that moment negotiating with the Germans, saw things in a very different light. Many Irishmen did go and fight for Britain, but the feeling was that Redmond was prepared to compromise over Home Rule and shelve it when it suited the British.

When in 1918 conscription was extended to Ireland even more people decided that Sinn Fein was the only party which could speak for them. It won all the Irish seats bar six. Redmond's party was finished. The only problem was that 44 of the Sinn Fein members were in English jails; those that were not, met in Mansion House and set up their own Dail Eireann. De Valera made an audacious escape from Lincoln prison and was elected the first President of the Irish Republic in April 1919. The Irish Volunteers became the Irish Republican Army and war was declared on Britain.

**THE NORTH:** For a moment, let me turn back to what was happening in the North. They had found a leader to defend the Union in the Dublin born Edward Carson. He was a leading barrister in London (he cross examined Oscar Wilde in that notorious law suit), and was openly supported by the Conservatives in England. A solemn Covenant of Resistance to Home Rule was signed by hundreds of thousands of Northern Unionists. They would fight with any means possible, not to come under an Irish Parliament in Dublin. After the Easter rising of 1916, Carson was assured by Lloyd George that the six north eastern counties could be permanently excluded from the Home Rule Act of 1914. When the War of Independence broke out in the South, the British offered them partition with their own Parliament whilst remaining within Britain. Today they still feel their ties are with a liberal Britain, not the Catholic South. Remember that in the Republic there is no divorce and no contraception, mixed marriages are discouraged, and the Welfare State is very limited. Protestants find it rather disturbing that the Roman Catholic Church's influence is so strong in every facet of social and political life.

**THE WAR OF INDEPENDENCE:** The British Government had been caught out by the Declaration of Independence by the Dail. The British were engaged in trying to negotiate a peace treaty at Versailles and the Americans had made it very clear that they sympathised with the Irish. Ammunition raids, bombing, burning and shooting began in Ireland, mainly against the Irish Constabulary. The British Government waited until the Versailles Conference had come to an end and then started to fight back. The Black and Tans were sent over to reinforce the police, Lloyd George tried to play it down as a police situation. The Black and Tans got their name from the mixture of police and army uniform they wore. Their methods were as brutal as those of the IRA and it became a war of retaliation after retaliation.

Michael Collins was in charge of military affairs and he set up an intelligence system which kept him well-informed about British plans; he waged a vicious well thought out campaign against the Black and Tans. By July 1921 a truce was declared because the British public wanted to try and reach a compromise. In October an Irish delegation, which included Griffith and Collins, went to London to negotiate with Lloyd George. They signed a treaty which approved the setting up of an Irish Free State with Dominion status, similar to Canada. The British were mainly concerned with the security aspect and they made two stipulations; that all Irish legislators should take an oath of allegiance to the Crown and that the British navy could use Irish ports.

**CIVIL WAR:** The Republicans or anti-treaty side in the Dail were furious, they regarded it as a sell-out, they did not like the oath, or the acceptance of a divided Ireland. Michael Collins saw it as a chance for the 'freedom to achieve freedom' and when it came to the debate on it in the Dail, the majority voted in favour of the Treaty. De Valera was against the treaty and as head of the Dail he resigned, Arthur Griffith succeeded him. In June, when the country accepted the Treaty, civil war began. The split in the Dail had produced a corresponding split in the IRA; part of it broke away and began violent raids into the North. The remainder of the IRA was reorganised by Michael Collins into the Free State Army. When he was assassinated, a man just as talented took over, Kevin O'Higgins. It is remembered as the War of Brothers, and it was bitter and destructive. Men who had fought together against the Black and Tans now shot each other down.

Finally, the Republicans were ready to sue for peace; De Valera, who had not actively taken part in the fighting, but had supported the Republicans, now ordered a cease fire. The bitterness and horror of the civil war has coloured attitudes to this very day. The differences between the two main parties, Fine Gael and Fianna Fail are historical rather than political, although perhaps in foreign policy Fianna Fail has taken a more anti-British line. Fine Gael held power for the first ten years and successfully concentrated on building the twenty-six county state into something credible and strong. In 1926 De Valera had broken with the Sinn Fein, because they saw the Dail and the government in power as usurpers, as bad as the British, and refused to take up their seats. De Valera founded his own party, the Fianna Fail. De Valera was a master pragmatist and succeeded in disappointing none of his supporters; the new state wanted a change and in 1932, he formed a government. He soon made it clear that Ireland was not going to keep the oath of allegiance or continue to pay the land annuities (this was the repayment of money lent to help tenants pay for their farms).

**DE VALERA:** In 1937 he drew up a new Constitution for Ireland, it declared Ireland a Republic and seemed a direct challenge to the Northern Ireland government. Article five went like this: *"It is the right of the Parliament Government established by the Constitution to exercise jurisdiction over the whole of Ireland, its Islands and territorial seas."* Article 44.1.2. recognised *"The special position of the Holy Catholic, Apostolic Roman Church as the guardian of the Faith professed by the great majority of its citizens."* Both parties had trouble with extremists in the 1930's; Fine Gael had to expel General O'Duffy of the Fascist Blue Shirt movement, and Fianna Fail were embarrassed by their erstwhile allies in the IRA. De Valera dealt with the situation by setting up a military tribunal and declaring the IRA an illegal organisation. The IRA did not die but went underground and continued to enjoy a curious relationship with the government and the public. When it got too noisy it was stamped on; but the IRA continues to be regarded nervously and with respect for their ideals and their intransigence seem to put them in line with Ireland's dead patriots.

**THE NORTH TODAY:** It is very difficult to be impartial about the troubles in Northern Ireland today – they are tragic and frightening. But if you are a traveller there is nothing to fear, as long as you keep out of parts of Derry and Belfast. Most of the troubles are contained within certain areas and the press always exaggerates. The basic reason for the troubles is that the Catholic minority in the North did badly with all the reshuffling that went on in the 1920's. Most Catholics are Republicans and want to be in the South, and have never given up hope that the Dublin Government might do something about it. The IRA view the North as an occupied state, the Protestants, who are in the majority in the North, have a completely different view of matters. They believed the Catholics would never co-operate with them and the IRA raids, started in 1922, confirmed that belief. The IRA were the enemy and the Catholics harboured them, therefore gerrymandering on the local councils was permissible and wise. The Catholics often found themselves with the worst jobs and housing. Another thing which the Protestants thought was necessary, but which to the Catholics was a constant irritant, was the 'B' Specials. (They were an armed part-time police force and most of them were in the Orange Order.) They knew who all the IRA supporters were and kept an eye on them. Some maintain they beat them up. The whole issue exploded with the Civil Rights movements which sought to reform local government in 1969. What happened after that? The rioting, bloodshed and bombings have appeared on your television set.

**THE ORGANIZATION OF GOVERNMENT:** The Irish Republic was set up in 1937 and has a President as Head of State, elected for seven years by the electorate. The President is empowered on the recommendation of the Dail to appoint the Prime Minister (Taoiseach), sign laws and invoke the judgement of the Supreme Court on the legality of Bills. He is also supreme commander of the armed forces. The Irish Parliament consists of the President and two Houses: the Dail and the Senate. The Dail is made up of 166 members elected by adult suffrage through proportional representation. The Senate is made up of 60 members: 11 are nominated by the Taoiseach; 49 are elected by the Dail and county councils from panels representative of the univerisities, labour, industry, education and social services. The average length of an Irish Government is three years.

**IRISH PARTIES TODAY:** Fianna Fail has established itself as the most natural ruling party and has hardly been out of office. Charles Haughey is its leader. Fine Gael came to power in 1973 and is in power at the moment because of a coalition with Labour, its leader at the moment is Garret Fitzgerald. Labour had found it difficult to get a foothold since the country is very conservative, socialist means atheist to many Irish Catholics. Sinn Fein has dropped considerably in the popularity charts; it is still the political arm of the official IRA.

In Northern Ireland there are many Unionist parties, but the main one is the Official Unionists, then the DUP led by the Rev. Ian Paisley. The predominantly Catholic party is the SDLP led by John Hume, followed by a few small Republican parties. The Alliance Party tries to build bridges between Protestants and Catholics and always loses out when things get more violent and attitudes harden.

# PART III
# THE PROVINCE OF
# CONNACHT

Oliver Cromwell thought of Connacht as a Siberia to which he could banish the troublesome Catholic landowners, and here on the crowded stony farms the famine struck the hardest in the 1840s. Today, it seems a wild paradise of mountains, heather and lakes into which the Atlantic makes spectacular entrances with black cliffs, golden beaches and island studded bays. This is the West, where in some parts the local people still speak Gaelic, and where they have clung to their own traditions in spite of the past invaders and the more insidious advance of modern life. On a bright day you might think that Cromwell did those 'transplanted Irish' a good turn – your aesthetic feelings are satisfied and you know that a good meal is waiting at the next hotel! The dismal grey rocks, and scraggy looking sheep, the turf ricks and misty mountains transform into a tumble of brownish purple with streaks of silver and cornflower blue where the lakes reflect the sky in the deep valleys. This is why the monks in early Christian times turned their backs on the court of Tara and the rich Celtic princes and built their tiny churches on the windswept islands off the coast.

Farming and fishing in this part of the world is a risky business and the history of Connacht closely reflects the barren countryside. The Norman invaders seem to have been less successful, or less persistent, than in other provinces, or else they became Irish themselves, like the family de Burgo who turned into Burkes. It's rather ironic that the Connacht people, who so strongly ignored the different influences at work, should be more anglicized now because of TV and the tourist trade than they ever were under the British. But the area known as the Gaeltacht, where Gaelic is still the first language, is protected by the government and incentives, by way of grants, have encouraged people not to move off to

America or England for jobs.

It would be a mistake to think that all Connacht is wild mountain scenery, a large part of it belongs to the limestone plain which covers the centre of Ireland making it rather saucer shaped, with its mountains on the rim. The whole of Roscommon, part of Leitrim, South Sligo and much of Galway is made up of neat fields, trees and heather, dotted with lakes and lined by the lovely river Shannon, The Shannon rises in the Iron Mountains of Cavan and flows south west into Leitrim, where it curves to form a moat round the eastern boundary of Connacht. This part of Connacht is wonderful, but it has not the instant splendours of Connemara or Joyce's Country. The Shannon widens to engulf huge lakes, rather like a snake swallowing down its prey whole, while it continues to coil down the countryside. The climate of the West is mild, though a misty rain often falls leaving you soaked through. The mountains seem to nudge the clouds above them into rain, but there is always a glimmer of sunshine about and in summer it can get superbly warm. Scarlet fuchsia grows along the coastal roads in place of the overbearing hawthorn hedges. In places where you would be hard put to find a blade of grass, a giant rhubarb plant will grow in early summer and purple rhododendron knows exactly how to place itself to its best advantage. All of Connacht, but especially **Connemara**, is rather like a piece of tweed cloth, with a thread of grey running through it, giving a speckled look, an impression given by the thousands of little stone walls.

Connacht has a lion's share of heroes, legends and battles. Back in the mists of pre-history, tradition holds that the Fir Bolgs, or men of bags, who had lived thinking themselves alone on the island, bumped into the tall, fair Tuatha de Danaan and there was a battle on the plain of Moytura; the Fir Bolgs were defeated and had to retreat to the islands and mountains of the West. Here they built themselves the marvellous ring forts of Dun Aonghus and Dubh-Chathair on the Aran Islands. They clung on whilst the centre of power shifted from the de Danaans to the invading Celts. The de Danaans are supposed to have brought with them the Lialh Fail, or Stone of Destiny, which was used in Ireland as the coronation seat. At some period it was taken to Scone in Scotland and has now landed up in Westminster Abbey! Connacht has produced two infamous queens. One told Queen Elizabeth I not to patronise her and was a sea pirate who ruled from Clare Island; the other is Maeve, the daughter of the High King in the 1st century BC, remembered in the epic tale *The Cattle Raid of Cooley*. What happened was this: she and her husband were measuring up their worldly possessions and found that they were equal in all things except one. He owned the most magnificent white bull which outclassed anything she could produce. However there was a brown bull in the Kingdom of Ulster that was equal to his and she was determined to have it. At certain times of the year, the Red Branch Knights, who were the guardians of Ulster, became as feeble as kittens because of the spell put on them. So choosing this time of the year, her raiding party thought the whole expedition would be a push-over; but at a crucial fording point, the young and untried hero Cuchulain challenged each Connacht man to fight, and he slew them all. Maeve, undaunted, decided to get the bull for herself and succeeded; only when she got the bull home it went into a mad frenzy and fought with the white bull until the earth shook. At last, the bull of Cooley caught the white bull by the horns and shook it to pieces, causing a loin to fall by the Shannon giving the town Athlone its name. Maeve is said to be buried at the top of Knocknarea Mountain in County Sligo and nearby on the slopes of the hauntingly beautiful Ben Bulben, the legendary hero Diarmuid met an untimely death in a boar hunt arranged by his enemy King Fionn Mac Cumhail.

# County Galway

Galway stretches from Connemara to the banks of the Shannon with Lough Corrib in the north. It is an area of contrast. There is rich farming land that a Meath man would not sniff at, and plenty to amuse ancient monument enthusiasts, and fishermen. Whilst amongst the mountains and along the coast the tiny clochan of white-washed stone cottages tells of a different way of life, where the Atlantic winds blow strongly and the cheerful red hens scratch away amongst a soil built up seaweed.

**Gort (Gort inse Guaire: field on Guaire's island)**, the main town on the road from Galway to Ennis, Shannon, Limerick, and the South, stands in a natural gap between the Slieve Auchty mountains and the **Burren**-the traditional roadway between Munster and Connacht. Guaire is the name of the 7th century King who built a castle here; he was supposed to have been so generous that his right hand, his giving hand, was said to be longer than his left. One day as he sat down to a sumptuous meal, the plates of food suddenly flew out of the windows; he naturally followed his meal on horseback, intrigued by such magic. After a few miles he came upon St. Colman who had just that minute finished a seven year fast by gobbling up the feast. Instead of being angry the king was impressed, and even more so when he found Colman was a relation and he granted him the lands of Kilmacdaugh where the saint founded a monastery.

**Kilmacduagh** is about four miles south west of **Gort** and is one of the most interesting collections of Church buildings in Ireland. There is a 12th century monastic church, called a cathedral; it's roofless now but has good carvings, one on the jamb of the door is an incised comic face with ear-rings. The round tower near the small lake was built in the 11th or 12th century. It is one of the most perfect in Ireland, its angle has something in common with the Tower of Pisa. The monks used to build the door of such towers about twenty-five feet from the ground, so that

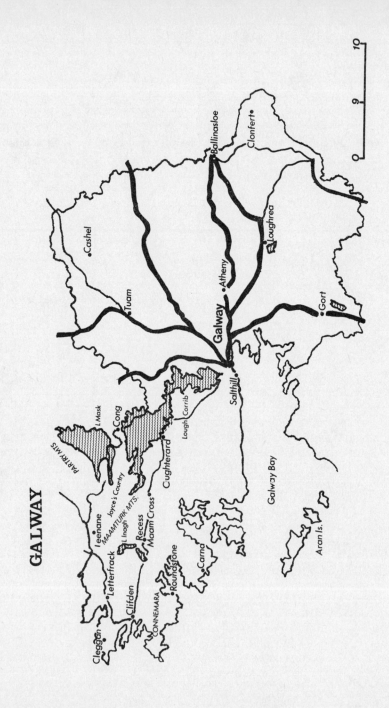

when marauders attacked they could whip up the ladder when they were safely installed with their treasures. In **Tirneevin**, just north of Kilmacduagh, is a small church with a very fine stained glass window of Christ, the sower, by George Campbell. Four miles south of **Gort** lies Lough Cultra and amongst some beautiful woods is a castellated mansion built in 1810 to designs by John Nash for Lord Gort.

Around **Gort** there are lots of little streams which suddenly disappear into the limestone; the river Beagh emerges to flow through a ravine called the Ladle and then into the Punchbowl. This is a huge funnel shaped hollow, surrounded by trees, with water swirling dangerously at the bottom. It is only a few yards from the road, so it's not difficult to see if you are in a hurry. The Gort area is full of literary associations: in 1917, W. B. Yeats bought a ruined tower house for £IR35 and called it Thoor Ballylee; he lived here until 1929, whereupon it once more fell into ruin. Bord Fáilte have carefully restored it, and many rare first editions of Yeat's work are on exhibit there daily from March to October. The hours are: 10 am-6 pm, in July and August 10 am-9 pm. There are tours and a tea room for the thirsty with some very good cakes. If you are in any doubt about times of opening Tel: Peterswell 8.

Lady Gregory's old home, Coole Park, is about two miles north east of **Gort**. Many remarkable people from the Irish literary scene stayed here, including Yeats, who found it a refuge when he was ill and little-known. Nothing is left of the house which was demolished for the value of its stone, such things always happened in Ireland, but the lovely spreading copper chestnut which was Lady Gregory's visitors' book, still grows in the walled garden. You can make out the initials of A. E. (George Russell, the mystical painter), Jack Yeats, Sean O'Casey and a bold G.B.S. – George Bernard Shaw. To prevent nonentities like you and I from getting out a pen-knife a high iron railing has been built round the tree. The demesne has been taken over by the Forestry Commission and is a wild life park open to all. Signs point the way to Coole Lake where Yeats saw nine and fifty swans and wrote a poem about them.

If you are interested in 16th century castles, five miles south of **Gort** are the ruins of Ardamullivan Castle, an O'Shaughnessy stronghold – notice the windows. Another of their strongholds is Fiddaun Castle, five miles south-southwest of Gort, the fine bawn is of an unusual plan. **Kinvara** is a charming fishing village at the head of a bay where there is a restored 16th century castle called Dunguaire. It is sited on a little jutting promontory beside the bay, a tower-house within the strong walls of its close-fitting bawn. On summer evenings you can savour the rather dubious delights of a *medieval banquet*, whilst you listen to readings from Irish literature. The Great Hall is rather bijou but the *Irish dancing* and *singing* are fun and through the windows of the castle to the north, you look over the waters of Galway Bay to the hills of **Connemara**. To the south you can make out the grey and hazy hills of the **Burren** in County Clare. Reservations by coach, Tel: CIE 091 62141 or if travelling privately contact the Galway Tourist Office 091 63081.

The road from **Kinvara** goes past the head of the peninsula on which is Doorus House, where Yeats and Maupassant used to stay; it is now a youth hostel.

Northwards from **Kinvara** the T69 runs inland with little side-roads turning west to the island waters of Galway Bay. One of these roads leads to the ancient monastic site of Drumacoo dedicated to a nun, Saint Sorrey. There is a very beautiful south doorway decorated in early Gothic style circa AD 1200. There is also a very weedy Holy Well outside the churchyard wall.

At **Clarinbridge**, on the main Galway/Limerick road, the bars come alive in September with oyster enthusiasts gathered there for the Oyster festival.

**Eating:** if you get the chance go to PADDY BURKES, OYSTER INN – Tel: 091 86107. It is a Cordon Bleu restaurant at night. For more ordinary fare there is O'GRADY'S RESTAURANT for hamburgers and steaks. There is lots to do if you are staying in the area: *Swimming* at Traught Beach, three miles from **Kinvara,** *golf,* and *pitch and putt* just outside **Gort.** *Fishing:* good sport can be had with mackerel, pollack, and bass in Kinvara Bay, and *good trout fishing* in the surrounding areas. You can go *dancing* in the ballrooms in **Gort** and there are ballad sessions in a number of hotels and bars; *'Seisiun'* – traditional music sessions are held in the Summers.

**Portumna** (Port Omna: the landing place of the tree trunk). This market town stands at the head of the huge and intricate Lough Derg, the furthest down-river of the Shannon lakes. The climb up the Slieve Auchty mountains is not too strenuous an exercise for the highest point is 1,207 feet. Enjoy the view, for it spreads over countryside full of sport for the fisherman, the antiquarian, boat enthusiast, and anyone hoping to shoot a pheasant. On the edge of the town is the forested demesne of the Earls of Clanrickarde. The 17th century castle is being restored by the Office of Public Works. I met an outraged little man who said it was disgusting that the government were restoring such symbols of oppression! A stone set in the crumbling walls of the double staircase is an affectionate epitaph to a dog that died in April 1797 'Alas poor Fury, she was a dog taken all in all, I shall not look upon her like again'. There is a Dominican Priory near the castle founded in 1410 with beautiful windows.

There are two castles really worth seeing: Derryhivenny Castle is three miles north west of **Portumna**; built 1653 by Donal O'Madden it is well preserved and one of the last Tower houses built in Ireland. Pallas Castle is about six miles from **Portumna** on the Loughrea road. Built in the 16th century by the Burkes, the lower stories are defensive, as in most castles and any openings are few and purely utilitarian – terrible places to have actually lived in. Amongst the lush and peaceful Shannon valley about 15 miles north east of **Portumna** is a monastery founded by Brendan the Navigator in 563. There is a superb example of Irish Romanesque art in the doorway of the miniscule church known as Clonfert Cathedral. Six receding planes are decorated with heads, foliage and abstract designs; within the pediment, sculptured heads peer down at you. The 15th century chancel arch is decorated with angels, rosettes, and a mermaid admiring herself in a mirror. Clonfert Catholic church houses a

13th century wooden Madonna and child, found in a tree hole it was probably hidden during Cromwell's time. **Meelick**, close by on the river Shannon, has mooring facilities for boats and a picnic area.

**Activities:** There is great *fishing, coarse and game* on the Shannon, Lough Derg, the Kilcrow River, the Cappagh River and Lough Atork. A new marina has been built at **Portumna** and boats can be hired from there as well as from numerous boathire companies along the river and the lough. Part of the lake has been especially developed for *swimming*, and a *tennis court* is available, free to visitors. Portumna Forest Park borders Lough Derg on its southern edge; it is a wild life sanctuary with lovely forest walks, often you come upon red and fallow deer. The entrance to the park is one mile outside **Portumna** on the Ennis road. *Golf* and *hunting* can be arranged, for this is the countryside of the famous Galway Blazers who have their headquarters at **Craughwell**. Early closing day is Monday.

**Loughrea** (the town of the grey lake): This bright colourwashed town, famous for its music and situated on a lovely lough started life as a stronghold of Richard de Burgo, whose family turned into Burkes and later Clanrickardes, you will come across the name often. The town is very affluent because at **Tynagh** there are lead and zinc mines.

What you must not miss if you stop in **Loughrea** is Saint Brendan's Catholic Cathedral. It's not very inspiring from the outside, but inside the decoration epitomises the development of the ecclesiastical arts and crafts in Ireland from 1903-1957. The stained glass windows are by Sarah Purser and other members of her Tower of Glass. The statue of the Virgin and Child is by John Hughes, and embroidered sodality banners are by Jack Yeats. Clonfert museum and the Carmelite monastery are worth a visit if you are staying in town, but the most impressive curiosity of all is the **Turoe Stone** which is found four miles north of town, signposted from the hamlet of **Bullaun**. This is a rounded pillar about three feet high, upon the upper part is carved a swirling mass of opposed spirals, La Tene style. It must have had some ritual purpose and dates from the 1st century AD; it is the finest of its type in Ireland and is similar to the pillar stones in Brittany. There is a circular cattle grid around it to protect it from the bovine itch.

**Activities:** There is *free fishing* on the rivers round about and the lake is well stocked with trout; contact Paddy Fitzgerald for details, Tel: 091 41269. Horses for *hunting* with the Galway Blazers can be hired from Aille Cross Equitation Centre, Loughrea, Tel: 091 41216.

Paddy Fitzgerald will also rent you a boat on which you can explore the lough and its little islands. There are lots of *good bathing* places on the shore.

**Eating:** if you have not had a picnic go for a meal at The MEADOW COURT, Clostoken, Loughrea; it's open all day and is very good for fish, Tel: 091 41051. In early June there is the Seven Springs Festival and in October there is a coursing festival. At night you can choose between the *theatre, cinema* or *dancing* at the Temperance Hall, it's always a bit of a gamble as to what the music will be like; too often it turns out to be country and western, but during the festival the locals get out their fiddles. Early closing day is on Wednesday.

**Ballinasloe** (Beal Atha na Sluaighe: town of the ford of the hostings): Ballinasloe is famous for its *Horse Fair* in October, when the quiet streets suddenly bustle with Carnival events which last for eight days. Horses are still put up for sale on the fair green, but not in the numbers that the ballads reminisce about.

There is a tower left from the castle which used to command the bridge over the river Suck an excellent river for *coarse fishing*. St. Michaels Church contains some of the best stained glass by Harry Clarke and Albert Power.

**Kilconnell** village, about six miles away on the road to Galway, has a Franciscan Friary. It was founded in 1353 by William O'Kelly, later it was unsuccessfully besieged by Cromwell. In the north wall of the nave are two 15th-16th century tomb chests one with flamboyant tracery; the west tomb has 'weepers', the figures of Saints John, Louis, Mary, James and Denis. Under the tower the corbel shows a little carving of an owl in high relief. Tradition alleged that the incompetent St. Ruth, who led the Irish against King William in 1691, was buried here after the Battle of Aughrim. If you are interested in battle mementoes there is a local museum in **Aughrim** village.

The abbey of **Clontuskert,** on the way to Lawrencetown, was rebuilt by the industrious monks in the 14th century; the money for this came from the sale of 10 years indulgences. The monks ignored the Reformation and carried on until Cromwell finally wrecked the place. The abbey has a pretty west door, and a mermaid carving. *Ballinasloe angling week* takes place annually on the River Suck, it is one of the biggest coarse angling competitions in Ireland. There are show jumping competitions which coincide with the Ballinasloe Fair. Ballinasloe tourist information Tel: 0905 2332, in the summer months only.

**Athenry** (Baile Atha an Ri: Town of the Kings Ford): Athenry is pronounced Athenrye and was founded by Meiler de Bermingham in the last half of the 13th century; the strong walls that were later built round it still remain in fragments. In the central square stands a 15th century cross head showing a crucifixion on one side and the Virgin and Child on the other. St. Mary's Parish Church was built in 1289, if not before. It became collegiate in 1484 and was suppressed in 1576 and burnt by Clanrickarde's sons (even though the mother of one of them was buried there). The graceful spire in the grounds dates from 1828.

Now ruined but full of interest is the Dominican Priory founded by de Bermingham in 1241; it has been a university and a barracks and has now been tidied up by the Office of Works. In a recess a small carving of a monk grins forever, and there is an interesting grave slab dated 1682 belonging to Thomas Tannain, on which are carved the bellows, anvil, auger, pinchers and horseshoe of his blacksmith's trade.

Moyode Castle, two miles south west of Athenry, is a ruined mansion with an ancient castle in its grounds; here in 1770 the nucleus of what was to become the Galway Blazers Foxhounds was formed. The big house was taken over by Liam Mellows and his Galway followers for several days during the Easter Week rising in 1916. **Claregalway** on the river Clare is now a suburb of Galway.

In Athenry the tennis courts are free and you can go *riding, trekking* or get *hunting instructions* from stables in Claregalway 091 88147 and Ballybeg, Corrandulla, Tel: 091 89202.

**Tuam** (Tumulas of the two shoulders) pronounced Choom: Tuam is a very uninspiring place, the streets smell of beer and chips. However there is fine 12th century cross in the town square and an imposing Church of Ireland cathedral. Although it is a Gothic revival structure, it still has a splendid wide and lavishly carved chancel arch of rosy sandstone which is a fine 12th century cross in the town square and an imposing Church of Dows, on one of the splays you can see the devil pulling Adam's ears.. The musty old place was full of the scent of flowers and the lady arranging them asked me if I would like to stay for the tour and talk the bishop was giving later on and then have tea at the vicarage; this is typical of the friendliness you find all over Ireland. She then told me that there were too many bachelors in Ireland and I thought of Merriman's poem *The Midnight Court* which challenged the Irish male for the same reason in 1750!

Four miles north of Tuam is Tollenfal Castle, ancestral home of the Lally's; one of them was the famous French general, Baron de Lally who has his name inscribed on the Arc de Triomphe in Paris. Lisacormack Fort, one mile east on the Dunmore road is the largest of the numerous earthworks scattered round this area. Tourist Information is available in the summer months only, Tel: (193) 24463. Unless you are really stuck, it's not a very nice place to stay in although there is plenty of accommodation. The Clare and Grange River are good for *brown trout* but permission must be obtained for some stretches. There is excellent pheasant and *woodcock, snipe* and *wild duck shooting*. Details of shoots may be had from Meehan's Game services Tel: 091 89202.

**Headford** (Ath Cinn the ford head): Set in countryside divided by stone fields, it's very tidy and neat and a favourite angling centre. Four miles away at Greenfields on Lough Corrib are mooring facilities. **Eating:** there is a good pub/restaurant, THE WHITE HORSE INN.

The surrounding countryside contains the ruins of many Norman castles. Knockma is traditionally held to be the home of King Finbarre and his Connacht fairies and the burial place of Queen Maeve. It is the only hill for miles. Ross Abbey is an important and well preserved 14th century ruin; the cloister remains intact, although not ornate, and the domestic buildings are complete, exhibiting perfectly the arrangements of a Franciscan Priory in the Middle Ages. There is a round hole in the floor of the kitchen, it is not a well but a fish tank, so the monks would always have fresh fish on Fridays. You will often notice that the monks knew how to choose the finest land, the best architects and well-stocked rivers for themselves.

## CONNEMARA

Connemara is not an area firmly drawn out by boundary lines, it is the name given to the western portion of County Galway which lies between Lough Corrib and the Atlantic Killary Harbour. Here at **Moycullen**, begin the real splendours of the west, although it is worth stopping only when you get to **Oughterard**. A pretty river, the Owenriff, runs though the charming village. It's right on the upper shores of Lough Corrib and a good place to base yourself if you are keen on *salmon* and *trout angling*. If you travel to **Costelloe** take the mountain road which gives you a vast panorama of watery landscape as you go up through a small hill pass. It's very wild, and the locals turn to stare at you as they load the turf into creels on the back of asses. There are shreds of shining water where you might find brown trout and turf cuttings, which gleam with black wetness when they have been newly cut.

When you arrive in **Costelloe,** you will find all the signs in English scrubbed out by a heavy hand. There is a coral strand here formed from fragments of a type of seaweed that develops a calcareous stem and lies beautifully white against the rocks and the green-blue sea. Beyond Greatman's Bay a series of bridges connects a chain of islands: **Lettermore, Gorumna** and **Lettermullen**. They are not visited very much by tourists though they are famous locally for poteen. The road from **Costelloe** (Casla) takes you to Galway via the coast, which is a disappointing route to drive through as new houses have been built up on either side so you can hardly see the sea.

For the moment, turn back to **Oughterard** and Lough Corrib to visit Aughnanure Castle three miles south east of **Oughterard**. It is an O'Flaherty building and said to be one of the strongest fortresses at that time Cromwell was blockading Galway. It was one of the outposts guarding Galway from attack. The six storey tower stands on an island of rock and in the days of its prosperity a portion of the floor of the hall was made to collapse; one of the flagstones was hinged downwards and an unwelcome guest might well find himself tipped into the fast flowing stream below. Nothing of the hall stands today, it collapsed into the stream, as did the cavern over which it was built. The Castle has been restored and you can climb right to the top. Ross Castle, five miles south east of **Oughterard** beside the shores of Ross Lake was the home of the Martins who bankrupted themselves trying to help out in the famine times. One of them 'Humanity Dick' was instrumental in setting up the Society for Prevention of Cruelty to Animals and Violet Ross was the Martyn Ross of Somerville and Ross fame. Her cousin Edith Somerville lived in Cork, but they succeeded in collaborating to produce some exquisitely humourous novel and stories. *The reminiscences of an Irish RM* and *Cousin Charlotte* are the best.

## INCHAGOILL (Inis an Ghaill: the island of the devout stranger)

Inchagoill is the largest of the hundreds of islands on Lough Corrib and is the prettiest and most interesting. There is a 5th century church, Teampall Pharaic and one of 10th century origin further to the south which was reconstructed in 1860. Then there is the Stone of Lugna, the navigator of St. Patrick which bears engraved Roman characters. It is supposed to be the earliest Christian inscription in Europe after the catacombs. You may get to the island by hiring a boat from Oughterard or Cong. The *fishing* is terrific for *brown trout, sea trout* and *salmon,* and you can hire a boat to explore the lough. *Bicycles are for hire* and there is a *golf course.* Tel: 091 82131. *Riding* is superb in the hills and lake countryside and *trekking* under supervision is available from Canrower Pony Stud. Tel: (091) 82120. The *tennis courts* in the village of Oughterard are free.

**Clonbur** is a centre for fishermen as it is situated on the limestone isthmus between Lough Mask and Lough Corrib, one mile to the west rises the lovely mountain where it is said the Fir Bolgs assembled before they made their last stand against the de Danaan. In the foot hills leading up to the highest peak Benlevy 1,370 ft is Lough Coolin, which in Edwardian days was the setting for lavish picnic parties which used to sally out from Ashford Castle about five miles away. You can get there by car although the road is very narrow, it is a peaceful, dreamy sort of place. If you want to climb the Connemara, Maamturk or Partry Mountains, **Clonbur** is well-placed. **Lough Nafooey** is one of the most beautiful in Connemara and in Irish means the lake of the spectre; lots of little streams run into the lake so there is never a ghostly stillness for the music of gurgling water plays continually in early summer accompanied by the smell of gorse and pine trees.

**Cornamona** is on the north-west shore of Lough Corrib on the Dooras Peninsula. It is in one of the most popular Irish speaking districts in North Connemara and on the edge of Joyce's Country. Joyce's Country is a mountainous area, named after a race of Welshmen who settled in Connacht after Richard de Burgo had conquered it. The native O'Flaherty's and the Joyce's eventually got on rather well and used to go and mob up the 'plainsmen'. As they often crossed swords on the isthmus it became known as the Gap of Danger. Not one of the roads around here are dull and the *fishing* on the little loughs, as well as Mask and Corrib, is good. On the road to Maam is a spectacular ruin, Hen's Castle on an island in the Corrib, it is said to have fallen into ruin after an O'Flaherty ate the hen which had been given to his family generations before by a witch. Cold historical fact states that the castle was built by the O'Connors.

## SOUTH CONNEMARA (IAR CHONNACHTA)

This includes most of the Irish speaking parts and stretches along the north coast of Galway Bay from **Bearna** (Barna) to **Casla** (Costelloe) and from there along the Atlantic to Carna. Its northern boundary runs from Gabhla through **Maam Cross** to **Bearna**. This part of the world is hilly and remote for there are very few roads into it. From **Galway** to **Spiddal** it is disappointingly built up, although you do get glimpses of the **Aran Islands**, looking far or near according to the clarity of the weather. There are good beaches and plenty of cafes on this stretch. At

**Spiddal** and **Knock** you can enroll in Irish summer school and stay with families whom you can practise your Gaelic on.

**Ros An Mhil** or **Rossaveal** has a cabin-cruiser called *The Queen of Aran* which runs regularly to Aran doing a brisk trade in turf, as Aran has no fuel resources of its own. By now you may have noticed the black beetle-like boats which the fishermen in Connacht use. They are very light and it needs a skilful man to handle the long heavy oars that have no blade. It is astonishing how much they can carry: cement, gas bombs, and even livestock, pig and sheep with their legs tied and muffled. The type of curragh varies considerably from the Donegal coast to the Kerry coast in the south. At Spiddal in June you cannot fail to get caught up in the excitement of the curragh races.

From Ros An Mhil you follow the road to **Casla** (Costelloe), which has a wonderful coral strand and a good *salmon fishing* river. There is quite a meeting of the roads here and you can go either to **Maam Cross** or follow a little road to **Carraroe** (An Cheathru Rua). At **Bealadangan** (Béal An Daingin) which is on the way to the islands of **Lettermore, Gorumna** and **Lettermullen** you can rent a traditional style cottage. This is rather deserted country, probably because the islands look rather dark and forbidding, but they attracted holy men long ago for there are remains of ancient churches and Holy Wells where now only the sheep munch.

Back on the main road again you come to **Scríb** or **Screeb** which has good *game fishing* and by turning left here you come to **Lough Aroolagh** and **An Gort Mor.** Here on a ledge of hillside above a small lake in the townland of **Turlough** you can go round the white washed cottage where the patriot Patrick Pearse used to write plays and poems. Back on the L102 four miles further on is the village of **Kilkieran,** here is scenery typical of the west; scattered houses with no nucleus nor clear distinction from the next village. You can see the brooding islands of **Lettermore** and, if the wind is in the right direction smell the rich seaweed which is dried in a factory here. **Kilkieran** and **Carna** are lobster fishing centres and there is a research station for shellfish, but you will find it difficult to buy a lobster for yourself – most of the seafood caught goes abroad or to the hotels. There is a three day festival in July at **Carna** with hooker (used for carrying turf), and *curragh races, sea angling competitions,* and arts and crafts.

You can get a boat from **Carna** to **MacDara's Island** where you get a marvellous view of the mountains of Connemara, and the hill of **Errisbeg** across **Bertraghboy Bay.** A side road from Carna takes you to **Mweenish Island** with beautiful sandy beaches, and out amongst the many islands that dot the Atlantic is **Oilean Mhac Dara** (MacDara's Isle) MacDara was a saint who was greatly honoured by the people of Iar Chonnachta, so much so that in the age of sailing boats, the fishermen used to dip their sails three times before passing the island. Most of the villages have halls where ceilithe, traditional Irish dances are held and you can hear Irish singers, musicians and story-tellers in the bars and hotels. The people who live here are very proud of their music and customs.

If you are interested in going to an Irish college where you join in the games, ceilithe and concerts write for details to: Comhchoiste na gColaisti Samhraidh, 86 Lower Gardiner Street, Dublin 1, Tel: 01 752231.

The tourist office for the area is Aras Failte, Victoria Place, Galway, Tel: 091 63081.

## WEST CONNEMARA

This is the district west of An Teach Dóite (**Maam Cross**) to the Atlantic, extending northwards to **Killary Harbour** and the Partry Mountains. This is a superb part of the world, much more exciting and untouched than the road that leads you round Iar-Chonnachta. You pass through lakes, rivers, forests and mountains where there is no hint of pollution or industry, even the machinery used on the farms is fairly traditional. **Maam Cross** is a place that you see signposted constantly, in fact it is the most unprepossessing place. But it is the centre of magnificent scenery and, rather like Piccadilly Circus, everybody travelling round Galway ends up there. **Maam Cross** has a petrol pump and a snack restaurant where you can stay as well. If you climb Leckavrey Mountain (2,012 ft) there are great views of the twelve Bens, Maamturks and Lough Corrib.

From **Maam Cross** you could go past **Recess** and take the road for **Roundstone. Recess** is a pretty village, where suddenly you come upon woods and Glendollagh Lough after driving through some spartan scenery. Lissoughter Mountain at 1,314 feet is worth climbing and you can see over to Lough Inagh and the mountains either side. This is where the Green Connemara marble is quarried.

**Cashel** is on a minor road and the village is right on Cashel Bay, an inlet of **Bertraghboy Bay,** it became famous overnight when General de Gaulle spent his holidays there.

**Roundstone** is a pleasant 19th century village and the name is an awful English corruption of the Irish Cloch na Ron which means Rock of the Seals. There is a pretty harbour which looks across the water to the low lying islands in Bertraghboy Bay. There is a good, friendly bar, O'Dowd's, where the fishermen contrast starkly with the Dubliners in their smart Aran sweaters. Incidentally there is a very good shop selling hand knitted jerseys next door to the post office. Errisbeg Mountain (987 feet) towers above the village. it is a short climb but the views are superb; look out for the flowers and plants for this is a place beloved of botanists as well as artists. Two miles on towards **Ballyconneely** are two of the best *beaches* in Connacht, you will have seen their silver lines beside the blue sea if you climbed Errisbeg. They are called Gurteen and Dog's Bay; this last name is another terrible mistranslation into English, for it is Bay of the plover or Port na Feadoige.

**Ballyconneely** is on the isthmus about nine miles from **Roundstone**. The road along this coast line is called the 'brandy and soda' road because of the exhilaration of the air. There is a newly developed *18 hole golf course* nearby at **Aillebrack** and beside the wide **Mannin Bay** is a

coral strand, the white sandlike debris of a seaweed similar to coral.
**Eating:** for an excellent meal try THE FISHERY RESTAURANT, Tel: Ballyconneely 31 and 38.

**Clifden** (An Clochan – Stepping Stones): is generally called the capital of Connemara, but it's not very big with a population of only just over a thousand. It's simply the biggest place around in a countryside of scattered hamlets and farms. It is in a sheltered bay and if you walk half a mile to the Atlantic shore and gaze out you are looking straight towards America. It is a well-planned early 19th century town and the two spires of the Protestant church and the Catholic cathedral give it a distinctive outline. There are plenty of places to eat and Millar's craft/tweed shop stock the lovely floor rugs, shawls and tweed that the Gaeltacht home industries have revived. **Clifden** is the centre for the *Connemara Pony Show* in August. The ponies are diminutive, shaggy little animals that look after themselves. Much more goes on besides selling and showing; there are bands, craft and cookery exhibitions and the wide streets are overflowing with people speaking Gaelic and English in a way which keeps the idiom and expression of the language.

There is a lovely road sign-posted Sky Road which takes you round the indented coast. Amidst sprays of fuchsia it climbs high above Clifden until it is above **D'Arcy's Castle,** the baronial style ruin of the D'Arcy who founded the town. From here you can see the waves crashing onto the rock islets of Inishturk, Inish-bofin and beyond to the north, Clare Island. The road continues into the quiet, sea weed fringed Streamstown Bay, where white Connemara marble is quarried. Four miles south of **Clifden** is the site where Alcock and Brown came to ground after the first ever transatlantic flight.

## GOOD RESTAURANTS AROUND THE CLIFDEN AREA:

KYLEMORE PASS HOTEL, Tel; Kylemore 10
ROSLEAGUE MANOR HOTEL, Letterfrack, Tel: Moyard 7
CROCARAW COUNTRY HOUSE, Moyard, Tel: Moyard 9
DOON RESTAURANT, MOYARD, Tel: Moyard 21
ABBEYGLEN HOTEL, Clifden, Tel: 33
HOTEL ALCOCK AND BROWN (modern decor) Tel: 134
CELTIC HOTEL, Tel: Clifden 115
O'GRADY'S SEAFOOD RESTAURANT, Tel: Clifden 263
For more information call the Clifden Tourist Office, Market St, Tel: Clifden 103 (open in summer only).

## ACTIVITIES IN CLIFDEN AREA

The *freshwater fishing* is some of the finest in Europe and Clifden is in the middle of many of the lakes and rivers. For information get in touch with Mr. Percy Stanley, Hon. Sec. of the Clifden Anglers' Association, Tel: Clifden 24. Boats and gillies are always available locally. There is an active *sea angling club* in **Clifden** which operates boats round the coast from **Roundstone** to **Leenne.** For details contact Mr. John Gilpin, Church Street, Clifden, Tel: Clifden 1. You can go out to **Inishturk, High Island, Omey Island** and **Slyne Head;** when the tide is out you can walk to Omey Island and the sand is so firm that *horse races* are held on it.

There are *riding* and *trekking centres* at: **Errislannan,** Tel: Clifden 27; and Angler's Return, Toombeola, Roundstone. Tel: Ballinafad 6. The Twelve Bens and Maamturks with their beautiful varying shapes are not much above 2,000 ft at their highest. Even though it may be sunny and dry at sea level, if you are going climbing it will be very wet underfoot. Many of the bars have notices in the windows about the ballad sessions you can go to and dances are held in Clifden town hall and other local ballrooms nearly every night.

You can explore round Cleggan Bay or make a spectacular drive through **Letterfrack** to the Kylemore Valley. **Cleggan** is the port for Inishbofin and the other islands. To find out about *boats* and *deep sea angling,* Tel: Cleggan 3. *Looking for holiday cottages to rent,* Tel: Cleggan 62.

**Inishbofin** has a very varied history, in the 7th century St. Colman founded a monastery here and in the 13th century, the O'Malley's won it off the O'Flaherty's to add to their sea board empire. Grace O'Malley is said to have fortified it though the locals say she could not dig through the rock to finish the deep ditch she was making. In 1652, Inishbofin was surrendered to the Cromwellians and was used as a sort of concentration camp for monks and priests. The barrack above the harbour has room for 6 cannons but now there are only red-beaked choughs to sound the alarm. Inishbofin has two hotels.

The mail boat leaves **Cleggan** at 1pm on Monday, Wednesday, Friday and Saturday (March to October), check on times in the winter. Bookings must be made and a return fare costs £4. Tel: Inishbofin 106. Other boats operate from Easter to September leaving at 11am. Tel; Cleggan 26.

**Letterfrack** was founded by the Quakers and there are wonderful bays for *bathing.* From Moyard onwards along the road are excellent craftshops. Nearby is the sparkling Diamond Hill, 1,460 feet. From Letterfrack a minor road leads to Tully Cross where there is a 'rent a cottage' scheme. These cottages are just like the traditional ones with a half door below the thatch, but the resemblance ends there, for the real cottages are very uncomfortable being badly designed with no electricity or water; families are abandoning them as quickly as they can. These holiday homes are an alternative to 'going native'. You can go *pony trekking* at Renvyle from Renvyle House Hotel and there are marvellous beaches from which you can *swim, sail* or *water ski.* Tel: Renvyle 3. A Teach Ceoil (music house) is open to everybody in the Summer at Tully Cross where the traditional musicians gather to play.

The Kylemore valley lies between the twelve Bens and the forested Doughruagh mountains in the North. Trees and rhododendrons grow beside the three lakes and the Dawros River which are well stocked with *salmon* and *sea trout* (Tel: Kylemore 7 for details). There is a splendid mock castle in the woods at Lake Kylemore which is now a girls school and a convent for the Benedictine nuns of Ypres. The nuns run a restaurant, a souvenir shop and cultivate beautiful grounds around which you can wander. The wealthy Liverpudlian merchant who built the castle, also built a fine mock Gothic chapel with pillars of Connemara marble inside. Nearby is a pre-Christian chamber tomb.

There is a lovely route just beyond the lake, dominated by the conical peaks of the Maamturks and the Bens, which cuts through the Inagh Valley to **Recess**. But if you follow the T71, you descend to the beautiful shores of **Killary Harbour**, a narrow fiord which reaches inland to **Leenane**. If you have time to go to Salrock on little Killary Bay; here shades of pagan customs existed until twenty years ago when tobacco pipes smoked at the wake of the deceased would be laid on their grave. The road from here to **Renvyle** follows a wild coastline and if you look towards Killary Harbour, the Mweelrea Mountain rises bare and massive. The road to the mouth of Killary Harbour is set between the dark blue fiord and green hill slopes that are rilled so as to give the effect of crushed velvet. Douglas pine, beech, hawthorn and purple rhododendron add to the luxury of colour. The Eriff River comes tumbling over the Aasleagh Falls at the bridge and enquiries for *salmon* tickets should be made to Chris Harper at Leenane 11 or Louisberg 20. At the bridge you will also find a grade A hotel.

From little Killary you can catch a curragh to the foot of Mweelrea or into **Killary Harbour**; there is no fixed charge and you must strike a bargain with the boatman. There is a very popular youth hostel here (even though it is miles from the shops, and the bus stop is a five mile walk away), so you must book well ahead. The harbour is 13 fathoms deep and one of the safest anchorages in the world. Here you can *fish for pollack, mackerel, ray, wrasse, whiting, flatfish* and *lobster*. If you want to climb Mweelrea Mountains begin at Delphi, follow the ridges to the fiord.

For full information and advice on holidays in Galway, or anywhere else for that matter, the principal office is Aras Fáilte, Victoria Place, which is just off Eyre Square and a few hundred yards from the rail and bus station in Galway City. Tel: 091 63081 Telex 8370.

**Galway City** is a bustling town which has been the centre of trade since the 13th century, despite a decline in the 18th and 19th century. Fragments of buildings and mutilated stone merchant houses still exist amongst the fast food signs and modern shop fronts. You have to go and seek out the strange and memorable animal carvings which have survived and the fine doorways and windows. The best example is Lynch's Castle in Shop Street which now houses a branch of Allied Irish Banks Ltd. There has always been some sort of settlement here, because of the ford on the Corrib River. However, Galway which takes its name from the river never achieved any importance until the de Burgos built a castle.

By the end of the 13th century many Welsh and English families had been encouraged to settle here and they built themselves strong stone walls to keep out the dispossessed and disgruntled de Burgos and the wild O'Flaherty's. There were 14 main families and they became known as the Tribes of Galway; fiercely independent they made an Anglo-Norman oasis in the middle of hostile Connacht. In 1549, they placed this inscription over the west gate 'From the fury of the O'Flaherties, good Lord deliver us'. They also put out edicts controlling the presence of the native Irish in the town 'that neither O nor Mac should strutte ne swagger thro the streets of Galway' So the Irish settlement grew up on the west side of the Corrib following completely different traditions. It is now renowned for the Claddagh Ring, which is a ring you will notice on the fingers of many Irish exiles; it is a circle joined by two hands clasping a heart and was used as a marriage ring. But the Claddagh settlement which inspired the Victorian travellers is gone, the thatched one storey houses have been replaced by a modern housing scheme.

The chief tribe of Galway were the Lynch family and there is a story of colourful and dubious origins about the Lynch who was Mayor in 1493. The tribes grew very prosperous through a trade in wine with Spain and Bordeaux, and this Lynch had the son of a Spanish merchant staying in his house who aroused the jealousy of Walter his son. Walter stabbed the young guests to death and because he was so popular nobody could be found to hang him. So his father, having pronounced the sentence, did the deed himself and filled with sadness became a recluse. Near the Church of St. Nicholas, in a built up Gothic doorway, there is a tablet commemorating the event. The modern Catholic Cathedral is an imposing hotch-potch of styles, and it is well worth going round the Church of St. Nicholas in the city centre where Christopher Columbus is supposed to have attended mass; it has interesting carvings and a peal of eight bells. There is a market held beside it on Saturdays. The Park in Eyre Square was opened by John F. Kennedy and is named in his honour; a doorway was salvaged from the Brown Mansion and now serves as the entrance to the Park; there is a statue by Albert Power of Padraig O Connaire, who wrote short stories in Irish in the 1920's.

By the Spanish Arch, there is a museum and Irish theatre (An Taibherc) open during the summer and the Druid Lane Theatre is open for evening performances in June, July and August, and concentrates on the works of Anglo-Irish writers. For *cinema programme details, ballad session, dances* and *plays* look in the local newspaper or the Tourist Guide to What's On. Larry Allen's Bar on Foster St. is the best place for traditional music.

There is the Galway Bay *International Sea Angling Festival* held in September and the *Galway Oyster Festival* with an oyster opening championship. The *famous Galway Races* take place two miles from the city. The most exciting races are held at the end of July and beginning of August and feature the Galway Plate and the Galway Hurdle, a mixture of high society and sweet talking bookies. If you want to study the local history join a Summer Course for foreign students at the University College. Reference material and books may be consulted in the reference library of the Court House. One of the nicest places to go and idle away the hours is the Salmon Weir beside the Catholic Cathedral. Shoals of salmon lie in the clear river before making their way up to the spawning grounds of Lough Corrib. You can *fish* in the weir for a fee, Tel: 091 63081. This narrow river is the only entrance from the sea to 1,200 miles of lakes.

**Salthill** is a very crowded holiday resort by the sea where there is lots to do. *Angling, golf* beside the promenade, *pitch and putt, tennis, squash, badminton, grey-hound racing, swimming* in a heated pool, and even flying lessons. The leisure land complex at Salthill has good amusements for all ages and there is a tourist information office on the promenade from mid-June to mid-September.

Galway is 134 miles from Dublin, 58 from Shannon, 190 from Belfast.

For full information on hotels, guest houses, bed and breakfast places pick up a complete list from the Bord Fáilte tourist offices. They will do your booking for you for the price of the telephone call.

---

## THE ARAN ISLANDS

The people and the Islands of Aran have been described so gracefully by Synge and filmed so beautifully by Robert Flaherty that any other descriptions are laborious, especially of the guide book kind. Another brilliant portrayal of the islands is Richard Powers' novel 'Apple on the Tree-Top' which is about living there and working amongst the Aran men in the building sites of Britain. He does justice to these barren limestone islands which a six hour rush round cannot hope to do. Gentian, maiden hair fern, wild roses and saxifrage blossom on the 11,000 acres which make up the three islands, but only 6% of the land is rated as productive. The soil has been built up over the years with layer upon layers of seaweed, animal manure and sand from the beaches, so that these limestone rocks can support a few cattle, asses and rows of potatoes.

The people of the islands speak Irish amongst themselves but out of politeness they will switch to English if there is a stranger around. Many of them have been to America or Britain for work. There used to be a distinctive Aran dress but this has died out, except for the waistcoat of unbleached wool called a bainin or bawneen. Sometimes you still see the thick, tweed trousers and the gay woven belt which is worn to keep them up and is now sold to tourists as the Aran kris or crios. The women used to knit the bawneens and heavy Aran sweaters with the family pattern, so that it would be easier to identify the bodies of drowned fishermen. The thick woollen shawl and red flannel skirt has died out, just as in the rest of the west.

**Inishmore** is the largest of the islands being about eight miles long. Its capital is **Kilronan.** When you get off the steamer you can either hire a bicycle, or a sidecar and jarvey to show you the sights. Kilronan has become rather touristy, but the people remain cheerful and courteous, even though the uncouthness and thick skinned attitudes of some of the tourists trying to take photos must jar.

Kilronan is linked by road to a chain of villages, and if you want to get to a friendly drinking house after the gruelling voyage, Daly's pub in **Killeeny** is the place. Amongst the fields separated by loose stone walls (the effect is rather maze-like), you will come upon ancient ecclesiastical sites, and most impressive of all, forts of stone built over 2,000 years ago, supposedly by the Fir Bolgs. The people of Aran, who could be descended from the Fir Bolgs, never bother with gates, they are too expensive to import. Instead, if they are herding livestock through different fields, they undo the stone walls and then calmly build them up again when the animals have got through.

**Dún Aonghus** or **Dun Aengus** covers some eleven acres; it consists of several concentric ramparts, 18 feet high and 13 feet deep which form a semi-circle with the two edges ending on the brink of the cliffs that fall nearly 4,000 feet to the Atlantic. The approach is guaranteed to cripple you if you don't advance with caution, for outside the middle wall, sharp spars of stone set closely in the ground form a chevaux de frise. Not far from Dun Aengus is **Dun Eoghanacha,** another stone ring fort. One and a half miles west of **Cill Einne,** on the southern side of the island, is **Dubh-Chathair**; some of it must have disappeared over the steep cliffs for it must have been even larger than Dun Aengus. At **Kilchorna,** Monasterkieran and Teampall an Cheathrair are more old and evocative ruins. With the coming of Christianity and St. Enda in 483 the island became Aran of the Saints; at Cill Einne there are the graves of 120 saints, for all Enda's followers seem to have reached the glorious state of sainthood after living their lives in the narrow confines of Clochans.

**Inishmaan Island** is not usually visited by tourists and you can see the huge fort of Dun Conor or Dun Chonchuir from the sound as you approach the shore. It is very likely, if you go to **Inishmaan** or **Inisheer** that you will have to do the last bit of the journey by currach; it is an exciting and quite alarming experience as you drop into the bouncing, frail looking craft and leave the security of the mail boat. If you see one on land, being carried upside down, it looks just like a giant beetle. Currachs are made of laths and canvas and then tarred over and the fishermen of the west handle them with innate skill; often they are heavily loaded with cargo ranging from hens to cement, so watch out for general mess when you get into one.

Dun Conor is the most impressive of all the Aran forts. Its three outer walls, with the exception of the remnants of the inner curtain, have disappeared; but the massive fortress wall, built of stones which only a race of giants could lift easily, is almost intact. Nearby is a freshwater spring which never dries up, called Saint Chinndheirg's Well; it's supposed to have curative properties. One of the most interesting churches is Cill Cean Fhionnaigh (church of the fair headed one). It is one of the most perfect primitive Irish churches in existence. There is another Holy Well here and you get to the place by walking south-west of **Trawletteragh**.

As you come through Foul Sound towards **Inisheer** you see O'Brien's Castle on the rocky hill south of the landing place. It is a 15th century tower set in a stone ring fort. Inisheer is the smallest island, only about two miles across, but it greets you with a broad, sandy beach. It also boasts a tiny 10th century church dedicated to St. Gobhnait, the only woman allowed on the three islands when the saintly men ruled these shores

Aran is a great place to stay, and you need at least a week. The views around the forts and churches are magnificent and you can wander around the rough roads, amongst the limestone rocks, watching for the little flowers and plants that somehow manage to grow. There are beaches on Inishmore and Inisheer and the water is comparatively warm; it is best to ask locally about the various beaches, and about *sea angling* which can be done from a currach, or the cliffs. Every evening in the summer there are ballad sessions in the public houses. You are not totally cut off from the outer world: there are two post-offices on Inishmore, at **Kilronan** *and* **Kilmurvey,** and a post-office on each of the other two islands. There is a phone service to the mainland and a travelling bank which comes out every Wednesday to Kilronan. Aran has a tourist office during the summer at Kilronan, Tel: Kilronan 29.

**Connections out there:** CIE provide a regular sea service from **Galway** to Kilronan which takes about three hours; if you are on a day trip you are allowed about six hours worth of sight-seeing. The boat goes daily during the summer, and in the winter twice a week, usually on Wednesday and Saturday. Timetables are determined by the tides and you can get them from CIE, Tel: 091 62141, or the Galway Tourist Office, Tel: 091 63081. These services also go to Inishmaan and Inisheer. A daily boat service also operates from **Rossaveal** about twenty-six miles from Galway, Tel: 091 63081

Aer Arann operates daily flights from **Carnmore** (four miles from Galway) to all the island. It takes about twenty minutes actual flying time. Contact Aer Arann at Dominick St, Galway, Tel: 091 65119 or 091 61282. They will also arrange scenic flights for groups.

## PLACES TO STAY IN COUNTY GALWAY

### Aran Islands

**Inishmaan**
Mrs Faherty, Creigmore.
**Inishmore**
Mr Dirrane, Gilbert's Cottage, Tel: (099) 61146
Mrs B Conneely, Beach View Hs, Oatquarter, Tel: (099) 61141
Mrs P O'Flaherty, Oughill, Tel: (099) 61157 (no CH)
Johnston-Hernons, Kilmurvey Hs, Tel: (099) 61218 (guesthouse grade B)
**Athenry**
Miss Gardner, Old Church St, Tel: Alhenry 17
**Ballinafad**
The Twelve Bens, Ben Lettery.
**Ballinasloe**
Mrs Lyons, Nephin, Kellysgrove, Tel: (0905) 2685

**Ballyconneely**
Mrs Laidlaw/Miss Welsh, Brandyburn Cottage, Tel: B'Conneely 11
Mrs S King, Coral View Hs, Derrygimla.
**Banagher**
Miss Kearns, Inishee, Esker, Tel: Banagher 146
**Cashel Bay**
Mrs O'Donoghue, Sunset Cottage, Tel: Cashel 12
**Clarinbridge**
Mrs O'Dea, Karaun, Stradbally, Tel: (091) 86182
**Cleggan**
Mrs de Courcy, Hazelbrook, Tel: Cleggan 54
**Clifden**
Mrs O'Toole, Taobh a Locha, Streamstown (farmhouse), Tel: Clifden 136
Mrs Walsh, Derrylea Hs. Derrylea, Tel: Clifden 224
Mrs Morris, Ben View Hs. Bridge St, Tel: Clifden 123
**Clonbur**
Mrs Burke-Glynne, Lakeview Hs, Loughnafooey, Finney, Tel: Clonbur 14
**Cornamona**
Mrs Joyce, Carrick West (no CH), Tel: Cornamona 128
Mrs P O'Sullivan, Oakland Hs, (farmhouse overlooking L. Corrib) Tel: 107)
**Costelloe (Casla)**
Mrs O'Toole, Post Office (NoCH), Tel: (091) 72122
**Craughwell**
The Jennings Family, Riversdale Hs, Tel: Craughwell 5
**Eyrecourt**
Mrs Lynch, Moyower, Eyrecourt, Tel: (0905) 5156
**Galway** and **Salthill** Area Code 091
There are plenty of places to chose from but the best and cheapest ones are in Salthill.
**City Centre**
Mrs Kennedy, 6 Loyola Park, College Rd, Tel: 64620
Mrs T Quinn, 134 College Rd, Tel: 61519
Mrs Lydon, 8 Lower Abbeygare St, Tel: 64914
**Renmore**
Mrs Carroll, Avila, 4 Glenina Heights, Dublin Rd, Tel: 65402
Mrs Leen, Arabella, 21 Woodlands Av, Tel: 64836
Mrs O'Connor, St Joseph's, 41 Dublin Rd, Tel: 63434
**Salthill**
Guesthouses: Rio, Salthill, grade A, Tel: 23580
Adare Hs, FR Griffin Pl, grade B, Tel: 62638
Glendawn Hs, Upper Salthill, grade B, Tel: 22872
Osterley Lodge, Salthill, grade B, Tel: 23794
Rockbarton Park Hotel, grade B, Tel: 22018
Mrs O'Halloran, Roncalli Hs, 24 Whitestrand Avenue, Tel: 64159
Mrs Flaherty, Loreto, 9 D'Alton Place, Tel: 22613
Mrs S Burke, St Annes, 11 Ardnamara, Tel: 23961

Mrs Bryne, Greenwood Hs, Gentian Hill, Tel: 22727
**Gort**
Mrs M Diviney, St Ritas, Ennis Rd, Tel: Gort 121
**Headford**
McDonagh Family, Balrickard Farm, Tel: (093) 21421. Bicycles for hire.
Mrs Hannon, Hillview, (farmhouse) Tel: (093) 21458
**Inishbofin**
Days Bofin Hs, grade B Hotel, Tel: Inishbofin 103
**Kinvara**
O'Connor Family, Burren View, Doorus, Tel: Kinvara 13
Youth Hostel, Doorus House, Kinvara.
Mrs Quilty, Teac Caoilte, Geehy North, Duras.
**Kylemore**
Mrs Naughton, Kylemore Hs, Tel: Kylemore 3
**Leenane**
Mrs King, Killary Hs, Tel: Leenane 6
Mrs O'Neill, Glen Valley Hs, Glencroft, (farmhouse) Tel: Leenane 34
Leenane grade A hotel, Tel: Leenane 4
**Letterfrack**
Mr McDonnell. Tullycross, Tel: Renvyle 36
**Loughrea**
Mrs Morrissey, St Anne's Hs, West Bridge St, Tel: (091) 41394
**Maam**
Mrs Kane, Tiernakill Farmhouse, Tel: (091) 71125
**Oughterard**
Mrs Harbem, Clonriff, Tel: (091) 82330
Mrs O'Neill, Creeve, Glan Rd, Tel: (091) 82210
**Recess**
Mrs Poulton, Caher County Hs, Tel: Recess 17
**Renvyle**
Mrs O'Toole, Tullycross, Tel: Renvyle 21
Youth Hostel, Killary Harbour, Rosroe
**Roundstone**
Mrs Burke, Letterdyfe, Tel: Roundstone 35
Ms Prynne, The Anglers Return, Toombeola, Tel: Ballinafad 6
Mrs Woods, St Joseph's, Tel: Roundstone 29
**Spiddal**
Mrs Feeney, Ardmor, Greenhill, Tel: (091) 83145
**Binge Places**
Rosleague Manor Hotel, Letterfrack, Tel:Moyard 7
Cashel Hs Hotel, Cashel, Tel: Cashel 9
Crocnaraw Hs, Tel: Moyard 9
Currarevagh Hs, Oughterard, Tel: (091) 82313
Renvyle Hs Hotel, Renvyle 3
Lisdonagh Manor (farmhouse), Caherlistrane Headford, Tel: (093) 21428
Ballynahinch Castle, Tel: Clifden 135

# County Leitrim

Leitrim is a long narrow country with a foothold in the sea, stretching back to mountains, hills and streams. It is divided in two by Lough Allen, one of the many lakes of the Shannon river. It is a very individual county, with a secret forgotten feel to it; a good place for a quiet holiday. Leitrim shares the beauty of Lough Gill and Lough Melvin and has countless lakes of its own; the conversation in hotels and bed and breakfast places will invariably be about fishing. The lakes by all accounts are teeming with bream, pike, perch, salmon and trout. If you are a walker and anxious to be alone, the mountains around **Manorhamilton** are full of wistful beauty; you will pass the remains of many deserted cottages on the slopes where only sheep and cattle graze.

## NORTH LEITRIM

**Manorhamilton** The town is situated at the meeting of four valleys in a setting of steep limestone hills and narrow ravines. It was founded by Sir Frederick Hamilton whose fine 17th century mansion is now a ruin cloaked in ivy. It is a good place to stop and explore all the various roads that spiral out from it. I found myself on a boggy little road which you take after going a few miles down the main road to **Belcoo**. It led me to some caiseail (stone forts) built about 500 BC; in the misty morning light they looked very mysterious and remote, only a pheasant's cry of alarm broke the silence. The land hereabouts belonged to the O'Rourke chieftains who took part with O'Neill and O'Donnell in the last great rebellion of the Irish nobility against Elizabeth I.

North of Manorhamilton, the Bonet Valley narrows towards the source of this pretty river into an equally pretty lake, the Glenade. The T54 runs beside its waters which are thickly edged with trees. The hills are high in the east, but to the west a line of crags rise from the grassy slopes. The road slopes down to Kinlough on the Melvin Lough and you are only three miles from the sea. If you want to taste the delights of **Bundoran**, a highly developed seaside resort in Donegal, it's only a few miles further on. Two noted *salmon* rivers flow into the Atlantic beside **Tullaghan**, Leitrim's only seaside village, they are the Bunduff and Bundrowes. Lough Melvin is very good for *salmon* and *trout*. *Fishing permits* for the Bundrowes can be obtained from Mr Jack Philips, West End, Bundoran, boats hired from Mr Kevin Clancy, Stracomer, Kinlough.

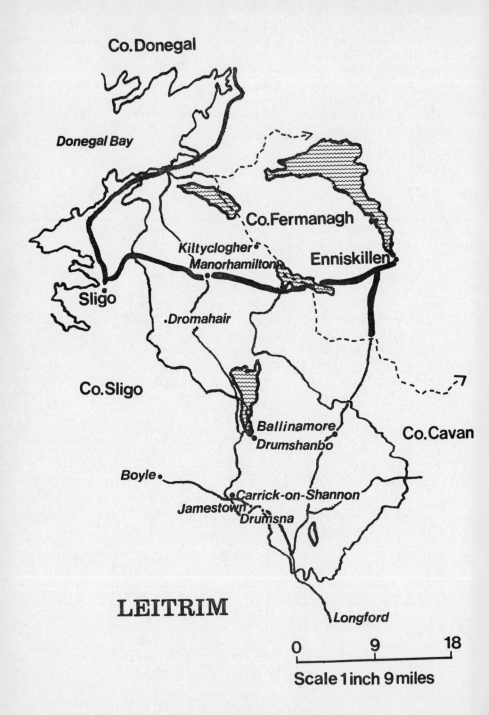

Co. Donegal

Donegal Bay

Co. Fermanagh

Kiltyclogher

Manorhamilton

Enniskillen

Sligo

.Dromahair

Co. Sligo

Ballinamore

Drumshanbo

Co. Cavan

Boyle.

Carrick-on-Shannon

Jamestown

Drumsna

LEITRIM

Longford

0        9        18

Scale 1 inch 9 miles

The many islanded Lough Melvin extends for eight miles, and a road follows its southern side from **Kinlough** to **Rossinver**. A sign by the road points to Rossclogher Abbey and Castle. You have to leave your car or bicycle and walk over long grass to reach them but it's worth it, for the view of the lough is superb. Notice the line of rushes going out to the castle, which is on a little island; probably an underwater causeway. At **Rossinver**, at the head of the southern end of the lake, are the remains of a church and a monastery of St. Mogue, and there is a Holy Well nearby. Modern gravestones look very out of place in the graveyard.

The road south to **Kiltyclogher** passes over the ancient earth work called the Worm Ditch or the Black Pigs' Race; it extends intermittently from Bundoran in the west to Newry in County Down. It was probably built by the Scotti, people who lived in the north, to prevent encroachment from the south. Legend as usual tells a much more colourful story: the ditch was formed by the slithering of a huge serpent over the land; or if it was not a serpent, then it was a monstrous pig that snuffled and rooted around, throwing up the earth as it went.

In the centre of **Kiltyclogher** village stands the statue, by Albert Power, of Sean MacDiarmada who was executed for his part in the 1916 uprising. There is a rock at **Laughty Barr** where people used to go to hear mass during the Penal times. Signposted from the road is Kiltyclogher Megalithic tomb; it is a court cairn built between 2000-1500 BC, known locally as Prince Connell's Grave. From Manorhamilton to Sligo there is a lovely valley in which lies Glencar Lough and Waterfall; the spray when it is in full spate would soak you in seconds on a windy day. Yeats wrote a poignant poem about this place called 'The Stolen Child'.

There are ballad sessions in the local lounge bars, but the big event in Manorhamilton is the Wild Rose Festival, which has *music, dancing,* and other fringe events. There is a registered camping and caravan camp at **Stracomer, Kinlough**. You can also go *shooting* on 7,000 acres for pheasant, snipe, duck, woodcock, hare and rabbit near Kiltyclogher. Rates are £IR20 per gun per day, which includes a guide, dogs for two guns, and a packed lunch. Contact F Hannon, Tel: Kiltyclogher 12.

**Dromahair** this is a very pretty village about eight miles from **Manorhamilton** through which the River Bonet flows until it gets to Lough Gill. It is the base for horse drawn caravans; contact Mr D Wall, Drumlease Glebe Hs, Dromahair, Tel: 071 74141. The road from Manorhamilton has the most beautiful views of Lough Gill and the wooded country around. Across the river in Dromahair is Creevelea Abbey founded in 1508 by Margaret, wife of Owen O'Rourke. The abbey has a pretty pillar representing St Francis talking to the birds, the branches and roots of the tree grow in Celtic patterns. In the middle of the town are the sparse remains of Breffni Castle, stones from it were used to build another mansion in 1630. It was the chief stronghold of the O'Rourkes and it was from here that Devorgilla, wife of Tiernan O'Rourke, eloped with Dermot MacMurrough at the age of forty-four. But she regretted her action for Dermot turned out to be even crueller than Tiernan and one day she slipped back to be reconciled with him. But her elopement was the turning point in the history of Ireland, for it eventually led to the flight of Dermot MacMurrough from Ireland and his conspiring with Henry II which resulted in the Anglo-Norman invasion of Ireland.

On the scenic road round Lough Gill, on the way to **Sligo**, you pass Parke's Castle, a fine example of a Planter's insecurity; it was built in the 17th century and well fortified against the Irish. There are plenty of laybys where you can park and look out over the water to the many islands. The Wall family who have the horse-drawn caravans, also have people to stay in their farmhouse and you can go *pony trekking* from there. Tel: 071 74141.

From **Dromahair**, take the L112 which joins the T54 for Drumkeerin and **Drumshanbo**, this road twists through hills past Lough Belhavel and Lough Allen. From now on the emphasis is on fishing and along the roads you will notice signposts pointing to the various lakes and the sort of fish you are likely to catch. Lough Allen is noted for its large pike, fish over 30 lbs are not uncommon. There is good *bream fishing* from the banks of the twenty lakes within the five mile radius of Drumshanbo. The Slieve Anierin range, or Iron Mountains dominate the landscape. You can hire a boat from Mr Joe Mooney, Tel: Drumshanbo 13. There is *tennis* and *swimming* in the village; it is also the setting for An Tostal, 'an Ireland at home' festival with everything Irish. The local groups of wren-boys perform, they are a variation on the mummers or rhymers who come round at Christmas.


## SOUTH LEITRIM

**Carrick-on-Shannon** this was always an important crossing place but now it is the centre of river cruising on the Shannon, boasting a marina and four cruising companies. It is a pretty place with very good shops and delicatessens. Nearby is the Lough Key Forest Park; it is very beautifully laid out with bog gardens, nature trials and boat trips on the lake. You can explore the Ariga Mountains, where coal is still mined, and experience the magnificent views down onto the lake country. Within six miles of Carrick there are 41 lakes and *fishing* is free and unrestricted. Contact Mr Des Keane, Bridge St, Tel: Carrick-on-Shannon 262. The river cruisers can be hired only for periods of one week or more, any travel agent can supply full details. There is a *canoe club* at **Summerhill**, and canoes can be hired from the Kennedy family at **Jamestown Bridge**. There is *golf, tennis, swimming, bingo, dancing, drama, cinema* and *cabaret* in Cartown House Hotel; *seisiun,* traditional Irish music, is played at the Bush Hotel on Friday nights during the summer.

The Festival of the Shannon runs for a fortnight in July, closely followed by the Shannon Boat Rally, in which all types of boats participate. If you get off your boat and want to hire a bicycle contact Mr Patrick Geraghty, Main Street or Mrs F Holt, Bridge St. Train services run from **Drumod** to **Sligo** and **Dublin** daily, bus services go to **Sligo, Galway, Limerick, Cork** and **Athlone**. The Tourist Office (open from June to September) is in Bridge St, Tel: 170. **Eating:** The JOLLY DOG

BAR and the BUSH HOTEL will fill you up with good things to eat, the latter is a B\* grade hotel.

**Drumona** on the Shannon is where Anthony Trollope lived for some time and the river scenery is lovely. When the Shannon was used for transporting produce **Drumona** was quite an important trading centre. **Fenagh**, up in the hills, has the ruins of a Gothic church which is all that remains of the monastery St. Columcille founded and which under the rule of St. Killian became internationally famous as a school of divinity. At **Ballinamore** you have the choice of staying at two farmhouses, a town or a country house. This is a lovely lake starred area where you can *fish* to your heart's delight. On an island in Lough Scur is an Elizabethan castle which in the past was often attacked by the O'Rourkes of Breffni Castle. At **Ballymagovern** is a site which used to be the scene of pagan worship. **Mohill** and **Carrigallen** are first class *fishing* centres.

The main tourist office for this region is Sligo, at Stephen St, Tel: Sligo 5336. You will find information on accommodation and anything else you want to know; they will book your room for you and give out lots of free literature on where to walk, fish, etc.

## PLACES TO STAY IN COUNTY LEITRIM

**Ballinamore**
The Thomas Family, Riversdale, Tel: Ballinamore 122
**Carrick-on-Shannon**
Mrs Griffin, Cartown Hs, St Mary's Close, Tel: Carrick-on-Shannon 131
Hotel grade B Tel: Carrick-on-Shannon 388
**Dowra**
Mrs O'Dwyer, Derrynahona, Ballinagleara, Tel: Dowra 29
**Dromahair**
Mrs Wall, Drumlease, Glebe Hs, Tel: (071) 74141
**Drumshanbo**
Mrs Earley, Kylemore Hs, Tel: Drumshanbo 19
Mrs McKeon, Woodside, Carrick on Shannon Rd, Tel: Drumshanbo 106
**Fenagh**
Mrs Curran, Foxfield, Carrick-on-Shannon, Tel: Ballinamore 179
**Mohill**
Mrs Carleton, Drumhirk Hs, Farnaught, Tel: Mohill 15
Mrs Slevin, Coolbawn Hs, Station Rd, Tel: Mohill 33
Sportman's Hotel, grade B, Tel: Mohill 12
**Rooskey**
Mrs Duffy, Kilianiker Hs, Tel: Roosky 16

# County Mayo

Mayo is a large county which towards the east is made up of limestone plains, which are interrupted by the sandstone hills of the Curlews, and further north by the Ox Mountains or Slieve Gamph. From **Ballinrobe** to **Ballintubber** and **Claremorris** you might turn round a corner and see the most unexpected things; perhaps the remnants of an old demesne, an eccentric looking folly, or some vast grey dolmen. If you stray to the south-west of the country and explore right up to the **Mullet Peninsula** and **Portacloy**, you will find yourself amongst some of the most spectacular scenery in the west quartzite, schist, and gneiss rocks form dramatic mountains and cliffs; and the Atlantic is a wonderful backdrop for the fuchsia covered inlets, the sandy beaches, the soft green drumlins and the stretches of wild boggy country. I love Mayo, especially the loughs of Furnace and Feeagh, and the hillside country looking to the Holy Mountain, Croagh Patrick and the wild Nephin range.

The Mayo Gaeltacht covers parts of north west Mayo including Curraun, parts of Achill and the Mullet Peninsula, plus a small area around **Tourmakeady** which is the centre of the Gaeltarra Eireann knitwear industry (soft colours and traditional patterns are used). Tourmakeady is also famous for its connection with the De Valera's - here Sinead taught Eamonn, who not only became one of her best pupils but her husband as well.

## EAST MAYO

Mayo has many holy sites and one of them, **Cong,** is beside the island studded Lough Corrib, just over the border from Galway County. Cong means isthmus and the Corrib and Mask Lakes are connected by a river which flows part underground and forms various caves in the limestone. A canal was built so that you could take a boat between the lakes, but the water never stayed in the porous limestone. Cong is a very friendly place and has one of the nicest ancient abbeys and a most attractive modern Catholic Church. They are both beside each other down by the tree lined river, and the graceful grey of the old merges with the flat asbestos sheets of the new. The abbey was founded in the 7th century by St. Feichin and it became the favourite place of Irish kings; the last of them Rory O'Connor spent his last years here after the traumas of the Norman invasion. The last of the O'Connor High Kings is a Jesuit priest living in Roscommon. The abbey was rebuilt in the 12th century for the Augustinians; there are four fine doorways left and the cloisters have been restored by Benjamin Lee Guinness. If you follow the path that leads into Ashford Castle and turn by the gate-lodge down towards the river, you come to a footbridge, here is the monks' fish house, a tiny stone building without a roof. It must have been a lovely place to contemplate whilst waiting for a salmon to take the bait. These monks became very rich because they possessed a fragment of the True Cross, for which Turlach O'Connor had made the most exquisite cross in which to enshrine it, and people came from far and wide to pray beside it. You can see it in the National Museum in Dublin.

Ashford Castle is now a renowned luxury hotel, but anyone may walk in the beautifully planted grounds for a small fee. There are some beau-

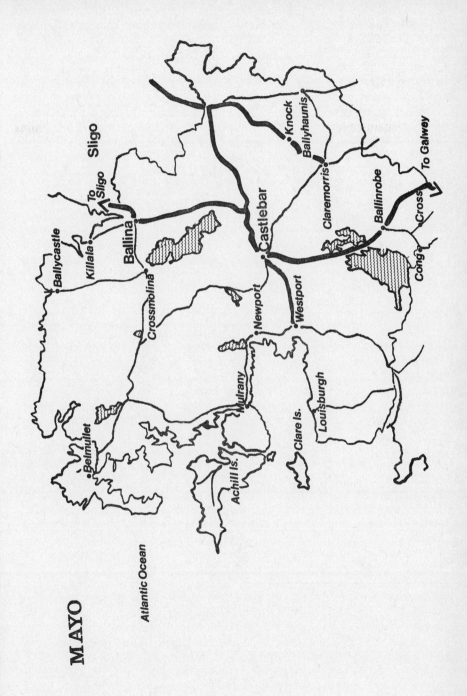

tiful walks around the caves of Cong, which have some interesting stories attached to them. Captain Webb's Hole was named after an individual who pushed his unfortunate mistresses down it, apparently, the thirteenth had the sense and the strength to push him into the hole instead! The Pigeon Hole is the most impressive, you climb down steep steps to the underground stream which is said to contain two white trout, an enchanted maiden and her lover.

About half a mile from **Cong** you might notice crusheens or little heaps of stone upon which a crude cross has been stuck; funeral processions still stop to pray by them. You could take the road to **Ballinrobe,** the fishing and touring centre of South Mayo - Loughs Corrib, Mask, Conncarra and Cullin are in easy reach and the waters are free for all sports. There are *race meetings* in June and September and an *international trout Angling Festival* at the beginning of August. On the way, between Cong and Ballinrobe is **Neale,** pronounced 'Nail', set in an area rich in ring forts. The Neale demesne contains 'the gods of Neale' which is a medieval tomb carving with a 19th century inscription claiming that 'the gods' go back to 'the year of the world 2994'. Lough Mask House, four miles south west of Ballinrobe, was the home of the hated Charles Boycott who was ostracised by his tenants during the land agitation of the 1880s. The ruined castle nearby was built by the De Burgos in 1480. About a mile from town is the great stone fort of Cahernagollum.

On the road to **Castlebar** you pass by the fretted shores of Lough Carra. On the eastern shore is the ruin of Moore Hall, burned in 1923; it was the home of George Moore, the novelist. He is buried on an island in the lake and the estate has been turned into a centre for *bathing, picnicking, boating* and *trout fishing.* Another member of the Moore family was proclaimed President of the Republic of Connacht after the success of the French invasion force at the Races of Castlebar, when they routed the English in 1798.

Situated one mile off the main Castlebar-Galway Road is Ballintubber Abbey known as 'The Abbey that Refused to Die'. Mass has been said there, continuously, for seven and a half centuries. The fame of Ballintubber goes even further back to St Patrick, who baptised his converts in a Holy Well there and founded a church. It was in the early 13th century that the king of Connacht, Cathal of the Wine Red Hand, built the abbey for the Augustinian Order. The abbey was nominally suppressed in 1542 and was attacked and burnt down by Cromwellian soldiers in 1653, but the stone vaulted chancel survived, and services continued. There is a pilgrim path from here to Croagh Patrick. When the guesthouse to the abbey was excavated many burnt stones were found near the stream over which it was built. The burnt stones reveal how the monks heated their water - red hot stones thrown into water brought it to the boil within minutes. The foot-weary pilgrims must have been in need of a good wash for the holy mountain is twenty miles away to the west. The restored Abbey is very plain, with bright modern glass in the windows.

Another noted place of pilgrimage is **Knock** situated in the Plain of Mayo, seven miles from the *freshwater fishing centre* of **Claremorris**. Here in 1879, the Blessed Virgin Mary, Saint Joseph and Saint John appeared to fourteen people. Although it rained heavily on the witnesses, the area around the apparition remained dry. Mary was wearing a white cloak and a golden crown on her head. Over 750,000 visitors and pilgrims visit the shrine annually. Unfortunately the quiet little village of Knock has been turned into a very ugly, commercialized centre with chapels, monuments and a huge Basilica. Holy water comes from chromium taps and there are endless car-parks.

For further information write to: The Presbytery, Knock, Tel: 094 88100, or the Secretary, Knock Shrine Society, Brigemount, Belcarra, Castlebar, Tel. Belcarra 3, they also have a phone number in Dublin 01 775965.

## SOUTH WEST MAYO

At the head of the Killary inlet are the handsome **Aasleagh Falls**, here you can take a beautiful and lonely route up to **Louisburg** through the pass of **Bundorragha.** Mweelrea mountain is on your left and Ben Gorm on your right. You soon come to **Delphi,** which somehow is rather an apt name, for the mountains and the wilderness have a sort of wisdom in birdsong and lapping water. Three lochs lie beside the road: Fin Lough, which means bright lake, Doo Lough, dark lake, and Glencullin Lough, the lake of the holly tree glen. Nearby is an old fishing lodge where you can park your caravan.

**Louisburg** is a very pleasant place, probably named after the Louisburg in Novia Scotia and pronounced Lewisburg. If you take a minor road from here over some low hills you will get to **Roonah Quay**, from here take a boat or currach to **Clare Island, Caher Island** and **Inish Turk**. Planning a trip to any of these islands depends on the weather, but if you have to wait a day or so in Louisburg, there are some nice places to stay and quite a lot to see. Kilgeever Abbey is one mile east of Louisburg, and has an ancient well and church; pilgrims to Croagh Patrick still include it in their itinerary. Then there is Murrisk Abbey, seven miles further to the east founded by Tadgh O'Malley in 1457. It has a beautiful east window. Just above it, is the pub where the thirsty pilgrims refresh themselves before and after the tough climb up **Croagh Patrick.**

**Croagh Patrick** is a sacred and beautiful mountain where Saint Patrick is believed to have spent forty days and nights in fasting and prayer. For this magnificent feat of endurance he is supposed to have extracted a promise from God that the Irish would never lose the Christian faith he had brought them. The mountain is made up of quartzite which breaks up into sharp-edged stones, so it is not very comfortable walking – some pilgrims do it in bare feet. At the top is a small modern chapel, 2,510 feet above sea level. The materials for building the chapel were carried up to the top of the mountain by devout pilgrims, all 716 bags of cement. If you are not interested in the religious aspects of the mountain, climb it just to see the magnificent views. Clew Bay lies below, its inner waters cluttered by green tear drop islands, formed by a glacier millions of years ago; further out you can see

**Granuaile's** islands.

Granuaile was an amazing woman otherwise known as Grace O'Malley; she was a pirate captain and her symbol was the sea-horse. People still talk of her, even though she died in 1600. Her territory includes Clare, Caher, Inishturk and Inishbofin. Her family had been Lords of the Isles for 200 years and in the forty years which it took the Tudors to extend their power to Ireland, Granuaile was the mainstay of the rebellion in the west. One of the stories which seems to explain her best is as follows: at the age of 45 she gave birth at sea to her first child, Toby. An hour later, her ship was boarded by Turkish pirates. The battle on deck was almost lost when she appeared wrapped in a blanket and shot the enemy captain with a blunderbuss. After that her men rallied, captured the Turkish ship and hanged the crew.

**Louisburg** is an excellent centre for *fresh water angling*. There are good runs of salmon and sea trout from June to September in the following rivers and lochs: Bunowen River, which flows though the town, the **Carrowniskey** which has deep pools, the Delphi/Doo Loughs; the Bundorragha River; and the Eriff Fisheries – fourteen miles away. *Sea angling* is superb; Clew Bay is famed for shark, skate, ray, pollack, coalfish, cod, wrasse, gurnard and mackerel. Carrowniskey is good for *surfing* and there are several *bathing beaches*: Old Head, Carramore, Bertra, Carrownisky and Thallabawn. There is an Ulster Bank branch open on Tuesdays and Fridays. The Tourist Information Office is open during the summer season, Tel: Louisburg 50.


## CLARE ISLAND

Clare Island has more land given over to farming than the other islands, though its higher slopes are covered in heather. It has superb cliffs up to 300 feet high, but even these are overshadowed by the Knockmore Mountain which drops from 1,550 feet in a few hundred yards to join the cliffs. As you come into the small stone pier, you will see Grace O'Malley's Castle now converted into a coastguard station. Legend has it that the young sea pirate was in the habit of mooring her ships by tying them together, then passing the main rope through a hole in her castle walls so that she retired to bed with the rope wound round her arm, in order to be ready at the first alarm. Her last years were fraught with difficulties and she was forced, aged 63, to sail up the Thames to parley with Elizabeth I. Elizabeth offered her a title, but Grace replied that she was a queen in her own right! Finally they made a deal; Grace would retain some of her old lands including Clare, in return she would keep down piracy.

There is a holy well at **Toberfelabride,** but the gem of Clare is its abbey which is about a mile and a half south of the harbour. It is a 15th century church with a tower, and is believed to be a cell of the Cistercian monastery of **Abbeyknockmoy.** On a plain round arch, leading from the roofless nave to the chancel, there is a coat of arms topped by a sea horse with the words *Terra Mare potens O'Maille (O'Malley powerful on land*

116

*and sea)*. The fresh water streams on the island hold small brown *trout* and there is *good surfing* and *bathing* on the beautiful strands. *Sub aqua* facilities are available at Bay View Hotel, Tel: Clare Island 104. This is the only hotel on the place. The Clare telephone service works between 8 am-10 pm on weekdays, 9 am-10.30 am and 7 pm-9 pm on Sundays. There is an annual regatta in July.

**Connections:** The mail boat operates between Clare and Roonagh Point every day. From 1 June-31 August twice daily: £IR4 return and £IR2 single. To go boating or sea fishing contact: Mr Chris O'Grady, Tel: Clare Island 104 for details. Getting to Caher is a matter for negotiation with a boatman.

## CAHER ISLAND

This island evokes the mood of early monastic settlements better than any other. The church is small and roofless and around it are twelve stone crosses, the most recent is not less than a thousand years old. One on the hilltop shows a human face, another a pair of dolphins. In the graveyard is St Patrick's bed with impressions said to be the mark of his hands, feet and hips. This used to be part of the Croagh Patrick circuit, but few people come nowadays to lie in his bed and hope for a miraculous cure. It is a lovely grey, green place of walls, donkeys, sheep and green pastures. But nobody lives there now.

From **Louisburg**, the T39 winds its way to **Westport** with lovely views of Clew Bay. **Westport** is a highly planned town, unusual in the west. James Wyatt, the well-known Georgian architect planned it for the Marquess of Sligo. There is a pretty walk called the Mall which runs beside the **Carrowbeg River** and is overhung with trees. There are some good restaurants and nice places to stay in Westport: ARDMORE HOUSE on the quay, specialises in seafood, Tel: Westport 636; also on the quay is CHALET SWISS RESTAURANT, Tel: 231 and the ASGARD TAVERN AND RESTAURANT for traditional Irish food, Tel; Westport 32.

In June the place is overflowing with people; there is the Westport International Sea Angling Festival and the Westport Horse Show. In August, there is a Cailin Deas Festival with sports, art displays, beauty competitions, music and dancing. There are ballad sessions in the pubs and hotels in the summer, a cinema in James Street and dancing in the Star-Light Ballroom, the Pavilion Ballroom and the Town Hall. All the shops close on Wednesdays. The Tourist Board office is open all the year round, Tel: Westport 269. Besides *fishing, golf,* at the 18 hole course, *tennis* and *mountain climbing* you could go and walk around one of the west's few stately homes. Westport House is full of old Irish silver, family portraits, and lovely furniture. There is a bedraggled zoo in the grounds. Entrance fee £IR2.25 to house and gardens. It is open from April to September. The *sea angling* grounds in Clew Bay are amongst the best in Europe and the Sea Angling Centre provides everything an angler might need. If you want to take things at a very leisurely pace, Connemara

117

horse drawn caravans operate from West Port House Country Estate, Westport, Mayo.

The *Clew Bay Diving Centre* is on lovely Clare Island, for details write to Bay View Hotel, Clare Island, Westport, or telephone Clare Island 104. Glenars Sailing School operates from Clew Bay.

**Newport** is a rather neglected looking village; moss and weeds grow on the roofs of the houses, it looks forgotten. However there is a very good hotel, NEWPORT HOUSE, which overlooks the river; even if you can not afford to stay there it is worth having a meal or drink. The old fittings and lovely furniture suit the gracious feel of the house. Bed and breakfast is from £IR12. Tel: 098 41222. There is quite a good pub called CHAMBERS, which has traditional music and food.

The coastline around here is full of little islands and inlets, but about half a mile outside Westport, take a little road signposted to **Furnace**; this takes you in the wild mountain country of the **Nephin Beg** range. When it's sunny the lakes go a deep, sparkling blue and the air is very bracing, rather like Switzerland. Lough Furnace (there used to be an old iron furnace here), is now a salmon research station as is the next lake along, Lough Feeagh. There are two lovely routes from here: the old mountain track beyond Srahmore, towards Glennamong (2,063 feet) and the old trade route to Ballycroy near the sea. The old grey house, wrapped in trees, which you pass on the way to Srahmore is supposed to be turned into a youth hostel soon. Everywhere – fuchsia, forests and rhododendron mingle with the stone walls and natural rock. Newport House Hotel has *fishing* on Beltra Lough, Furnace and Feeagh.

On the road to **Mulrany**, there is a turn off to Rockfleet Castle (also known as Carraignahooley Castle). It stands on firm but seaweedy rock, a complete tower house looking over Newport Bay. A key to go inside can be got locally, but much of the charm of the place is the story which goes with it. The tower was built by the Burkes and passed to Grace O'Malley by means of a trick. She married Richard Burke with the understanding that either of them could end the marriage after a year by a simple declaration. She used the year to garrison the castle with her own men and kept it when she declared the marriage ended.

Numerous tantalising beaches fringe the road. When you get to Mulrany on the neck of the Curraun Peninsular you will find it has a beautiful long strand looking out to Croagh Patrick across Clew Bay. The climate is mild and fuchsia and rhododendron bloom with even greater luxury than is usual in the west. There are myriads of yellow flags growing in the fields another common and lovely sight in **Connacht,** though not so to the local farmers. You will notice lots of guest houses and B&B places along the road between Newport and Mulrany for this area is very popular in the summer. The attractions are: a nine hole *golf course, very good swimming, fishing* in Clew Bay and on the Owengarve River. There is good mountain climbing on the Claggaun, the Cuchcamcarragh (2,343 feet) and Nephin Beg (2,665 feet).

The **Curraun Peninsula** is a wild nob of land through which you can pass on the way to Achill Island. There are three mountain peaks over 1,700 feet and lovely views over the sea to Clare Island and Achill. There is a youth hostel overlooking the Achill Sound. The single track road round the Curraun gives you a fine introduction to Achill Island, which has all the nicest characteristics of Connacht, amongst them are the sleepy white washed cottages you can see across the water and the smell of turf floats with the breeze. Placid looking donkeys are everywhere, one stuck his head through my car window and demanded a biscuit.

## ACHILL

Achill is connected to the mainland by a bridge, and because it is one of the easiest islands to reach, it is the most touristy. The dramatic cliff scenery and long golden beaches make it very popular. The island has a splendid atmosphere; you wind up and down through the valleys, past lakes, where a few swans idle, and see before you the surging ocean where the Achill fishermen hunt for basking sharks. Achill is 53 square miles and the largest of the Irish islands, so the best introduction to it is to take the Atlantic drive. You pass a small, ruined early church and then a slender tower, which is supposed to have belonged at some time to Grace O'Malley. There is always a boat or two drawn up by the little quay beside it which adds to its charm. The road follows the line of the shore round the south tip and there is a ferry to **Achillbeg Island**, which contains the remains of an old hermitage.

The road now goes north winding high up the sides of the cliffs – a route not recommended for horse or motor drawn caravans. **Keel** is a big village with restaurants, and craft shops. It has the attractions of a large sandy beach and cathedral rocks which are covered in fantastic fretwork. If you walk three miles to the end of Trawmore Strand, you come to a Holy Well and if it is low tide you can see clearly the Gothic arches and pillars of the rocks, above which, rise the Minaun Cliffs (800 feet). **Keem Bay** is a lovely sandy little cove obvious from the cliff road. It is a favourite haunt of the basking shark but have no fear if you want to bathe, its food is plankton, not human flesh. **Dugort** is a little fishing hamlet in the shadow of **Slievemore Mountain** (2,204 feet). Nearby are the Seal Caves, you can hire a boat to get to them and enjoy the superb bathing beaches. The people of **Achill** are friendly and helpful though one woman confessed that she much preferred the winter, when they had the island to themselves.

Outer Clew Bay and the area between Achill and Clare Island is paradise for the *angler*; here in abundance swim porbeagle, blue shark, tope, dogfish, skate and ray. The smaller inland fish include ling, conger, grey and red gunard, whiting, cod, bream, pollack and mackerel; even tuna (tunny) have been caught in these waters. In September there is a shark safari at Purteen Pier. There is white trout in the Dooega River and brown and sea trout in the two loughs. Licences cost very little and can be obtained from Achill Sporting Club. Boats can be hired in all the villages. There is *sub-aqua* at Keem Bay; *surfing, tennis* and a 9-hole *golf course* at Keel; and *hang-gliding* on Muleelin Mountain. For *mountain*

climbers Croghaun drops 2,000 sheer feet into the sea and its crescent
arms provide impressive scrambling. The western sky with its tumbled
cloud formation is one of the beauties of the west, and the rocks, mountain and crouching cottages on Achill must be seen in relation to it.
Dances are held in Parish halls and hotels, and ballad sessions in the
pubs. There is a Tourist Office at Achill Sound open during the summer,
Tel: Achill Sound 51 or Keel 27.


## NORTHWEST MAYO

From Mulrany, the T71 runs over a vast bog; the edges are enlivened by
splashes of purple rhododendrons and a few fir trees. Turf is used much
less nowadays in heating and cooking; bottled gas has made life much
easier for the housewife, but many farmers and country people have
rights to turf turbaries, which they cut every year. The tool used to cut
the neat sods from the bog is called a slane; while the man cuts, the
women and children gather the sods and arrange them in little piles to
dry. The pattern of the piles varies from area to area but they often
resemble little clochauns, such as the early Christians built.

**Bangor Erris** is a small place on the long, lonely road to **Belmullet.**
This region is still known as Erris, one of the ancient baronies of Ireland.
The **Carrowmore Lough** just off the route is a *good fishing lake*,
Belmullet is one of the loneliest towns in Connacht, it stands on a slender
piece of land just wide enough to prevent the Mullet from becoming an
island. All the commerce of the peninsula is channelled through
Belmullet, so on market day it is surprisingly full. If you want to base
yourself here before exploring the wild and lonely peninsula, there is
plenty of accommodation. Belmullet is famous for *sea angling*, there is an
international festival held in September. The Mullet is almost divided
into little islands, by the deep bays which cut into it on either side. The
beaches and fishing are excellent and there are superb views of Achill ,
the Nephin Beg range, and the mystical islands of Inishglora and Inishkea.

## INISHGLORA

Inishglora has the ancient remains of a monastery founded by St Bren-
don, the Navigator; a car will take you within half a mile of the
monastery, stopping at Cross Abbey, a medieval church. On Inishglora,
the island of the voice, the children of Lir regained their true form after
being turned into swans by their jealous step-mother. The spell was to be
broken when St Patrick's bell was heard ringing out over Ireland, but
unhappily for the children of Lir, their immortality only lasted whilst
they were swans. They came ashore blind, senile and decrepit to die
almost at once. Inishglora has been a sacred island for thousands of
years, the Holy Well there is supposed to turn red if the water is touched

by a woman's hand. There are lots of bones where the soil has been washed away by rain and sea-spray, for it was believed that the more serious a dead man's crimes the more important it was to have him buried on a holy island. This not only improved his chances of salvation, but ensured that he could not come back to haunt you since the spirits of the dead can not pass over water.

## INISHKEA

Inishkea means Isle of the lonely heron. Legend tells of Mulhenna who was unfaithful to her husband and banished here for 1,000 years, condemned to take the form of a heron. **South Island** has a little hill-top deserted village, though fishermen camp here when they are fishing round the shores. The islanders moved to the mainland after ten men were drowned in 1927, in a freak gale. Moondaisies, grass, sheep and sandy beaches will be your reward, if you persuade a boatman to bring you out here.

On the mainland again you could make your way up to the fishing hamlet of **Pollathomish** on **Sruwaddacon Bay**. This is invigorating country for the walker. Some people like to tramp along the cliffs between **Benwee Head** and **Belderg**, and admire the views from the **Cliffs of Ceide**. There is a youth hostel in Pollathomish. **Blacksod Bay** and **Broadhaven** used to be considered the best places to fish years ago when fishermen used to come here from the Skerries and Howth. The little **Belderg River** is good for *salmon*.

**Ballycastle** is very typical of the villages in the west. The streets are wide, and the air smells faintly of turf and everybody seems to be asleep. A 'rent an Irish cottage scheme' has been developed on the outskirts of the village, write to or phone the resident supervisor, Ballycastle 3 for reservations.

This is a good place to base yourself because there is much to explore and very few tourists in the summer. The cliffs of **Downpatrick Head** are full of wheeling birds; terns, gulls, skuas, razorbills and guillemots plus less active ones such as puffins; all seem to have nests somewhere on the cliff edges. There are picnic tables set out overlooking the Atlantic, but it does not look as if anyone has ever eaten off them and now the birds and seapinks have taken over, visited by the occasional hare. There is ugly wire fencing on the head to prevent you from falling into the crevasses and holes around the cliff edge. One of the most spectacular holes is a puffing hole called **Pollnashantinny**. The story is that St Patrick was having a fight with the devil, and dealt him such a blow with his crozier that the devil was hammered clean through the rock and down into the sea-cave below. In their fight they also knocked a bit of the headland off into the sea, the stack of **Doonbristy** is proof! An old promontory fort was built on Doonbristy, before it became separated from the headland. There is a pattern (pilgrimage) to the Holy Well and ruined church of St Patrick on Garland Sunday.

About two miles north west of Ballycastle is **Doonfeeney** graveyard, where there is a ruined church and a standing stone, about 18 feet high, with a cross carved on it. A large ring fort stands close by, where according to old beliefs fairies hold their revels. The grave yard is scattered with ancient stone slabs and it's rather a quiet secret place.

In spring, on the way to **Killala Bay**, the banks of the roadside are covered in daisies and primroses. Killala was the scene of French landings in 1798, when Humbert brought 1,500 French soldiers, uniforms and weapons for the rebels. It is a very beautiful bay and now has a new sea angling centre at Killala Pier where modern deep sea fishing boats can be hired. Killala Bay is rather like a lagoon, having calm sheltered waters. Before you get to the town, a road leads you past a ruined but fine Dominican friary. Killala town is very pretty and rather higgledy-piggledy, with a round tower rising from the middle of it. Two miles west is a 15th century ruin called **Moyne Abbey** on the lovely salmon river **Moy**. Just a mile or two upstream is another abbey, **Rosserk**, which is less complete but has some interesting carvings.

**Ballina** — pronounced bally-nah is a port town on the estuary of the River Moy and is a good place to stay if you are in Ireland for the fishing. It's a very good shopping centre as well, especially after the remoteness and lack of choice in Erris. *Trout fishing* in the Moy, and the Loughs Conn and Cullen is free and excellent. Lough Talt, 15 miles away to the east is full of trout and very beautiful, lying as it does in the Ox Mountains. Salmon fishing is good from June onwards. **Crossmolina** on the Deel River is also a *good fishing centre.* There is *golf* and *horse riding,* Tel: Knockmore 110. The Ballina Salmon Festival is a really big event and one of the towns greatest tourist attractions. Imaginative programmes and events are staged for every age and taste. The climax is the choosing of the Queen of Moy. Ballina is closed all day on Wednesday. There are ballad sessions in the bars, Thursday evenings and Sunday lunchtime in BELLEEK CASTLE HOTEL. Tel: 096 22061. For pizza-lovers the COFFEE BEAN in Pearse St., is worth a visit. Tel: Ballina 096 22078.

Just outside Crossmolina and half a mile from Lough Conn is a caravan park with TV and a souvenir shop. **Foxford** is a good place to stay if you are fishing on the Loughs Conn and Cullin. The summit of **Nephin Mountain** is of whitish quartzite so it looks perpetually snow-capped and when the sun is shining is a lovely background to the deep blue waters of Lough Conn. **Pontoon** is on the isthmus between the two Loughs and there are two hotels there.

It is well worth stopping at **Strade,** if you are going to **Castlebar**. It is the birthplace of Michael Davitt, who started the land league, and it has a ruined Franciscan Abbey with a wonderful series of sculptures. The pieta is especially good, the Virgin sits with the limp body of Christ in her lap, guarded by two angels. There is an elaborate tomb chest in the same style.

**Castlebar** is the administrative centre of Mayo and is busy enough to have a small airport. Castlebar started as a settlement of the de Barry's.

It became more important in 1611 when James I granted it a charter, and is remembered for the ignominious scattering of the British garrison in 1798 when the French General Humbert advanced with a motley crowd of French and Irish troops. The event is known today as the 'Races of Castlebar'. The remains of John Moore, the first and only president of the Connacht Republic are buried in the Mall and there is a Memorial to 1798 beside his grave. For a good meal there is a restaurant called LA PETITE FRANCE, Tel: 094-22709.


## PLACES TO STAY IN COUNTY MAYO

**Achill:**
Mrs Lyons, Glenfarne, Achill Sound, Tel: Achill 29
Mrs McHugh, Ailblin, Dooagh, Tel: Keel 38 (No CH)
Mrs McAndrew, Teach Nambrack, Valley Dugort, Tel: Dugort 17
**Ballinrobe**
Mrs Sheridan, Alder Hs, Cushlough Bay, Tel: Ballinrobe 148
**Ballina**
Mrs Ryan, Waterville Hs, Killala Rd, Tel: (096) 22072 (youth hostel Pollathomish)
**Belmullet**
Mrs O'Malley, Glenribbon Lodge, Carne, Tel: Belmullet 38
Mrs Maquire-Murphy, Drom Caoin, Ballinavode, Tel: Belmullet 171
**Castlebar**
Mrs Fitzgerald, Turlough Park Hs, Tel: (094) 22438
Mrs Moran, Lakeview Hs, Westport Rd., Tel: (094) 22374
**Clare Island**
Bay View Hotel, grade B, Tel: Clare 104
**Claremorris**
Mrs Merrick, Ballyhowley Hs, Knock, Tel: (094) 88339
**Cong**
Mrs Lydon, Corrib View, Gortacurra Cross, Tel: Cong 36, (farmhouse)
Mrs Lydon, Cong, Tel: Cong 53
**Crossmolina**
Mrs Fair, Glebe Hs.
Mrs Moffat, Kilmurray Hs, Castlehill, Tel: (096) 31227
**Foxford**
Mrs Gannon, Providence Rd.
**Killala**
Mrs West, Bay View Hs, Ballysorkery, Tel: Killala 121
Mrs Caplice, Avondale Pier Rd, Tel: Killala 137
**Louisburg**
Mrs Sammon, Cuaneen Hs, Carrowmore, Tel: Louisburg 121
Mrs O'Toole, Sycamore Hs. Louisburg 28
Old Head, grade B* Hotel, Tel: Louisburg 3
**Newport**
Mrs M McGovern, Carrowbawn, Tel: (098) 41162
Mrs Chambers, Loch Morchan, Kilbride, Tel: (098) 41221

**Tourmakeady**
Mrs King, Mask View, Treen, Tel: Tourmakeady 21
**Westport**
Mrs O'Brien, Rath a Rosa Farmhouse, Rossbeg, Tel: Westport 297
Mrs Ree, Fair Lawns, Lecanvey, Tel: Murrisk 22
Mrs O'Malley, Rosbeg, Tel: Westport 211
Riverbank Hs, grade B, guesthouse, Tel: Westport 76
Hotel Cavanaugh's, grade B*, Tel: Westport 18
**Mulrany**
Avondale House, grade B, guesthouse Tel: Mulrany 5. Youth hostel,
Currane, Achill Sound.
**Binge Places**
Newport Country Hs, Tel: (098) 41222 (where Grace Kelly stays).
Breaffy House, Castlebar, Tel: (094) 22033
Ashford Castle, A* Hotel, Cong (only if you are feeling very rich), Tel:
(094) 22644

---

# County Roscommon

County Roscommon has the placid River Shannon to form its eastern
boundary but it is the only county in Connacht without at least a touch
of sea shore. There are plenty of lakes to make up for this, the largest
being Lough Ree; it is a good region for the *coarse fisherman* as there are
bream, perch and pike in the loughs and trout in the rivers. Do not expect
any magnificent scenery, for Roscommon's terrain consists of plain, bog
and river meadows. However there are many ancient remains and associations with the warriors and heroes of long ago.

**Keadue** is near the Sligo and Leitrim borders. It is in one of the most
attractive parts of the county with the Slieve Anierin rising to the east.
By the shores of Lough Meelagh is an ancient church site and a holy well
called Kilronan; they are both associated with the St. Lasair and Ronan.
You are far away from the bustle of life in this enchanted and weed-high
graveyard, and in the ruined church is a modern monument to Turlough
O'Carolan who died in 1738. He was the last in a line of harpists and
poets who used to have such status in the minor Gaelic kingdoms; he is
supposed to have composed the melody of the *Star Spangled Banner*.
Nearby surrounded by ash trees, and sacred to the Druids, is a lovely
clear well which flows into the lough. Rosaries and rags ornament the
ground and a large rectangular stone slab is supposed to heal those
suffering from backache. The cure entails crawling under the slab which
is balanced on two other stones.

**Boyle** is one of the nicest towns in Ireland situated between Lough Key
and Lough Gara, the Curlew Hills rise to the northwest and the River

Boyle flows through it. By the river bank is a Cistercian Abbey, an ivy clad ruin founded by Maurice O'Duffy in 1161 and closely asociated with the great Mellifont Abbey in County Louth. It was not completed until 1218 and reflects the change of fashion from the round arches of the Romanesque period to the pointed lancet of the Early English style. The monastery was suppressed in 1569 and occupied by Cromwellian soliders later on, you can see their names carved on the door of the porter's room. The capitals of the pier arches are lavishly carved.

East of the town is the great demesne of Rockingham House which was burnt to a shell in 1957; its grounds have been planted with conifers and form part of the Lough Key Forest Park. Here you may go *boating, fishing, swimming* or *walk on a nature trail* through the woods. Pedestrians can enter free of charge whilst for those with cars the entrance is 30p. There is a caravan park here, for details Tel: Boyle 212. A small company operates *pleasure cruises* on the Lough round the islands – they are licensed to carry booze and take about 45 minutes, commentaries are given on the sights. For details phone or write to Shannon Cruisers, Cootehall Boyle, Tel: Cootehall 7. **Eating:** There is a restaurant on Rockingham Harbour overlooking the lake.

About two miles away at Dromonone is one of the largest dolmens in Ireland, known locally as Druid's Atlar; it may have been a monument to someone living in the Bronze Age. It is found by following a grassy lane to a railway crossing. On the waters of Lough Carra, three hundred crannogs (artificial islands) have been found.

**Frenchpark**, south east of Lough Gara, was the birthplace of Douglas Hyde, the founder of the Gaelic League and the first President of Ireland; he was born in the rectory and retired to Rattra House in his old age. In the grounds of Frenchpark House is a five chambered souterrain. Six miles south-east of **Frenchpark** is the Hill of Rathcroghan. The ancient palace of the kings of Connacht once stood in this desolate spot and many of the kings who reigned at Tara were crowned here. About a quarter of a mile to the south are several tumuli and raths, reputed to be the burial ground on Conn of the Hundred Battles and the three Tuatha De Danaan Queens: Eire, Fodhla and Banba. There is also a redstone pillar which marks the grave of the last pagan monarch, Dathi. According to the Book of Leinster, he conquered Scotland, invaded the Continent and died in the Alps from a stroke of lightening about AD 428. Here at Cruachan, Queen Maeve launched her expedition to capture the Brown Bull of Ulster. It is difficult to imagine these legendary figures and this place as the seat of power, for the plain is now empty, crisscrossed by stone walls and modern farms.

Just east of **Castlerea** stands Clonalis House, home of O'Conor Don, descendant of the ruling family of Connacht. Two of the O'Connors were High Kings of all Ireland. The house is Georgian and open to the public. Inside you will find Sheraton furniture, Victorian costumes, military uniforms, four-poster beds, and rare glass and china. But the special feature of the house is the paintings, manuscripts and documents relating to a proud Gaelic past. It is open on weekends in May, June and September (to the 15th) 2pm-6pm. In July and August the house is open every day, except Tuesday, from 2pm-6pm. Entrance fee is 65p.

Four miles south east is **Ballintober of Bridget** (named after St. Bridget's Well), there is a ruined O'Connor Castle that withheld many sieges, including one by the Cromwellians. Glinsk Castle, south of Ballintober and just over the county border is well worth a visit. It is the shell of one of the best fortified houses in Connacht, it has four storeys of mullioned and transomed windows, and stacks of chimneys, now used by the starlings and crows. There is *trout fishing* in the upper reaches of the River Suck, the Francis and Derryhipps Rivers, and at Lough O'Flynn. There is a *9 hole golf course, tennis* and an *outdoor swimming pool*. The shops are closed all day Monday.

**Strokestown** is at the foot of Slieve Bawn, which at 864 feet is quite something in this low lying countryside. It is a very handsome town with a wide main street. There is an attractive Jacobean house at the lower end of the street. It was laid out by Maurice Mahon who was created Baron Hartland in 1800. The Slieve Bawn Co-operative Handcraft Market which produces wicker baskets, lovely tweeds, etc., is open to visitors all year round. There is *coarse fishing* on the Kilglass and Grange Lakes four miles north-east. There is very good *shooting* and *horse riding* round the lakes, Tel: Strokestown 47. You can hire boats and go *fishing* and *boating* from the grade B Percy French Hotel around the Kilglass Lakes. If you climb Slieve Bawn you get a lovely view of the meandering Shannon. The famous Ardkillen Brooch which is in the National Museum was found near here. **Eating:** If you are just passing through, the PERCY FRENCH is a very good place for a meal with plenty of atmosphere.

**Roscommon** is the county town and the main shopping centre of the county and a popular *angling* resort. The dominating feature of the town is the old jail and in it you can find the Tourist Office of the region; the last hangman of the jail was not a man, but a woman known as Lady Betty. The Georgian court house is worth a visit, its lovely rounded windows have been rescued by the Bank of Ireland. St. Comán founded a monastery here in the 8th century from which the town gets its name, but there is nothing left of it today. But south of the town centre is a ruined Dominican friary founded by Felim O'Connor, King of Connacht in 1253. His tomb is sculptured with figures representing gallowglasses, these were the fierce warriors from the west of Scotland who were hired by the Irish kings to fight the Norman and English invaders.

Roscommon Castle, north of the town was built in 1269 by Roger d'Ufford, Lord Justice for Ireland. Four years later it was razed to the ground by the Irish, built anew, and taken again by the O'Connors in 1340, who held it for more than 200 years. The Roman Catholic church, off Abbey Street is built of local cut limestone and has lovely glass mosaics constructed by the famous Italian firm of Salviati and Co. It also has a replica of the famous Cross of Cong. Beyond the village of **Fuerty**, where there is an ancient graveyard, and across the River Suck is the Castlestrange demesne. The house is a ruin, but under some trees is an Iron Age boulder known as the Castlestrange Stone. This is egg-shaped and covered in whorls and spirals which seem to have been very potent symbols and used often in the Celtic La Tene style.

The road to **Athlone** stays close to Lough Ree but not close enough to get a proper look at it. If you cut down a small lane to Galey Castle, you will see the island, **Inishcloraum** in Lough Ree where Queen Maeve retired to ponder on her eventful life and to find some peace. She used to bathe in a clear, fresh pool but an enemy pursued and killed her with a stone. From **Lecarrow** another minor road leads you down to the Castle of Rinndown; it was a great fortress with a rectangular keep within curtain walls and in the shelter of its strong walls a medieval village grew up along Norman lines. A ditch was built across the peninsula on which it was built and it became one of the bases for the conquest of Connacht. Now it is an ivied ruin and a place of peace for few wander down the mile long peninsula.

## PLACES TO STAY IN COUNTY ROSCOMMON

**Boyle**
The Burke Family, Riversdale Hs, Knockvicar, Tel: Cootehall 12
Mrs Graham, Rushfield, Tel: Boyle 276
Mrs Mitchel, Abbey Hs, Tel: Boyle 385
**Carrick-on-Shannon**
Mrs Harrington, Glencarne Hs, Tel: Cootehall 13
Mrs O'Riordan, Clooneigh, Tel: Carrick-on-Shannon 400
**Castlerea**
Mrs Dockery, Oakview, Tel: Castlerea 116
**Roscommon**
Mrs Dolan, Munsboro Hs, Munsboro, Tel: (0903) 6375
Golden Family, Lisheen, Castlecoote, Fuerty, Tel: (0903) 7413
Mrs Frawley, St. Gabriel's, Galway Rd, Tel: (90903) 6395
**Strokestown**
Mrs H Cox, Church View Hs, Tel: Strokestown 47
Mrs E Cox, Gayfield Hs, Kilglass, Tel: Strokestown 74

---

# County Sligo

Mrs S C Hall writing in the 19th century about her tour of Ireland, dismisses Sligo in a few words 'in scenery and character it so nearly resembles the adjoining county of Mayo that we pass over Sligo'. Nothing could be further from the truth. Sligo is somehow civilised, unlike the other counties in Connacht; there is order among the lakes and the glens, the great table mountains and open beaches. Sligo is Yeats, just as Wessex is Hardy, for there is hardly a knoll or a stream which did not stir his imagination. His brother Jack uses paint instead of words to capture the faces of old men at the Sligo races, or the special quality of light which bathes the figures on the beaches; the light is very like that which plays around the coast of Brittany. Jack is always quoted as saying 'Sligo was my school and the sky above it' and it was William Butler Yeats' wish that he should be buried 'under bare Ben Bulben's head'. All the places which inspired W B Yeats are still largely untouched; they are brought to your notice by discreet Bord Fáilte notices which quote the name and the line from the poem in which they are mentioned. Most Inishfree enthusiasts do not know but the place is referred to locally as Cat Island! You can enrol in Yeats Summer School which has as its theme his poetry, plays, prose and his historical background, plus Irish myths, legends, and the Abbey Theatre, founded by the energetic Lady Gregory. For details write to The Director, Yeats International Summer School, Yeats Memorial Building, Douglas Hyde Bridge, Sligo, Tel: 071 2693.

**Sligo Town** is the largest town in the north-west. It has a great deal of colourful charm, and your best guide to the beautiful countryside is a copy of Yeat's collected poems. There are tinkers near the town and they are bound to come and ask you for your loose silver; some of the women still swathe the upper part of their body in a thick plaid shawl which is used as a sling to support their latest baby. There are lots of tinkers in Ireland who move from place to place with an amazing collection of modern caravans, cars, donkeys, cats, dogs and children; the local people say that they are all as rich as Midas. Sometimes you will find them selling old brass ornaments and light fittings along the roads at very high prices.

In the Anglican cathedral, designed by Richard Cassels, is a brass memorial to Susan Mary Yeats, the mother of William and Jack whose family, the Pollexfens, came from Sligo. The Catholic cathedral made out of local limestone is next door. Sligo Abbey, a Dominican priory, was founded in 1252, but was rebuilt in the 15th century after being burnt; it then suffered the usual fate of Irish monasteries by being destroyed by the Cromwellians. Inside are some graceful monuments to the local Gaelic nobility, and some very fine cloisters. Sligo County Museum and Art Gallery is very interesting with objects dating from pre-Christian times up to the Anglo-Irish war of 1919-1921. There is a special section devoted to W B Yeats. Opening hours are: 10 am-5pm on Tuesdays, Wednesdays, Fridays and Saturdays; 12 noon to 5 pm on Thursdays. Closed on Sunday and Monday.

**Doorly Park** is by the **River Garavogue**. The park has some lovely walks with wonderful views of **Lough Gill** and the mountains. Inside the park is the Sligo Race Course; the Sligo races take place in April, June and August. In the evenings during the summer, Sligo Drama Circle put on plays in the Town Hall every Tuesday and Thursday, usually by Irish playwrights. There are two cinemas: the Gaiety in Wine Street and the Savoy in High Street. For dancing and cabaret you can go to the Baymount Entertainment Centre in Strandhill which has dances nightly, or to the Sligo Rugby Club on Saturday nights. There are discos

SLIGO

Co.Donegal

•Mullaghmore

Rosses-Pt.
Coney Is.
Easkey
Strandhill•    •Sligo

•Enniscrone

OX MTS

Ballymote

-Tubbercurry

Co.Mayo        Co.Roscommon

0        9        18

129

in a number of Sligo hotels at weekends. Buy a copy of the *Sligo Champion* which tells you what's on. Every Wednesday in the summer, there is an Irish night at Dolly's Cottage, Strandhill. Comhaltas Ceoltóirí Eireann have traditional music sessions at Sligo Trades Club in Castle Street every Tuesday, and at the Baymount Entertainment Centre every Tuesday and Thursday. You can hear traditional music in: Conway's Wine Cellar and Beezies in O'Connell St; at McLynns, Old Market St, Feehily's in Stephen St and Hennigans, Wine St. One of the nicest places to have a jar and enjoy some music is Ellen's Bar on the Drumcliff/ Donegal Road. Jazz sessions are held every Tuesday and Friday night in Beezies, Yeats Country Hotel, Rosses Point and on Saturdays at Sligo Park Hotel.

**Lough Gill** is as wooded and pretty as the Killarney lakes and less crowded. The best way to enjoy it is to go on a cruise; the trip takes two and a half hours and Yeats' poetry is recited where it refers to various parts of the lake. There is a half an hour stop near the **Lake Isle of Inishfree** for tea and coffee at the Craft shop. Trips aboard the luxury cruiser take place every Wednesday and Sunday during May, June and September and daily during July and August. Departure times: 11 am and 3.30 pm. Rates are £IR2 per adult, students £IR1.50 and children £IR1.

*Boats* for *fishing* or *pleasure trips* on Lough Gill can be hired from Mr P Henry, Blue Lagoon, Riverside, Sligo, Tel: (071) 2530 and from Mr Frank Armstrong, 14 Riverside, Sligo. *Rough shooting* is available from the Sligo Gun Club, rates are £IR15 per gun per day which include a guide and two dogs – contact Mr Hugh Loftus, 2 Garavogue Villas, Sligo, or the Tourist Office. *Sailing* tuition is available at the Yacht Club, Rosses Point – contact the clubhouse. *Sub aqua* enquiries to Francis Sexton, 17 Doorly Park, Sligo. **Markievicz Park** is the centre of Gaelic football and hurling if you want to go along and watch. Coach tours on day trips operate from June to September; they go to Bundoran, Hills of Donegal, Ballintubber Abbey, Knock Shrine, Yeats Country, Lissadell House and Lough Key Forest Park. Departures from Sligo Railway Station.

There is an 18 hole championship *golf* course at Rosses Point and another one at Strandhill, Tel: 071 78188. There is *game* and *coarse fishing* on the local loughs and rivers: Tel: 071 2356 and 071 2651 or the Tourist Office for details and boat hire. Sligo School of *Landscape Painting* run courses in July and August, write to Truskmore, Strandhill Rd, Tel: 071 3410. There is an art gallery in the Yeats Memorial Building which holds frequent exhibitions and you can see Sligo Craft Pottery in the Market Yard, open Monday-Saturday, 10am-6pm. Most shops are closed all day Monday. There are good caravan and camping parks at Rosses Point and Strandhill. Buses go frequently from town out to these resorts.

For meals, good value can be found at the COFFEE BEAN in the Mall, Sligo (salads and pizza). More expensive but very good is KNOCKMULDOWNEY RESTAURANT, Ballisodare, Tel: 071 71270 (about five miles south of Sligo town).

**Strandhill** is a typical sea resort, five miles from Sligo. It has too much concrete and consequently is not very attractive but the strand is superb. The sand stretches for miles and the waves are good for surfing. Nearby is Dolly's Cottage, which is open to the public being a typical example of an early 19th century rural dwelling. Open daily during July and August from 3pm-5pm. From here you take the little road marked Glen which takes you up into the lower slopes of **Knocknarea Mountain.** You get a lovely view of the hummocky green fields down to the shore. The climb to see the gigantic cairn on the summit of the mountain (1,978 feet) is very easy and very rewarding. The cairn, which is reputed to be the burial place of Maeve, Queen of Connacht, is awe inspiring in its size, and completeness, however it is probably Bronze Age, so far older than the celtic Queen Maeve. But no-one has evacuated it, probably because it would be very expensive to undo its massive structure and it would be sad if they did. The walk to the cairn is partly through an old man's farm and along the track of curiously moulded limestone, with orchids and primroses growing either side.

About three miles on is **Carrowmore**, a Stone Age cemetery, which spreads over many fields. There are circles, passage graves and dolmens; each one has a little notice warning that it is a national monument, but unfortunately quite a few stones have disappeared. Nearby is the Sligo Riding Centre Tel: 071 2758.

**Rosses Point** is a seaside resort five miles from Sligo with two magnificent *beaches.* There is a *golf course, a yacht club* and a *caravan park*. There are regular buses between here and Sligo in the summer.

Between Strandhill and Rosses Point is **Cumeen Strand**, an expanse mentioned in Yeats poem 'Red Hanrahan's Song' and here the Garavogue River flows into the sea. You can walk or drive out to **Coney Island** when the tide is out from the Strandhill side, it is supposed to have given its name to the New York pleasure island.

A ten minute drive from Sligo takes you to **Glencar Lough** and two waterfalls which are on the borders of Leitrim. In Yeats' poem 'The Stolen Child' he talks of the Glencar pools 'that scarce could bathe a star'. Unfortunately the pools now have a concrete path, but it is very beautiful still with a noisy stream and a mass of rhododendrons.


## NORTH SLIGO

**Drumcliff:** Saint Columcille founded a monastery here in the 6th century before sailing away to Iona. Among saints, St. Columcille seems to have been the 'enfant terrible', for whilst a guest of St. Finian he borrowed his psalter and secretly copied it out. Finian found out and said that the copy should be his, but Columcille refused to hand it over. The High King was asked to settle the dispute and he ruled in favour of Finian, saying that just as every calf belongs to its cow, so every copy belongs to the book from which it is made. St. Columcille did not accept the king's judgement and gathered an army. He fought the king and won, but with the loss of 3,000 lives. His friend St. Molaise of Inishmurray advised him to leave Ireland for ever, as a penance, and convert as many people as he had caused to die. All that remains of Columcille's monastery is a fine carved high cross, with lovely panels carved with Biblical scenes, and the stump of a round tower.

W B Yeats' great grandfather was the rector of the plain church built in Georgian times and the poet is buried in the graveyard under his beloved Ben Bulben. He has a very plain headstone with his own epitaph 'Cast a cold eye on life, on Death, Horseman, pass by'. In Yeats' Tavern across the road they serve very good Guinness. West of Drumcliff is **Lissadell House**, its grounds swallowed up in Forestry Commission conifers. It is the home of the Gore-Booths and Yeats was a frequent visitor here. He wrote of his two friends, Constance and Eva as 'two girls in silk kimonos, both beautiful, one a gazelle'. Constance married a Polish artist and became Countess Markievicz, she also became deeply involved with the struggle for independence. Having won a seat for the Sinn Fein party, she, like the rest of them, refused to take up her seat in Westminster and sat instead in the Revolutionary Parliament in the Dail. One of her nieces, Miss Gore-Booth, will take you round the Italianate house which has some interesting furniture, china and curiosities. The house is very large and a little run down; it takes courage to try and keep it going and they charge a very small entrance fee – only 60p per person. Downstairs in the vast kitchen, you can have tea and coffee, made under conditions reminiscent of the 1920s. There is no drinking water or electricity in this part of the house and buckets of water have to be lugged down the stairs. You can buy handsome Aran sweaters, warm socks and various other things made locally. The house is in a lovely situation looking onto the sea, Knocknarea and Ben Bulben.

All around the coast are wrecks of the warships of the Spanish Armada. It is not surprising that the people of **Inishmurray**, four miles off the coast, abandoned their lands and houses in the 1950's for life was very hard. Inishmurray used to be famous for its brand of poteen, now it is famous for the early Christian relics which have survived: Beehive huts, small stone rectangular oratories, open air altars, pillars and tombstones are dotted all over the island. The monastery was probably built on a druidic site, for one of the oratories is known as the Temple of Fire, and roundabout are quite a few cursing stones. After the Vikings struck in 807 AD, the monks left and the islanders took over the old monastic buildings; one oratory became the men's chapel and another for the women. The Irish like to separate the sexes whenever they can! Often, in a country church the men will sit on one side and the women on the other. If you want to go to Inishmurray, contact Mr Christy Herrity, Carns, Moneygold, or Mr Mulligan, Dun Ard, Mullaghmore, Tel: 071 67126.

The **Gleniff Horseshoe** is a superb drive; turn off at **Cliffony** for **Ballintrillick**, the road runs into the heart of the **Dartry Mountains** with their tumbling steams, and desolate grey limestone cliffs. One of these caves is supposed to be where Diarmuid and Grainne slept when they were fleeing from the wrath of King Fionn Mac Cumhail. They are the Irish equivalent of Tristan and Iseult, every cave, dolmen and cromlech seems to be named after them.

North of Cliffony, a rock peninsula projects into Donegal Bay, its
sandy beach has encouraged the growth of a small resort, Mullaghmore.
On the headland you will see a Victorian Gothic castle, this is
**Classiebawn**, the old home of Earl Mountbatten of Burma. In 1979 he
and members of his family and crew were killed when his boat was blown
up by the IRA in the bay below. In Grange you can watch craftsmen hand
cut crystal at Sligo Crystal, the factory shop. Open Monday-Friday
8.30am-5.30pm and on Sundays in July, August and September from
2pm-6pm.

There is good bathing at **Mullaghmore, Lissadell, Raghly** and
**Streedagh. Bundoran** nearby has an indoor heated *swimming pool*.
Pollack, mackerel, and flatfish are common catches off the rocky
headlands; in Mullaghmore Bay you can catch conger, skate, and ling.
Contact Mr M Conroy, West End Bundoran, Tel: 072 41280 for boat hire:
£35 per boat per day. For salmon fishing on the **River Drumcliff** *riding*
and *donkey trekking* at **Cliffony**, Tel: 071 76152; a horse per week costs
£60. **Ben Bulben, Benweskin** and **Truskmore** are good peaks for
*climbing*. The nearest Tourist Office is at The Bridge, Bundoran, Tel:
072 41350. The Beach Hotel, Mullaghmore has cabaret sessions at
weekends during the summer months, but for discos, cinema, etc, Bundoran is the best bet.


**WEST SLIGO**

**Enniscrone** is a holiday resort on Killala Bay with a long, sandy strand
ideal for sea bathing. There is a *marina,* and a *golf course.* Two miles
north is **Castle Firbis**, the ruined stronghold of a family well-known for
their poetry and annals. One of the MacFirbis Clan compiled the 'Book
of Lecan'. Each year one weekend is devoted to Irish folklore and history.

**Easkey** is an old monastic village eight miles from Enniscrone on the
coast road; it is guarded by two martello towers built to raise the alarm if
Napoleon tried to invade. Two miles east, by the roadside is Split rock, or
Fionn MacCumhail's Fingerstone; this huge rock is said to have been
split by MacCumhail's sword – Irish heroes always have superhuman
strength. Easkey is good for *surfing* enthusiasts, so is Dunmoran Strand
and Aughris. From **Skreen** a minor road, with fabulous views, climbs
into the Ox Mountains over **Ladies' Brae**, passing Lough Achree. This
stretch of the coast is famous for its *sea angling*. Contact Mr Jim Byrne of
the Alpine Hotel, Enniscrone Tel: 096 36144. For salmon and trout the
Easkey River is one of the best spate rivers in the west, and fishing is free
on most of it. There is a camping and caravan camp at Easkey. You can
hire a bicycle at Helly's, Enniscrone. The Tourist Information Office is in
the main street Tel: 096 36202, open June to September.

**PLACES TO STAY IN COUNTY SLIGO**

**Ballymote**
Mrs Tansey, Gratton Lodge, Tel: Ballymote 3385

**Cliffoney**
Mrs McLoughlin, Villa Rosa, Bunduff, Tel: (071) 76173
**Collooney**
Mrs Hosie, Castle Dargan Hs, Ballygawley,Tel: (071) 71127
**Drumcliff**
Mrs Blighe, The Old Rectory, Tel: (071) 73221
**Enniscrone**
Mrs I. Maquire, Massabielle, Pier Road, Tel: (096) 36296
Mrs Bolger, Rinroe Hs, Tel: (096) 36183
St Martins, grade B guesthouse, Tel: (096) 36111
**Easkey**
Mrs Clark, Swan Hs, Tel: Easkey 7
**Grange**
Miss M McGovern, Breadhwy Hse, Ballinfull, Tel: (071) 73136
**Mullaghmore**
Pier Head Hs, grade B guesthouse, Tel: (071) 76171
**Rosses Point**
Mrs Henry, The Farmhouse, Cregg, Tel: (071) 77189
**Sligo and area around**
Mrs Carter, Primrose Grange Hs, Knocknarea, (071) 2005
Mrs Cullinan, Culbree Hs, Carrowmore, Tel: (071) 78189
Stuart Family, Hillside, Kilsella, Ennishkillen Rd, Tel: (071) 2808
Mrs Blighe, The Anchor, Quay St, Tel: (071) 3002
Mrs Coyne, Beaupré, Cornageeham, Dublin Rd, Tel: (071) 2548
Bonne Chere, grade B guesthouse, Tel: (071) 2014
**Riverstown**
Mrs O'Hara, Coopershill, 12 miles from Sligo, farmhouse, Tel: (071) 75108
**Strandhill**
Ocean View Hotel, grade B, Tel: (071) 78115
**Binge Places**
Ballincar Hs, Sligo Town, Tel: (071) 5361

# PART IV

# THE PROVINCE OF

# LEINSTER

Most travellers who come to Leinster head straight for Dublin City, the magnet which promises the most fun, history, culture and comfort. They might make a few sallies out into the countryside, perhaps to the beautiful **Glendalough** or a tour of the fascinating **Boyne Valley** burial grounds, and **Tara**, in Co. Meath, the seat of the High Kings. If they are epicureans, a meal at the Restaurant Mirabeau in Sandycove, Tel: (01) 809873, or Dunderry Lodge, Navan Tel: (046) 31671, might be worth an expedition. But Dublin City draws them all back and the rest of Leinster pales into insignificance. If you arrive at Rosslare in Wexford, the province probably gets a fairer chance of being explored. There are many beautiful places in **Wexford, Wicklow, Kilkenny**, and **Carlow**. The centuries of history are marked by castles, monasteries and the more mysterious landmarks left behind by the Celts and those who went before. Most striking of all are the lordly mansions built by the Anglo-Irish, and Leinster has more than its fair share of them. Many are open to the public, Castletown and Russborough are the best. The Bog of Allen, which takes up most of Kildare and Offaly, is counterbalanced by the gentle rolling hills of the Blackstairs; the peak of Mount Leinster (2,610 feet) gives you a wonderful view and some exciting ridge climbing. The spiky mountains and rounded summits of the Wicklow range, the bogland and mountain pools make a happy contrast to the noise and crowds of Dublin City. On a clear blustery day it is not difficult to imagine yourself a million miles away from civilisation, though the city is only an hour's drive.

# County Carlow

South west of Wicklow lies Carlow, the second smallest county in Ireland. There are no mountains, except for the Blackstairs Mountains on the Wexford border, and the undulating plains are rich farmland. In the west, the River Barrow threads through a limestone region which forms the boundary with Kilkenny; in the northeast the River Slaney flows through the granite fringe shared with the Wicklow mountains.

**Carlow Town** is at the crossing of the River Barrow in the north west of the county and is steeped in history. It was an Anglo Norman stronghold, and much later it was the scene of a bloody scrimmage in the '98 rebellion. Nowadays it is involved in the manufacture of beet sugar, which was introduced in 1926 as part of the Irish self sufficiency programme. Sights to see include the Norman castle, whose ruins were further reduced by a Dr. Middleton building a lunatic asylum there in 1814. (Permission should be obtained from the Corcorans Mineral Factory on whose property it now stands.) There is a prominent Gothic Revival Catholic church; a handsome court house with a Doric portico, after the Parthenon. You may like to visit the Carlow Museum: open May to September weekdays 11am-5.30pm with a 12.30pm-2.30pm lunch break. Sundays 2.30pm-5.30pm. During the rest of the year it is open Sundays only. Admission: adults 25p, children 10p.

Outside **Carlow**, two miles to the east, is the largest capstoned dolmen in Ireland, the Brown's Hill dolmen. At **Killeshin**, three miles west of Carlow town, is a ruined 12th century church with an exceptionally fine Romanesque doorway. In the graveyard, you will find the oldest decorated font in Ireland. The Kings of South Leinster are buried at nearby St. Mullins, a very pretty village.

**Eating:** If you are staying in Carlow Town try the ROYAL HOTEL, Dublin Rd, Tel: (0503) 31021 for a meal with all the trimmings at a cost of £IR5-£IR9 per person. There is also Reddy's Grill, Tullow Street, Tel: (0503) 42224 for cheaper fare. For tourist information in July-August, Tel: (0503) 31554. Early closing day is Thursday.

If you want to do some inland *water cruising* Ireland's rivers are beautiful and unspoilt. The River Barrow connects with the Grand Canal to Dublin, and links up with the Shannon. A small book called *Guide to the River Barrow* price £IR1.65 is useful and available in most book shops and from Easons, 40 Lower O'Connell Street, Dublin 1. Following the lovely Barrow you come to **Leighlinbridge**. Beside the river are the ruins of the Black Castle erected in 1181. Nearby is the Hill of the Kings of Leinster.

**Eating:** Out of town is a highly recommended and expensive restaurant, The Lord Bagenal, Tel: (0503) 21668 or 21679; it is only open for dinner. **Muine Bheag**, formerly **Bagenalstown**, was destined by Walter Bagenal, to become an Irish Versailles! Perhaps more impressive is Ballymoon Castle, built in the 14th century, and one of the earliest Anglo-Norman strongholds built in Ireland. Legend says that it has never been occupied.

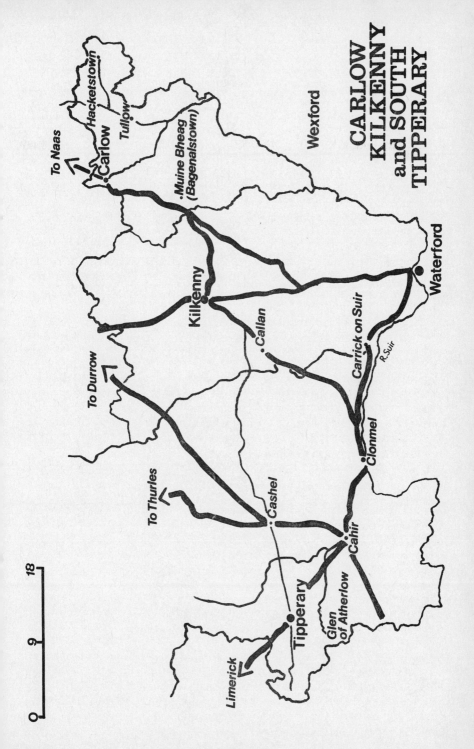

CARLOW
KILKENNY
and SOUTH
TIPPERARY

To Naas

Carlow

Hacketstown

Tullow

Muine Bheag
(Bagenalstown)

Wexford

Kilkenny

To Durrow

Callan

Carrick on Suir

Waterford

R. Suir

To Thurles

Clonmel

Cashel

Cahir

Tipperary

Limerick

Glen
of Atherlow

0    9    18

Travelling down the east side of Carlow you will come to the principal town of the region, **Tullow**. If you are interested in archaeology the raths ringing the town will be worth a visit. Three miles east, there is the ancient stone fort of Rathgall.

North of Tullow lies **Hacketstown**, situated in the Wicklow foothills; this was the scene of a desperate engagement between the insurgents and the yeomanry in 1798.

## PLACES TO STAY IN COUNTY CARLOW

**Borris**
Mrs R Curran, Borris Lodge, Tel: (0503) 73112, full board offered. Attractive setting.
**Carlow Town**
Carlow Lodge, Tel: (0503) 42002. Expensive £IR11 per night, but each room with bath or shower.
Dolmen Hs, guesthouse, Tel: (0503) 42444 reasonably priced, offering full board.
**Muine Bheag (Bagenalstown)**
Mrs B Young, Lorum Old Rectory, Kilgreaney, Tel: (0503) 75202, dinner, tennis and croquet lawn.
Mount Leinster Arms, guesthouse, Tel: (0503) 21253
**Tullow**
Tara Arms, guesthouse, Tel: (0503) 51305

---

# County Dublin

The city sprawls over a large part of this county and threatens to dominate it completely for the average tourist, but if you follow the example of the fun loving Dubliner you will follow him to the jaunty sea resorts along the coast, to the lavish gardens of the Howth, or to the unique collection of Irish furniture and portraits at Malahide Castle. When you are in the National Gallery, search out Nathaniel Hone's 'Cattle at Malahide' for he has caught the glancing light of the east coast perfectly. Those James Joyce disciples who are travelling by themselves around the *Ulysses* landmarks in Dublin (you can pick up a map from the Tourist Office) should not neglect the museum of Joyceana in the Martello Tower, and Sandycove where Gertie McDowell showed Mr. Bloom her garters! Unfortunately today it has become highly developed. Further to the south sweeps the lovely Killiney Bay, whilst to the north of Dublin, the flat, tidy fields of the Skerries and Rush slope down to the sea, where you may bathe, fish, sail or play golf before going to the theatre in Balbriggan or Dublin, which is only 19 miles away.

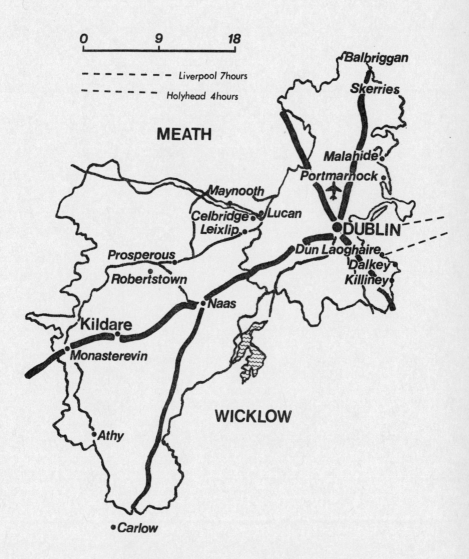

**DUBLIN and KILDARE**

## NORTH COUNTY DUBLIN

**Skerries** and **Balbriggan** are noted for their dry, sunny climate. The locals are involved in the fish industry, but both have every facility someone on holiday could want. Try the Balrothery Inn, Balbriggan which has a theatre and traditional entertaiment every night; Tel: (01) 412252. You may visit St Patrick's Island off the Skerries and the ruin of a church said to have been built by St Patrick. **Rush** is another attractive fishing village; look round Lusk Round Tower and the Church of Ireland church which contains some fine medieval tombs. Fetch the key from the shop 50 yards back from the entrance to the churchyard. There is an excellent museum in Channel Road featuring old machinery and agricultural tools. Looking out to sea is Lambay Island with its 500 foot cliffs rising out of the sea. You have to get permission to land there from the Steward, for it is the sanctuary of many rare birds, but the beauty of the island can be seen by sailing round it.

**Malahide** is another seaside resort with a wonderful old castle, which was the seat of the Talbots of Malahide from 1185 to 1976. Today the castle is publicly owned and a large part of the National Portrait collection is housed there. It is open from Monday-Friday, 10am to 5pm; Saturdays 11am to 6pm; Sunday and Bank Holidays 2pm-6pm. These times change slightly in December. The Boswell Papers, which give us such an insight into 18th century travel were found here in a croquet box. You can get a meal or a snack here. If it is a sunny day, a better idea is to have a picnic on 'the Island', where terns nest and the air is heavy with the scent of thyme flowers. There is a *golf course*, so watch out for golf balls. For *water-skiing*, Tel: (01) 451365, and for *sailing tuition* Tel: (01) 451979. Sea fishing can also be arranged.

**Swords** just inland from Malahide has a very interesting monastic settlement founded by St. Colmcille in 563 AD. The 12th century castle is five sided and under restoration; at the moment you have to shut your eyes very tight to imagine the richly clothed ecclesiastics who ruled here. At the nearby Dublin Airport is an Aeronautical Exhibition which is open everyday. **Portmarnock** further along the coast has a three mile long beach nicknamed 'velvet strand' which is very safe for *bathing*, and a championship *golf* course. Two miles outside is St Doulagh's Church which incorporates a 12th century anchorite cell and a small subterranean chamber covering a sunken bath, known as St Catherine's Well. In the summer it is open at the weekends. The velvet strand stretches up to the neck of Howth, whilst a mile out to sea is **Ireland's Eye**, a great place for a picnic – you can take a boat out there from Howth Harbour. Its name comes from the corruption of Inis Eireann which means Island of Eire (or Eira, a Gaelic princess).

**Howth** comes from the Danish word Hoved, meaning a head. Before the Anglo-Norman family of St. Lawrence muscled their way into the area, Howth was a Danish settlement. The castle still remains in the hands of the St. Lawrence family; now Gaisford St. Lawrence. The public are allowed to walk around the tropically bright gardens; in late spring the gardens are gloriously coloured by the rhododendrons. Try to go on a weekday. The gardens are open from 8 am to sunset all year round and there is a small admission fee during April, May and June. There is a lovely story attached to the gardens which concerns Grace O'Malley, the famous pirate queen from Co. Mayo. She stopped in at Howth to replenish her supplies of food and water, and decided to visit the St Lawrences. The family were eating however, and she was refused admittance. Enraged by this rudeness she snatched Lord Howth's infant son and heir and sailed away with him to Mayo. She returned the child only on condition that the gates of the castle were always left open at mealtimes and a place set at the table for the head of the O'Malley clan. This custom is kept right down to the present day.

At **Howth** you can play *golf*, and from Claremont Strand you can go *boating* or *deep sea fishing* or *swimming* whilst Fitzgibbon Cove is ideal for *diving*.

**Eating:** In the evenings you can eat in the famous Abbey Tavern and listen to traditional music, though it is a little touristy. Tel: (01) 322006. The King Sitric, East Pier, Tel: (01) 325235 has made a good name for itself specialising in seafood. Look in the national newspapers for what's on in Dublin itself.

**Lucan** used to be a sort of minor Bath and is placed on a beautiful stretch of the Liffey. James Gandon, Ireland's most famous architect, lived here and is buried in Drumcondra graveyard.

**Eating:** Henri's Restaurant in the Mall will produce a good meal and then you can return, if you like, to Dublin via **Strawberry Beds** and **Phoenix Park.**

**Dun Laoghaire** (pronounced Doon Laye-reh) in the south of Co. Dublin is a huge terminus for car ferry services from Britain. This prim Victorian town, with its bright terraced houses, is also a holiday resort where you can have a lot of fun before exploring the wilder delights of the Wicklow mountains. The Marine Parade, laid out with trees and flowers, takes you to James Joyce's Tower in Sandycove. In fact the Martello Tower was rented by Oliver St. John Gogarty, whose witty book *As I walked down Sackville Street* is a must for all true Hiberniphiles! Joyce stayed with him for the weekend, he uses the visit in the opening scene of *Ulysses.* Oliver, 'stately plump Buck Mulligan' and James Joyce later quarrelled, now their names are perpetually linked. Few Irishmen and women have read *Ulysses,* and for a long time it was banned by the heavy handed Irish censor for revealing too much of the earthy Dublin character. But the Tower is a holy shrine where other more discerning foreigners, especially Americans can worship and ponder over the collection of Joyceana. It is open from May to September Monday to Saturday 10am-1pm, 2pm-5.15pm. During the rest of the year it can be seen by special arrangement with the Eastern Tourism Organisation, Tel: (01) 808571.

**Eating:** back in **Dun Laoghaire** you can eat well and expensively at the Restaurant Creole, 20a Adelaide St, Tel: (01) 806706 and Le Chateau, 9/10 Upper George's St, Tel: (01) 804802. Somewhat cheaper is Pavani's Bistro, 2 Cumberland St, Tel: (01) 809675 or Graham O'Sullivan's Delicatessen Marine Rd, Mall. For the active there is *golf, sailing, fishing,*

141

*bathing, tennis* and *scuba diving* at Killiney and Dalkey, *horse riding* at Leopardstown Racecourse. Very often there are *open air concerts* at the People's Park, East Pier; Black Rock Park and Sorrento Park, Dalkey. One mile away at Monkstown is the headquarters of the Irish Cultural Institute which presents a number of traditional entertainments like seisiun and dance. For details Tel: (01) 800295. **Monkstown** also has the Lambert Mews Puppet Theatre, whilst the more usual type of theatre can be found at the Pavillion in **Dun Laoghaire**. Wednesday is half day closing for the shops. Tourist information and room reservation service Tel: (01) 806984/5 or (01) 807048.

**Dalkey** is a small fishing village where Bernard Shaw used to stay and admire the skies from Dalkey Hill. A boat may be hired from Coliemore Harbour to Dalkey Island where there is a Martello Tower and the remains of an ancient church. The Vico road runs along the coast unfolding beautiful views of Killiney Bay. If you climb Killiney Hill you will have an even clearer view of the Bay, the mountains and the Liffey Valley. On the south side of the hill is an old church and a collection of Druid stones.

## PLACES TO STAY IN COUNTY DUBLIN
Telephone code for the area is 01

**Balbriggan**
The Grand, grade B hotel, Tel: 412813
**Blackrock**
Mrs Kennedy, Erne Lodge, 104 Rowanbyrn, Tel: 893149
Mrs Wheland, St. Judes, 72 Monkstown Rd, Blackrock, Tel: 807237
**Dalkey**
Mrs Jackson, Desmar, 15 Railway Rd, Tel: 858203
Mrs Seaver, Rockview, Coliemore Rd, Tel: 858205
**Dun Laoghaire**
Mrs Cowley, Rossmore, 16 Corrig Avenue, Tel: 807015
Mrs Hefferman, Gleneagles, 6 Mellifont Ave, Tel: 806265
Mrs Kavanagh, Roisin Dubh, 54 Patrick St. Tel: 809921
Mrs O'Sullivan, Duncree, 16 Northumberland Ave. Tel: 806118
**Howth**
Mrs McMahon, Highfield, Thormanby Rd. Tel: 323936
Mrs Dunne, Morven, 14 Nashville Park, Tel: 322164
**Malahide**
Mrs P Darcy, Shanida, 23 Biscayne, Coast Rd, Tel: 450076
Mrs Geraghty, 578 Biscayne, Coast Rd, Tel: 451459
**Portmarnock**
Mrs Dermody, 251 Limetree Ave, Martello Estate, Tel: 463471
Mrs Lynch, 325 Limetree Ave, Martello Estate, Tel: 463282
**Rathcoole**
Mrs Shanley, Calliaghstown House, Kilteel Rd, (farmhouse) Tel: 589745
**Sandycove**
Mrs E Power, Dunmore, Castlepark Rd, Sandycove, Tel: 804158

**Swords**

Mrs McGrath, Erne House, Lispopple Cross, Tel: 402994 (on Ashbourne Rd).

---

# Dublin City

Dublin has a worldwide reputation for culture, wit, friendliness and beauty and this image perpetuates itself as the casual Dublin charm works its way into the heart of every visitor. Irish people themselves call it 'dear dirty Dublin' and at first glance you may think that they are right and discount the affection in their voices when they talk about it. For there is no doubt that Dublin can be a dismal disappointment and you may ask yourself what on earth all the fuss is about; the rosy coloured Georgian squares and delicate, perfectly proportioned doorways are jumbled up together with the most grotesque adventures into modern architecture. Fast food signs and partially demolished buildings mingle with expensive and often second rate shops, and the slums and housing estates through which you pass on the way in and out of the centre are depressing. The tall houses north of the Liffey are divided into squalid tenement flats and through the doors and windows you catch glimpses of their former glory – elegant staircases and marvellous plasterwork. The modern Dubliners seem bent on tumbling the past or ignoring it so that it crumbles away on its own. When you are in Dublin ask about Wood Quay and the official attitude to the complete Danish settlement which was found there!

But gradually the atmosphere of Dublin, and atmosphere is what it is all about, begins to filter through that first impression, and things really begin to pick up. Get up early in the morning and explore the ancient streets in the morning sunlight, walk down Dawson Street, where noisy, laughing shoppers mingle with some genuine eccentrics, relax and notice the pleasant things about Dublin which have been staring you in the face all along.

**HISTORY:** Ptolemy mentioned Dublin in 140 AD when it was called Eblana, but it really came to prominence under the Danes during the 9th century because of its importance as a fording place and as a base for maritime expeditions. The name Dublin comes from the Irish Dubhlinn (Dark Pool) athough the Irish form in official use at the moment is Baile Atha Cliath: the town of the Hurdle Ford. After the Norman invasion (which was actually invited over by an aggrieved king) Dublin began to play a dominant part as the centre of English power. The Anglo-Normans fortified themselves with strong castles and the area surrounding Dublin, where they settled, was known as the Pale; anything outside was dangerous and barbaric – hence the expression 'beyond the Pale'! But it was during the 18th and early 19th centuries under the rule of the Anglo-Irish gentry that Dublin acquired her gracious streets and squares which amaze one with their variety. Each door is slightly different and the patterns of the wrought iron balconies and railings change from house to house. You will not see iron work like this in London as most railings were ripped up and melted down during the First World War. Many of the houses were built in small groups by speculators when Dublin was the fashionable place to be – hence the variety.

Throughout the centuries Dublin has produced great writers: Swift (who suggested that the ruling class in Ireland ate all new-born babies to 'cure' the problems of poverty and over-population!) Bishop Berkeley, Edmund Burke, Thomas Moore, Sheridan, La Fanu, Wilde and Goldsmith to name but a few. Towards the end of the 19th century Dublin became the centre of the cultural movement, which resulted in the formation of the Gaelic League, which became entangled with the nationalists' aspirations of the time. How much influence this movement had on the next flurry of great writers it is hard to say, but G B Shaw, George Moore, James Stephens, Yeats, James Joyce and later Samuel Beckett draw much of their inspiration from the streets of Dublin.

The 19th century and early 20th century violence became increasingly common in the streets of Dublin, and buildings and lives were shattered by nationalist clashes with British troops. However, today the streets are safe and the buildings have been rebuilt to their former grandeur.

**ARRIVAL AND DEPARTURE FROM DUBLIN:** The airport bus runs frequently between the the airport, six miles from the city and Busarus (about £IR1.50) or you can get a cheaper 41A bus which drops you in Lower Abbey St. All buses with An Lar labels are going to the city centre. If you arrive by ferry at Dun Laoghaire a train from the pier will take you to Pearse Station on Westland Row, and then continues on to Connelly station, Amiens Street. Buses 7A and 8 run from the ferry to O'Connell Bridge which is right in the centre of the city. If you arrive at the Dublin ferryport there is no trouble finding buses on the Alexandra Road to the city centre and vice-versa. Connelly train station serves the north and north east of the country and Heuston Station the west and south west. Pierce and Tara Stations serve the suburban areas to the south and north west. Those hitching out of Dublin should take a bus to the outer fringes before trying their luck.

**GETTING AROUND DUBLIN:** Look back to the section on 'Getting To and Around Ireland' for details of concession tickets, etc. The best and cheapest way of getting round Dublin is by walking, because most of the museums, shops, galleries are fairly near to each other. The Tourist Office should give you a free street map of Dublin, or you can buy one at countless stationers. Pick up a Dublin District Bus and Train timetable from the CIE office, 59 Upper O'Connell St. Drivers in Dublin may be amazed at the custom of jumping the red lights, it happens constantly, so be on your guard. Driving in Dublin is mostly a matter of nerve and panache! Using your horn is the worst insult – so keep it as a last resort.

**USEFUL ADDRESSES IN DUBLIN:** 01 is the telephone code for Dublin
The Tourist Offices are listed on page 58 and are open Monday/Friday 9am-5.15pm, Saturday, 9am-1.30pm. Tel: 747733
Irish Student Travel agency (USIT) 7 Anglesea St, off Dame St. Tel: 778117. Open Monday-Friday 9.30am-5.30pm, Saturday 10am-1pm.
Telephone numbers of CIE bus and train stations on page 24.
Four Hour Dry Cleaning available at Esquire Dry Cleaners, 35 Grafton St. Tel: 770613
Taxis: Try calling 766666, 761111, 772222, 683333 or 783333; minimum fare 60p.
Emergency Services dial 999
An Oige (Irish Youth Hostel Assoc.) 39 Mountjoy Sq. Tel: 745734 Open Monday 10am-2pm and 7.30pm-9.30pm Tuesday-Friday 10am-5.30pm, Saturdays 10am-12.30pm.

**Vital Publications whilst you are in Dublin:**
The 'In Dublin' magazine was started by a group of students and was so successful that you can now buy it at every newstand. Bord Fáilte publish a guide to 'What's On In Dublin' which is very useful as well. Also check with Friday Folk column in the Evening Press for music venues. Check with the Irish Times for reviews of plays, concerts, films. Every Saturday, it also lists something special happening in Dublin and the Provinces. Comhaltas Ceoltoiri Eireann at 32 Belgrave Sq. Monkstown (take bus 8 from O'Connell St) have a booklet on what's on in the traditional music scene. Tel: 800295. Hodges and Figgis, Top floor, Dawson Street, is the best shop for books of Irish interest.

**MUSEUMS, GALLERIES AND LIBRARIES:** The National Museum is absolutely vital for anyone who has not yet realised that Ireland between 600 AD and 900 AD was the most civilised part of Europe. The Museum is open Tuesday-Friday 10am-5pm and Sunday 2pm-5pm. In the Antiquities Department you can see the beautiful filigree gold whorl enamelling and design which reaches perfection in the Tara brooch and the Ardagh Chalice. The many beautiful torcs, croziers, and decorated shrines on display, together with a long look at the Book of Kells (in Trinity Library) will leave you amazed at the sophistication and skill of the craftsmen in those days. Also very interesting are the findings of the Stone and Early Bronze Ages.

Besides the Antiquities department, you will find the Art and Industry departments. The entrance for these is Kildare St, but if you are in search of Natural History (the museum seems to have thousands of stuffed birds) approach from Merrion St. **The Dublin Civic Museum,** in a fine 18th century Assembly House in South William St, has a collection of old newspapers, cuttings, prints, pictures and coins which build up a very clear picture of old Dublin. **The National Gallery** in Leinster Lawn is where you are greeted by a statue of George Bernard Shaw. This is a very fine gallery with some superb works by Renaissance masters, the Dutch 17th century school and Italian painters of the 16th and 17th centuries. There is a Spanish room with a lovely Goya, and an Irish room which includes work by J B Yeats (the father of the poet and a very good portrait painter) by Lavery, Hone, and Orpen. Gainsborough is well represented with ten major works. Between rooms you can have a cup of coffee or a meal at the excellent GALLERY Restaurant. (Open weekdays 10am-6pm, Thursday to 9pm, Sunday 2pm-5pm.) Gallery tours on Saturday at 3pm free admission.

**The Municipal Gallery** of Modern Art is in a Georgian mansion on the north side of Parnell Sq. It was founded by Sir Hugh Lane (W B Yeats wrote a poem about his bequests) and has a small but wonderful collection of works by well known artists, plus portraits of W B Yeats, Synge and a bust of Lady Gregory by Epstein. (Open Tuesday-Saturday 10am-6pm, Sunday 11am-2pm free admission). **The Chester Beatty Library** is one of the gems of Dublin and is tucked away in Dublin's most fashionable residential area at 20 Shrewsbury Rd Ballsbridge. A bus can drop you just by the entrance to Shrewsbury Rd. It has one of the most valuable private collections of Oriental manuscripts and miniatures in the world, as well as albums, picture scrolls, and jades from the Far East. (Open Tuesday-Friday 10am-1pm, 2.30-5.30pm, Saturday 2.30pm-5.30pm.)

**Kilmainham Jail** is now a historical museum. It is rather a grim building where countless patriots were imprisoned (Open Sunday 3pm-5pm). Also worth going round, if not for the books at least for newspapers, 15,000 volumes worth, is the **National Library** in Kildare St and **Marsh's Library** next door to St Patrick's Cathedral, it is the oldest public library in the country and was founded in 1707.

**CHURCHES IN DUBLIN: Christchurch Cathedral** is at the western end of Lord Edward St. The present building was founded by Strongbow in 1172 and heavily restored in the 19th century. The magnificent stonework and graceful pointed arches are well worth a visit, as well as the effigy representing Strongbow, who was buried in the church. **St Patrick's** a short distance south in Patrick's St was founded in 1190 and is Early English in style. In the 14th century it was almost completely rebuilt after a fire and during the 17th century it suffered terribly from the fighting, and was not restored until the 1860's. It is here that Dean Swift preached his forceful sermons in an effort to rouse some unselfish thoughts in the minds of his wealthy parishioners; over the door of the robing room is his oft quoted epitaph 'He lies where furious indignation can no longer rend his heart'. Nearby is the grave of Stella, Swift's pupil and greatest love. Notice the monument to Richard Boyle, first Earl of Cork, (you will come across him again in the county he named himself after) and the monument to the last of the Irish bards, O'Carolan.

**St. Michan's** is a 17th century structure on the site of an 11th century Danish church, and although it has some very fine woodwork inside, most people are interested in getting to the more ghoulish vaults where bodies have lain for centuries without decomposing. The skin of the corpses remain as soft as in life and even their joints still work! Coffins layered upon each other have collapsed into each other exposing arms and legs; you can even see a crusader from the Holy Land and the body of Robert Emmet, hero and leader of an abortive uprising in 1803, is said to be buried here. The only things that live down in this curiously warm and fresh atmosphere are spiders who feed on each other and there are so many types that people come from afar to study them. It is said that a Dublin lad has honourable intentions if he takes his girl' there! The reason for this mummification is that the air is chemically impregnated by the remains of an oak forest which grew there in ancient times, so as long as the vaults are kept perfectly dry decay ceases.

**St. Werburgh's Church** in Werburgh St off Christ Church Place is worth visiting for the massive Geraldine monument and the pulpit, a fine piece of Gothic sculpture. This church was for a long time the parish church of Dublin and the Viceroys were sworn in here. **St. Audoen's Church** in High Street is partially a ruin, but go there to look at the beautiful Norman font and make a 'wish at the 'lucky stone' of St. Audoen's which has been cherished for many centuries. The Franciscan Church, opposite the Four Courts and known as **Adam and Eve's**, has some fine murals, and **St. Catherine's Church** in Thomas St. has a fine facade, built in 1769 and in front of which Robert Emmet was hanged. The **Rococo Chapel** in the Rotunda Hospital is very sumptuous. **St. Anne's Church** in Dawson St is one of the finest 18th century churches in Dublin.

**FAMOUS BUILDINGS OF DUBLIN: Parliament House**, now **The Bank of Ireland** is the brainchild of Lovat Pearce and was finished in 1785 by James Gandon, Dublin's greatest architect. It was between these walls that Gratton stunned everybody with his oratory when he demanded constitutional independence from the English Parliament, and that later in 1800, a well-bribed House, voted for the Union. To profit from the many interesting exhibitions held in the building consult your **What's On in Dublin** guide. Just opposite is **Trinity College,** notice the water-fountain sculpture on your way over. As you enter through the facade, you leave bustling Dublin far behind and come upon a giant square laid out with green lawn and cobbled stone and surrounded by gracious buildings. Stop to look at the Museum Building which has stone carving by the O'Shea brothers who also created the amusing monkeys which play round what used to be the Kildare St Club. Your main objective will probably be to visit Trinity College Library to take a look at the priceless Book of Kells. Everyday one of the thick vellum pages are turned to present more fantastic and intricate designs. Someone said that the book was made up of imaginative doodles! But the man who was copying out the gospels and enlivening them with such 'doodles' was able to draw so perfectly that sections as small as a postage stamp reveal no flaws when magnified. The book is probably 8th century and comes from an abbey in Kells, Co. Meath. Have a look at the Book of Durrow and the Book of Armagh which are also beautifully illuminated. One of the most restful parks to take a stroll in is Trinity College Green, on your way

147

there notice the skilfully designed Arts Building. Quite often there is music of some sort in the J C R and an exhibition of art at the Douglas Hyde Gallery.

**The Custom House** is on the north bank of the River Liffey, near Butt Bridge, and is the most impressive building in Dublin. It was designed by Gandon and completed in 1791. Gutted by fire in 1921, it has been perfectly restored so that the graceful dome crowned by the figure of Hope still rises from the central Doric portico. **The GPO** in O'Connell St is memorable not for its beauty but for the events of 1916 when a free republic was proclaimed from here. Later it was shelled by an English gunboat from the Liffey and completely gutted by fire. Inside is a memorial to the 1916 heroes in the form of a bronze statue of the dying Cuchulainn. It's quite useful to remember that the GPO keeps very long hours and you can buy stamps here until 11pm.

**Dublin Castle** is well worth a visit, not only because of the place it has in Irish history; it was the seat of English rule, but because of the State Apartments which are beautifully decorated, and for the Church of the Most Holy Trinity, designed by Francis Johnston, in the Lower Castle Yard. The State Apartments are open every weekday from 10am-5pm with a break for lunch, and on Saturdays and Sundays from 2-5pm.

**The Four Courts** Down here by the quays, you get one of the most characteristic views of Dublin, although the skyline once dominated by spires and domes is now one of skyscrapers around O'Connell Bridge. The Four Courts was designed by Gandon and was almost completely destroyed in the civil war of 1921. The Public Record Office next door was burnt down completely with an irreparable loss of legal and historical documents. Powers Court Town House in South William Street built in 1771, is typical of the town houses of the Ascendency. It has fine Rococo and Adamesque plasterwork. Open 9.30am-5.30pm on weekdays.

**PARKS AND GARDENS IN DUBLIN: St. Stephens Green** at the top of Grafton St is a major landmark in Dublin, its cool, green gardens make a perfect setting for a picnic. The gardens are formal, there is a lake with a waterfall, trees and some interesting statues. At the western edge of the Green is Henry Moore's graceful monument to W B Yeats. The Green opens at 8 am and closes when it's dark. **The Botanic Gardens** in Glasnevin consists of 50 acres of plants and flowers, many of them rare, a sunken garden, rock garden and a lily pond. Parnell and O'Connell are buried in the cemetery nearby. The gardens are open in summer from 9 am to 6pm and in winter until sunset. Take a 13, 19, 34 or 34A bus from the centre of town.

**Phoenix Park** is huge expanse of pleasureland which you might not realise is actually within walking distance of central Dublin. The Dubliners themselves are very proud of it, with good reason. The Earl of Chesterfield laid out Phoenix Park, it finds room in its 2,000 acres to house the Arus an Uachtarain, the residence of the President, the residence of the American Ambassador and a hospital. In 1882, the Chief Secretary Frederick Cavendish and the Under Secretary were stabbed to death in the Park; the press called these deaths the Phoenix Park murders, now they are referred to as a military skirmish in the Anglo-Irish War (1169-1921). But forgetting the depressing subject of Irish history, it is memorable as a park where cattle still graze and deer can be glimpsed through the trees. At the northern end is the Phoenix Park Race Course and at the southern end, near the Parkgate St entrance, is The People's Flower Gardens. Between the two lie the Zoological gardens, one of the oldest in Europe, they are attractively landscaped and represent almost every animal under the sun, or at least it seems like it! It is open from 9.30am-6pm on weekdays and from noon to 6pm on Sundays: in the winter it shuts at sunset.

**INDOOR ENTERTAINMENT:** To find pubs for drinking and music check the listings in the 'In Dublin' magazine. Dublin pubs are famous for their congenial atmosphere and the literary types that are supposed to 'live' in them. Each area has its own type of pub and crowd, so it's simply a matter of finding one which suits you. Here are a few suggestions, most have traditional, folk, or blues music a couple of nights a week.

**The Bailey**, on Duke St. A very different set-up to James Joyce's time, smart, touristy but still a good place to meet friends.

**McDaid's**, Harry St.

**Mulligans**, Poolbeg St. Traditional and folk music.

**Ryan's**, Parkgate St.

**The Brazen Head**, Bridge St. Off Usher Quay, licensed since 1666.

**The Lincoln**, Nassau St. Definitely only for those who like a Trinity College student atmosphere: lots of people and noise. Sometimes a venue for traditional music.

**The Abbey Tavern**, Howth. Traditional music every night.

**The Stag's Head**, 1 Dame Court, off Dame St. Old fashioned furnishings, often the venue for traditional music.

**O'Donoghue's**, Merrion Row. Traditional music and casual sessions.

**The Meeting Place**, Dorset St. Traditional music Monday and Thursday nights.

**The Sportsman's Inn**, Mountmerrion. Traditional music, and very untouristy.

**The Chariot Inn**, Ranelagh. Traditional music

**Slatterys**, Capel St. Traditional music most nights.

**The JCR**, lunchtime. Trinity College often has casual sessions going on.

**The Magnet**, Pearse St. Friday night local groups play Rock and Blues Jazz.

**The Merrion Inn**, Merrion Rd. Ballsbridge.

**Bruxelles**, Harry St. Off Grafton St. Jazz and Rock

**CHEAP PLACES TO EAT** in central Dublin.

**The Granary**, 34-36 East Essex St. Pasta, salads, self-service buffet meals from £IR4.00 upwards.

**Nico's Italian/Irish Restaurant**, Dame St. Delicious meals from £IR4 upwards, at night.

**Solomon Grundy's**, Suffolk St. Off Grafton St. Amusing decor, large

helpings and an extensive menu, meals from £IR4 upwards Tel: 774804.
**Club 76,** Brown, Thomas and Co., Grafton Street.
**Kilkenny Design Shop,** Nassau St. Imaginative salads, cakes and a great view over Trinity Green.
**Auric Austrian Patisserie,** 32a Dawson St.
**All Bewleys Cafes:** Westmoreland St, 78/79 Grafton St and 13 South Great Georges St. Coffee and cakes especially good.
**The Blackboard Restaurant,** 2 Balfe Street (behind Woolworths off Grafton St). Bistro type meals, £IR3.50 upwards. Also good for a binge meal.
**Flanagan's Pizza Cellar,** 61 Upper O'Connell St.
**Murph's,** 21 Bachelors walk. Steaks, salads, hamburgers in restored warehouse.
**Murph's,** 99 Lower Baggot St. £IR4 upwards.
**The Pancake H.Q.,** 5 Beresford Place. £IR1.80 upwards.
**Jonathan's** Irish Life Mall, Talbot St. Gateaux, sandwiches, light lunches.


**BINGE PLACES**

In Dublin
Snaffles, 47 Lower Leeson St, Tel: 762227 country house style, restaurant from £IR10 upwards per person.
Shelbourne Hotel, Saddle Room, St Stephen's Green, Tel: 766471. Roast beef a speciality; £IR10 upwards per person.
The Golden Orient Restaurant, 27 Lower Leeson St, Tel: 762286; £IR6 upwards per person.
The Grey Door, 23 Upper Pembroke St, Tel: 763286; £IR12 upwards per person.
Mitchell's Cellars, 21 Kildare St, lunch only, Tel: 766234; £IR5 upwards per person.
Sandford House, Sandford Rd, Ranelagh, Dublin 6, Tel: 974383, £IR8 upwards per person.


**NIGHTCLUBS, DISCOS AND DANCING:** Nightclubs are very expensive and mediocre, you either pay masses to get into a club or else pounds on a drink once there. They get very crowded at weekends and particularly after the pubs close. Admission fee is £IR2.50-3.00.
**Annabels,** Burlington House, Upper Leeson St, Dublin 4, Tel: 785711.
**Barbarellas,** Night Club, 76 Fitzwilliam Lane, Baggot St, Dublin 2, Tel: 762270.
**Lord John Knight Club,** 14 Sackville Place, Dublin 1, Tel: 786294.
**Waves Disco,** Asgard House, Balscadden Rd, Howth, Co. Dublin, Tel: 324978.
**Bouzy Rouge** (supper/night club), 23 Upper Pembroke St, Dublin 2, Tel: 763286.
**Bojangles,** 26 Lower Leeson St, Dublin 2 Tel: 789100.

**THEATRE:** It is much more worth while to spend money on the theatre. The most convenient place to book your tickets is at the stall in Brown Thomas's in Grafton St, or at Switzers. You can also get them in the Tourist Office or at the theatre itself. Tickets start at £IR2-3, for established theatres, less for fringe shows and pub theatre.

**The Abbey Theatre,** Lower Abbey St, Tel: 744505, was founded by the indomitable Lady Gregory and W B Yeats. The old building was burned down and the new one houses **The Peacock Theatre** which concentrates on plays in Irish, and experimental poetry and mime. The Abbey has made the Anglo-Irish idiom famous throughout the world with plays such as *Playboy of the Western World* by J M Synge and *Juno and the Paycock* by Sean O'Casey.

**The Gate Theatre,** Parnell Sq, Tel: 744045, stages productions of international and classic dramas.

**The Gaiety** in South King St provides a venue for opera, musicals and pantomime. Tel: 771717.

**The Olympia,** Dame St, Tel: 778962 has drama, ballet, revue and pantomime. Fringe Theatre includes **Focus,** Pembroke Place, **Eblana,** Busarus, Shore St, Tel: 746707.

**The Project Arts Theatre,** East Essex St, Tel: 781572 is perhaps the most inventive and stimulating with art exhibitions and films. **An Damer,** St. Stephens Green, produce Irish plays. **The Lambert Mews,** Clifden Lane, Monkstown, Co. Dublin is a puppet theatre. Pub theatre includes **Beavers Theatre,** Pallinteer Ave, Dublin 14 and the **Balrothery Inn,** near Balbriggan, Co. Dublin.

**The Threadbare Theatre Company,** provides lunchtime theatre at Trinity College, Tel: 774673. The students often put on very exciting plays, look on the JCR notice board.

Theatre really takes off in Dublin during the festival with new plays by Irish authors, some of which have become Broadway hits! Most theatres are not open on Sundays and performances in the evening begin at 8pm. If you have a ISIC card you get a discount off tickets for the Abbey, Peacock and Focus Theatres.


**EXTRA SPECIAL SHOPS AND THE STREET MARKETS OF DUBLIN:**

The best shopping is to be found in a very small area around Dawson St. Ib Jorgensen an Irish clothes designer has a shop in Molesworth St worth visiting and next door you can buy very reasonable prints at the Sentanta Gallery.

Beneton in Grafton St sells jerseys, T shirts and trousers in bright colours.

The Kilkenny Design Shop, Nassau St has everything of high quality and design that is being produced.

Pat Coley, Duke St, sells evening clothes and dresses.

There are antique shops and delicatessens in Duke St.

Lad Lane Gallery, 34 Lad Lane, Baggot St. and

David Hendrik's Gallery at 119 St Stephen's Green, give you a good idea
of contemporary Irish art.
Anastasia sell very pretty dresses and the Antique Clothes Shop opposite
is superb. Both in the arcade in South Great George's St.

**STREET MARKETS:** Moore Street gives a taste of Dublin life, mostly
fruit and vegetable stalls.
The Dandelion Market, through the Gaiety Green Arcade, is good for
jewellery, used books, nice junk and clothes.

**CINEMA AND CABARET:** All the latest films will be showing in
Dublin, Sunday night is especially popular, so it might be wise to book.
Look in the evening papers or *In Dublin* for cabaret and cinemas. There
is cabaret at the Burlington Hotel, Upper Leeson St, Tel: 785711 and
Fitzpatrick's, Killiney Castle Hotel, Killiney, Co. Dublin, Tel: 851533
and at Jury's Hotel, Pembroke Rd, Ballsbridge, Tel: 767511.

## PLACES TO STAY IN DUBLIN

**Hostels**
The International Student Accommodation/Activity Centre (ISAAC, 2-4
Frenchman's Lane, Tel: 788159, is just around the corner from Busarus,
the mainline bus depot, off Lower Gardiner St. This huge hostel requires
neither IYHF or student ID card. It has extensive facilities: free hot
showers, cafe, free luggage holding, USIT travel office, and bicycle
rental. However bring your own sleeping bag although you can rent one.
The hostel costs about £IR2.50 a night.
An Oige, Morehampton House, 78 Morehampton Rd, Donnybrook,
Dublin 2, Tel: 680325. This is about 10 minutes from city centre. You
cannot stay here more than three consecutive days.
YWCA, 64 Lower Baggot St, Tel: 766273. Special weekly rates, and very
central, costing about £IR5 a night.
YWCA, Radcliff Hall, St. John's Rd, Sandymount, Tel: 694521. Rooms
have baths. It is about £IR5 per person although there are special weekly
rates.
Salesian Sisters Youth Hostel, for women only, 40 Morehampton Rd,
B&B around £IR5.
Trinity College sometimes has spare rooms for students with ID cards.
Write to Trinity Hall, Dartry Rd, Rathmines, Tel: 971772.

**B&B in Central Dublin:** If you are planning to spend a considerable
amount of time in Dublin you can stay with an Irish family in the Dublin
suburbs and get breakfast and a four course evening meal. Write well
ahead of your visit to:
The Educational Travel Office, 51 Dawson St, Dublin.
Miss M Mcmahon, Sinclair St, off North Frederick St, Tel: 788412
The Grey Door, 23 Upper Pembroke St, Tel: 763286. It is a very central
Georgian house costing about £IR9 B&B. Its famous for its restaurant.

Burtenshaw's Marion, grade B guesthouse, 21 Upper Gardiner St, Tel: 744129. Costs £IR8 single B&B.
Harveys Viona, 11 Upper Gardiner St, grade B guesthouse, Tel: 748384 £IR8 B&B.
Stella Maris, 13 Upper Gardiner St, grade C guesthouse, Tel: 740835
If you arrive in Dublin with no bookings, the Tourist Board's accommodation service comes in very useful; for 50p they will make endless phone calls to find you a room in the area and price range you want. Tel: 747733.

**SOUTH EAST DUBLIN** (Ballsbridge, Donnybrook, Sandymount, Mount Merrion): These areas are well served by buses and are only 10-15 minutes away from the city centre. They are very quiet, and attractive and are fast becoming the smart places of Dublin.
Ballsbridge, Sandymount buses 2, 3, 5, 6, 7a, 8

**Guesthouses**
Elgin, grade B, 23 Elgin Rd, Dublin 4, Tel: 684497
Embassy, grade B, 35 Pembroke Rd, Dublin 4, Tel: 684130
Lisava, grade B, 46 Northumberland Rd, Dublin 4, Tel: 688572
Montrose Park, 16 Pembroke Park, Dublin 4, Tel: 684286
Mrs Abbott Murphy, 14 Sandymount Castle Park (off Gilford Rd), Sandymount, Tel: 683861
Mrs Chambers, 25 Anglesea Rd, Ballsbridge, Dublin 4, Tel: 687346
Miss MacNamara, 73 Anglesea Rd, Ballsbridge, Dublin 4, Tel: 689302
Mrs O'Connor, St John's Hs, 23 Pembroke Park (off Herbert Pk), Ballsbridge, Dublin 4, Tel: 684847
Mrs Doyle, 35 Sea Fort Avenue, Sandymount, Dublin 4, Tel: 689850

**Donnybrook** Buses 10, 11, 46a, 64a
Mrs Corrigan, Glenfield, 176 Stillorgan Rd, Tel: 693640
Mrs O'Connor, 39 Glenomena Park, Stillorgan Rd, Tel: 692519
Mrs O'Louglin, 174 Stillorgan Rd, Tel: 693155

**Mount Merrion** Buses 5, 46a, 62, 63, 64a, 84
Mrs Finn, Brookside House, Stillorgan Grove, Tel: 887062
Mrs Hickey, 51 North Av, Mount Merrion, Tel: 882304


**SOUTH WEST DUBLIN**

**Rathmines, Rathfarnham, Ranelagh, Dartry** Buses, 11, 11a, 12, 13, 14, 14a, 15a, 15b, 44, 47a, 48, 48a, 61, 62

Misses M and E Coman, 26 Butterfield Crescent, Rathfarnham, Tel: 908699
Mrs McCann, 11 Prince Arthur Terrace (off Leinster Sq), Rathmines, Tel: 972874
Mrs McColgan, 40 Belgrave Sq, Rathmines, Tel: 975619
Mrs McKenna, Suncroft, 110 Sandford Rd, Ranelagh, Dublin 6, Tel: 971375

Mrs O'Connell, 15 Butterfield Orchard, Rathfarnham, Dublin 4, Tel: 900521

**NORTH EAST DUBLIN**
**Clontarf** Buses 30, 44a
Mrs Bryne-Poole, Sea Front, 278 Clontarf Rd, Tel: 33618
Mrs C. Connolly, 362 Clontarf Rd, Tel: 332546, no C.H.
Mrs Egan, 144 Kilcora Rd, Clontarf, Tel: 339990
Mrs Haire, 73 Dollymount Park, Clontarf, Tel: 333685
Mrs Hunt, Cheznous, 7 Kincora Drive, Clontarf, Tel: 333892
Mrs Mooney, Aisling, 20 Lawrence Rd, Tel: 339097
Mrs O'Keeffe, Eagle Lodge, 12 Clontarf, Tel: 336009
**Drumcondra** Buses 3, 11, 13, 16, 16a
Mrs Creagh, St Aiden's, 150 Clonliffe Rd, Tel: 376750
Mrs Crofton, 90 Walnut Rise (off Griffith Av), Tel: 375431
Mrs Fitzgerald, Clonfert, 94 Walnut Rise (off Griffith Av), Tel: 379813
McGuinness Family, 71 Whitworth Rd, Tel: 303961
Mrs Moore, 45 Hollybank Rd, Tel: 372671
Mrs O'Neill, 6 Whitworth Parade (off St Patrick's Rd), Tel: 304733
**NORTH WEST DUBLIN**
**Glasnevin** Buses 13, 19, 19a, 34
Mrs T Ryan, Parknasilla, 15 Iona Drive, Tel: 305724
Egan's grade A guesthouse, 7/9 Iona Park (good value), Tel: 303611
**BINGE PLACES**
Kilronan House, 70 Adelaide Rd, Dublin 2, grade A guesthouse, Tel: 755266
Mount Herbert, 7 Herbert Rd, Dublin 4, grade A guesthouse, Tel: 684321
Ariel, 52 Lansdowne Rd, Dublin 4, grade A guesthouse, Tel: 685512
Iona House, 5 Iona Park, Glasnevin, grade A guesthouse, Tel: 306217
Buswell's Hotel, B* Molesworth St, Dublin 2 (central and expensive), Tel: 764013
Lansdowne Hotel, B*, Pembroke Rd, Dublin 4, Tel: 762549
Rooms are more expensive and you are wise to book well ahead, during Easter, the RDS (Spring Show) in May, The RDS Horse Show at beginning of August and all Ireland finals and Rugby International matches.

---

# County Kildare

Kildare is a county of bog and plain: the Bog of Allen leads into the Curragh Plain where some of the fastest horses in the world are bred and exercised. This county also contains two of the grandest houses in Ireland: Carton, where Lord Edward Fitzgerald, one of the leaders of the United Irishmen was brought up, and Castletown, now the centre of the

Irish Georgian Society. The River Liffey meanders through the countryside, it's perfect for *canoeing*, whilst the Grand Canal yields plentiful catches of *bream, rudd, eel, pike* and *perch.*

**Naas,** only 21 miles from Dublin is a busy industrial town, it used to be one of the seats of the kings of Leinster. Jigginstown House, just a mile southwest on the Kildare Road is now a massive ruin, it was built by Thomas Wentworth when Charles I proposed to visit him. The visit never came off and 'Black Tom', one of the most unpopular men in Ireland was executed in 1641 before it was finished. If it had been completed it would have been the largest unfortified house ever built in Ireland.
**Eating:** there are several good eating places in town, try LAWLOR'S in Poplar Sq, famous for its beef; or GEM RESTAURANT, Tel (045) 97268 in Main Street.

**Punchestown** is famous for its standing stone and for the races. The stone is three miles southeast of Naas, off the Woolpack Road and is 23 feet high with a bronze age burial chamber at its base. For details of *race meetings* at Punchestown and the Curragh, look in the national papers or the Bord Fáilte calendar of events.

North of Naas, the countryside becomes more interesting and **Robertstown** on the banks of the Grand Canal is ideal for a quiet leisurely visit. The locals are very proud of the town's 18th century associations and the waterfront has been restored to look as it did in the days when travellers used to alight from their boats for an overnight stop. Some of the barges have been restored and you can go for short trips on the canal, Tel: (045) 60204/60236. For those interested in *birds of prey*, a tour of the largest falconry in Europe can be made every day from 11 am for a small fee. Every night except Sunday, from April to October, 18th century banquets are recreated in the Grand Canal Hotel. The evening begins with a visit to the falconry, followed by a horse drawn barge cruise, and then the meal at 9.30pm Tel: (045) 60204. During the weekends in July and August, there are concerts, lectures on the Georgian and canal era and lots of festivities.

Two miles from here is **Prosperous,** another canal side village, famous for its *coarse fishing.* Contact the secretary of the Coarse Fishing Club in Prosperous for more details. **Eating:** there is a fairly lavish restaurant in a Georgian farmhouse, CURRYHILLS HS, Tel: (045) 68150.

**Celbridge** is a must for all Georgian country house lovers; within a few miles of each other are Castletown and Carton. Sadly the future of the latter is at the moment rather precarious and it is difficult to view it. It was the seat of the Earls of Kildare, a powerful Norman family who became 'more Irish than the Irish', and the grounds were laid out by Capability Brown in a park where 'art and nature in just union reign.'

Castletown at the eastern end of Celbridge village is approached through a fine avenue of lime trees. It was built for William Connelly, speaker of the Irish House of Commons from 1715-1719, and contains some elaborate plasterwork by the Francini Brothers. It has the only 18th century print room in Ireland and some superb 18th century furnishings. The house is open everyday except Tuesday from April to September, from 11am to 6pm; during the winter it is open on Sunday from

2pm-5pm. A *music festival* is held in the house during June, details from the Irish Georgian society, Castletown, Celbridge. One of the hunt balls held during the Dublin Horse Show week takes place in its gracious rooms. Period banquets are also held and there is a restaurant in the West wing, Tel: Mrs Marks (01) 288502. From the windows of the Long Gallery you can see the extraordinary Connelly Folly. It is an obelisk supported on arches, it was built by the widow of Speaker Connelly to provide relief work after a particularly hard winter.

**Maynooth** has ancient associations with the great Geraldine family, the Fitzgeralds, later Earls of Kildare and Dukes of Leinster. The fine ruins of the 12th century castle may be explored if you get the key from Castleview House, across the road from the Castle. Today, it is more closely associated with St. Patrick's College, one of the greatest Catholic seminaries in the world. *The Ecclesiastical Museum* is open by arrangement, call at the lodge gate. **Leixlip** is on the banks of the Liffey and is one of the prettiest villages in Ireland. It's name comes from the Danish Lax-Plaup which means salmon leap. Before the falls were utilised for hydro electric power, it was a wonderful sight to see the salmon do just that. The 12th century Norman castle is owned by Desmond Guinness, the force behind the Irish Georgian Society, and the whole village is steeped in Guinness family history. The *Salmon Leap Canoe Club* welcomes visitors and can offer campsites to canoeist free of charge!

**Kildare** is on the edge of the Curragh and is now an important centre for *horse breeding*. It is said that St. Brigid spread her handkerchief over enough land on which to build a convent and a monastery and the ruling king had to grant it to her. The Church of Ireland cathedral is well preserved, it incorporates part of the 13th century structure, and beside it there is a round tower which you can climb. *The Japanese gardens* in the grounds of the National Stud at **Tully** are perfect : they symbolize the life of man, from the cradle to the grave. The gardens are open from Easter to October, 10.30am-12.30pm, 2pm-5pm on weekdays and on Sundays, in the afternoons.

The green spring grass of the Curragh stretches for miles with the blue hills of Dublin on the horizon. The land is said to be so good for rearing horses because it is a limestone plain, so the pasture is the best in the world for bone-making. But it is the skill of the breeders in choosing the sires which has made them so successful and the excitement at the *races* when their skill is put to test is phenomenal; the chat is fast and furious, porter is downed in the tents, and the horses are splendid thundering along in the green distance. Numerous meetings are held between March and November, the most famous are the Irish Sweep Derby in midsummer, the Irish 2,000 Guineas, the Irish Oaks and the Irish St. Leger.

The Hill of Allen (676 feet) is famous in Irish Legend as the other world seat of Finn MacCumhail (MacCool). Together with Naas, and Dun Aillnne (Knockaulin) they were the residences of the Kings of Leinster, straight lines joining them form an equilateral triangle, with sides nine miles long. **Newbridge** (Droichead Nua) is an industrial centre on the Liffey.

**Athy,** has developed from a 13th century Norman settlement at a fording point on the River Barrow. In Irish Athy means Ford of Ae, Ae was the King of Munster, who in the 11th century was killed trying to take control of the Ford. A 16th century castle looks over Crom-a-boo bridge, the name refers to the war cry of the Desmond branch of the Fitzgerald family. There is a lovely old market house in the town, and the modern Dominican Church is worth looking at: it is pentagon shaped and built of massed concrete. Half a mile out of town Woodstock Castle still survives in the form of a rectangular tower. The LEINSTER ARMS HOTEL is a friendly place for a *meal* before you move on to explore the Ardscull Motte, used by Edward Bruce in 1315 to defeat an English army, and the Moone High Cross, one of the most famous and beautiful of all the High Crosses. The Moone High Cross is eight miles from Athy and is also known as Saint Colmcille's Cross, it is 17½ feet high and has 51 sculptured panels depicting scenes from the Bible. It stands in the demesne of Moone Abbey.

Nearby at **Timolin**, the art of pewter making has been restored and you can visit the workshop between 11am and 5pm. The village of **Ballitore** was once a flourishing Quaker settlement. The old meeting house is is now a library and museum; it can be visited free of charge. It is open Wednesday 7pm-9pm, Fridays 4pm-6pm and Saturday 11am-1pm. Sundays 3pm-5pm. Edmund Burke, Napper Tandy and Cardinal Cullen were all pupils at the school which was famous for its high standard of education. Nearby is the Rath of Mulaghmast, an earthen fort where it is said that Garret Og Fitzgerald, the 11th Earl of Kildare sleeps, emerging once every seven years.

**Castledermot** is famous for the remains of its Franciscan Abbey, high crosses and round tower. A few miles outside it is Kilkea Castle, once the home of the Earls of Kildare, now a luxury hotel and health farm.
**Eating:** on the Naas-Carlow Road, OS DOYLES SCHOOLHOUSE, is a restaurant with Irish style food. Tel: (0503) 44282. Castledermot was a walled town and was sacked by Cromwell; notice the lovely 12th century Romanesque doorway beside the round tower.


## PLACES TO STAY IN COUNTY KILDARE

**Athy**
Leinster Arms. B* grade hotel. Tel: (0507) 31265
**Ballymore Eustace**
Mrs Dennison, Bridge View, Tel: (045) 64125
**Celbridge**
Mrs McCabe, Green Acres, Dublin Rd, Tel: (01) 271163
**The Curragh**
Mrs McCann, Dara Lodge, Pollardstown, Tel: (045) 21770
**Kilcullen**
Mrs Hickey, Bulhill Hose, Calverstown, Tel: (045) 83243
**Kildare**
Mrs Winters, St. Marys, Maddenstown, Tel: (045) 21243

**Kill** nr. Naas
Mrs Kearns, Thorn lodge, Broguestown, Tel: (045) 62166
**Naas**
Mrs Phelan, Silverspring Hs, Clane, Tel: (045) 68481
Mrs MacNamara, Rosstree, Hollywood Park, Sallins Rd, Tel: (045) 76490
**Prosperous**
Mrs Travers, Curryhills Hs, Tel: (045) 68150
Mrs Duffe, Lissadel, Downings, Tel: (045) 68314
Mrs O'Brien, Hill View, Curryhills, Tel: (045) 68252 (6 rooms with bath.)
**Binge places**
**Leixlip**
Springfield Hotel, grade B Tel: 280453
**Casteldermot**
Kilkea Castle, grade A Tel: (0503) 45156

---

# County Kilkenny

The countryside round Kilkenny is lush and well cultivated, reminiscent of England, so too are the villages with their neatness and mellowed cottages. Places to visit from west to east include **Urlingford** on the border with Tipperary, near which are the ruins of at least four castles. **Ballyragget** on the Nore River has more to recommend it to historians: it was the scene of a dramatic trial of strength between Black Tom, Earl of Ormonde, Lord Lieutenant of Ireland in Queen Elizabeth's time and Owen MacRory O'More; it ended in the capture of the Earl. Further east, about 7 miles north of Kilkenny are the dramatic Dunmore Caves. During the Viking raids people took refuge here, but the Vikings found them and killed nearly 1,000. However it continued to be used as a shelter by local people. You can now go on an informative guided tour, Tel: 056-27720 (Closed Mondays mid-September to mid-June).

**Gowran** town deserves your attention if you love horse racing, and is also a centre for the manufacture of ornaments and other objects from the black Kilkenny marble (you may find Kilkenny marble mantlepieces pointed out to you in many big houses). Going south of Kilkenny you reach lovely **Thomastown** (on the Waterford road) with its mellowed grey stone buildings. Near here, at Dysart Castle was the home of the famous idealist philosopher, George Berkley (1685-1753). He gave his name to the city and the university of Berkley, California. About two miles from here is one of the best kept estates in Ireland, Mount Juliet, where the *Kilkenny Hunt Kennels* are located. Continuing towards Waterford are the ruins of Jerpoint Abbey which appear to have been built by the same masons who raised Baltinglass in Wicklow. You should

158

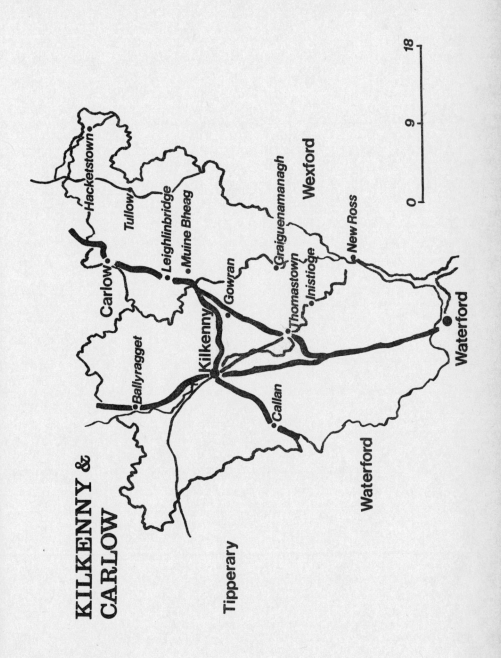

KILKENNY & CARLOW

Hacketstown

Tullow

Carlow

Leighlinbridge

Muine Bheag

Ballyragget

Gowran

Kilkenny

Graiguenamanagh

Thomastown

Inistioge

Wexford

New Ross

Callan

Tipperary

Waterford

Waterford

0   9   18

159

take a look at the cloisters with their sculptured lords and ladies. (Open June to September 10.30am-7.30pm)

Due east rises the hill of Brandon which gives you a clear view of this well worked countryside, you can see the Blackstairs Mountains to the east on the Carlow-Wexford border. On your way here you will pass the charming town of **Inistioge** home of the Tighes. This family was connected with a pair of remarkable ladies who exercised a great influence on taste in the 18th century. The ladies of Llangollen, Eleanor Butler and Sarah Ponsonby, exemplified the Romantic and the Gothic by running away together to live in a Welsh cottage. North of Inistioge is **Graiguenamanagh**, right on the Carlow border. The town boasts an early Cistercian abbey called Duiske, which survived the suppression of the monasteries in the 16th century, as did the Catholic church which has some 9th century crosses in the graveyard. At **Ullard**, three miles north, there are remains of another foundation. St. Fiachre set off from Ullard, he is one of the saints that chose the isolation of a foreign land in preference to a lonely island hermitage. He is the patron saint of Parisian taxi-drivers, because the first carriage conveyances in Paris used to congregate round the Hotel de St. Fiachre. Just outside **Kilkenny** town on the way to **Thomastown,** is a well dedicated to St. Fiachre, patterns are held here around the time of the Festival. Before leaving the Graiguenamanagh district take the opportunity to investigate the woolcrafts; the Cushendale Mills produce very finely woven goods.

West of **Kilkenny** town is the ancient town of **Callan** which seems to have nourished a fair number of Ireland's great men. One of them, Edmund Ignatius Rice a candidate for canonisation, founded the influential teaching order of the Christian Brothers who not only educate most of Ireland's politicians, but also some of the Third World's. Robert Fulton, born in 1765, designed the world's first steam engine, and James Hoban, architect of the White House, came from near here.

**Kilkenny town** (Cill Chainnigh, St.Canices's Church) This old city was the focal point of the Anglo-Norman and Irish resistance to the Cromwellians in 1642 where they formed a confederate parliament. Before that it was the seat of power for the 'old English', the first foreign war lords. The city takes its name from St.Canice who established a monastery here in the 6th century, the cathedral now occupies that site and you can see the finest collection of 6th century sepulchral monuments in Ireland. The 100 foot round tower beside the church also dates from this earlier time. This grouping of ecclesiastical buildings with the Church of Ireland vicarage is curious but charming, and represents the strength of the Anglicising influence in its best aspects. In the town centre, the great fortress of the Ormondes, Kilkenny Castle, remains a dominant feature. Kilkenny Design Workshops promote Irish goods, their label is almost a guarantee of good taste and quality workmanship.

Architecturally the town is one of Ireland's most interesting because it is so old. You should try to visit Rothe House, a unique example of an Irish Tudor merchant's house, built in 1594. The Kilkenny Archaeological Society, a pioneer of its kind in Ireland and forerunner of the Royal

Society of Antiquities in Ireland, houses its collection there. It is open everyday April to October between 10.30am-12.30pm and 3pm-5pm. Admission: adults 30p, students and children 20p. Nearby in Abbey St is the Black Abbey that gives the street its name, it has some interesting antiquities on show. The only surviving gate of the medieval walled city, the Black Freren Gate (because of the black habits of the Dominicans) is worth a visit. Further into the town, in the High Street, you can see the beautiful Tolsel, formerly the Toll House or Exchange, now the City Hall, which was built in 1761

Kilkenny Castle acts as an exhibition centre during the Festival. Until 1935 it was the principal residence of the Butlers, now you can go round it and enjoy the lovely gardens sheltered behind the castle walls. Opening times for the castle are weekdays except Mondays 10.30am-6.30pm June-September. Admission: adults 30p, childen 10p. Opposite the castle are the Kilkenny Design Centre workshops which you can visit and you can explore fascinating streets with intriguing names.

Across the Nore river, which the Castle overlooks, is Kilkenny College, a handsome Georgian building where some of Ireland's greatest writers were educated: the satirist Dean Swift, the philosopher Berkley and the dramatist Congreve.

The city also acts as host to one of the nicest cultural festivals in Ireland, the Kilkenny Festival. It takes place at the end of August and includes all the arts, visual, performing and gustatory, if you go by the number of people in the smarter pubs drinking the home brew, Smithwick's, a beer which is as popular as Guinness.

**Eating:** for atmosphere KYTELER'S INN would be hard to beat. Dame Alice Kyteler, who carried on a despised but powerful business as a moneylender in the 13th century was convicted as a witch. This unfortunate woman went through about four husbands which added further suspicion. You eat in the cellars of her house in Kieran St. Tel: (056 21800). Try MULHALL'S RESTAURANT in the High St. Tel: (056 21329) for a bit of glamour (lunch from £IR4, dinner £IR7.50). You can get pub lunches at EDWARD LANGTON'S PUB, a great venue, Tel: (056 21728) from £IR3. There is a very atmospheric old hotel, the CLUB HOUSE HOTEL, Tel: (056 21994). For fast service grill meals go to the NEWPARK HOTEL, Tel: (056 22122) (£IR5-£IR9), you can also tuck into haute cuisine meals if you are prepared to pay.

Tourist information enquiries should be made to the office on the Parade. Room reservations can be made here (and even in the crowded festival time they will do wonders) Tel: (056) 21755.


## PLACES TO STAY IN COUNTY KILKENNY

### Graiguenamanagh
Mrs A McCabe, Brandon View Hs, Ballyogan, Tel: (0503) 24191. Attractive setting and putting green.
Mrs B Neary, Brandon Villa, Tel: (0503 24198), near good fishing.
The Anchor Guesthouse, Tel: (0503 24207).

**Inistioge**

Mrs D Cantlon, Cullintra Hs, The Rower, Tel: (051) 23614. Situated underneath Mount Brandon, with rough shooting.

Mr & Mrs L Rothwell, Nore Valley Villa, Tel: (056) 31318. Pony trekking and near Jerpoint Abbey.

Round Way Guesthouse.

**Kilkenny**

Mrs M Neary, Tara Troyswood, Freshford Road, Tel: (056) 27619, outside the town, and near good fishing.

Mrs E T Milne, Lunar Lodge, Bawnlusk, Cuffes Grange, Tel: (0409) 5362.

Mrs N O'Connor, Sundown, Freshford Road, Tel: (056) 21818.

Central Guesthouse, Tel: (056) 21926

**Other guesthouses round Kilkenny town** include the Ryans, Drumherin, Ballyfoyle Tel: (056 27626), with an enjoyable atmosphere and plenty of out door activities. It is near Dunmore Caves.

Also Tennypark Guesthouse, Tel: (056) 21572.

**Urlingford**

Urlingford Arms Hotel, Tel: (056) 31188.

**Youth hostel**

Jenkinstown, Foulksrath Castle. Open all year round.

**Binge Places**

Rose Hill House, Tel: (056) 22603.

---

# County Longford

If you are a coarse fisherman or a Maria Edgeworth enthusiast you may decide to venture into this county which shares a characteristic with all the middle counties – dullness. This will probably annoy anyone who actually lives in the area, though one man I talked to thought it a good idea to just describe it as 'a terrible beauty' and leave it at that!

**Longford** is set on the Camlin River. It is a pleasant if somewhat run down town, which grew up around a fortress of the O'Farrels which has long since disappeared. You cannot fail to notice the dominating limestone 19th century cathedral with its lofty towers. **Eating:** The SPINNING WHEEL and WEAVERS LOFT in Ballymahon St are very good places for a quick meal.

Five miles to the west is **Clondra** a pretty village on the Royal Canal that links up with the Shannon. During the summer you can go to Teach Cheoil or the Irish Music House where traditional song, music and dance are held. Times and days of performances can be checked up on at the Tourist Office in the main street of Longford, Tel: (043) 6566. **Newtownforbes** three miles northwest of Longford boasts a fine 17th century

162

# LONGFORD & ROSCOMMON

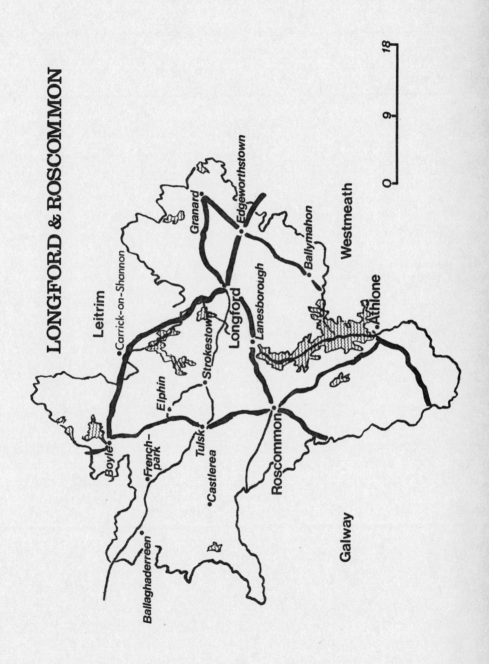

mansion, the seat of the Earls of Granard. Visitors must ask permission if they wish to view the grounds. There is plenty of *trout* and *coarse fishing* plus an 18 hole *golf course*. For *cruising* on the Shannon, Tel: (043) 6633 and for *hunting* with the Longford Harriers Tel: Edgeworth Town 26.

**Ballymahon** is all Oliver Goldsmith country and his connection with these parts are proudly remembered. Ballymahon itself is a good place from which to explore the River Inny and the Shannon. **Pallas** five miles to the east is Goldsmith's birthplace and at **Auburn (Lissoy)** you can have a drink in a pub named after the Inn in *'She stoops to Conquer'*, called the Three Jolly Pigeons. **Ardagh** is a lovely village surrounded by woods where it is said that St. Patrick founded a church which can still be visited. **Abbeystrule** on the banks of the Inny has the sad remains of a Cistercian Abbey.

**Eating:** If you find yourself slightly depressed by the indifference the Irish seem to have for their past, cheer yourself up with a delicious meal at the RUSTIC INN, Tel: (044) 5424/5469.

**Edgeworthstown** (Mostrim) is not a very noteworthy place, except that Maria Edgeworth and her innovative father lived here. The family home is now a nursing home and has been terribly altered. The Maria Edgeworth Museum is very interesting and situated in St. John's Church of Ireland, and the old school. The key may be got from Mrs. Mahon, Main St (opposite the Ulster Bank).

**Lanesborough** is famous for its *coarse fishing* and is on the northern tip of Lough Ree. You may tour the power station which is fuelled by turf – one fossil fuel Ireland has a lot of! On Inchleraun Island in the Lough are the remains of a monastery founded early in the 6th century and the remains of several churches and some ogham stones. You can hire a boat out there from Mr Kelly, Elfeet Bay,, Lanesborough. You could try your hand at the popular Irish pastime of bingo in the Ballyleague Hall on Thursday nights, or listen to traditional music at Fermoyle National School on Monday nights – it's free.

## PLACES TO STAY IN COUNTY LONGFORD

**Abbeystrule**
Mr Mallon, Ratharney Hs, Tel: (044) 5460.
**Clondra**
Mrs Stusche, Maryville Hs, Tel: (043) 5443. Small restaurant attached.
**Edgeworthstown**
Mrs Keogh, Treel House, Lenamore, Tel: (044) 5418. Farmhouse no C.H.
**Lanesborough**
Mrs Gallagher, Corrigeen.
The O'Loughlin Family, Lakeside, Rathcline Road. Tel: (043) 21343.
**Longford**
Mrs O'Kane, Sancien, Dublin Rd, Tel: (043) 6187. 3 rooms with shower.
Mrs Cunningham, Eye-Kay-Ne, Dublin Rd, Tel: (043) 6495.
**Newtownforbes**
Mrs Farrell, Curry Lodge, Tel: (043) 6814.

Mrs Flynn, Tel: (043) 5071.

---

# County Meath and County Louth

**The Boyne Valley** is a gloriously green valley which has a crumbling estate at every corner of the road, and ancient tumuli at every curve of the river. The valley was the centre of power in Ireland for thousands of years. Here you will come upon the **Hill of Tara**, the seat of the priest kings in pre-historic times and later of the High Kings of Ireland. You can easily cover all the ancient places and monasteries in a few days at a leisurely pace on a bicycle. In the summer it is the most enjoyable way to travel along the country lanes laced with cow parsley.

**Kells** is not actually in the Boyne Valley but in the wooded valley of the Blackwater. The village is extremely pretty, but has some dark assocations in the form of its round tower where a claimant to the High Kingship of Ireland was murdered in 1076. It used to be the headquarters of the Columban monks who moved here from Iona in 807 after being pillaged repeatedly by the Vikings. You can go inside St. Columcille's house, an unpretentious cell with a stone roof and a well nearby. Incidentally it's worth making the extra effort to go to Saint Ciaran's, three miles away on the south bank of the Blackwater, where there is a very attractive holy well. You may only drink from it, for if you wash in it the well would lose its holy properties. A rather sane law of hygiene! Back at Kells, you can see in the church a facsimile copy of the famous Book of Kells. It is open all day.

**Trim** is the most usual starting point for a tour of the Boyne Valley. You should approach it from the Dublin Road if you can, for suddenly all the ruins, towers and moats through which the River Boyne winds its way burst upon you. King John's Castle built in 1172, is the largest Anglo-Norman castle in Ireland, it is a well preserved ruin which dominates the town. The Duke of Wellington's family came from this area, as did that strange adventurer Bernardo O'Higgins, hero of Chile.
**Eating:** Try the WELLINGTON COURT HOTEL for a steak, the inevitable but delicious basis of every Irish menu. The Education Centre in Castle St mounts some very interesting exhibitions: art, history, and oriental collections and all free! About two miles away is the small village of Laracor, where Jonathan Swift and Stella lived for a while; he must have been a curious rector, as least not the sort the local gentry felt at ease with. In St. Patrick's Cathedral, Dublin you can read his final comment to the world 'rage and savage indignation no longer lacerate his heart'.
**Eating:** DUNDERRY INN RESTAURANT near Trim Tel: (046) 3167 is possibly better than ARBUTUS LODGE in Cork, and much cheaper.
All that is left of **Tara** is a green hill in green fields, so do not be

# LOUTH and MEATH

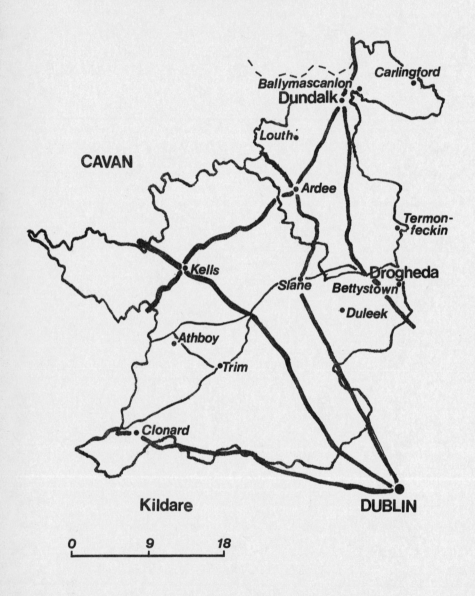

Carlingford

Ballymascanlon
Dundalk

Louth

CAVAN

Ardee

Termon-
feckin

Kells

Slane

Drogheda

Bettystown

Duleek

Athboy

Trim

Clonard

Kildare

DUBLIN

0       9       18

disappointed; just shut your eyes and imagine the pagan rites which were enacted and later the great triennial feis, where tribal disputes were settled and laws were made. The Book of Leinster describes Tara in its heyday (1160 AD) as being full of warriors who combined fierceness with elegance; the great wooden buildings resounded with the clamour of people going about their business. The pastures around would have been thick with herds of cattle representing the wealth and importance of the High King, so many of the legendary battles seem to have centred round a bull or a prize cow. The Great Assembly Hall was built by the Irish King Solomon, Cormac, who presided over the massive banquets and laid down lists of protocol – even meat was portioned out according to rank : the king, queen and nobles of the first rank ate ribs of beef, buffoons got shoulder fat, and chess-players shins, harpers and drummers got pig's shoulders as their portion, whilst historians were entitled to the haunches! The most important of the earthworks that remain are the Mound of the Hostages, Cormac's house, the banquet hall, and the Lia Fail (the coronation stone of ancient kings) and an awful modern statue of Saint Patrick. The whole place was dug up by enthusiastic but misled British Israelites who believed that the Ark of the Covenant was buried in one of the large mounds. They got this ridiculous information from a second hand book shop in the Charing Cross Road and in those days – sixty odd years ago no one did anything to stop them. Daniel O'Connell held one of his monster meetings here in 1845 when he was campaigning for the repeal of the Union with Britain, about a million people turned up to hear him speak; the Red Branch Knights and other heroes must have been stirring in their graves.

**Slane** is one of my favourite villages. Notice the four Georgian houses arranged in a square, they were built for the four spinster sisters of one of the Conynghams who could no longer stand their inquisitive chattering and quarrelling. They detested each other but could not bear to be parted, so he thought of that perfect solution; you can imagine them watching each other through lace curtains. The castle which overlooks the Boyne River makes a romantic picture from the bridge.

**Eating:** You can get a very good dinner in the CASTLE itself. Tel: (041) 24207/24163. The CONYNGHAM ARMS produces excellent ham sandwiches in a bar decorated with a fascinating collection of old china cups and plates. On the hill above, Saint Patrick kindled his historic fire in the 5th century AD which proclaimed Christianity throughout the land. Fishing permits for *salmon, grilse* and *sea trout* may be had from the Earl of Mount Charles, Slane Estate, Slane.

Past Townley Hall and along a twisting road you come to a piece of land which is enclosed by the Boyne on three sides. Here is **Brugh na Boinne,** the Palace of the Boyne, which is a huge cemetery with at least 15 passage graves from Neolithic times. The three main sites are at Newgrange, Knowth and Dowth. It is fascinating to go to Newgrange, its mound sparkling with white quartz pebbles like a beacon in the landscape. In the tourist shop at the car park there is an exhibition of the Brugh na Boinne; try to see it after your tour of the grave because it has most of the answers you will be provoked into asking by the sophistication of the building. Try to avoid going at the weekend in mid-summer when the place is crowded, you can not appreciate the age or the impressive atmosphere when you are squashed up sideways against a sacred stone, decorated with a lozenge or not! The guide gives you a very polished talk, one of the most impressive facts amongst all the conjecturing that goes on is that the corbelled roof of the chamber has kept the place dry for 45 centuries. There is a small entrance fee to the tumulus and it is open daily except from September-May it is shut on Mondays.

**Dowth** has not been tamed to satisfy the curiousity of the inactive, be prepared for a certain amount of scrambling if you want to see the two tombs inside and the early christian souterrain at the entrance. This site is open from June to September (though you can get the key to it at other times, instructions are posted on the site). **Knowth** has wonderfuly lavish kerbstones placed round the mound, they are decorated with spirals and lozenges. At the moment extensive excavations are being carried out, so the site is closed. The main tourist office for Meath is at Newgrange. Tel: (041) 24274.

Between Drogheda and Dublin are numerous *beach resorts*, the only really noteworthy one is Laytown/Bettystown where the Strand Races are held one day a year either in June, July or August. If you wish to experience an Irish day out, this is for you. Contact Mr Joseph Collins, 27 Fair St, Drogheda. If you want to find a quiet undiscovered village along the coast make for **Termonfeckin** with it's own 10th century High Cross and the headquarters of the Irish Countrywomen where you can attend courses in pottery, weaving, etc. From here you can easily visit Mellifont and Monasterboice, two ancient ecclesiastical centres. Set amongst peaceful woods and fields you can not fail to notice the Bord Fáilte signs pointing to the Battle of the Boyne where the Protestant king outflanked and outnumbered Catholic James Stuart, who deserted his Irish followers. **Mellifont** is a gracious ruin six miles west of Drogheda, it was built in 1142 by the first Cistercians to come to Ireland. Their arrival and the new ideas in architecture and church organisation were the result of the efforts of Saint Malachy who did much to bring the Irish church more in line with Rome. It is a great place for a picnic and you can even stay in the grounds, in the youth hostel. **Monasterboice**, a 5th century monastic settlement contains the most perfect High Cross, the Cross of Muireadach made in the early 10th century. Nearly every inch of the cross is covered in scenes from the Bible, the only way the poor and illiterate could 'read' the scriptures. The West Cross is almost as nice and less squat. You can climb the damaged round tower that must have been the tallest in the country in its time. One of the best things about Irish ruins is that you are not accompanied everywhere by officious guides or directed by smart painted notices to 'keep off the grass' or 'away from the edge' so you still feel the spirit of adventure.

**Drogheda** conjures up images of the cruelty of Cromwell for which he is notorious in Ireland, but it has been a famous place in Ireland since the Danes settled there and today is bustling with energy. In the Church of St Peter is the preserved head of St Oliver Plunkett, Archbishop of

Armagh, who sadly became caught up in the panic of 'the popish plot', fabricated by Titus Oates in 1678. He was hung, drawn and quartered at Tyburn, but his goodness is remembered amongst the extremism and violence of that century. Tourist Office Tel: (041) 7070. Bicycles for hire; P J Carolan 77 Trinity St, Drogheda, Tel: (041) 8242.

**The Cooley Peninsula** is one of the most beautiful, untouched places in Ireland. First, go to **Carlingford** which looks across the Lough to the Mourne Mountains. This town is full of castellated buildings, King John's Castle with arrow slits in the outer walls, is impressive. Seek out Faughart Hill where Edward Bruce was killed in battle in 1318; you go through **Moyry Pass**, along the ancient road into Ulster, to an overdone shrine to St Brigid who is supposed to have been born in Faughart. It really is hideous, so pass on to the cemetery on the hill where a slab marks Bruce's Grave. From here, the whole of Leinster spreads out below you, you can see the Wicklow Hills rippling across the plain to join the Slieve Bloom and the Cooley hills behind. All this part is touched by the splendour of myth – Cuchulain was born in these heather coloured hills.

It was at **Ardee,** now a very attractive market town, that Cuchulain slew his friend Ferdia in a four day combat to stop the raiding party stealing the bull of Cooley for Queen Maeve. Ardee was an outpost of the Pale, and often used by the English as a base for attacking Ulster, that is why you will find along the main street two old castles. **Collon,** a small place on the way to Ardee has an excellent antique shop.


## PLACES TO STAY IN COUNTY MEATH

**Drumconrath** (near Ardee)
Mrs A Ward, Inis Fail, Bawn Rd, Tel: (041) 54161.
**Kells**
Mrs M Roundtree, Deerpark Farm, Crossakiel, Tel: Crossakiel 9.
Mrs C Woods, Latimor House, Oldcastle Rd, Tel: Kells 133.
Miss L Sherlock, Balreask, Carlanstown, Tel: Carlanstown 2.
**Laytown**
Tara guesthouse, grade B, Tel: (041) 27239.
Mrs P Downey, Ardilaun, 41 Beach Park, Tel: (041) 27033.
**Navan**
Mrs E McCormack, Balreask House, Tel: (046) 21155 (farmhouse on Dublin-Navan Rd).
Mrs N Whelehan, Ballinlig Hs, Clonmellon, Tel: (046) 33118 (no C.H.)
Mrs R Naughton, Moondyne, 61 Academy St, Tel: (046) 23366 (no C.H.)
**Oldcastle**
Mrs H Pallin, Purchanmone Hs, Tel: Oldcastle 72. A great centre for fishing and archaeology enthusiasts.
**Slane**
Mrs Murren, Monknewtown Tel: (041) 24295 (on Slane-Drogheda Rd).
Mrs Fortune, 3 Castle Hill, Tel: (041) 24394.
Conyngham Arms, grade B hotel, Tel: (041) 24155.

## PLACES TO STAY IN COUNTY LOUTH

**Carlingford**
Slieve Foy, grade C guesthouse, Tel: (042) 73116.
**Castlebellingham**
Mrs B Campbell, Newrath Hs, Newrath, Dromiskin, Tel: (042) 72240.
**Drogheda**
Mrs M Flanagan, Tubbertoby, Clogherhead, Tel: (041) 22124. On the coast road between Termonfeckin and Clogherhead. Dairy farm.
Mrs S Dwyer, Harbour Villa, Mornington Rd, Tel: (041) 7441.
Mrs M O'Leary, Aghina, 8 Greenhills Villas, Tel: (041) 8023.

**Binge Places**
Glenside, Smithstown, Tel: (041) 7449. Grade A guesthouse with a private bathroom for every room.

---

# Counties of Offaly and Laois

To many travellers the only significance of these two counties is that you travel through them on your way to Tipperary or Cork. They lie in the centre of Ireland's saucer shape, in the flat plains and boglands, separated from Galway and Roscommon in the west by the Shannon. In **Offaly,** formerly King's County one place stands out: **Clonmacnoise,** near the Shannon, one of Ireland's most celebrated holy places. In 548 AD St. Ciaran founded a monastery which became one of the most famous of all the monastic settlements in Ireland. In the great hymn on the downfall of heathens which begins the Martyrology of Aengus, the opening words are:

> 'In quiet Clonmacnoise,
> Around Ciaran's feet
> Everlasting choirs
> Raise a concert sweet...'

The words of Rolleston's adaptation of an early Gaelic poem express the importance of this centre of worship.

> 'In a quiet watered land, a land of roses
> Stands St. Ciaran's city fair.
> And the warriors of Erin in their famous generations
> Slumber there.'

In the early 12th century the famous 'Book of the Dun Cow' was compiled by Mael Muire (his father was Ceileachar, Bishop of Clonmacnoise), who was killed by robbers in the Cathedral Church in 1106. It was the favourite church of the O'Connor kings; Turlough and Rory were buried there. The coming of the Normans spelt the decline of Clon-

170

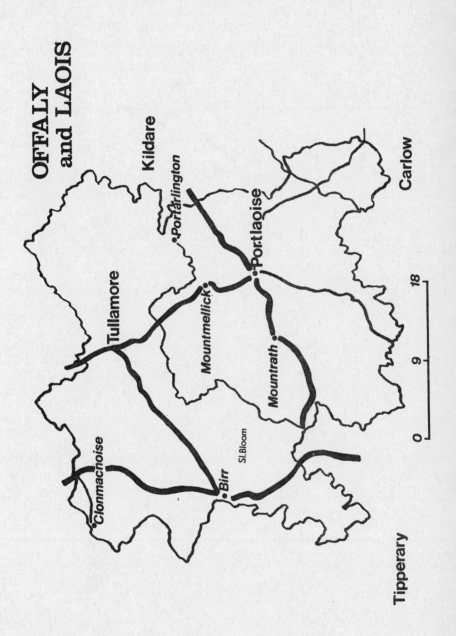

OFFALY and LAOIS

Kildare

Portâr-lington

Portlaoise

Tullamore

Mountmellick

Mountrath

Clonmacnoise

Birr

Sl.Bloom

Carlow

Tipperary

0    9    18

macnoise, for they built a fort by the river, and an English garrison was built at Athlone. Nowadays the monumental slabs with inscriptions dating from the 6th and 11th centuries are of special interest. There is a pilgrimage held here on September 12th, the feast of St. Ciaran. During the summer months there is a Tourist Information Centre open at the entrance to Clonmacnoise (Tel: 0905 4134) though the site itelf is open all the year round. **Durrow** in Laois is a centre of early Christian Art. The manuscript book of Durrow was written here in 700 AD, and now rests in Trinity College Dublin.

If you travel south towards **Birr** from Clonmacnoise and Shannon-bridge (L27) you will pass a lovely little castle at **Clononey** built in Henry VIII's time. From there, go on to **Banagher**, an attractive little canal village on the east bank of the Shannon. Anthony Trollope spent a few happy years here as Post Surveyor in 1841, and it was here he tried his hand at writing novels. The Crannog pottery at **Banagher** is interesting because you can see the potter 'throwing' the pots on his wheel. (Open daily in summer 9.30am-8pm; and on Sundays, 2.30pm-6.30pm. No charge). Banagher is also a good base from which to go *cruising* on the Shannon, contact Silverline Cruisers Ltd, Tel: Banagher 25, boats are available from Brosna Hotel, Banagher for *trout* and *coarse fishing,* contact Mr Smyth at the Marina. Early closing is on Thursday.

**Birr** is an attractive stopping place. It is a pleasantly laid out town and the hand of the landlord's family (it used to be called Parsonstown after them) is evident. Their castle, formerly an O'Carroll stronghold is close to the town, and the gardens are open to the public. Times of opening (gardens) 9am-1pm, 2pm-6pm. Admission: adults 80p, children 40p. In August there is a *Birr Vintage Week.* The recreational facilities are numerous, one can *fish, golf,* or go *orienteering, pitch and putt* on the green, and *ride.* For details go to the Birr Tourist Office (open only in summer), Emmet Square, Tel: Birr 206. Sadly the Birr Theatre, almost a pioneer in its field has closed down, it provided the inspiration for such companies as the Shakespearian travelling company which is now based in Dublin.

With the best will in the world it is difficult to wax lyrical about the scenery in Offaly and Laois. The latter county has had quite a few name changes: it started off as Queen's County, named after the unfortunate Queen Mary, then became Leix; similarly the county town **Port Laoise** was Maryborough, then Port Leix. It suffers from the proximity of a well publicised prison. If you are interested in veteran and vintage cars you might time your visit for the *July Rally.* The town itself is built on a sand and gravel embankment (an esker ridge), so this suggests that the site was the boundary of some ancient sea. Tourist information can be obtained from James Fintan, Lalor Avenue, Tel: 0502 21178 in the summer season.

North of Port Laoise is the canal town of **Portarlington**. It was founded at the end of the 17th century and became an important centre for Dutch and French Protestant refugees. In 1696, Henri de Massue, Marquis de Ruvigny, also the Earl of Galway, was granted title to the lands round here; he was one of William III's foreign favourites who excited

much jealousy among English courtiers. The connection is commemorated by the Festival Français of Portarlington in September, and by
the so called French style of the old town houses, their gardens stretch
down to the river rather than into the street.

**Mountmellick** and **Mountrath** north of Port Laoise are Quaker towns,
which were quietly prosperous through linen manufacture. These
towns are set in the Slieve Blooms, and through this country, you get to
the boundary between the two counties, Offaly and Laois. Until quite
recently an annual tug of war took place between the 'Kings' and the
'Queens' (Offaly and Laois). Arderin, the 'Height of Ireland', was
thought to be one of the major elevations in Ireland (1,734 feet high); it's
a proud but not a true title.


## COUNTY OFFALY

**Banagher** (see also p105)
Brosna Lodge, Tel: Banagher 50. Some rooms with bath, no extra charge.
**Belmont**
Mrs P Griffith, Lisderg Hs, Tel: Belmont 23. Near good trout, coarse
fishing and riding.
**Birr**
Mrs A Stanley, Woodville, Shinrone, Tel: (0505) 47278. Own river,
attractive setting.
Mrs C Shiels, Emmet Square, Tel: Birr 172.
Dooly's Hotel, Tel: Birr 32. Moderately priced, bath is extra.
**Portarlington**
Mrs E Brennan, Ashmount House, Cloneygowan, Tel: (0506) 53533. On
the Tullamore-Portarlington Road, lovely setting.
**Tullamore**
Mrs M Smith, Clodiagh, Tullabeg, Rahan, Tel: (0506) 55966. On the
river.
Mrs J O'Reilly, Charleville Road, Tel: (0506) 41283.
Oakfield Guesthouse, Rahan Road, Tel: (0506) 21385. Bath extra.


## COUNTY LAOIS

**Abbeyleix**
De Vesci Arms, Tel: (0502) 31231, small reasonably priced hotel.
**Borris-in-Ossory**
Mrs M Phelan, Castletown Hs, Donaghmore, Tel: (0505) 46415,
farmhouse.
**Port Laoise**
McLoughlin Family, Jamestown Hs, Ballybrittas, Tel: (0502) 26163,
fishing nearby, 38 miles from Dublin (off the road to Cork).
Mrs C Haslem, Mayview, Glynnside, off Abbeyleix Road, Tel: (0502)
21484.
Donoghues guesthouse, 1 Kellyville Park, Tel: (0502) 21353.

**Rathdowney**
Mrs P Carroll, River House, Tel: Erill 4 (between Rathdowney and Templemore).
Central Hotel, Tel: (0505) 46261.

---

# County Westmeath

This is one of the most fascinating counties for those who enjoy *Irish history, fishing* and exploring the wooded lake country through which magnificent old fashioned pubs and ruins are scattered; this land has a quiet beauty. **Athlone**, half of which is in Co. Roscommon but dealt with here, is a good touring centre on the Shannon River, which immediately spreads into the lovely Lough Ree. Here, you can either head for Connemara or Dublin. Westmeath is rather flat, but the little hillocks, never more than 850 feet high are well placed and attractive.

**Athlone** (Ath Luain: the Ford of Luan) has always been important as the crossing place on the Shannon between the kingdoms of Leinster and Connacht; many raids were launched from here by the fierce Connacht men who wanted the fat cattle of Meath. Later, when the Anglo-Normans had established themselves in Leinster, Athlone became the last outpost of that civilisation, for behind it stretched the world of the Gaels. The castle was built by King John and from it the English attempted to govern Connacht. Over the centuries, the castle and walls had to be rebuilt many times, but the most memorable stories surround the seige of Athlone when the town was held for James II against the Williamite forces. Sergeant Custume (after whom the present barracks is named) and ten volunteers gave their lives in hacking down the temporary wooden bridge over which the enemy was about to swarm into the breach in the walls. Unluckily for the Irish, their leader, a French general called St Ruth, was a prize idiot and having secured what he thought was victory decided to throw a grand party, even though Patrick Sarsfield, our Limerick hero, begged him to take the rumours of further attack seriously. Thus the Williamite forces were able to take the city whilst the Irish troops were drunkenly sleeping over their cups. Westmeath became a separate shire to Meath because Henry VIII needed tougher measures to subdue it. The ruling Gaelic family were the Mac Geoghegans whose lands remained intact up to the time of Cromwell.

**Athlone** is a thriving market town, a major rail and road terminus, and has a harbour on the inland navigation system. It has a well-developed marina and quite a few river cruiser companies operate from here. One of the most striking buildings in the town is the enormous Roman Catholic Church of St Peter and St Paul built in the Roman Renaissance style. Overlooking the bridge, almost opposite the church is St. John's Castle

174

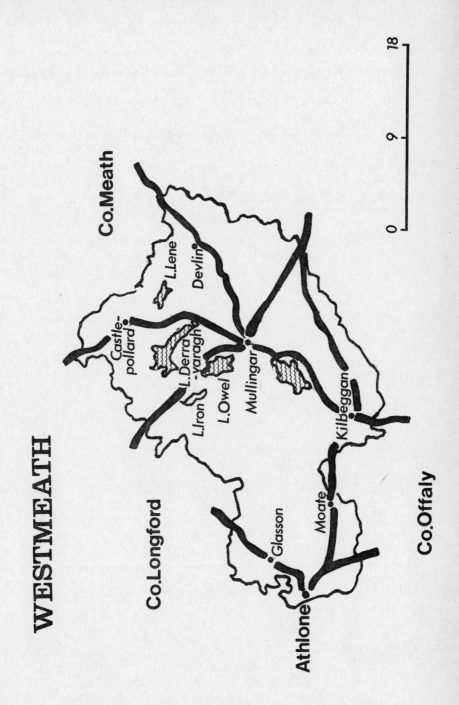

WESTMEATH

Co.Meath

Co.Longford

Co.Offaly

L.Lene

Devlin

Castle-
pollard

L.Derra
-varagh

L.Iron

L.Owel

Mullingar

Kilbeggan

Moate

Glasson

Athlone

0    9    18

which now houses a museum, open June to September 11.30am-6pm. If you want to immerse yourself further in times past wander into St. Mary's Church (C. of I.) where in imitation of the past, Tudor squires kneel with their ladies in perpetual prayer, the atmosphere is like that of a village church in England. You get the same atmosphere in the Church of Ireland church in **Raphoe**, Co. Donegal. The tower bell is one of those removed at the despoiling of **Clonmacnoise.**

Athlone is full of good shops and places where you can have a good jar and listen to *traditional* or *jazz music*. The Green Olive is very Guinness orientated, whilst Shaws Bar, decorative in the old fashioned style and providing a great venue for traditional music is sadly lacking in that respect. The Goldsmith Tavern sports a 16 piece jazz band in the summer, with jazz for regular fans on Sunday mornings all year round. You can get a very cheap and filling meal at lunchtime.

**Eating:** more touristy is the JOLLY MARINER BAR and RIVERSIDE RESTAURANT where you hear traditional music in the summer. The place to eat is the UPSTAIRS DOWNSTAIRS RESTAURANT in Northgate Street. Tel: (0902) 4074.

If you are staying in Athlone, you might find time to explore the many islands on Lough Ree. Ask down at the marina about hiring a boat to Hare Island, Inchmore, Inchbofin and Saints Island, all of which in ancient times were the homes of saints. *For short cruises* contact Mrs P Furey, 5 Retreat Heights, Athlone, Tel: (0902) 2894. For one week in April, Athlone is brimming with people when people come for the All-Ireland Amateur Drama Festival and the side shows. Bicycles can be hired from Hardimans, 48 Connaught St, and for breathtaking views take the High Road from **Ballykeeran** which looks down on Lough Ree.

**Moate** is an important market town right in the middle of cattle raising country and gets its name from the mound of Mota Grainne Oige which rises beside it, Mota was the wife of O'Melaghlin, a chief of the district. At **Bealin** on a little road between Moate and Athlone is a sculptured cross from the 8th century called the Twyford Cross and at Ballinderry Lake two miles east of Moate are some excavated crannogs. But this area is not very inspiring and it is better to read about it than explore it. So, unless you want to catch a train or bus from **Moate**, it is more interesting to press on towards **Mullingar** and **Castle Pollard**. If you are on your way to Dublin you might visit **Kilbeggan** and its famous monastery founded in the 6th century by St. Columcille; amongst its attractions are a Holy Well, and in the disused graveyard the Durrow High Cross.

**Eating:** at **Kinnegad,** you can get a good meal at HARRY'S Tel: (044) 75128, or at THE DUNNER ARMS.

**Mullingar** was a garrison town and has now become a noted *angling* centre with a busy, brightly painted main street, several excellent pubs and grocery shops that sell brie and salami! It is one of the nicest market towns in Ireland with a feeling of energy which is often lacking in some of the dreary, identical-looking towns scattered through the middle of Ireland. The countryside around Mullingar is great shooting, fishing and hunting country, but the new squires who lead the way in these sports are

German and French – which explains the brie! Three miles from Mullingar is Lough Ennell which John Betjeman mentioned in one of his longest poems, describing a modern scandal, fast becoming a legend, of Lady Concurry who was seduced for a bet.

The *trout* and *coarse fishing* in Lough Ennell, Owel, Derravaragh and several of the rivers is considered very good. Ask about *boat hire* in the Grenville Arms Hotel, Mullingar. There is a very interesting little museum in the Columb Barracks; you must seek permission to view from the officer in charge. Tel: (044) 8391. Five and a half miles from Mullingar, east of **Crookedwood Village** is St. Munna's Church, this fairy tale church was built in the 15th century and has a castle-like tower and battlements. The key is kept in the house opposite the graveyard. Twelve miles west of Mullingar on the Ballymore Road is Uisneach Hill, from where you can see a vast expanse of country. In ancient times, before Christianity, it was an important meeting place and the seat of kings, but now there is little left but a field with a broken wall around it. The Tourist Office for the whole of Westmeath is in Dublin Road, Mullingar. Tel: (044) 8650.

In **Crookedwood**, at the southern tip of Lough Derravaragh, the scenery is really charming. Take the little road through **Collinstown** to **Fore**, once an important ecclesiastical centre, it has the same magic atmosphere as **Glendalough**, but has not really been looked after. Seek out St. Feichins' Church which dates from the 10th century, it has a cross in a circle on the massive door lintel. The Benedictine priory is very well preserved and has an anchorite cell which was later turned into a family vault for the Grenville-Nugents of Delvin. From the hills around **Fore** are some lovely views of Meath, Cavan and Longford.

Three miles on is **Castlepollard**, another fishing centre; *trout fishing* is good in the White Lake, Lough Gore and Lough Sheelin (nine miles away). You can go *swimming* at 'The Cut', Lough Lene near Collinstown, or explore Tullynally Castle (which used to be Pakenham Hall) the seat of the Earls of Longford. The hall became a Gothic Castle in the 1840s; seen from a distance, in a romantic setting, it makes you think of a castle in an illustrated medieval manuscript. The castle has a fascinating collection of family memorabilia in the museum, kitchen and tower. Maria Edgeworth was an enthusiastic visitor here and described it as 'the seat of hospitality and the resort of fine society'. The grounds are beautiful and the castle looks down to Lough Derravaragh, which is one of the loughs associated with the story of the Children of Lir. It was here that their jealous stepmother transformed the children into swans. The castle grounds and the museum are open from June to September on Sundays and Bank Holidays from 2.30pm to 6pm.


## PLACES TO STAY IN COUNTY WESTMEATH

**Athlone** Tel: code 0902
Mrs Monaghan, Ballycreggan Hs, Kiltoom (off Athlone-Tuam Rd) Tel: 38101 (farmhouse).

Mrs Denby, Shelmalier, Cartrontroy, Tel: 2245
Mrs Farrell, Marian, Dublin Rd, Bonavalley, Tel: 4300
Mrs N Mangon, 7 Erris Grove, Willow Park, Tel: 75447
Newpark House, grade B hotel, Tel: 39130
Cloghanderry, grade B guesthouse, Tel: 2405
**Finea**
Mrs O'Reilly, Inny Side Hs, Tel: Finea 24
**Kinnegad**
Mrs P Cooney, Annascanan Hs, Killucan, Tel: (044) 74130
Mrs Miller, The Old Glebe Rectory, Killucan, Tel: (044) 74263
**Mullingar** Tel: Code (044)
Mrs Austin, Grasslands, Dysart, Tel: 26146 (farmhouse).
Miss Potterton, Craddenstown Hs, Raharney, Tel: 74165 (farmhouse).
Mrs Casey, Hill Top, Delvin Rd, Rathconnell, Tel: 8958 (all rooms with private bathroom).
Mrs T Carroll, Glencar Hse, Kilbeggan Rd, Tel: 8545
Mrs Nolan, Keadeen, Irishtown, Longford Rd.
Grenville Arms, grade B* hotel, Tel: 8563

Ask in the Tourist Office, **Mullingar** if you want accommodation near **Castlepollard.**

---

# County Wexford

If you are invading Ireland from the south, as the Normans did, you will land at **Rosslare Harbour**, the warmest, driest part of the whole country. The countryside of Wexford is said to be similar to that of Normandy with low hills, rich valleys and extremely tidy farms. Along the coast are gloriously sandy beaches and the centuries-old buildings have been treated with a bit more care than is usual in Ireland. Wexford is perhaps the most 'planted' of all the Irish counties; the foreigners moved in gradually and not with the systematic force with which the Scots moved into the north. In the ancient Baronies of Forth and Bargy, in the southeast corner, you may still come across a dialect which might make you think that by some amazing twist of time you were back in Chaucer's England. Obviously this is changing rapidly but you could start chatting with someone to whom Puck and Queen Mab were not just fairies out of a play by Shakespeare but beings that their parents or grandparents talked about.

Wexford, besides being an invasion target for the Normans, and so bursting with stories of battles between the Celts and the Anglo-Normans, has some more recent history to dwell on. You will notice that many of the towns have memorials to the heroes of the 1798 rebellion and

# WEXFORD

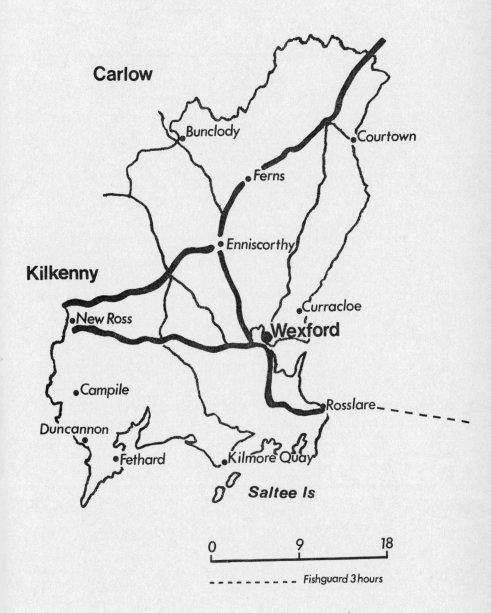

Carlow

Bunclody

Ferns

Courtown

Enniscorthy

Kilkenny

Curracloe

New Ross

Wexford

Campile

Rosslare

Duncannon

Fethard

Kilmore Quay

Saltee Is

0      9      18

- - - - - - - - - Fishguard 3 hours

179

the thousands of peasants who were mowed down like grass before the trained English soldiers. Nearby **Enniscorthy** is Vinegar Hill, often mentioned in ballads, where Father John Murphy and the rebels held off the English for a month.

*Birdlovers* will find herring gulls, kittiwakes, razorbills, puffin colonies, petrels, gannets, Greenland white fronted geese and terns. This only touches on the variety of fowl you can see on the **Saltee Islands**, Ireland's largest bird sanctuary and the slobland around **Wexford Harbour**. The locals are mad about *hurley* and they are reputedly the most skilful players in Ireland, so if you have a chance, try and watch one of their legendary matches, preferably against the Kerry boys.

**Wexford Town** is one of the most atmospheric of all Irish places with a past. It was originally settled by a Belgic tribe called the Menapii, and later by the Vikings who gave it the name Waesfjord. They ruled from the 9th to the 12th century and built up a flourishing port around the River Slaney and its outlet to the sea. Then the Normans, allies of Dermot McMurrough, captured it and built walls, castle and abbeys in their usual disciplined pattern. Many of the winding streets are so narrow that you could shake hands across them. Cromwell has left behind him here as bloody a reputation as in Drogheda. Most people come to Wexford for the Opera Festival held every year in October. Programmes of lesser known operas are produced with world famous soloists, an excellent local chorus and the R.T.E. Symphony Orchestra. Its reputation is world wide for originality and quality. Many fringe events, exhibitions, revues, and plays take place at the same time. For details write to the Tourist Office in Crescent Quay or Tel: (053) 23111.

The Maritime Museum floats in the Quay, and the displays are kept in a disused lightship. It is open during the festival and the months of July, August and September. Other things of interest are the 12th Century ruins of Selskar Abbey near Westgate Tower, (the only remaining fortified gateway of the original five). In 1172, Henry II spent Lent there, doing penance for the murder of Thomas Becket. Notice the John Barry Memorial on Crescent Quay. He was born ten miles away at Ballysampson and is remembered as the father of the American navy.

Three miles from town is a wild fowl reserve where the Greenland white fronted geese rest in winter. *Salmon* and *brown trout fishing* is good on the Slaney and *sea fishing* in the estuary. Your visit might coincide with a race meeting at **Bettyville**, ask locally about the more casual *races* held on the strands where you really see the local people in their element.

**Eating:** THE TALBOT HOTEL is without doubt, the best place to eat, followed closely by CAPTAIN WHITE'S SEAFOOD RESTAURANT. Both are expensive, so the less affluent should try the BOHEMIAN GIRL or THE GRANARY. WHITE'S HOTEL has a cheapish grill room and the more sophisticated SELSKAR RESTAURANT. It is well signposted from the Bank of Ireland on the Quay.

Evening entertainment consists of ballad singing in pubs such as the Mayflower Lounge, the Gaelic Bar, and the Stonebridge Lounge. For a simple chat and drink, with delicious sandwiches thrown in, try Tim's

Tavern, in South Main Street, on the corner of Cinema Lane. Night life begins to brighten up in the summer; there is cabaret and dinner theatre at the Talbot Hotel, seisiún, traditional Irish entertainment, at White's Hotel once a week at 9 pm. You can watch last year's films at the Abbey cinema. Early closing for shops is on Thursday and the Tourist and room Reservation Service is in Crescent Quay, Tel: (053) 23111.

Three miles south of **Wexford**, near **Murrintown** is Johnstown Castle. Built in 19th century Gothic style, it is now a State Agricultural College and visitors can tour round the landscaped gardens, lakes and the folk museum.

Five miles north of **Rosslare Harbour** is the resort town of **Rosslare**, with six miles of curving strand. It has a championship *golf course* and the usual resort amenities.

**Eating:** an excellent restaurant in KELLY'S STRAND HOTEL. Reservations essential, Tel: (053) 32114. The coastline beyond, starting with **Lady's Island** is well worth travelling around. In a sea inlet, Lady's Island is linked to the mainland by a causeway. The rare roseate tern can be heard, if not seen, and the woolly cotton- weed plant still grows on the sea bar, even though it died out on the English south coast a couple of centuries ago. The island is sacred to the Blessed Virgin and is still a favourite place of pilgrimage. Nearby **Carne** has a rather good restaurant 'THE BAKEHOUSE' Tel: (053) 31234.

**Kilmore Quay** is an attractive thatched fishing village where you can get a boat, weather permitting, to the fowl-full Saltee Islands. You can join in a *fishing* spree for mackerel, sole, ray, and plaice, run by the Sea Angling Club. The view from the harbour along the headland looks rather like the landscapes by the Norwich School of painters. Keeping close to the sea the road passes through **Carrick**, and you can visit historic **Bannow**, the first corporate town established by the Normans. The town is now buried deep under the shifting sands, a process which began in the 17th century, though the benighted steeple and a couple of chimneys still returned MPs to the Irish Parliament until 1798! All that is left today of this proud Norman town is the ruin of St. Mary's church and an old graveyard.

**Fethard** is a quiet resort and there is a lovely walk over the sea pinks and grass to the ramparts at Baginbun, which the Normans hastily built to repel the Norsemen and the Gaels. The Normans won the day by driving a herd of cattle into the advancing army. The road continues down to the tip of Hook Head where the 700 year old lighthouse still keeps the light burning. There is a passenger and cyclist ferry only which ploughs backwards and forwards from **Ballyhack** to **Passage East** on the Waterford shore.

Near to **Campile** is Dunbrody Abbey beside the winding River Barrow. It is one of the most underestimated ruins in Ireland, and was built by the Monks of St. Mary's Dublin in 1182. The West door is magnificent and so are the lancet windows over the high altar. **New Ross**, on the river Barrow, has some ancient gabled houses and a medieval feel to it. It was built by Isobel, Strongbow's daughter, and has seen fighting against Cromwell and during the 1798 rebellion. Though there was much brutal-

181

ity on both sides, the massacre of Scullabogue is still not forgotten; hundreds of British prisoners were burnt alive by the frightened rebels after they had fled from the fight in **New Ross**. Visit the **John F Kennedy Park** and **Arboretum,** a superb picnicking place with marvellous young trees and shrubs, (open May-August everyday, April and September, only weekends). **Eating:** you might want to cruise along the river valleys of **New Ross** and **Waterford** and enjoy a delicious meal at the same time. Tel: (051) 21712, bookings essential. Lunch and cruise from £IR 7.50.

The Kennedy ancestral home is actually in **Dunganstown.** In 1848, Jack Kennedy left his family homestead for a new life in America after the dreadful years of the famine, from there the Kennedy success story needs no further telling, suffice to say, his great grandson is remembered all over the world, and especially in Ireland. There are plenty of singing pubs in New Ross and you can go pony trekking from Horetown House Equitation Centre at Foulksmills.

**Eating:** THE CELLAR RESTAURANT in the same place, serves generous country house meals. Tel: (051) 63633, whilst THE HORSE AND HOUNDS RESTAURANT in **Ballynabola** has unbeatable prawns. From **New Ross** you could follow the old N129 along the side of the Blackstairs Mountains. Sometimes you meet a lone deer making its way between these hills and the Wicklow Mountains; the tiny farms on these slopes are more reminiscent of the west than the neat prosperity of the rest of Wexford. Stop in **Killane** at Rackards Pub, one of the friendliest traditional pubs in Ireland; it is a local dive with no hint of 'the singing pubs for tourists' style.

**Enniscorthy** is the most attractive town in Co. Wexford, it is a thriving market town on the River Slaney presided over by Vinegar Hill from which there is a great view of the river and rich farming land around. You might time your arrival for the Strawberry Fair in early July. The county museum is in the Castle built by Raymonde le Gros and later owned by the Roche family. It has an interesting folk section. All around Co. Wexford the mummers or rhymers act out in dance the characters of Irish heroes to the rhythm of Irish reels; this tradition actually sprung from England In other parts of Ireland, custom differs; the mummers dress themselves in strawsuits and tinsel and act out the perpetual struggle of good over evil. Ask at the Tourist Office in Castle Hill Tel: (054) 2341, or in any of the other Wexford towns if you are interested in seeing them in action.

**Curracloe** strand on the way back to **Wexford** is one of the nicest for bathing, it has six miles of golden beach and attractive whitewashed houses. **Eating:** ESKER LODGE, Ballinesker, three quarters of a mile from Curracloe is a family run restaurant good for a binge. Tel: (053) 37171. The Blackwater is another attractive resort.

**Ferns** is rather like **Swords** in Co. Dublin, full of memories and former glory. In the 12th century the King of Leinster, Dermot McMurrough (the one who invited the Normans to invade) made it his capital and founded a rich abbey there, but after the Norman conquest, the town declined. The 13th century castle is one of the finest of its type in Ireland.

**Gorey** and **Courtown** are tourist orientated and conveniently placed for those who want to visit the beauty spots of Co. Wicklow. Hunting, fishing, golf, theatre, dance, seisiún are all available; ask at the Tourist Office, Lower Main Street, Gorey Tel: (055) 21248. Open June/July/ August. MARFIELD HOUSE has earned itself a good reputation for food. Tel: (055) 21572.

## PLACES TO STAY IN COUNTY WEXFORD

**Arthurstown**
Youth Hostel, Cottages No. 1,2,4, Coastguard Station.
Mrs Cummins, St. Helens Country Hs, Kilhile, Tel: (051) 88125
**Boolavogue**
Mrs Gough, Ballyorley Hs, Tel: (054) 6287 (farmhouse).
**Curracloe**
Esker Lodge, grade B Guesthouse, Tel: (053) 37171
**Courtown Harbour**
Mrs Doyle, St. Jude, 25 Skuna Bay,
**Donaghmore**
Seamount Hs, grade B guesthouse, Tel: (055) 25128
**Enniscorthy**
Mrs Healy, Glen View Farmhouse, Glonhaston, Tel: (054) 2377
Mrs Colliver, The Haven, Monart, Tel: (054) 2011
Mrs Delany, St. Judes, Munfin, Tel: (054) 2011
Miss Heffernan, Ivella, Rectory Rd, Tel: (054) 2475
**Ferns**
Mrs Breen, Clone Hs, Tel: (054) 6113 (farmhouse).
**Fethard on Sea**
Naomh Seosamh, grade B hotel, Tel: (051) 07129
Foxfield Hs, grade B guesthouse, Tel: (051) 97118
**Foulksmills**
Mrs Crosbie, farmhouse, Tel: (051) 63616
Mrs Redmond, Mill Hs, Tel: (051) 63683 (farmhouse).
Mrs Young, Horetown Hs, Tel: (051) 63633 (riding holidays).
**Gorey**
Mrs Magourty, Meldan Farm, Tel: (055) 21535
**Kilmore Quay**
Mrs Bates, Coral Hs, Grange, Milmore Tel: (053) 29640
Hotel Saltees, grade B, Tel: (053) 29601
**New Ross**
The Crosbie Family, Park View Farm, Curraghduff, Campile, Tel: (051) 88178
Misses Fitzpatrick, Ballywilliam Hs, Tel: (051) 24542
Misses T&M Kent, Aclamon, Campile, Tel: (051) 88235
Mrs Furlong, Mountain View, Gobbinstown, Tel: (051) 24552
Mrs Michels, Venroode, (Off William St.), Lr. South Knock, Tel: (051) 21446

**Rosslare Harbour**
Mrs Threadgold, St. Josephs, Kilrane, Tel: 33285
Mrs Roche, Four Seasons, Hayeslands, Tel: (053) 33132
Mrs Walshe, Kilrane Hs, Kilrane, Tel: (053) 33135
**Wexford**
Misses E&H Bennett, Johnstown, Castlebridge, Tel: (053) 22726 (overlooking bird sanctuary).
Mrs Allen, Westmount, Westgate, Tel: (053) 22167
Mrs Browne, Carrig Hill Hs, Barntown, Tel: (053) 23304
Hollyville Hs, grade B guesthouse, off Francis St, Tel: (053) 22705
**Binge Places**
Marfield Hs, Gorey, Tel: (055) 21572 grade A
The Talbot, grade A hotel, Wexford, Tel: (053) 22566

# County Wicklow

Wicklow is a mountainous county known as the 'garden of Ireland' because of the variety, and diversity of its charms. Certainly the drive out of Dublin, south towards Bray and the Wicklow Hills is very scenic, perhaps because of the great contrast to the hustle and bustle of Dublin city life. During winter months the Wicklow Hills are severe and savage, but look at their beautiful lines: some sharp and conical, others long and gentle. In the mountain hollows there are deep lakes such as Lough Dan, Lough Naharaghan and Lough Tay. The hills are full of streams which tumble from the remote, harsh high ground to the green valleys.

**Bray** is one of Ireland's principal coastal resorts and has all sorts of amenities. Bear in mind however that it is very tourist orientated and prices are in line with this image. Three miles west of **Bray**, is Powerscourt Estate and the gardens at **Enniskerry**. Tragically the house, one of the most beautiful in Ireland, was gutted by fire, in the 1950s. However the gardens remain and the setting of the house, facing the Sugar Loaf Mountain, makes it an unforgettable sight: you walk towards the house thinking it is still intact, but it is a mere shell. The Italianate and Japanese style gardens, and the Monkey Puzzle Avenue, are all open every day between Easter and October 10.30am-5.30pm. Admission adults £IR1, children (5-16 years) 45p. On the Powerscourt Estate there is a breathtakingly beautiful waterfall, the highest in Ireland. The water falls from 400 feet into a pretty stream which winds its way through numerous walks. Another local beauty spot is the Glen of the Dargle to the west of **Bray**. In the thick woods a massive rock juts out over a narrow defile which leads along the river; this spot has been nicknamed 'the lovers leap'.

In Bray itelf there is plenty to do. You can enjoy *golf, tennis, bowling, riding, fishing* (river and sea), *sailing;* contact the local Tourist

# WICKLOW

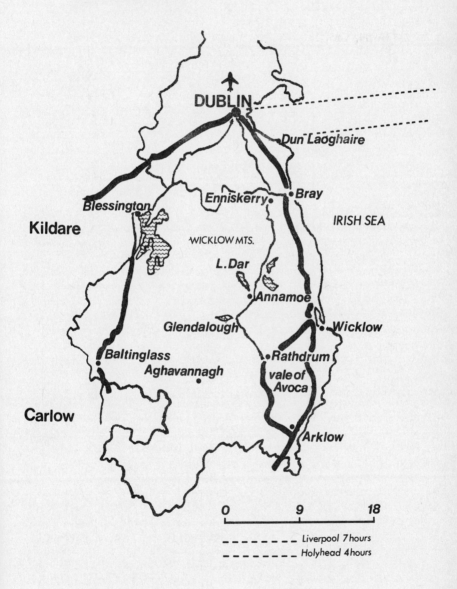

DUBLIN

Dun Laoghaire

Blessington

Kildare

Enniskerry · Bray

IRISH SEA

WICKLOW MTS.

L. Dar

Annamoe

Glendalough

Wicklow

Baltinglass

Aghavannagh

Rathdrum

vale of Avoca

Carlow

Arklow

0         9         18

– – – – – – – Liverpool 7 hours

– – – – – – – Holyhead 4 hours

Information Centre, Tel: (01) 867128, half day closing Wednesday. Choice of accommodation includes caravan parks at Shankill and Killiney.

From Enniskerry follow the road through the Scalp – a glacier formed gap. The forests surrounding the Scalp have some lovely trails. In **Glencree Village** there is a yoghourt making factory; for tours around the factory you must make arrangements through the Tourist Office, Tel: (01) 867128. If you want to glut yourself on forest scenery take the 'Military Road' which runs through the mountains from Rathfarnham to Aghavannagh. This road bisects the country and takes you through mysterious glens and remote valleys; you see turf cutting country and some stupendous mountain scenery. At Laragh the military road joins another coming down the valley of the King's River. Near here, north east, is the village of **Roundwood**, which is reputedly the highest village in Ireland being 780 feet above sea level. The high ground in these mountainous areas was the realm of the 'mountainy men' – the Irish who had been deprived of their lands in the plain by the English settlers. Up here in the hills the rule of Dublin Castle had little influence and the Gaelic customs lingered on.

**Glendalough**, the valley of two lakes has overwhelmed people with its peace and isolation for many centuries. An enclave of holiness amongst the wilderness. The composition is unforgettable and uniquely Irish, it is high in the hills, with two small lakes cupped in a hollow, a tall round tower and a grey stone church. The round towers in Ireland have been a distinctive and curious feature of Irish architecture (read Petrie on the subject if you are interested). The generally accepted theory is that they were built as bolt holes from the plundering Danes. The tower doors are high off the ground, so that the ladder could be drawn up after the community had scrambled up. At Glendalough you have the remains of a famous monastic school, founded by St Kevin in 520 AD. The story goes that the saint came here to recover from the effort involved in rejecting the advances of a beautiful girl named Kathleen. However she chased him to the monastery and he had to hit her with stinging nettles to lessen her ardour. Another version of the tale recounted by Thomas (Tom) Moore is that he cooled her off by pushing her into the lake. Despite Kevin's wish to be a hermit, the saint's refuge became a centre of learning and later a place of pilgrimage. You can see St. Kevin's kitchen, the church with its corbelled roof, and the ruins of the cathedral with its 12th century chancel. More intrepid visitors should walk up to St. Kevin's Bed; this is the cell where St. Kevin stayed before the seven churches of the settlement were built. The views of the lakes are remarkable. You can get to Glendalough by bus from Dublin. Buses run daily from 1st June to 15th September leaving from St. Stephen's Green 11.30am and leaving from Glendalough at 4.30pm (Tel: (01) 818119 for further details).

Further down stream from **Glendalough** is the little priory of St Saviour, a 12th century foundation associated with St. Lawrence O'Toole. The cathedral's east window shows signs of Danish influence. Continuing south on the military road, you go through **Rathdrum** and enchanting woodland before you turn north to **Wicklow Town**. On the way you might visit **Avondale**, birthplace of that great Irishman Charles Stewart Parnell. The county town, **Wicklow** overlooks a crescent shaped shingle bay. Maurice Fitzgerald built the Black Castle when he was granted land here; and there are ruins of a Franciscan friary. The town is a good centre for *golfing, horse riding,* and *fishing;* for further details consult the Wicklow Community Tourist Office, Market Square, Tel: (0404) 4169. At **Ashford**, four miles north of **Wicklow**, you can find out about more adventurous pursuits. The Tiglin Adventure Centre (Tel: (0404) 4169 for details) offers weekend and weekly courses in *orienteering, mountain climbing* and *hang-gliding.* Mount Usher gardens, renowned for the exotic trees and shrubs, can be found in Ashford (open Monday-Saturday 10am-5.30pm all year. Sundays, May-September 2pm-5.30pm). Admission: adults 75p, children (5-16) 35p.

Travelling further down the coast you will reach **Arklow**, which is a *fishing* centre and a popular resort. Visit the Arklow Maritime Museum if you are interested, open June-September daily 10am-5pm. Admission: adults 20p, children 5p. You can also visit the famous Arklow pottery centre. For full details Tel: (0402) 2134. For evening entertainment check in the *Wicklow People,* the local weekly newspaper, and this advice goes for anyone staying in the area.

Inland, retracing your footsteps towards **Rathdrum**, visitors will pass through the Vale of Avoca, immortalized in Thomas Moore's poem 'The meeting of the Waters' (where the rivers Avonmore and Avonbeg meet). You can understand the appeal of such scenery to the Romantics of the day. High above Avoca Village and the rivers is Castle Howard, and the Motte Stone, which is a glacial boulder of granite perched on the summit of an 800 foot hill; it commands a spectacular view. Along the valley road are shops selling the well known Avoca weave rugs which make lovely presents. You can visit the weaving centre in Avoca village, which is open every day from May to October. **Woodenbridge** at the end of the 'sweet vale' was the site of a gold rush in 1796, and supplied much gold for Ireland's earlier goldsmiths. Nearby Croghan Mountain was also the scene of another 18th century gold rush.

Wicklow offers the perfect setting for any walking enthusiast. Glencree acts as stage one of the Wicklow Way (covering the eastern flanks of the Dublin/Wicklow Mountains the largest area of unbroken high ground in Ireland). Useful walking books are listed below:

1. The Open Road by J A Malone, 1950.
2. Walking in Wicklow by J A Malone, 1964.
3. The Irish Walk Guides/No 4 by Herman, Casey and Kavanagh, 1979 (£IR1.25).
4. The Scouting Trail, 1980 £IR2.50 (available at the Scout Shop, in Dublin).
5. Dublin and Wicklow Mountains Access Routes for Hill Walkers, Irish Ramblers Club, 19.

**West Wicklow** is relatively unexplored, and ruggedly attractive. Travelling south west out of Dublin one comes to **Blessington**, which is a small town on the northern arm of the Poulaphouca reservoir. This huge reservoir, formed by the damming of the River Liffey, is picturesque enough to warrant a visit. Other attractions are Russborough House and its art collection. The house is the most perfect Palladian styled house in Ireland, and it houses a magnificent art collection which belongs to Sir Alfred and Lady Beit. It is open between 2.30pm-6.30pm on Sundays and Bank Holidays from Easter to the end of October; on Wednesdays from June to September; and on Saturdays from July to August. You can tour the main rooms and the art collection. Admission: adults 80p, children 40p. You can see the bedrooms and an outstanding collection of Irish silver for an extra 30p. For information Tel: Naas 65239.

South from Blessington you will come to the Poulaphouca lake, which forms the Wicklow gap, and the lovely Hollywood Glen, before you arrive at **Laragh**. The nearby Glen of Imaal is beautiful. **Baltinglass**, which lies 19 miles south of Blessington, has a transport museum (Tel: (01) 311287/977543) and a late romanesque Cistercian Abbey.

While you are in the south eastern region take note that the main Tourist Office is in Dun Laoghaire and they should be able to clear up any difficulties and supply information. May to September Tel: (01) 8069 84, October to April, Tel: (01) 807048.

**Eating:** because of its proximity to Dublin there are many expensive, haute cuisine retaurants. If you are based in Bray and want to enjoy a moderately expensive evening out try CAPTAIN'S TABLE RESTAURANT, Sea Front, Tel: (01) 862585. For fast service there is BAMBI'S RESTAURANT, Queensboro' Rd. Tel: Bray (01) 867606; it is also a delicatessan and bakery. It is worth going to Greystones or Enniskerry if you want to eat out of Bray. There is ENNISCREE LODGE, (01) 863 542. Woodland Hotel, ELYSEE RESTAURANT, Greystones, Tel: (01) 874423. Round Wicklow town there is the HUNTERS HOTEL, Rathnew, Co. Wicklow, Tel: (0404) 4106; it is on the banks of the River Glen. More expensive is ARMSTRONG'S BARN at Annamoe, Tel: (0404) 5194. In Wicklow Town itself you can get a quick service meal in THE STEAK AND ALE BAR at the GRAND HOTEL, Tel: (0404) 2337 and the à la carte menu runs from £IR5.50. THE OLD RECTORY RESTAURANT, Tel: Wicklow (0404) 2048 specialises in French cuisine and sea food dishes.

## PLACES TO STAY IN COUNTY WICKLOW

**Arklow**
Mrs F N Sharpe, Ballinaskea, Tel: (0402) 2242 B & B Own beach.
Mrs D Forster, Keliba, Beech Rd, Raheen, Tel: (0402) 2737 B & B, off the road.
Mrs E Porter, Iona, Ferrybank (town), Tel; (0402) 2197 B & B.
Hotels: The Bridge and Royal are cheap, Tel: (0402) 2458 and (0402) 2451, both are grade B.
Guesthouses: Butler Hs, Tel: (0402) 2143. Grade C.
**Ashford**

Mrs M Byrne, Ballyknocken Hs, Glenealy, Tel: (0404) 5627 full board, tennis.
Bel Air Hotel, Tel: (0404) 4109 à la carte meals, room with bath, grade B*.
**Avoca**
Mrs F Sutton, Rose Linn Farm, Kilmacoo, Tel: (0402) 5247 B & B,
Mrs M Caswell, The Arbours, Tel: (0402) 5294 B & B.
Riverview Guesthouse Tel: (0402) 5181, grade B
Vale View Hotel, Tel: (0402) 5236. Rooms with private bath are expensive, grade B*
**Blessington**
Mrs O Boothman, Miley Hall, Tel: (045) 65119 scenic.
Mrs K. Hayden, Lake Forest, Burgage, Tel: (045) 6517 B & B near Russborough.
**Bray**
Mrs M J Crombie, 5 Sidmonton Sq. Tel: (01) 863727, high tea.
Mrs A Fanning, Neptune Hs, Esplanade, Tel: (01) 860346, high tea.
Mrs M McGrory, Innisfree, Esplanade, Tel: (01) 863058
Crofton Bray Head, Tel: (01) 867182. For rooms with bath, extra payable.
Doon-a-Lawn, and Esplanade Hotels are cheaper hotels. Tel: (01) 882058 and (01) 862056
Also cheap, but less classy, the Antler, Tel: (01) 867472 and Mellifont Tel: (01) 862362
**Dunlavin**
Mrs I Waters, Rahoon Farm, Colbinstown, Tel: (045) 53138
**Enniskerry**
Mrs E Cummins, Corner Hs, Tel: (01) 860149
**Greystones**
Mrs S Healy, 4 Ashlawn, Kilcoole, Tel: (01) 876558
There are two expensive hotels, La Touche and Woodlands.
**Rathdrum**
Mrs E O'Brien, Abhainn Mor, Corballis, Tel: (0404) 6330
Mrs E Sheehan, The Hawthorns, Corballis, Tel: (0404) 6217
**Roundwood**
Mrs M Malone, Ballincor Hs, Derralossary, Tel: (01) 818168 near Glendalough.
Mrs N O'Brien, Woodside, Tel: (01) 818195
Derralossary guesthouse Tel: (01) 818133, à la carte meals.
**Wicklow**
Mrs A Bittel, Knockrobin Hs, Tel: (0404) 23447, restaurant.
Mrs C Crennan, Sea Crest Hs, Ashtown Lane, Tel: (0404) 27721, 4 rooms with bath.
Mrs E Wright, Bella Vista, St Patrick's Road, Upper. Tel: (0404) 2325, good views.
**Wicklow Town**
Mrs G Murphy, Marine Villa, Church Hill, Tel: (0404) 3252
Mrs E Tallon, Sunnyside, Bayview Road. Tel (0404) 2417
Mrs A Solon, Heather Ridge, Dunbur Road. Tel: (0404) 2656

There are two medium priced hotels. The Grand Tel: (0404) 2337 and Strabreaga (0404) 2383

Also the Old Rectory guesthouse, Tel: (0404) 2048 with lots of baths (expensive).

**Woodenbridge**

Two hotels: grade B, The Valley, Tel: (0402) 5200 and the Woodenbridge Tel: (0402) 51463, both moderately priced.

**Youth hostels**

Ashford, Tiglin, open all year.

Aughrim, Aghavannagh Hs, open all year.

Blessington, Baltyboys, open all year.

Donard, Ballinclea, open all year.

Enniskerry, Lackan Hs, Knockree, open all year.

Enniskerry, Stone Hs, Glencree, open all year.

Glendalough, open all year.

Greenane, Glenmalure, Greenane open weekends only.

Valleymount, Glenbridge Lodge, open all year.

**Binge places**

There are many in Wicklow, you need quite a few punt to fuel your expedition:

Delgany Inn B* grade hotel: Delgany Tel: (01) 875701

La Touche, grade A hotel, Greystones, Tel: (01) 874401

Avonbrae Hs, grade A, guesthouse, Rathdrum, Tel; (0404) 6198

The Old Rectory, Wicklow, Tel: (0404) 2048

Downshire House Hotel, Blessington, grade A, Tel: (045) 65199

# PART V
# THE PROVINCE OF
# MUNSTER

**Munster** is a mixture of everything you consider Irish: the purples of the mountains melt into chessboards of cornfields, in which the stooks stand like golden pieces. Houses are whitewashed, glens are deep and the coastline is made ragged by sandy bays and rocky cliffs. It is a land of extremes, a large placid fertile plain, brooding mountain scenery, luxurious vegetation and harsh barren land. The extreme south westerly coast is swept by westerly gales, trees have been distorted into twisted bent shapes. The moonscape of the Burren contrasts with the softness of Killarney, so the dairy land of Cashel of the Kings contrasts with the thrashing sea around Dingle and the Iveragh Peninsula. This is the island of the Mumonians, the ster suffix is a Scandinavian addition to the more ancient name of Muma, as it is with Ulster and Leinster. The people are warm, relaxed and musical, they are also backward-looking and quarrelsome. The Dubliners say that Munster is a little England. The Anglo-Normans certainly had a part in moulding the towns, so did some of the adventurer types of the Elizabethan times, but Cork city is the creation of lively Irish minds, whether original Celts or later arrivals. Cork people think their city ought to be the capital rather than Dublin! You can exchange the activity of the city for the gentler pace of the countryside, for within an hour's drive, you may come across those west Cork women who still wear the heavy cloaks which their great grandmothers wore, the hoods pulled almost over their faces to hide from unwelcome glances and to keep out the rain.

The Irish have a way with words but the Kerryman is something else, from the cradle he is taught that language was invented to conceal thought! At least this is what the rest of Ireland thinks, and not surprisingly, Kerry jokes, not Irish jokes, are common. If you are interested in botany Munster has a great collection of southern and northern plants growing together, notice the bog violet and arbutus in Kerry and the alpine/arctic plants of the Burren.

---

# County Clare

Clare was known in the past as the Kingdom of Thormond, the whole county still echoes with signs left over from a tempestuous past. There are nearly two hundred castles and 2,300 stone forts or cahers dating back to pre-Celtic times. In the tales of ancient Ireland the countryside was fraught with the battles of the O'Briens, O'Deas, MacNamaras and MacMahons who, when they weren't waging fierce war on foreigners, filled in the time by fighting amongst themselves. Yet it was a Clare man, Brian Boru, who is still remembered today as the one who was able to draw all the fighting factions together to defeat the Vikings at Clontarf in 1014. Clare is part of the wild west of Ireland, when Cromwell heard that a large part of Clare had no trees to hang a man from, nor enough water to drown him, nor enough earth to bury him, he thought it would be just the place to banish the rebellious Irish. Clare is wild and beautiful and unspoilt by tourism, even though it boasts the huge Shannon Airport on its edge.

Nearly three quarters of the county boundary is formed by water, its neighbour in the south is Co. Kerry, but they are separated by the Shannon Estuary, though there is a car ferry from **Tarbert** to **Killimer**. Most people go inland, almost to the centre of Ireland, to find the Limerick bridge and then only shoot through Clare on their way to the delights of Connemara. But Clare has its plunging cliffs and strange karst landscapes to attract the more adventurous. The **Barony of Burren** looks like some misplaced section of the moon, white, crevassed and barren, but springy turf grows in the earth filled fissures and cattle manage to graze quite happily around the cracks that could catch them in a leg breaking fall. In late May the place becomes starred with gentians, cranesbill, geraniums, and orchids. Arctic Alpine mountain avens sprawl lavishly over the rocks and Irish saxifrage tufts cover sea sprayed boulders. No one has yet been able to explain fully how such a profusion of northern and southern plants came to grow together, some of which are unknown in continental Europe. The temperate winter and warm limestone beneath the turf suit the plants, and their colonies grew up helped by the barrenness of a land which was never cultivated. There are many places to sea-bathe and fish around the coast, whilst the scenery and walking around the lakes and hills of Slieve Bernagh is some of the best you will ever find.

**Killaloe** is right on the great Shannon and connected to Tipperary by a bridge of thirteen arches. Not far from the bridge is the gem of **Killaloe**,

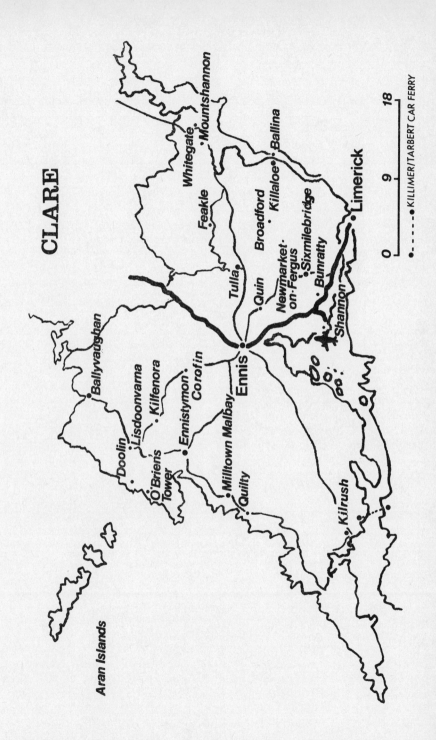

CLARE

Aran Islands

Ballyvaughan

Doolin

Lisdoonvarna · Kilfenora

O'Briens
Tower

Ennistymon · Corofin

Milltown Malbay

Quilty

Ennis

Tulla

Feakle

Whitegate · Mountshannon

Quin

Newmarket-
on-Fergus

Broadford

Killaloe · Ballina

Sixmilebridge

Bunratty

Shannon

Limerick

Kilrush

0        9        18

● ----- ● KILLIMER/TARBERT CAR FERRY

193

the fine 12th century cathedral built by Donal O'Brien on the site of an earlier church founded in the 6th century by Lua. There is a magnificent Hiberno-Romanesque door which is better than anything else of its kind in Ireland; the bold and varied carvings of animals and foliage on the shafts and capitals, and the pattern of the chevrons on the arches are not merely decoration, they are so modelled as to make the entire conception an integral and organic whole. Nearby, is the shaft of a cross bearing a runic and ogham inscription of about the year 1,000 AD. The view from the top of the square tower is superb, you can see all the mountains that crowd round the gorge of Killaloe and the beautiful Lough Derg. In the grounds of the cathedral is St. Flannan's Oratory with a lovely high stone roof, a splendid contrast to the Cruciform Cathedral with its Gothic doorway. The oratory has a Romanesque west door but the inside is dark and gloomy. The Roman Catholic church standing high above the town is believed to be on the site of Kincora, the great palace of Brian Boru where riotous banquets were the order of the day. Inside the church are some good Harry Clarke stained glass windows and in the grounds is Saint Molua's Oratory, reconstructed here after being removed from an island in the Shannon, before it was flooded by the great Shannon Hydro-electric scheme in 1929.

A mile or so out of **Killaloe** is Crag Liath, known locally as the Grianan overlooking the road north wards to Scarriff. It was written in 1014 in the annals of Loch Ce that this was the dwelling place of Aoibhill, the celebrated banshee of the Dalcassian Kings of Munster. A banshee (bean-sidhe) or fairy woman is a ghost peculiar to people of old Irish stock; her duty is to warn the family she attends of the approaching death of one of its members. Thus it was that Aoibhill appeared to Brien Boru on the eve of Clontarf and told him that he would be killed the next day, though not in the fury of the battle, which is exactly what happened, for he was murdered in his tent when the battle was over and the victory his. All around is beauty; woods, water and mountain and the short climb to the fort is lovely.

If you crossed the Shannon at Limerick, you will find yourself heading for **Bunratty Castle** on the Newmarket road. Bunratty is a splendid towerhouse standing beside a small stone bridge over River Ratty. The present castle dates from 1460, though it is at least the fourth to have been built on the same spot. It was built by the MacNamaras, fell into the hands of the O'Briens, and then occupied by the parliamentarian Admiral Penn, the father of William Penn who founded Pennsylvania. After years of neglect it was bought by Lord Gort who restored it with the help of Bord Fáilte and the Office of Public Works. They have managed to recreate a 15th century atmosphere and there is a wonderful collection of 14th - 17th century furniture. It is open daily from 9.30am - 5pm (£1 entrance) and in the evenings it provides a memorable setting for expensive medieval style banquets. Tel: 061-61788 for further details. In the grounds surrounding the castle, a folk park has gradually grown up with examples of houses from every part of the Shannon region; many of them were re-erected after being saved from demolition during the Shannon Airport extension. *The Folk Park* is open from 9.30am - 5pm.

You can see buttermaking, basket weaving and all the traditional rural skills which made people so self sufficient in days gone by. There is a very good collection of agricultural machinery.

**Broadford, Tulla** and **Feakle** are all pleasant villages where you can stay in farms or town and country houses and explore the Clare lakelands. Lough Garney is especially beautiful with its wooded shores; most of the loughs are well stocked with bream and pike. There is a 'Rent an Irish Cottage' centre at Broadford. Near Feakle the witty and outrageous poet Brian Merriman earned his livelihood as a school master and produced his masterpiece 'The Midnight Court'.

The pretty village of **Mountshannon** on Lough Derg is a centre for pleasure cruisers and a favourite haunt of *anglers*, it is also possible to get a boat to Iniscealtra, about half a mile from the shore. The Christian settlement is attributed to St. Caimin who lived on the island in about 640. Today there are five ancient churches, a round tower, saints graveyard, a hermit's cell and a Holy Well. The church beside the incomplete round tower has a wonderful Hiberno-Romanesque chancel arch, impressive in it's simplicity. The festival at the Holy Well was famous for the Bacchanalian revelry that accompanied it. It was stopped because the local squireens would steal the girls at it! The memorial stones are still in place in the saint's graveyard for the period covering the 8th to the 12th century. Unfortunately the whole effect is rather spoiled by the modern tombstones and garish plastic wreathes. At Mountshannon, there is a youth hostel, a country house hotel and some very good local restaurants and bars.

**Newmarket on Fergus**, takes its name from a 19th century O'Brien, Lord Inchiquin who was very enthusiastic about horses. In the grounds of his Neo-Gothic mansion, now a luxury hotel, is Moohaun Fort, one of the largest Iron Age hill forts in Europe, enclosing 27 acres with three concentric walls. You can get to it through Dromaland Forest signposted off the road to Ennis. Maybe it was people from this fort who buried the enormous hoard of gold ornaments which were discovered nearby in 1854 by workmen digging the way for a rail line to be laid. Unfortunately, much of it was melted down, probably by dealers, but a few pieces 'of the great Clare gold find' have found their way to the National Museum in Dublin.

At **Craggaunowen** off the Quin-Sixmilebridge Road is a reconstructed Crannog or lake dwelling and a four storey tower house; this complex is open daily from April to the end of September with a small admission charge. Nearby is Knappoque Castle on the same lines as Bunratty Castle with medieval banquets in the evenings. Contact Castle Tours at Tel: (061) 61788. At the next crossroads a right turn leads to Quin Abbey which is very well preserved and so subject to countless coach tours. It was founded for the Franciscans in 1402 and incorporated with a great castle built by one of the de Clares. Buried here is the famous duellist with the wonderful name of Fireballs MacNamara.

**Ennis** (Inis: river meadow) the county capital is sited on a great bend of the River Fergus. The streets are narrow and winding and in the centre is a hideous monument to a great Irishman, Daniel O'Connell. He contested the Clare seat in 1828 even though the repressive laws of the time disqualified Catholics, and he won the election with a resounding victory. Ennis Friary is rich in sculptures and decorated tombs although the building itself has been rather mucked about with additions and renovation. On one of the tombs is the sculptured device of a cock crowing, standing on the rim of a pot he cries in Irish 'the son of the Virgin is safe', a reference to the story of the cock that rose from the pot in which it was cooking to proclaim that 'Himself above on the Cross would rise again' to the astonishment of the two Roman soldiers who had questioned the prophesy. The Friary was founded for the Franciscans by Donchadh O'Brien, King of Thormond, just before his death in 1242. You get the key to the friary from the office at the Franciscan Church, Francis St. There is a small museum open Monday to Friday in Harmony Row which specialises in objects associated with famous Clare people. The shops are closed on Thursday. Information on *salmon fishing, golfing, walks* etc. is obtained from the tourist office in Bank Place. Tel: Ennis 21366. Fans of Percy French can go and look at the old west Clare steam engine immortalized in his song 'Are you right there, Michael, are you right?'.

**Eating:** you can get a very good meal in the OLD GROUND HOTEL and a quick snack at BROGAN'S.

On the way to **Corofin** is the famous religious settlement of Dysert O Dea. It was started in the 7th century by St Tola, but he probably lived in a cell of wattle and daub; the present ruin is a much altered Hiberno-Romanesque church with a badly reconstructed west doorway that now stands in the south wall. The door is sumptuously carved, and the arch has a row of stone heads with Mongolian features with proud but rather sad expressions. The idea for the heads came from Northern France. Monks and Scholars moving between Ireland and the Continent had much more influence on building and style than previously thought. Beside the church is the stump of a round tower and about a hundred yards east is a High Cross belonging to the 12th century; Christ is shown in a pleated robe and below him is a bishop with a crozier. **Corofin** village lies between two pretty lakes, the Inchiquin and Atedaun. There is good *fishing* and plenty of caves, for it is marginal shale and limestone countryside in which the River Fergus plays some tricks.

Nearby is **Kilnaboy** where the remains of a round tower rest in the graveyard of a ruined church. Over the south door is a Sheela-na-Gig, a grotesque and erotic figure of a woman. These Sheela-na-Gigs are often carved and fixed to ecclestiastical buildings, probably as a sort of crude warning to the monks and laity of the power of feminine sexuality. There are many gallery graves around here. A mile north-west from Kilnaboy, just over a stile and in a field is the Tau Cross, shaped like a T, in each of the arms is a carved head. Several like this have been found in a Celtic sanctuary at Roquepetruse in France, and it is likely that is is pre-Christian.

On the main road leading to **Kilfenora** is the ruined **Lemaneagh Castle** which belonged to Sir Donat O'Brien; it is a really lovely old ruin with a tower dating from 1480 and an early 17th century fortified house. Sir Conor O'Brien who built the more comfortable four storied house had a very strong minded wife called Red Mary, many of her exploits have passed into folklore. To ensure the inheritance of her son Donat she married an influential Cromwellian (after her husband had been killed) to prevent the expropriation of her lands. One day her husband made an uncalled for remark about her first husband and she promptly pushed him out of the window. **Kilfenora** is on the fringe of the Burren and it is worth staying awhile if only to look at the Burren display centre which explains the flora/fauna, butterflies and rock formations of the Burren; but also because it has four 12th century carved crosses, all of the same excellent standard, which suggests that they might have been produced by the same workshop or even by a single carver. The 12th century church is still called the cathedral and its bishopic is still held by the Pope! There is one **farmhouse** where you can stay. One of the amazing things about the Burren is that its 200 sq miles are dotted with signs of ancient habitation, stone forts and megalithic tombs. They blend perfectly with a landscape which is strewn with strangely shaped rocks, one I saw looked just like a cream bun.

On the road to **Ballyvaughan**, six miles past Lemaneagh Castle, is the great dolmen of Poulnabrone (the pool of Sorrows) with a massive capstone, and nearer Killnaboy in the upland part of the Burren is the great stone fort of Cahercommaun. A Harvard excavation team reached the conclusion that it was occupied during the 8th and 9th centuries by a community that raised cattle, hunted the red deer and cultivated some land for growing grain. The fort is situated on a cliff edge across some ankle breaking country, but notice the flower life between the stones. Also on the road to Ballyvaughan, a few miles out of Kilfenora, is one of the finest stone forts in Ireland, known as Ballykinvarraga. It has a very effective trap for those trying to launch an attack: chevaux de frise, which are sharp spars of stone set close together in the ground. The great fort of Dun Aengus on the Aran Islands has a similar arrangement.

At **Ballyvaughan** on the north of the Burren you can rent yourself an Irish cottage and explore Black Head which looks over the shimmering Galway Bay. There is a clear view of the Aran Islands from Black Head, and the Cliffs of Moher. The islands are made of the same grey limestone as the Burren and have the same bright flowers in the springtime. Ballyvaughan village is set in a green wooden vale, an oasis after the bleached plateaux of limestone, mighty terraces and escarpments. There are a couple of tower houses, built in the 16th century, to explore. Gleninagh, signposted between Black Head and Ballyvaughan, was occupied by the O'Loughlins until 1840. Newtown castle is unusual in that it is round with a square base. It is not sign-posted, you will find it down a lane, two miles south of **Ballyvaughan**.

You must visit Aillwee Cave, the entrance has been tamed to make it easier for the less intrepid; all over the Burren there are hundreds of caves formed by the underground rivers, great sport for the spelaeologist. The Aillwee Cave dates back to BC 2,000,000. When the river dried up, or changed its course, it became the den of wild bears and other animals, today it is festooned with stalagmites and stalactites. The cave is two miles southeast of **Ballyvaughan**, just off the Ennis road and open everyday from April to October and during the other months by special arrangement. Tel: Kilfenora 26. You can get refreshements from outside the cave.

**Eating** There are some good places to eat: GREGAN'S CASTLE HOTEL grade A, specializes in seafood, Tel: Ballyvaughan 5, HYLAND'S HOTEL grade B is good, you can also hear traditional music. On the main coast road to Lisdoonvarna is a cottage style restaurant called SEAFOOD HOUSE Tel: Craggagh 205.

By taking the cork screw road to **Lisdoonvarna**; Lios Duin Bhearna – (the enclosure of the gapped fort) you get a series of lovely views of Galway Bay. Lisdoonvarna, since the decline of Mallow is the most important spa in Ireland. The waters are said to owe much to their natural radio-activity; there are sulphur, magnesia and iron springs, a pump room and baths for those who come to take the waters. Hotels, guest houses and bed and breakfasts have sprung up everywhere for the place is very crowded in the summer and there is much courting inspired no doubt by the invigorating properties of the water. Dancing and concerts are held at the SPA WELLS HEALTH CENTRE which also provides such things as massages and saunas.

There is a sandy cove at **Doolin**, three miles away, good for bathing and fishing. This little fishing village is famous for its traditional music at O'CONNERS and McGANNS and there are two good places to **eat**, both specialising in seafood: THE BRUACH NA HAILLE Tel: Lisdoonvarna 120, or KILLILAGH HOUSE Tel: Lisdoonvarna 183. Mid-July is crowded in Lisdoonvarna with musicians for the folk festival. There is a championship golf course and you can take a course in *painting*, contact Mrs Christine O'Neill, O'NEILL'S GUESTHOUSE Tel: Lisdoonvarna 13. The Tourist Office is open during the summer.

In the area are curious mineral nodules formed by limestone and shale which look just like tortoise backs. There are three of these tortoises built into the wall beside the IMPERIAL HOTEL. The coast road from Lisdoonvarna leads to the Cliffs of Moher, which drop down vertically to the foaming sea. Seabirds somehow manage to rest on the steep slopes: guillemot, razorbill, puffin, kittiwake, various gulls, choughs and sometimes peregrines. The cliffs stretch for nearly five miles and are made of the darkest sandstone and millstone grit. On a clear day there is a magnificent view of the Twelve Bens and the mountains of Connemara. O'Brien's Tower, built in 1835 by a notorious landlord as an observation post, is now a *Tourist Information Centre* and a craft shop. You can get a boat from Doolin to **Innisheer**, the smallest of the Aran Islands, it takes about 40 minutes and a return fare costs £IR6.

**Liscannor**, a little fishing village where the fishermen still use currachs, is where John P Holland, who invented the submarine, was born, but it is more famous locally for the Holy Well of St. Brigid. The Well is an important place of pilgrimage and an aura of faith and devotion lingers in the damp air and amongst the trivial offerings of holy pictures, bleeding hearts and plastic statues of the Pope. You approach by a narrow stone passage, probably still feeling slightly amazed by the life sized painted plaster model of Saint Brigid next to the entrance of the

Well, it is sufficiently naturalistic to be macabre when first glimpsed.

**Lahinch** is a small seaside resort with a pretty arc of golden sand and waves big enough for surfing. For details on salmon *fishing*, and deep sea *angling* contact the Tourist Office which is open during the summer months. Tel: Lahinch 48.

**Ennistymon** is two and a half miles inland in a wooden valley beside the cascading River Cullenagh. There is a good old family-run hotel here called THE FALLS. The *golf course* at **Lahinch** is champion standard and there is an amusing story of one enthusiast who putted a winner and got the trophy; he remarked with the skill and colour only the Irish can summon 'I declare to God I was that tense I could hear the bees belchin'.

Southwards down the coast, from **Lahinch** you come to Spanish Point, where a great number of ships from the Spanish Armada were wrecked. Those sailors who struggled ashore were slaughtered by the locals on the orders of the Governor of Connacht. From **Milltown Malbay**, you can climb Slieve Callan, the highest point in west Clare, and on the way, rest at the little lake at Boolynagreana, which means the summer milking place of the sun. To get there you must follow the road southwards to the Hand Crossroads and then walk over rough land for about a mile. All round these foothills the ancient agricultural practice of transhumance, known in Ireland as "booleying" was practised. Just above the lake is a false Ogham pillar around which countless tales have been woven. Miltown Malbay has a summer school, held as a tribute to Clare's greatest piper Willie Clancy.

**Quilty** is a strange name for an Irish village and comes from the Irish 'coillte' for woods, but there are no trees on this flat part of the coast, however the great lines of stone walls are bestrewn with seaweed that is being dried for kelp making. The seaweed is either burnt, and the ash used for the production of iodine, or exported for the production of alginates – they produce the rich creamy head on Guinness. There is a church here that is reminiscent of the early Christian churches, but was built with money given by some French sailors who had been rescued by the villagers when their ship was wrecked one stormy night in 1907. There are deep sea *fishing boats for hire* and good beaches nearby.

**Kilkee** (Cill Chaoidhe: Church of Saint Caoidhe) is a really nice place for a holiday by the sea, it is built along a sandy crescent shaped beach, and the Duggerna Rocks, acting as a reef, make it safe for bathing at any stage of the tide. There is *salmon* or *trout fishing* on the Creegh and the Cooraclare rivers, deep sea *angling* and *skin diving*. Tel: Kilkee 211. The coast lying south westwards, for about 15 miles from here to **Loop Head**, is an almost endless succession of caverns, chasms, sea-stacks and wierd and wonderfully shaped rocks, the cliff scenery is on a par with the Cliffs of Moher. There is a colourful legend about Ulster's hero, Cuchulain, who was well loved by women, but this time he was being pursued relentlessly by a termagant of a women called Mal. Eventually he came to an end of edge of the cliffs on Loop Head and leapt onto a great rock about 30 feet out to sea. Mal was not to be outdone and made the same leap wth equal agility and success. Cuchulain straight away performed the difficult feat of leaping back to the mainland and this time Mal faltered, fell short, and disappeared into the raging ocean below. Out of this legend came the name Loop Head, in Irish Leap Head. As for poor Mal, she must have been a witch for her blood turned the sea red and she was swept northwards to a point near the cliffs of Moher called Hag's Head.

**Eating**: There is a good seafood restaurant which does delicious steaks as well Tel: Kilkee 211. On the way to Doonbeg is a small *folk museum* Tel: Kilkee 169. You can get details on *fishing*, accommodation (There is a *caravan* and *camping site*) from the Tourist Office in O'Connell St. Tel: Kilkee 190 (Only open in the summer months).

**Kilrush** (Cill Ruis – the church of the Promontory) is a busy place overlooking the Shannon estuary with a good harbour at Cappagh. Two miles out into the estuary, Scattery Island (Cathach's Island), founded by St Senan in the 6th century has some interesting monastic remains; but an island in the broad Shannon was easy meat for the Vikings who raided it several times. The round tower is very well preserved and has its door at ground level, so the unsuspecting monks must have been surprised by the aggressive Norsemen. The five ruined churches date from medieval times. *Boat trips* to Scattery island are available in the summer Tel: Kilrush 272

**Killimer** has a car ferry that links Clare with Kerry and it is otherwise distinguished only by its connection with the Colleen Bawn, otherwise known as Ellen Hanly, who is buried in the graveyard. Sadly nothing remains of her tombstone, it has been chipped away by souvenir hunters.

## PLACES TO STAY IN COUNTY CLARE

**Broadford**
Mrs E McGuire, The Lodge, near to Bunratty and Shannon Airport, Tel: (061) 73129
**Bunratty**
Mrs Rohan, Gallows View, Bunratty East, Tel: (061) 72241
**Corofin**
Cahill Family, Caherbolane Farm, Tel: (065) 27638
**Cratloe**
The O'Brien Family, Little Orchard, Sixmilebridge Rd, Tel: (061) 97135
**Doolin**
Mrs E O'Brien, Atlantic View, Ballaghaline, Tel: Lisdoonvarna 189
**Ennis**
Derrynane guesthouse, grade B, Tel: (065) 21464
Mrs B Lynch, Hillcrest, Limerick Rd, Tel: (065) 21536
Mrs Meere, Four Winds, Limerick Rd, Tel: (065) 22831
**Ennistymon**
Falls Hotel, grade B*
Mrs E Carroll, Tullamore Farmhouse, Kilshanny, Tel: Ennistymon 187
Mrs K Cahill, Station Hs, Ennis Rd, Tel: Ennistymon 149
**Feakle**
Mrs J Tuohy, The Biddy Early, Kilbarron, Tel: Feakle 44
**Kilfenora**

Mrs Doorty, Ballybreen West, Tel: Kilfenora 46 (farmhouse).
**Kilkee**
Mrs Fitzpatrick, Billows, West End, Tel: Kilkee 205
**Killaloe**
Mrs. McKeogh, Lakeside Hs, Tel: (061) 76295
**Kilrush**
Mrs. Fennell, Balleykett, Tel: Kilrush 230
Mrs Vallot, Greenfield Hs. Leadmore East, Tel: Kilrush 314
**Lahinch**
M van der Linden, Derry Hs, Tel: Ennistymon 228
**Lisdoonvarna**
The Linnane Family, Fernhill Farmhouse, Doolin Rd, Tel: Lisd. 40
Mrs Carey, Emohruo, Cliffs of Moher Rd, Tel: Lisd. 171
Mrs M Petty, Loretto Hs, Tel: Lisdoonvarna 35
**Miltown Malbay**
Mrs. Hannon, Leagard Hs, Tel: M'Malbay 174
**Mountshannon**
Youth Hostel
**Quilty**
Mrs A O'Conner, Clohauninghy Hs, Seafield, Tel: Quilty 81
**Binge Places**
Gregans Castle, Bullyauhan, grade A hotel, Tel: Ballyaughan 14
Ballykilty Manor, Quin, B* hotel, Tel: (065) 25654

# County Cork

Imagine quiet flowing rivers in green wooded valleys, a coastline which combines savage rock scenery with the softest bays, hillslopes which are purple in the late summer with bell heather, an ivy clad castle standing amongst hayricks in a field and you have captured something of Cork County. The city is something else, the country people may be slow, but the city people have produced a cosmopolitan centre humming with energy and confidence, full of grand buildings and shops, industry and culture, aided by a wit and business sense that would be hard to beat. Dubliners alternate between jealousy and heavy sarcasm in trying to describe the place – the best I heard was 'God's own place with the devil's own people'. Ireland's second city is built on marshy land on the banks of the River Lee, and has crept up the hills. The river flows in two main channels, crossed by lots of bridges, so that central **Cork** is actually on an island. It's a bit confusing if you are driving there for the first time, with its one way roads and the crossing and recrossing of the river that goes on. If the worst comes to the worst, dump your car and get a bus or walk, the CIE city transport service is excellent. For anyone trying to get out of Cork by train, the *station* is on *Lower Glamire Rd*, Tel: Cork 54422 for

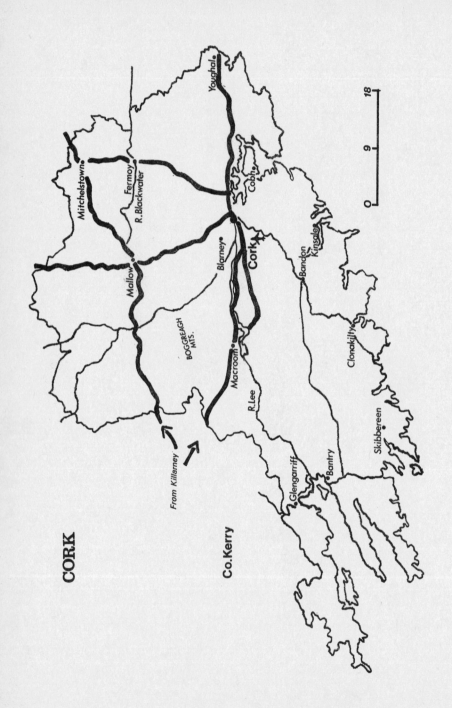

CORK

Co.Kerry

Mitchelstown

Fermoy
R.Blackwater

Mallow

Blarney

Cork

Youghal

Cobh

Bandon

Kinsale

Clonakilty

Skibbereen

Bantry

Glengarriff

BOGGREAGH MTS.

Macroom

R.Lee

From Killarney

0    9    18

202

information. The county bus and long distance *coach terminal* is at *Parnell Place* and *Cork Airport* is at **Ballygarven**, three miles south of the city, Tel: (021) 25341. The *car ferry terminal* is off Lower Glanmire Rd, Tel: (021) 504100. B&I, Brittany Ferries Tel: (021) 507666.

**Cork**, until the Anglo-Norman invasion, was largely a Danish stronghold though it first became known in the 6th century as an excellent school under St. Finbar. The Cork citizens were an independent lot and although after 1180 English laws were nominally in force, it was really the wealthy merchants who were in charge and decided things. In 1492, they took up the cause of Perkin Warbeck and went with him to Kent where he was proclaimed Richard IV, King of England and Lord of Ireland. They lost their charter for that piece of impudence, but Cork continued to be a rebel city. William III had to lay siege to it in 1690 and in the 19th century, it became a centre for the Fenian movement. During the War of Independence 1919-1921, the city was badly burned by the Black and Tans and one of Cork's mayors died on hunger strike in an English prison. But Cork is also famous for a more moderate character, Father Theobald Matthew, who persuaded thousands of people to go off the drink, though the effect of his temperance drive was ruined by the potato famine and the general misery it bought. Cork still has a reputation for clannish behaviour amongst its business men and an independence in the arts and politics, but you would be hard put to find a friendlier city to wander around.

The first thing you will notice about **Cork** city is the skyline which like Derry is still 19th century. **Cork** has spires and gracious wide streets; St. Patrick's St. curves alongside the river, one side of which is lined with old buildings the other by uninspiring modern office and shop fronts built after the burning in 1920. Cornmarket St. has a **flea market** usually called 'Coal Quay' where you can bargain for trifles and observe the sharptongued store owners. The South Mall and Grand Parade have some pretty buildings. North of the river is St. Patrick's Church in Lower Glanmire Rd. built by one of the Pain brothers in 1836. Some of the streets here are literally stairs up the steep slopes and open only to pedestrians. The lovely tower of Shandon with its two faces – white limestone and red sandstone, looks down into the valley. You may ring the bells of Shandon for a small fee and conjure up Father Prout's lyrical poem about the wild spells that they wove for him; nearby are Skiddy's 18th century almshouses.

South of the river is St. Finbar's Cathedral, its great spires dominate the city, the building itself is in the Gothic style of 13th century France and was built by a convinced medievalist, William Burges, between 1867-79. His eye for detail was meticulous, but the whole effect is vigorous, a defiant gesture to Catholic Ireland. The Church of Christ the King at Turner's Cross was designed by an American architect, Barry Bryne, in the 30s. The carved figure of Christ crucified with his arms spread above the twin entrance doors is very striking. If you want to explore the city in detail pick up one of the pamphlets called *Cork city and County* from the Tourist Office in the Grand Parade, Tel: (021) 23251. During July and August this office is open from 9 am - 9 pm every day. Riverside

House, Glanmire, built in 1602, has exquisite plaster work by the Francini brothers. It is open in the afternoons Thursday–Sunday, May to September.

Guided *walking* tours of **Cork City** depart from the Tourist Office two evenings a week in July and August. *Fishing, riding, swimming, sub aqua,* and *golf* are all easily available – details from the Tourist Office. Twenty minutes walk from the city centre via Barrack Street and Bandon Road is the Lough, a freshwater lake with ferel geese. Douglas estuary via Tivoli (15 minutes from the centre by car) has hundreds of black tailed godwit, shelduck and golden plover. Cork shops are well known for their quality and helpfulness, the Cork Craftsman's Guild, Savoy Centre, Patrick St, has a good range of pottery, woodwork and enamels.

In the evenings there are plenty of *films* to chose from but if I were you I would try and see a production by the Theatre of the South, at the Cork Opera House. They tend to produce only contemporary Irish writers' work and sometimes it can be very good. Theatre of the South is open for about eight weeks every summer, otherwise go to the Everyman Theatre which does not restrict itself in any way; tragedy, farce, comedy by any author as long as he or she is good. For the programmes of both cinema and theatre look in the *Cork Examiner* and the *Evening Echo.* Disco *dancing* at Kojaks, Carey's Lane (near the Pavillion Cinema) Swingers, Oliver Plunkett St. and Chandras, Grand Parade. *Traditional music* and *dance* can be found at Dun Mhuire on the Grand Parade, make sure that you go after 9 pm when the instruction is over and the fun begins, no charge. *The Cork and Kerry Tourism Entertainment Centre* at the rear of the Tourist Office puts on a programme of music and entertainment at least five nights a week during the summer, they usually start about 8.30 pm, full details from the Tourist Office.

Cork is host to some great festivals: in May the *Cork Choral Festival,* and in June the *Film International,* documentaries, art films, short fiction and sport films, plus a special competition for Irish film makers. It is not too expensive to see about 75 films and go to some fun parties as well. Make sure you have a room booked well ahead as the city will be very crowded. In September the *Mobil 14th Irish Rally* is held, which everybody in the city watches with great interest.

*Car parking:* A disc system operates in city centre areas. One disc at 10p allows either one or two hours parking depending on the area. Parking discs are sold in booklets and you can get them in the Tourist Office, from many shops and petrol stations.

**Eating:** THE METROPOLE HOTEL, Jazz 12-2 pm on Sundays. Grill/ snack or full-blown meal in dining room. Tel: (021) 508122. MURPH'S (part of the successful Dublin chain) in the Savoy Centre is closed on Sundays, Tel: (021) 504333. THE WILLOW PATTERN Pembroke St. Imaginative and cheap, closes after serving high tea. THE STAR, 77 Grand Parade. Chinese food, Tel: (021) 23999. TUNG SING, 23A Patrick St. Chinese food. THE OYSTER TAVERN, Market Lane, 56 St Patricks St, Tel: (021) 22716. Delicious for both lunch and dinner. ARBUTUS LODGE, Montenotte, at the head of Glanmire Rd, Tel: (021) 51237. One of the best and most expensive restaurants in the country. MAHARAJA, Market Parade, Patrick St. Fiery Indian food at moderate prices, Tel: (021) 22559. O'GRADY'S, 5 Patrick St. Self service, good for salads, also licensed bar. HALPINS DELICATESSEN, 14 Cook St. Cheap, good pizza. By the way when you are in Cork, nobody drinks Guinness, natives drink Murphy's and Beamish, what the local breweries make.

Cork is 160 miles from Dublin, 263 from Belfast and 128 miles from Galway.

**Blarney** is five miles from Cork city. This small village has a fame out of all proportion to its size because it is the home of the Blarney Stone. Whoever kisses it will get the gift of the gab. It is a magnet which attracts almost every visitor to Ireland so expect to find the place crowded and full of knick-knacks. This magic stone is high up in the castle walls. In the days of Queen Elizabeth I the castle was held by Dermot Mac Carthy, who had the gift of plamas, the Irish word for soft flattering or insincere speech. Elizabeth had asked him to surrender his castle, but he continued to play her along with fair words and no action. In the end the frustrated Queen is supposed to have said 'it's all Blarney – he says he will do it but never means it at all'. The stone is probably a 19th century invention and today you can even buy yourself a certificate which guarantees you have kissed the Blarney stone, try showing that to your prospective employer! The castle is well worth seeing for its own sake as one of the largest and finest tower houses in Ireland, built in 1446 by the MacCarthy clan.

**Cobh** – pronounced Cove, 15 miles from Cork city, is the great harbour of Cork and handles huge ships. The town is nearly entirely 19th century and is dominated by the Gothic cathedral, the work of Pugin and Ashlin. The museum, a converted church, has displays on the Lusitania disaster and the maritime history of Cobh. There is an International Dance Festival here in July; it is a rather a nice place to stay, near to the city but without its bustle.

**Kinsale** (Ceann Saile: Tide Head) is 18 miles from Cork city. It hit the headlines as a quaint, seaside town years ago but its popularity only seems to increase, along with the delicious restaurants and carefully preserved buildings. In the olden days it used to be an important naval port; in 1601 the Spanish fleets anchored here before the disastrous battle which led to the 'flight of the Earls'. There are some superb sandy beaches at the nearby resort of **Garrettstown** and splendid cliff scenery at the Old Head of Kinsale. This is the perfect place for a relaxed holiday and you can mix *deep sea angling, sailing, walking,* and *swiming* with a little bit of culture. Multose Church is the oldest building in town, parts of it dating from 13th century, inside are the old town stocks. The church yard has several interesting 16th century grave stones which in spring are covered in white-bells and blue-bells, and in summer red valerian grows casually out of crevasses in every wall. The interesting museum is in the old courthouse, and near **Ballinspittle** is a ring fort circa 600 AD. Round the Old Head of Kinsale the remains of a 15th century de Courcy castle overlook the blue and white flecked sea. The Charles Fort, in the attractive village of **Summercove** is shaped like a star and you can wander

205

round its rather damp nooks and crannies. It was occupied until 1922.

**Pubs in Kinsale:** The Spaniard, White Lady, The Shanakee, and Coakley's Hotel at Garretstown. *Disco* and *carbaret* in the White Lady. Acton's Hotel does a candlelight *dinner/dance* on Saturdays from Easter to October. (The Spaniard is the liveliest spot).

**Eating:** THE BLUE HAVEN. Seafood is speciality, quite expensive £IR9 a head, Tel: (021) 72209. THE VINTAGE, Main St. Original, and delicious food, Tel: (021) 72502. SKIPPERS RESTAURANT Lower O'Connell St. Seafood, steaks etc., Tel: (021) 72664. KINSALE DELICATESSEN, Smoked mackerel, quiches. MAN FRIDAY RESTAURANT, Tel: (021) 72260 (opposite the Spaniard pub).

**Crosshaven** 13 miles from Cork city is the playground of the busy Cork business men and their families. There are lovely beaches at **Myrtleville** and **Robert's Cove**, and a crescent shaped bay filled with yachts and boats of every description. Myrtleville has a very relaxed drinking and eating place, you can even stay there. Look for an old rambling house called BUNNYCONNELAN, perched on the cliffs, it has a fabulous view over the bay. Sea *Angling* Tel: Mr Barry Twomey (021) 504314. *Sailing*, the Royal Yacht Club, which is the oldest in the world, is based here, Tel: 831440.

**Youghal** (pronounced Yawl from Eochaill, a yew wood) is 30 miles from Cork city. If you are starting from Cork city there is a very fast main road that by-passes **Cloyne**. Turn off at **Midleton** if you want to stop and visit the monument to the philosopher, Bishop Berkeley, in the vast ancient cathedral. This area has system of unexplored caves. A smallroad from here leds down to **Ballycotton**, a little fishing village set in a peaceful unspoilt bay, there is a pretty view out to Ballycotton islands which protect the village from the worst of the sea winds. Nearby is **Shanagarry**, famous for its pottery and the old home of William Penn, the founder of Pennsylvania. **Ballymaloe House** has won many awards for its *restaurant*, Tel: (021) 65231. You might be approaching **Youghal** from the lovely **Blackwater Valley** which has some of the best *driving* and *walking* country in Ireland if you like wooded banks, green fields, old buildings and twisting, unfrequented roads. If you get to **Youghal** for lunch, stop at **Aherne's** seafood pub for some memorable food, it's not too expensive if you stick to their snacks. Their freshly squeezed orange juice is delicious, and the whole atmosphere is very friendly. For an evening meal, try CHOUCAS in Mistletoe Castle; Tel: (024) 2666, another out of the ordinary Irish restaurant.

But **Youghal** is not all about food, it is also one of the most attractive seaside towns in Ireland. It was founded by the Anglo-Normans in the 13th century and was destroyed in the Desmond rebellion of 1579; then it was handed over to Sir Walter Raleigh in the Elizabethan plantations when he become Mayor of the town and lived in a gabled house by the churchyard gates called Murtle Grove. It is not open to the public. Raleigh is said to have planted the first potato in the garden, an act which was to have far reaching consequences for Ireland's population. The inside of St. Mary's Collegiate Church is crowded with interesting monuments, including one of the Earl of Cork, Richard Boyle looking very smug surrounded by his mother, his two wives, and nine of his sixteen sons. A monument was erected to the extraordinary lady, Countess of Desmond, who died in 1604 at the age of 147 after falling out of a tree when gathering cherries! Bits of old abbeys, castles, and old walls make Youghal an interesting place to walk around. The Clock Gate in South Main St is very pretty and houses the Tourist Office and the museum, Tel: (024) 2390. *Boats* are available for sea *fishing*, either off the Ballycotton rocks or for shark, Tel: Mr Vastenhuse, Stonebridge Cottage, (024) 2313. Sandy *beaches* stretch from here to Ballycotton and at **Ballymona** there is a *bird sanctuary*. The Moby Dick bar is quite fun for a bit of chat. *Cabaret, sing-songs* and *band concerts* are held on the promenade during the summer season. Early closing is on Wednesday. There are plenty of B&Bs along the seafront on the Cloyne Road and two caravan parks.

**Fermoy** (Mainistir Fhearmuighe or the Abbey of the Plantations) used to be a garrison town for the British army and is built along both sides of the darkly flowing Blackwater River. People hereabouts are familar with every fascinating detail of the salmon, and if you are a **fisherman**, your gillie will lead you to the best roach, dace and perch. Salmon fishing costs £IR6 a day. For details contact Mr Jack O'Sullivan, Tel: (025) 31110. I heard a curious story about the battle of the rooks and the starlings; the latter were invading the nesting places of the rooks and this went on for about a week until about 2,000 rooks rose as one cawing mass above the starlings and flew around them until the starlings gave way and fled.

Lord Fermoy, an ancestor of the Princess of Wales is said to have gambled away his Fermoy estates in an evening. The Protestant church built in 1802 contains some grotesque masks. Just outside **Fermoy** is one of the most beautiful houses in Ireland, the Georgian mansion Castle Hyde, which was the home of Douglas Hyde, first president of the Irish Republic and the founder of the Gaelic League. Today it is owned by an American. KATE O'BRIEN'S and the GRAND HOTEL are the places to drink. The *golf* course is 18 hole and the only heath course in Ireland. **Mitchelstown** is famous in Ireland for butter and cheese and also for its caves, ten miles to the north on the Cahir road. The countryside around becomes richer as you enter the Golden Vein.

**Doneraile** and **Buttevant** are in Edmund Spenser country between the Blackwater and the Ballyhoura Mountains. Here he is said to have written the *Faerie Queene,* inspired by the sylvan beauty of the countryside. Tragically, his home was burned and he and his wife had to flee Kilcolman Castle leaving their baby daughter to perish in the flames. Kilcolman is now a sombre ruin, in a field beside a reedy pool northeast of Buttevant. There are plenty of old castle ruins roundabout built by the Desmonds or the Barrys; Doneraile Court is a house with an interesting story behind it; here Elizabeth Barry, wife of the first Viscount Doneraile hid in a clock case to observe a masonic lodge meeting held in the house. Perhaps she laughed, whatever happened she gave herself away and all the masons could do was to elect her as a mason – the first woman mason in history. Doneraile Court is in the process of being restored by the Irish Georgian Society, you are welcome to look around it. Off the L37 is a marsh with a bird observatory about 3 miles north-east of **Buttevant.**

**Mallow** used be to a famous spa where the gentry of Ireland came to take the waters and have a good time. The spa inspired the verse which begins 'Beauing, belling, dancing, drinking,/Breaking windows, damning, sinking,/Ever raking, never thinking,/Live the rakes of Mallow'. It has pretty 18th century houses, a timbered decorated Clock House and Mallow Castle, which is a roofless ruin but still impressive; the original owners live in what were the stables, across the river from the castle. The old spa house is now a private house and the once famous water gushes to waste. The *Mallow Races* is the only time the place really comes alive.

**Macroom** (Maghcromtha; sloping plain) is on the direct route to Killarney and is a favourite place for tourists and music enthusiasts Van Morrison has played in their musical festival. This is a gorgeous part of Ireland, scenes are lush with green pasture and bright-flowered with fuchsia and heather. The route from **Cork City** follows the lovely Lee River through **Dripsey** and **Coachford**, Dripsey woollen mills produce an excellent wool. If you are heading for Killarney try and plan your journey to include the **Pass of Keimaneigh** and one of the most beautiful forest parks in the country – **Gougane Barra,** the 'rock-cleft of Finbar'. It is a dramatic glacial valley with a shining lake in its hollow into which run silvery streams. In the lake is a small island, approached by a causeway, where St Finbar set up his oratory in the 6th century, nowadays there is his Holy Well and a modern chapel. There is a small admission fee to the park. After the **Pass of Keimaneigh,** strewn with massive boulders, you come into the colourful valley of the **Owvane** with views of Bantry Bay. At **Kealkill** there is an ancient stone circle reached by an exciting hilly road.

**Bantry** has one of the nicest views in the world, but otherwise little of note except the modern statue of St. Brenden and the fact that in these parts undertakers call their premises 'funeral homes'. What you must not miss is Bantry Bay House which has a glorious view and is directly above the town so you do not see nasty petrol stations, etc. You can go round the house on your own (accompanied only by the faint strains of classical music) with a detailed guide written by the owner which you then hand back when you have finished. Rare French tapestries, family portraits, china still have a feeling of being used and loved. The house and garden have definitely seen better days, yet this is one of the most interesting houses in Ireland and certainly the least officious open to the public. £IR1.50 entrance fee. *Cruising* is available on Bantry Bay, round the oil tankers and islands, everyday except Wednesday and Sunday. Contact Mr M J Carroll, Main St, Tel: Bantry 275. Just outside the town on Glengarriff Road are the Donemark Falls, a very pretty waterfall on an island. The rather eccentric owner of this land has made it into a garden, a mixture of natural and commercial charm with gnomes etc.

**Bandon** (20 miles from Cork city) was founded by Richard Boyle, the Earl of Cork, in 1608. Over the gate of the then walled town it is said that there were the words 'Turk, Jew or atheist may enter here, but not a papist'. A Catholic wit responded, 'He who wrote this wrote it well, the same is written on the gates of hell'. The Bandon River and its tributaries make for good *fishing* and *walking,* and if you want to explore **Kilbrittain, Timoleague** and **Courtmacsherry Bay** are very unspoilt while the wooded valleys, and rolling fields do not have the hedges you find in Tipperary. Here you find the typical Irish bar cum grocery shop with the old fashioned lettering displaying the proud name of the owner.

**Rosscarbery** is a charming old fashioned village. In the valley of the little Roury River stands the ruin of Coppinger's Court which gives shelter to cows in winter. It was burnt out in 1641. From Roury bridge a country road winds to Drombeg Stone Circle, from where you can see across pastures and cornfields to the sea. It is dated between the 2nd century BC and 2nd century AD and was used for some rite involving human sacrifice.

**Glandore** is a pretty fishing village, on the Ownahincha Beach where you can go *yachting* or *boating* in the magnificent Bay.

**Castletownshend** is a neat Georgian village on a steep hill, in the middle of which grows a huge tree. This used to be the home of Edith Somerville, co-author of the humourous *Reminiscences of an Irish RM.*

**Skibbereen** is a rather nondescript market town, but it does have a year round Tourist Office in the Main St, Tel: (028) 21766 and some good places to eat especially GERRADS DELICATESSEN. All round **Skibbereen** and particularly to the west is some lovely country where knuckles and fingers of land reach into the sea breaking off into islands like the Sherkin and Clear. Near to **Baltimore** is the beautiful Lough Inne, just the place for a walk or picnic. This region used to be an O'Driscoll stronghold until it was sacked by Algerian pirates in 1631 and the Irish people captured and sold as slaves along the Barbary coast. **Ballydehob** is a colourful little village, while at **Rosbrin** the ruin of an O'Mahony castle stands by the sea, the home of the 14th century scholar Finin. A spectacular road runs from Skull up the Glaun Valley, and you can easily climb Gabriel Mountain, the view is out of this world and you can watch out for pre-historic copper mines dug into the slopes. The road curls round the head of lovely **Toormore Bay,** past **Goleen** with its sandy beach (the gulf stream means that swimming is quite a possibility here) to **Crookhaven** with its boat filled harbour. Barley Cove is a sandy beach along which you can stretch your legs before you get to the splendid, sheer heights of **Mizen Head**, the soft red sandstone cliffs banded with white fall down to the sea whilst flurries of birds glide on the air currents beneath you.

**Glengarriff's** humpy hills and wooded inlets look over limpid water and isles, Mulroy Bay in Donegal is similar.\ The trip out to **Garnish Island** is short and a must, for it is a dream island full of sub-tropical plants, with a formal Italian garden, rock gardens and a marble pool full of gold fish. Bernard Shaw stayed here often. The return trip costs approximately £IR2, and the island is open weekdays 10am-5.30pm and Sundays 1-6pm. You might *walk* in Glengarriff Valley 'the bitter Glen' and up to the hills hidden in the Caha Range; or go up to **Healy Road**, with its lovely mountain scenery gazing down on the indented sealine and the green woods.

## PLACES TO STAY IN COUNTY CORK

**Bandon**
Mrs M P O'Brien, Valley View, Knocknagallough (off Bandon/Timoleague Rd), Tel: (023) 41173 farmhouse.
Mrs J O'Shea, Mount Grellam Hs, Kilbrogan, Bandon, Tel: (023) 41569
Mrs K Hunt, Beech Lodge, Tel: 023 41273
The Munster Arms, grade B* (21 rooms with bath/shower).
**Bantry**
Youth Hostel at Cahermeelabo, Allihies
Numerous B&Bs: 12 farmhouses, 8 town and 7 country houses in the area.
Mrs Cronin, Ninorc Farm House, Gurtycloona, Tel: Bantry 178
Harnedy Family, Mountain View Farm, Mealagh River Valley, Droumclough, Tel: Bantry 347
Mrs O'Connor, Rooska Farm, Tel: Bantry 11
Mrs E Andrews, Ferndeene, 4 Slip Lawn, Tel: Bantry 146
Eagle Point, Carvans and camping site, 4 miles on Glengarriff Rd.
**Blarney**
The Gables, Stoneview, Tel: 021 85330
Mrs Dooley, Valley View, Woodlands, Gloghrow, Tel: (021) 85384 (all rooms with shower).
Mrs K Moyland, Clonliffe, Kerry Pike Rd, Tel: (021) 85352
Blarney Hotel, grade A, 76 bedrooms with bath, Tel: (021) 85281
**Cobh**
Miss M O'Driscoll, 1 Upper Park, Tel: (021) 811506
**Cork City**
Youth hostel is at 1-2 Redclyffe, Western Rd, Tel: (021) 432891
The B&Bs are plentiful in the £IR5-6 range and are clustered round four districts near Cork Airport and the B&I Ferry

1) Summerhill (Bus 7)
Mrs S Keane, Mountain View, Summerhill, Tel: (021) 501045
Mrs M Leonard, Ardskeagh, Gardiners Hill, Tel: (021) 501800

2) Wilton Rd (Buses 5, 8, 9, 10, 11)
Mrs M Vaughan, Ouvane Hs, Connacht Av (off Donovans Rd), Tel: (021) 21822

3) Western Rd, Mardyke area (Buses 5, 8)
Mrs O'Brien, Redclyffe Hs, Western Rd, Tel: (021) 23220

4) Douglas Rd (Buses 6, 6a, 7, 7a)
Mrs J Wolfe, Glenfael, 4 Douglas Hall Lawn, Well Rd, Tel: (021) 293225
The Cork Caravan and camping site, Togher Rd, very well equipped.
**Fermoy**
Mrs K Healy, The Rectory, Kill St Anne, Castlelynos, Tel: (025) 36238
Mrs B Lomasney, Beechmount Hs, Kilworth, Tel: (025) 27255
**Glandore**
Mrs. M Watson, Killeenleigh, farmhouse to Glandore, Tel: (028) 33103
Mrs O'Donoghue, Riviera Lodge, Tel: (028 331£73

**Glengarriff**

Mrs A Guerin, Sea Front (centre of town), Tel: Glengarriff 79

Mrs O'Sullivan, Island View Hs, Tel: Glengarriff 81

**Kinsale**

Youth hostel at Summercove, Tel: (021) 72309 (very popular).

Mrs H Griffin, Hillside Hs, Camphill (beach nearby), Tel: (021) 72315

Mrs K O'Donovan, Guardwell, Tel: (021) 72428

The Folk Hs, grade B guesthouse, Tel: (021) 72382

**Macroom**

Mrs Mullen, Normandale, Killarney Rd, Tel: Macroom 196

Mrs O'Sullivan, Findus Hs, Ballyvoige, Kilnamartyra, Tel: Kilnamartyra 623

**Mallow**

Mrs E Coleman, Kilquane Farmhouse, Mourne Abbey, Tel: (022) 29137

Mrs M Fitzpatrick, Beechmount Farm, Tel: (022) 21764

Youth hostel, Bridge Hs, Ballingeary.

**Rosscarbery**

Miss M Horrigan, Post Office Hs, Tel: (023) 48161

**Skibbereen**

Mrs J Griffin, Glencar, Cork Rd, Tel: (028) 21638

**Youghal**

Mrs E Long, Cherrymount Farmhouse, Tel: (024) 7110 (signposted from Youghal Bridge).

Mrs M Muir, Blackwater Hs, Kinsalebeg, Tel: (024) 2176

Miss C Hennessy, Maryville, Front Strand, Tel: (024) 2162

Devonshire Arms, Tel: (024) 2872 guesthouse.

**Binge Places**

Ardnavaha House Hotel, Ballinascarthy. Hotel and Restaurant, Tel: (023) 49135

Assolas Country Hs, Kanturk, Tel: Kanturk 15 (Lively surroundings and delicious food).

Ballylickey Country Hs and Restaurant, near Bantry, Tel: Bantry 71 and 124

Ballymaloe Hs, Shanagarry, Midleton, Tel: (021) 652531

---

# County Kerry

You must not miss Kerry for this county is packed with some of the most beautiful scenery in Ireland and the nicest people. It boasts the opulent Lakes of Killarney, set amongst wooded mountains, the grandest range in the land. The Peninsula of Iveragh and Dingle where mountains and sea are jumbled together in a glory of colour and every year the small farmer recreates a pattern of golden hayricks, cornfields and handkerchief fields where the black Kerry cow grazes, when she is not creating a traffic jam

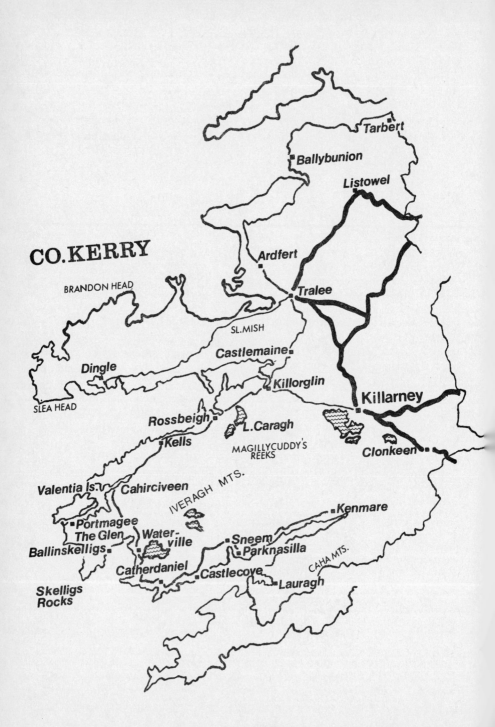

CO.KERRY

Tarbert

Ballybunion

Listowel

BRANDON HEAD

Ardfert

Tralee

SL.MISH

Castlemaine

Dingle

Killorglin

SLEA HEAD

Killarney

Rossbeigh

L.Caragh

Kells

MAGILLYCUDDY'S
REEKS

Clonkeen

Valentia Is.

Cahirciveen

IVERAGH MTS.

Kenmare

Portmagee

The Glen

Water-
ville

Sneem

Parknasilla

Ballinskelligs

Catherdaniel

Castlecove

CAHA MTS.

Lauragh

Skelligs
Rocks

212

on the narrow country lanes. For those interested in the past, Kerry is scattered with ogham stones, standing stones, forts, and clochans (the stone huts of holy men). Off the coast are some fascinating islands: on the Skelligs Rocks the word God was praised and celebrated for 600 years; Valentia is a soft, easy island by comparison, while the Blaskets, three miles out to sea, are beautiful but deserted.

The N71 route into **Kerry** via Cork is spectacular. However, instead of going straight to Killarney explore around **Lauragh** and **Cloonee** for the waterfalls and lakes are lovely, and there is a beautifully planted garden at Derreen Woodland. Open to the public between April and September on Sundays, Tuesdays and Thursdays in the afternoons, Tel: Lauragh 3. This is marvellous walking country, and you can base yourself either at the Youth Hostel at **Bonane** or in **Kenmare**, a pretty 19th century town. **Eating:** the best place is the PURPLE HEATHER, then go out and savour the view of the Kerry Hills, the Macgillycuddy's Reeks, the Caha range on the Cork border and the broad estuary of the Kenmare River. In the Convent of the Poor Clares, Tel: (064) 41385, you can look at a display of the point lace and other varieties made by the nuns. Three quarters of a mile from the town on the Killarney road, is a much visited Holy Well and shrine to Our Lady, reputed to have very strong healing powers. The river is famous for *salmon* and *sea trout fishing*, seek advice and permission from Mr Tony O'Shea, Tel: (064) 41264.

**Killarney** is a dedicated to making money out of tourists and not attractive in itself, yet the surrounding countryside remains beautiful and unspoiled. If you are willing to walk in the mountains and away from well worn tracks, you will find that the luxuriant green of the woods, the soft air, the vivid blue of the lakes and the craggy mountains above will have the same charm for you as they had for the countless stream of travellers since the 18th century. Remember to bring a raincoat and expect at least one day when the mists will creep over everything.

The actual town of **Killarney** has one thing to offer sightseers, St. Mary's Cathedral, built in silvery limestone in the 1840s to the designs of Pugin. It is a very successful 'Early English style', austere and graceful. The Tourist Office in the Town Hall, Main St, will help you chose accommodation from the countless rooms offered and explain the intricacies of all the 'excursions' to local beauty spots, to be made by side-car, Tel: (064) 31633. These excursions take up to a full day and during the trip you are regaled with stories by jarveys. They have built up an international reputation for telling visitors exactly what they expect to hear – leprechauns, legends – you name it!

For those who prefer to be more independent and economical, *hiking* or *biking* will get you to the Gap of Dunloe, Muckross Abbey and Castle, Ross Castle and Innisfallen Isle. The trick is to start form the opposite end to the average tourist by going first to Ross Castle. *Bicycle hire* shops are numerous, try O'Neill's, Plunkett St, Tel: (064) 31970 or O'Meara, High St and O'Callaghan's, College St, Tel: (064) 31465 where they also rent out *camping equipment*. Ross Castle, one mile and a half from the town centre on a peninsula, is a fine ruin dating from the 14th century. It is not possible to go inside the castle but from here you can hire a boat to

**Innisfallen Island**, which is like a country in miniature: with hills and valleys, pasturelands and dark woods, holly and other evergreens grow very thickly here. Near the landing stage are the ruins of Innisfallen Abbey founded about 600 AD, a refuge for Christians during the dark ages in Europe. The Annals of Innisfallen, a chronicle of world and Irish history written between 950 AD and 1380 are now in the Bodleian Library, Oxford.

**Muckross House** and **Abbey** are part of an 11,000 acre estate given to the nation by Mr and Mrs Bowers Bourne of California and Senator Arthur Vincent; it has been made into a National Park and covers most of the lake district with walks and drives to all the beauty spots (motorcars are not allowed to parts of the estate). Muckross House has been transformed into a museum of Kerry folklife with a craftshop in its basement, you can see a potter, a weaver, and blacksmith at their trades. It is open 9am – 9pm July and August, during the rest of the year it is open daily (except Monday) from 11am – 5pm. Admission adults 60p. Muckross Abbey is a graceful Early English ruin founded for the Observantine Franciscans in 1448. In fact this area is a stage set for everything the tourist wishes to see and the natural beauty of the setting is enhanced by superb gardens.

**The Gap of Dunloe** is further along the main Killarney/Kenmare Rd. Notice the strawberry tree or arbutus growing with the ferns and oaks, and the pink saxifrage on the wayside. You could stop and take the woodland path to the **Torc Waterfall**, or once past the Galwey Bridge you could follow the stream up into the hills to the **Derrycunnihy Cascades**, and maybe you will come upon a few sika or red deer. Six miles on past Ladies View (which gives you a marvellous view of the Upper lake) and a hideous tourist shop/cafe, turn off left before Moll's Gap and left again along the dirt track. You are now in the **Gap of Dunloe**, a beautiful wild gorge bordered by dark, mysterious tarns above, and towering above everything are the Macgillycuddy's Reeks, The Purple Mountain and Tomies Mountain. When you get to the head of Upper Lake, a boatman will take you across the rapids. This is some of the best ridge *walking* country in Ireland; there is a very enthusiastic *mountaineering club* in **Killorglin**, contact Mr Sean O'Sullivan, Langford St, Tel: Killorglin 27. The Macgillycuddy's Reeks include Carrantuohill (3,414 feet) the highest mountain in Ireland. At the other end of the Gap is Kate Kearney's Cottage – most people start from this end, where you can hire *side-cars* and *ponies*. Tel: Beaufort 7 or 27 for enquiries.

On the main road to **Killorglin**, past Dunloe Castle a signpost points to a collection of ogham stones in a wired enclosure high on the bank. This is the best place in Kerry to see this weird writing, the only form that existed before the arrival at Christianity; the lateral strokes incised into the stone crossing a vertical line give the name of the ancient dead man.

**Eating:** places are not too good in the Killarney area, so buy yourself a picnic in the daytime or pastries from the CONTINENTAL COFFEE SHOP in Glebe Place, off Plunkett St. If you are not eating supper at your guest house, try GABY'S SEAFOOD RESTAURANT, 17 High St, Tel: (064) 32519 or book in at the CHEF'S SPECIAL RESTAURANT at the Linden House Hotel, Tel: (064) 31379, the restaurant is closed to non residents on Wednesday, Friday and from November through to mid-January. The food is very cheap, plain and deliciously cooked. DEE-NACH RESTAURANT, 10 College St, Tel: (064) 31656 is also good.

**Killarney Town** in early May plays host to a Pan Celtic week, when Celts from Brittany, Wales, Cornwall, Scotland and the Isle of Man come together to play traditional music, dance and play sports, including hurling matches. In July, there is a *Bach Festival* and hard on its heels the *Killarney races* when the place is crowded with Irishmen. They come in their thousands for the Killarney Easter Rally, part of the Benson and Hedges circuit of Ireland. The place is a hive of activity during all these events, but at other times you might seek entertainment in **Tralee** at the *National Folk Theatre* for Siamsa – merrymaking and a recreation of rural life acted out in mime, dance and song. Book your ticket through the Tourist Office in Tralee or Killarney. Buy a copy of the local newspaper *The Kerryman* for a list of events; *cinema, ballet, Gaelic football* matches etc. Do not miss *Puck Fair* held in August at **Killorglin**, the atmosphere is fantastic; a mountain goat is crowned King of the Town in a ceremony which has pagan undertones.

**The Ring of Kerry** and the **Dingle Peninsula** (the Peninsulas of Iveragh and Corcaguiney). If you have to choose between the two, explore **Dingle**, for it is still relatively deserted and the scenery around the coastline is full of drama and beauty. Whatever you do give yourself plenty of time. The road which makes up the **Ring of Kerry** is 112 miles long and doesn't venture deeply into the interior of the peninsula, but you should do just that by travelling from **Killorglin** to the lake area of **Caragh, Glencar** and Lough **Cloon**. Then take the lonely road over the **Ballaghasheen Pass** to **Waterville** or alternatively, the **Ballaghbeama Gap** to **Sneem**. The latter route takes you through a tortuous and breathtaking channel between two mountains, named in Irish after the golden gorse that grows on their slopes. **Sneem** is a quiet village divided by the Sneem river.

**Eating:** it has a good seafood restaurant CASEY'S Tel: (064) 45147, the 'BLUE BULL' country pub has provençal cooking in the evenings, Tel: Sneem 76.

A few miles outside is a Bord Fáilte sign to Staigue Fort, it is isolated at the head of a desolate valley, and about 2,500 years old. The beautiful valleys are wonderful walking country and it is a delight to swim from the beaches of **Kenmare Bay.** One mile from **Catherdaniel** is Derrynane House, the home of Daniel O'Connell, the Great Liberator. It contains many of his possessions and is beautifully kept as a museum, the grounds have exceptionally fine coastal scenery. It is open daily from April to October, 9am – 6pm (Sundays 11am – 7pm) and during the rest of the year from 1pm – 5pm. **Derrynane Bay** has a glorious strand.

**Waterville** is the main resort of the Ring and has some good eating places; palm trees and fuchsia embue it with a continental air. The people speak gaelic, the Munster variety, and **Ballinskelligs** is crowded every year with Gaelic students. Do not miss the breathtaking view from **Bolus Head** looking out to the Skelligs, and the view from the mountain road at Ballynahow over a high col to **Valentia** is even better. You can visit the **Skelligs** to see the ruins of the old monastic settlement on **Skellig Michael**, the largest rock. Contact Mr Sean O'Shea, Tel: Catherdaniel 29, for boats leaving from Bunvalla Pier in the morning, or contact Mr Dermot Walshe Tel: Valentia island 15. It is amazing to think that over a thousand years ago, men hacked a stairway out of stone, 540 feet up to a barren rock half a mile long and threequarters of a mile wide. There was little they could do except pray and meditate. The way of life must have been hard, sometimes the waves crashing around the rock reach enormous heights. You can see beehive huts, stone crosses, Holy Well, oratories and cemeteries.

A theatrical tower guards the bridge and the inlet at **Cahirciveen,** it used to be the police barracks but is now derelict. This area is dominated by turf cutting and the holy mountain, Cnocknadobar. The Holy Well is at its base and from the summit (2,267 feet) you get a wonderful view of the Dingle Peninsula and the Blasket Islands. At **Glenbeigh** you can blow some of your money at the TOWERS HOTEL RESTAURANT famous for its prawns, Tel: Glenbeigh 12.

Make straight for **Dingle** unless you want to stop in **Tralee** for the Rose of Tralee Festival in late August, or for the Siama Tire Theatre; enquiries about both can be made at the Tourist Office in the The Mall, Tel: (066) 21288. The best way to get to **Dingle** is via **Camp** and the **Glennagalt Valley,** the Glen of the Madmen. Mad people were dropped off here to recover, helped perhaps by the magnificent scenery between the Beenoskee Massifs. The Irish phrase for someone who has gone mad is that 'he's away with his head'. This is the way the old railway used to go, dropping down to **Annascaul** where you can get a drink at the famous **South Pole Inn. Dingle** became famous overnight after the film 'Ryan's Daughter' and has become a little commercialised as a result. You must stop for a meal at **Doyle's Seafood Bar** in John St, where you can get excellent snacks or a full-blown gourmet meal, Tel: Dingle 144. Another famous stopping place is O'FLAHERTY'S PUB in Bridge St. After ten in the evenings you can listen to traditional music or singing, which just happens when the locals get together. CAFE LITERATA, off the Main St, sells a happy mixture of books, salads and teas. Dingle is a wonderfully onomatopoeic word and comes from the Irish Daingean, meaning a fortress, but nothing remains of one now, although the Peninsula is crowded with antiquities. The local people speak Irish amongst themselves, though you will find that they will switch to English when you are around, for courtesy's sake. If you have hitched down here, you can rent a *bicycle* from J. Moriarty, Tel: Dingle 66, or M O'Sullivan, Waterside, Tel: Dingle 46. Then explore west of Dingle into marvellous austere country battered by the Atlantic wind and sea.

**Ventry** has a lonely white strand on which it is said the King of the World, Daire Donn, landed to subjugate Ireland. The great Fionn Mac Cumhaill and his Fenian knights won the day, of course. On the road to **Shea Head**, past **Ventry** are the Fahan group of early Christian clochans, 414 in all. 19 souterrains (underground passages and storage places) and 18 standing stones, two sculptured crosses and seven ring forts are strewn all over the slopes of Mount Eagle; the most prominent is the powerfully built Doonbeg Fort. Local farmers still build little clochans as storehouses for animals, and the continuity of style is such with the unmortared stone that you can not tell the old from the new. The road from **Fahan** winds around the countryside to **Shea Head** from which you can see the **Blasket Islands**. Some beautiful writing has sprung from the Great Blasket, 'The Islandman' by Thomas O'Crohan 'Twenty years a-Growing' by Maurice O'Sullivan and the autobiography of Peig Sayers. All are worth reading for the humour, pathos and command of the Gaelic language which comes through even in translation. You can get out to the Blaskets from the quay at **Coumeenole**, if not by canoe or curragh, then by motor boat from **Dunquin,** where you can also buy good pottery.

In the Bays around here are Kerry diamonds – sparkly pieces of quartz, a nicer souvenir than anything you could buy. At **Ballydavid**, the ancient industry of curragh making goes on and at **Ballyferriter**, there is an active and friendly co-operative which grows parsley to export to France. They are also very keen on preserving their heritage: the Gaelic Language, antiquities, and beautiful scenery. There is a self catering cottage complex here, plus a hotel Tel: Ballyferriter 33.

East of **Ballyferriter** lies the perfectly preserved oratory of Gallarus – a relic of early Christianity. It is built of corbelled stone and is so watertight that not a drop of rain has entered it for a thousand years. Nearby is the Saint's Road up the Brandon Mountain, St. Brendan climbed up to is summit to meditate and saw in a vision Hy-Brasil, the Island of the Blessed, and afterwards he voyaged far and wide looking for this ideal land. An easier climb can be made from the village of **Cloghane** and the views from it are magical, it's not surprising that St. Brendan saw Utopia from here.

The main road from Dingle to **Stradbally** and on to **Tralee** take you over the **Connor Pass**, the summit of which is 1,500 feet with great views over Dingle Bay. There are several dark loughs in the valley and giant boulders are strewn everywhere. At the foot of the pass, branch roads lead off to **Cloghane** and **Brandon** – both good bases for exploring and climbing the sea cliffs around Brandon Point and Brandon Head. If you are planning to go west to Clare and Galway you can avoid Limerick city by taking the Ferry at **Tarbert**, across the Shannon, to **Killimer**. Ferries sail every hour on the hour from Tarbert and every hour on the half hour from Killimer. In summer they start from Killimer at 7.30 am and stop at 10 pm from Tarbert, in winter they start at 9.30 am and stop at 7 pm. The journey takes 20 minutes. North Kerry has none of the splendour of Dingle but rather a quiet charm, a taste of which you will get on the ferry trip.

Other places to go in North Kerry are: **Ardfert Cathedral**, a noble Early English Romanesque building dating from the 13th century; **Banna** and **Ballyheige** have lovely strands; whilst **Listowel** has ambitions as a cultural centre and puts on a 'writers week' every year in

May, with a book fair, art and photgraphy exhibitions, plus workshops for short story writing.

## PLACES TO STAY IN COUNTY KERRY

**Kenmare**
Mrs T Hayes, Ceann Mara, Killowen, Tel: (064) 41220 Farmhouse.
Mrs O'Sullivan, Waterfalls, Glengarriff Rd, Tel: (064) 41461
Mrs L O'Shea, Mountain View, Gengarriff Rd, Bonane, Tel: (064) 41394
Mrs H Boland, Muxnaw Lodge, Tel: (064) 41252
Mr and Mrs T Fahy, Rockvilla, Templenoe, Tel: (064) 41331
Mrs M Murphy, Rose Cottage, Tel: (064) 41330, very central.
**Killarney**
Is surrounded by youth hostels. Aghadoe Hs, an old manor house, very friendly, and quite noisy at nights. Tel: (064) 31240
Black Valley Hostel, Beaufort, great base for hiking around Gap of Dunloe, no Tel.
Corran Tuathail, Gortboy, Tel: Beaufort 87
Loo Bridge Hostel, Clonkeen, Tel: Clonkeen 2 (15 miles from Killarney on Cork Rd).
The Climber's Inn, Clencar, a friendly, unofficial hostel – a meeting place for climbers.
**Guesthouses:**
Lindon House, grade B, on the New Road, Tel: (064) 31379
Loch Lein Farm, Fossa, grade B, Tel: (064) 31260
Marian Hs, Woodlawn Rd, Tel: (064) 31275, grade B.
Tuscar, Fossa, Tel: (064) 31978, grade B.
Mr and Mrs Beazley, Carriglea House, Muckross Rd, Tel: (064) 31116 (farmhouse).
Mrs N Brosnan, Brosnan's Farmhouse, Woodland Rd, Tel: (064) 31328
Mrs M Kearney, Gap View Farm, Firies, Via Ballyhar, Tel: Farranfore 72
Mrs O'Sullivan, Lios na Manach Mill Rd, Muckross, Tel: (064) 31283 (farmhouse).
Mrs C Gorman, Sunset Villa, Tralee Rd, Tel: (064) 31124
Mrs B Moriarty, Briry Bungalow, Gap of Dunloe, Tel: Beaufort 113
**Cork Rd Area**
Mrs M Connell, St. Anthony's Villa, Park Rd, Tel: (064) 31534
Mrs C O'Meara, Breffni, Cork Rd, Tel: (064) 31413
**Muckross Rd Area**
Mrs A O'Mahoney, Mystical Rose, Woodlawn Rd, Tel: (064) 31453
**Town Centre**
Mrs O'Connor, Shangrila, 7 New Rd, Tel: (064) 31448

## THE RING OF KERRY
**Sneem**
Mrs A O'Sullivan, Woodvale Hs, off Quay Rd, Tel: (064) 45181
Mrs Hussey, Avondale, Sportsfield Rd, Tel: (064) 45221
Cantherella County Inn, grade B Tel: (064) 45187 delicious food

**Castlecove**
Mrs E McGuillicuddy, Birchgrove Farm, Tel: Catherdaniel 6
**Waterville**
The O'Shea Family, Benmore Farmhouse, Oughtive, Tel: Waterville 143
**Ballinskelligs**
Prior Hs Youth Hostel, Tel: Ballinskelligs 9
**Valentia Island**
Mrs P Lavelle, Tel; Valentia 24
Valentia Island Youth Hostel, Tel: Valentia 54
**Cahirciveen**
Mrs T Sugrue, Valentia View Farmhouse, Tel: Cahirciveen 219
Mrs Laanders, San Antoine, Valentin Rd, Tel: Cahirciveen 83
**Glenbeigh**
Mrs K O'Sullivan, Sea View Farmhouse, Mountain Stage, Tel: Glenbeigh 109
Mrs P Shearley, Glen Caragh, Tel: Glenbeigh 58
**Killorglin**
Mrs O'Callaghan, Aglish Hs, Cromane, Tel: Caragh Lakes 25
Mrs F Mangan, Riverside Hs, Tel: Killorglin 84

**THE DINGLE PENINSULA**
**Castlegregory**
Mrs K Griffin, Griffin's Country Farmhouse, Goulane, Tel: (066) 39147
**Cloghane**
Hillside Farmhouse, Ballynalackon, Tel; (066) 38124
**Dingle**
Guest houses both grade B: Alpine, Tel: Dingle 15 and Milltown Hs, Tel: Dingle 62
Strand Accommodation is an unofficial Youth Hostel (cheap)
Mrs T O'Connor, Dykegate St, Tel: Dingle 78
**Ventry**
Mrs S Birmingham, Ballymore Hs, Ballymore Ventry, Tel: Dingle 140
**Ballydavid**
Mrs Ni Gearailt, Bother Bui, Baile na nGall, Tel: Ballydavid 42
The Hurley Family, An Dooneen Farmhouse, Kilcooley, Tel: Ballydavid 12
**Tralee**
Heatherville Farm, Blennerville, Tel: (066) 21054
Mrs Ferguson, Dunkerron, Oakpark Rd, Tel: (066) 21110
**Binge Places**
Carash Lodge, Caragh Lake, Tel: Caragh Lake 15
Riversdale Hs, grade A hotel, Kenmare, Tel: (064) 41299
Butler Arms, grade A hotel, Waterville, Tel: Waterville 5

# County Limerick

A limerick is a nonsense verse, and it is also a lovely county in Ireland. The quiet farming country is dotted with the ruins of hundreds of castles and bounded on the north by the spacious Shannon spreading like the sea and on its other sides by a fringe of hills and mountains.

The city of **Limerick** is largely Georgian in character, but was founded long ago by the Norsemen, for it has always been an important fording place on the River Shannon. In parts where modern buildings have sprung up, it is rather tinpot, but if you go down to the river and look across to the massive rounded towers of St. John's Castle you feel something of its romance and history. Limerick is like Londonderry in the North, full of memories of the 1690s. During the 1690s, there were three struggles going on: the struggle of Britain and her Protestant allies to oppose the ascendancy in Europe of Catholic France, the struggle of Britain to subdue Ireland, and the struggle of the Protestant planter families and the Catholic Irish for the leadership of Ireland. The Irish army had been beaten at the Boyne under St. Ruth and had retreated to Limerick whose walls were said to be paper thin. Patrick Sarsfield led a daring raid on the siege train from Dublin and destroyed it. When William III eventually did break through the Limerick walls he sent in 10,000 men to wreak havoc, but the women and children of the city fought with anything that came to hand alongside their men and they beat back the invaders. The second siege started a month later and they held out for four weeks, but time ran out and Sarsfield signed an honourable treaty.

You may wander around King John's Castle in the summer months and in one of its towers hear Irish music (seisiun), twice weekly in the evenings. St. Mary's Cathedral is the only ancient church building left in the city and was built in 1172 by Donal Mor O'Brien, King of Munster. Inside are some superb 15th century misericords (choir stalls) carved into the shapes of fantastic beasts. Old English Town and its Irish counterpart across the river are the most interesting parts of Limerick to wander in. St. John's Square is full of lovely old buildings circa 1750, some of which are being restored after years of neglect. Beautiful lace is made by the Good Shepherd Sisters in Clare Street, you can visit them during working hours and perhaps buy something exquisite which might in time become a family heirloom! The Hunt Collection at the National Institute for Higher Education is on view during the weekdays, it contains a mixture of bronze age weapons, 18th century silver, and medieval art.

This is great *hunting* country, ask at the Tourist Office for the telephone numbers and addresses of the various hunts. Remember you have to be experienced, the hire of a mount for the day is at least £IR30. The Tourist Office is at 62 O'Connell Street, Tel: (061) 47522 the rail and bus

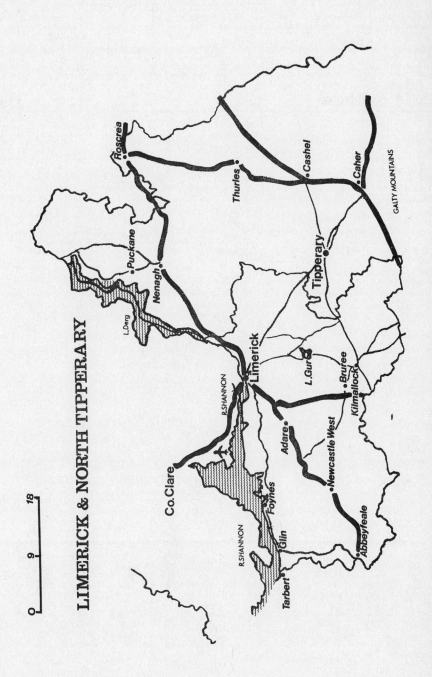

# LIMERICK & NORTH TIPPERARY

0    9    18

Roscrea

Puckane

Nenagh

L.Derg

Thurles

Cashel

Caher

GALTY MOUNTAINS

Tipperary

Limerick

L.Gur

Brulee

Kilmallock

R.SHANNON

Co.Clare

Adare

Newcastle West

Foynes

Glin

Abbeyfeale

R.SHANNON

Tarbert

terminal Tel: (061) 42433 is at Parnell Street, and Shannon airport is 16 miles away. **Shannon Airport** is a free port area in which custom duties and formalities are suspended, also there are hundreds of bargains for those flying out. The Shannonside Entertainment Guide will give you details on what is happening in Limerick city, pick it up from the Tourist Office or any hotel.

**Eating:** THE CURRY POT, 56 O'Connell St, Tel: (061) 46027; THE GALLEON GRILL, 122 O'Connell St, Tel: (061) 48358; HARVEST RESTAURANT, Cecil St, (Health food and seafood) Tel: (061) 40314; STELLA RESTAURANT 116/117 O'Connell St, Tel: (061)45349; JONATHAN'S, 112 O'Connell St, expensive but delicious (if you like dancing to piano music), Tel: (021) 46020.

**Lough Gur**, about 12 miles from Limerick, is in an area rich in field antiquities and guarded by two strong castles built by the Desmonds. According to legend the last of the Desmonds is doomed to hold court under the waters of Lough Gur and to emerge, fully armed, at daybreak on every morning of the seventh year in a routine that must be repeated until the silver shoes of his horse are worn away.

**Adare** (Ath Dara – the Ford of the Oak Tree) is set in richly timbered land through which the little River Maigue flows and pretty thatched cottages blend with graceful ruins. Finest of all the ruins is the Franciscan Friary, best seen from the long narrow bridge of 14 arches. It was founded by the Earls of Kildare, and above the fine old doorway is the Geraldine Shield. Other ancient foundations are the Trinitarian Abbey, founded for the redemption of Christian captives during the Third Crusade, the Augustinian Abbey and St. Nicholas' Church. Looking at Desmond Castle and Adare Manor on the river, one could have taken a step back into history.

**Eating:** THE FARRIERS RESTAURANT and the DUNRAVEN ARMS are excellent for food and drink and you can wander round the Manor House, built of finely worked limestone, and its gardens. The area round **Adare** is known as the Palatine because of the number of German Lutherans who settled here in the 18th century.

**Kilmallock** should have been twenty times more gracious than Adare but nothing was protected or cherished. If you are heading for **Tarbert** to catch the car ferry to Killimer in Clare, keep an eye out for the pretty village of **Glin** and the castle of the Knight of Glin, his family have been there for 700 years.

**PLACES TO STAY IN COUNTY LIMERICK**

**Limerick**
The Youth Hostel, 1 Pery Sq, usually very busy, very central.
Miss M Collins, St. Anthony's, 8 Coolraine Terrace (Ennis Rd Area), Tel: (061) 52607
Mrs C Gavin, Shannonville, Ennis Rd, Tel: (061) 53690
There are plenty of other B&Bs along this road which is on the direct route to Shannon Airport, buses are constantly passing so it's easy to

reach from the centre of town.
Clifton House has plenty of private bathrooms and is a grade B guesthouse, Tel: (061) 51715
**Centre**
Mrs T A Walsh, St. Mary's, Clancy Strand, Tel: (061) 55919
**Adare**
Mrs E Walsh, Knockwadra Hs, Tuogh, Tel: (061) 94173
Mrs M Fitzgerald, Woodlands Farmhouse, Knockanes, Tel: (061) 94118
**Bruree**
Mrs E McDonagh, Cooleen House, Tel: Bruree 84
**Kilmallock**
Misses A & M O'Shea, Roseville, Kilbreedy East, Tel: Martinstown 9
**Newcastle West**
Mrs Buckingham, Glenastar Lodge, Ardagh, Tel: Ardagh 28

**Binge Places**
Dunraven Arms, grade A hotel, Adare, Tel: (061) 94209
Colonel S. O'Driscoll, Castle Matrix, Rathkeale, Tel: Rathkeale 139

---

# County Tipperary

**Tipperary** (Tipperary the well of Ara – a spring near the main street in the town of Tipperary)
To get a clear idea of how beautiful Tipperary is – even though it lacks a stretch of coastline – climb or rather walk to the top of Slievenamon which in early summer is scented with the almond fragrance of gorse blossom. Up there you get the feeling of space and a wide, splendid view; to the south are the Comeraghs and the silver ribbon of the Suir, to the west, the Galtees and to the north, the Rock of Cashel rising out of the flat, rich farmland. Slievenamon means in Irish, mountain of the fairy women of Fevin; Finn and the Fianna warriors had dallied with them a little so when he decided to wed, to prevent any of the fairy women becoming jealous, he said he would marry the one who reached the summit of the mountain first. However, the wily man had set his heart on Grainne, the daughter of King Cormac and so he whisked her up to the top the evening before the race. When the panting winner reached the top 'there sat the delicate winsome Grainne and not a feather of her ruffled'.
**Clonmel** in the south (in Irish, the Honeyed Meadow) has a lovely setting by the River Suir and the Comeragh mountains. It has got a prosperous bright look about it which is not surprising as most of Tipperary consists of very fertile land. Lawrence Sterne, who wrote one of the first ever novels 'Tristram Shandy', was born here, as was the enterprising Italian pedlar Charles Bianconi who gave Ireland its first

public transport service when he ran his celebrated Bianconi Long Cars from **Clonmel** to **Cahir** in 1815. The Parish Church of St. Mary has a fine east window. You could look in at the art gallery and museum in Parnell Street and about a mile outside town is St. Patrick's Well in a pretty glen. *Fishing* on the Suir, the Nire, the Tar and the Anner, *horse racing* meeting at Powerstown Park Racecourse and an 18 hole *golf course*. Tel: (052) 21138 for details. Clonmel is the big centre for *greyhound racing* enthusiasts – it all happens twice weekly at Davis Road.

**Carrick-on-Suir** is a thriving market town founded largely by the Quakers, though in the past it was a stronghold of the Ormond clan, the chief family of Tipperary. Black Tom, in the last years of the reign of Elizabeth I, built a magnificent mansion which still stands outside the town. There is nothing else quite like this Tudor mansion in Ireland, for the transition from the fortified castle to the undefended house had not begun, and when it did the Tudor Style had given way to other architectural fashions. The Office of Public Works has sympathetically restored it, returning the great fireplace to the long gallery; it had adorned Kilkenny Castle for many years. There are not guided tours but the house is open on request. *Golf*, and brown trout *fishing* on the Suir are available.

**Eating:** you can get a snack at the TWIBA FOOD AND WINE BAR in Kickham St.

**Ahenny** (the ford of Fire) on the border with County Kilkenny boasts two elaborately carved stone crosses from the 8th century in a sleepy old churchyard. The bases are carved with wonderful figure scenes and the crosses themselves with involved spiral, interlaced and fret designs. Around the neighbourhood are some very extensive slate quarries; the vast spoil heaps and water-filled holes are softened by many kinds of orchids, and flags, known locally in Gaelic as felistroms.

Near **Fethard** is Kiltinan Castle and Kiltinan Old Church where you can see some Sheela-na-Gigs, they are pretty revolting, and smothered in ivy. **Fethard** itself has a lovely old church with fine 15th century windows and a square tower. Kilcooly Abbey is one of the outstanding examples of a cistercian building in Co. Tipperary, the other is the Abbey of Holy Cross. The former was founded in 1183 and nearly ruined in 1445 with subsequent reconstruction, but despite being a muddle, it is a very handsome ruin with a superb six light east window. The tomb flags are exquisitely carved by one Rory O'Tunney and the south doorway is set in the midst of a highly ornamented screen with a carved crucifixion, and a scene of St. Christopher bearing Jesus over a river symbolised by a shoal of fishes. Amongst the other carvings is a coy mermaid holding a looking glass, a motif also found in Connacht. This area was settled by Palatines when some of them fled here from religious persecution in Germany.

**The Rock of Cashel**, Cashel of the Kings is a steep outcrop of limestone rising out of the Golden Vein, the name reflects the richness of this agricultural land. The grouping of the bare, broken buildings against the sky is memorable and worth travelling many miles to see. The rock was the seat of ancient chieftains and later the early Munster Kings, and upon the naturally well defended rock, there was very likely a stone fortress or caiseal. In 450 St. Patrick came to Cashel to baptise either Corc the Third, or his brother and successor, Aengus. During the ceremony Patrick is supposed to have driven the sharp point of his pastoral staff into the king's foot by mistake, and the victim bore the wound without a sign, thinking that such pain was all part of becoming a Christian! Brien Boru was crowned at Cashel in 977. In 1101 King Murtagh O'Brien granted the Rock to the church for its political importance had declined and it became the See of the Archbishopric of Munster.

Cormac's Chapel was built in the 1130s by the bishop-king of that name; it is a fascinating building, architecturally it has been influenced by the Germans though it is often described as Hiberno-Romanesque. The most Irish thing about Cormac's Chapel is its steep stone roof, as for the rest, the twin towers, the storeys of blank wall arcading, the high gable over the north doorway and most of the stone cut decoration, it could be German or English.

Inside the Chapel is a splendid but broken stone sarcophagus of 11th century work, the ribbon beast interlacement was probably re-introduced into Ireland by the Vikings. Inside a gilt copper crozier head was found, it is now preserved in the National Museum; the head is late 13th century French, richly ornamented with animal and fish forms in enamel, turquoise and sapphire.

As you enter the complex of buildings through the restored Vicars Choral Hall you will see the Cross of St. Patrick probably of the same date as the sarcophagus, Christ is carved on one side and an ecclesiastic, perhaps St. Patrick, carved on the other. The massive base on which it is reputed to be the coronation stone of the Munster Kings. The immense ruins of the cathedral built beside the chapel dates from the second half of the 13th century and was the scene of two deliberate burnings during the Anglo-Irish wars of the Tudors and Cromwell. In 1686, the cathedral was restored and used by the Church of Ireland, but then it was left to decay until **Cashel** became a National Monument and everything was tidied up. What remains now is a fine example of austere Irish Gothic architecture with a rather short nave, the end of which is taken up with what is known as the Castle, a massive tower built to house the bishops in the 15th century. Everything about the cathedral is superbly grand and delicate in marked contrast to Cormac's chapel. The round tower is about 12th century, you can see the top of it perfectly if you climb to the top of the castle, plus a wonderful view of the Golden Vein, the Devil's Bit Mountain, the hills to the East and West and Slievenamon in the South. Just below, in the plain, is Hore Abbey, built by the Cistercians from Mellifont. The Rock looks superb at night, particularly during the summer when it is floodlit. You can go round it for a very small fee, except on Monday in the winter months.

**Cashel Town** is a thriving place with a very good hotel, the **Cashel Palace**. It used to be the residence of the Church of Ireland archbishops and was built in gracious Queen Anne style in 1730; it's worth having at least a coffee there so you can get a glimpse of the panelling and carving. The Diocesan Library, in the precincts of the St. John the Baptist Cathedral, has one of the finest collections of 16th and 17th century books in Ireland. There are several on exhibition, but you have to contact Dean Clarke if you want to get inside the cathedral. **Cashel** has a very good craft shop specialising in handwoven Shanagarry tweed, and leather work. In Padraig O'Mathuna's Gallery you can buy enamel and silver objets d'art.

**Eating:** CHEZ HANS, nestling at the foot of the Rock, is a very imaginative and fairly expensive restaurant, it is actually a small Gothic chapel. A good cheap place is the very unromantic but clean ESSO RESTAURANT by the Esso petrol station on the Dublin Road.

Every year there is a festival of traditional Irish music, song and dance. a Tourist Office in the Town Hall, Tel: 062 61333, will give you all the necessary details.

Deep in the countryside, reached by tiny roads hemmed in by hawthorn hedges, is the **Holycross** Abbey, unfortunately right next door to a rather grotty looking lounge bar. It lies between **Thurles** and **Cashel** on the banks of the lazy Suir, it was built so that a portion of the True Cross, presented by Pope Pascal II in 1110 to Murtagh O'Brien, might be properly enshrined. In 1182, the Abbey was transferred to the Cistercians who magnificently embellished it so that it became a popular place of pilgrimage. The building was rebuilt and changed over many centuries and most of the finest work belongs to the 15th century. Inside is a sedilia of perfect workmanship and design, so delicate that it resembles the work of a woodcarver rather than a mason working in hard limestone. The Abbey is in full use today, having been restored by skilled workmen, who had to give their best to equal the standard of past centuries. Nearby is LONGFIELD HOUSE the home of Charles Bianconi, now a grade B* hotel.

**Cahir** (the Stone Fortress of the fish abounding stronghold). This is the nicest sort of Irish town on the River Suir at the eastern end of the Galtee Mountains, at the meeting of the Dublin/Cork and Limerick/Waterford roads. It has a magnificent fully restored 15th century castle on an island in the River Suir, the castle houses the Tourist Office. Here in 1599, the Earl of Essex achieved the only important success of his Irish Campaign when he took the place after a 10 day siege. Swans float on the river and the Cahir House Hotel is where you should settle if you plan to go *walking* in the Galtees or *fishing* in the Suir. It has a plush old fashioned bar and everybody eats Sunday lunch there, the ladies is unusually luxurious with wooden loo seats and fresh flowers!

**Eating:** the EARL OF GLENGALL describes itself as a luxury restaurant, it has a cocktail bar, whilst the lobsters crawling around in an aquarium can provide your meal. You can go *beagling* with the Ardfinnan and Kilfeacle packs from October to March. **Ardfinnan** has a ruined castle built by the Earl of Morton, afterwards King John of England. There is *dancing* in the Galtee Hotel every Friday and in the Cahir House Hotel. There are *ballad* sessions in Silver Sands at **Balldrehid**, and the Welcome Inn, Lower Abbey St. **Cahir.**

The Vee Road from **Cahir** passes beautifully wrought iron gates and then plunges you deep in the countryside. It is a route through the Knockmealdown Gap which crosses the county border into Waterford.

You pass through **Clogheen** before the road curves up the slopes thick with pine forest, then it suddenly turns back on itself in a wide vee or hairpin and you get the most fabulous view over the patchwork of fields; you are 1,114 feet above sea level. Forest gives way to bracken and heather and a lonely mountain tarn, the steep cliff rising up behind it is covered in a bright green mass of bog oak and rhododendron. It's sometimes quite misty and as you go down towards **Lismore** you look through the rain and sparks of sunlight at shifting vales. Just before **Lismore** the trees, oak and beech grow with tropical thickness, festooned with moss and ferns, then suddenly, the spires of Lismore Cathedral stand against the skyline.

The **Glen of Aherlow** between the Galtee mountains and the Slievenamuck Hills is not really a glen at all but a lush and colourful valley. The road runs parallel with the Aherlow River and signposts point to the numerous tarns and lakes set in the beautifully shaped Galtees. This pass used to be the scene of many battles and the refuge of the mountain men and outlawed Irish.

**Tipperary** lying in the Golden Vein is a great farming centre, and known by many from the soldiers song 'It's a long way to Tipperary'. The town has a fine bronze figure of Charles Kickham, a patriot and novelist; read his novels, *Knocknagow* and *The Homes of Tipperary* if you can. The Manchester Martyrs and John O'Leary, a fenian leader and journalist, have memorials worth looking at, also try to take a look at the Catholic church, a limestone Gothic building. The Galtees are a magnificent huddle of peaks formed from a conglomerate mixture of old red sandstone, and silurian rocks; the ridge **walking** is fantastic especially around **Lyracappul**. The Galtees stretch from Tipperary into Limerick where they merge with the Ballyhoura Hills which border Cork. The Tourist Office is in the main street, Tel: (062) 51457.

The mountain splendour between **Toomyvara** and **Nenagh** is worth exploring; round here you will hear stories of Ned of the Hill, the local Robin Hood, who plundered the English planter families and made up the lovely song *'The Dark woman of the Glen.* **Nenagh** is the administrative capital of the north riding of Tipperary, it has an impressive Keep called the Nenagh Round which was built as part of a strong pentagonal castle in 1200 by the first of the Ormond line. The Bishop of Killaloe did it an injustice in 1858 by adding a castellated crown, but it is still beautiful.

## PLACES TO STAY IN COUNTY TIPPERARY

**Bansha**
Ballydavid wood Hs Youth Hostel, Tel: Tipperary 54148
**Ballina** (beside Killaloe).
Mrs T Lucus, Derry Cottage, Derry Castle, Tel: (061) 76209
**Borrisoleigh**
Mrs Brown, Killoschehane Castle, Tel: Borrisoleigh 5
**Cahir**
Mrs English, Brookfield Hs, Dublin Rd, Tel: Cahir 373
Mrs FitzGerald, Ashling, Cashel Rd, Tel: Cahir 601

Cahir Hs Hotel, grade B*, Tel: Cahir 207
Youth Hostel, Mountain Lodge, Burncourt
**Cashel**
Mrs O'Brien, Knock Saint Lour, Tel: (062) 61172
Mrs P Higgins, Castlelake Manor, Tel: (063) 61480
Mrs Foley, Rahad Lodge, Tel: (062) 61052 (on outskirts of town).
**Clonmel**
Phelan Family, Mullinarkinka Hs, Tel: (052) 21374
Mrs O'Connell, Benuala, Marlfield Rd, Tel: (052) 22158
**Dundrum**
Mrs T Grene, Cappamurra Hs, Tel: (062) 71127 Farmhouse near the
Holycross Abbey.
**Emly** (near Glen of Aherlow).
Mrs Burns, Monemore Hs, Tel: (062) 57122
**Nenagh**
Mrs Delaney, Tyrone Hs, Tel: (067) 32053
Mrs Kennel, farmhouse, nr. St. Joseph's Abbey, Tel: (0505) 41258
Mrs Fallon, Cregganbell, Birr Rd, Tel: (0505) 21421
**Thurles**
Mrs Cambie, Killoran Hs, Moyne, Tel: (0504) 45271
Mrs E Maher, Parkstown Hs, Horse & Jockey, Tel: Littleton 15
Mrs Molony, Holycross Hs, Holycross, Tel: Holycross 78
**Tipperary**
Mrs N O'Dwyer, Barronstown Hs, Emly Rd, Tel: (062) 55130
Mrs Ryan, Ballyryan Hs, Conard, Tel: (062) 51321
Mrs L Haye, Ballincourty Hs, Glenof Aherlow, Tel: (062) 56230
Mrs M Quinn, Cork-Galbally Rd, Tel: (062) 51637
**Binge Places**
Inislounaght Hs, Marlfield, Clonmel, Tel: (052) 22847
Cashel Palace Hotel, Cashel, Tel: (062) 61411

# County Waterford

Waterford is a fertile county with rugged mountain beauty and a pretty
coastline, dotted with fishing villages cum holiday resorts and plenty of
interesting ruins. The south east coast also has the reputation for being
sunny.

**Waterford City**, is famous in Waterford for its nouveau riche business
men who annoy the local fishermen at weekends with their ostentation!
Most tourists will recognise the name because of its cut crystal glass; if
you are over 12 years old you can go round the famous Waterford glass
factory but make arrangements with the Tourist Office first. Reginald's
Tower, a massive circular fortress with a wall ten feet thick, is worth a

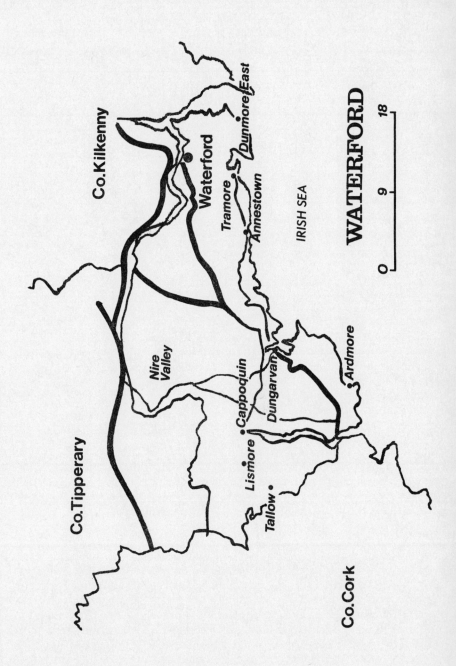

WATERFORD

Co.Kilkenny

Waterford

Dunmore East

Tramore

Annestown

IRISH SEA

Nire Valley

Cappoquin

Dungarvan

Lismore

Ardmore

Tallow

Co.Tipperary

Co.Cork

0    9    18

visit as well. The city was founded by the Danes, eventually they traded with the Irish and became Christian; nothing remains of their timber fortifications, and although Reginald's Tower is named after a Dane of that name, it probably was not built until the 12th century. When the desperado Strongbow landed in 1170 and took the city, Reginald's Tower became a Norman stronghold and has since then served as a royal residence, a mint, a military barracks and a city prison, and is now the civic museum.

Waterford city has many beautiful buildings worth visiting. Christ Church Cathedral built in 1779 and designed in the English Classic style is a lovely building; inside are several monuments, one of them being a carved tomb of a 15th century mayor named Rice, who chose to depict himself in a state of decay with frogs, toads and other wriggling things emerging from his entrails. The French Church, now a ruin, was nicknamed thus because it was used by Huguenot refugees from 1695 onwards, but in fact it was originally a Franciscan foundation built in 1240. The key and permission to view may be obtained from the Board of Works, Catherine St. The Chamber of Commerce building is a Georgian building with a lovely staircase and carving, open from 9.30am-5pm, Monday to Friday. The City Hall in the Mall was built by the same architect who built Christ Church and inside is a splendid cut glass Waterford Chandelier, a copy of which hangs in the Hall of Independence in Philadelphia. The City Hall also houses two old theatres, the Theatre Royal has frequent productions by leading professsional touring companies.

There is quite a lot to do in Waterford, with *golf, tennis, river cruising* and CIE operated *coach tours* from the quay to The Vee, and the Nire valley. In the evening there are three *cinemas* to choose from and two hotels, the Tower and the Ardee have *dancing*. There is some rather sub-standard music at the Showboat, The Glen, O'Donaghue's and other singing pubs.

**Eating:** costs about £IR12 a head; particularly good is BALLINA-KILL HOUSE, two miles from Waterford off the Dunmore East Rd, Tel: (051) 74138 and the SITRIC RESTAURANT in the Mall, Tel: (051) 55611. Cheaper places are the GLANVILLE HOTEL, BIANCONI GRILL at the quay, and the REGINALD GRILL ROOM in the Mall.

In September **Waterford** holds the *International Festival of Light Opera*, so make sure you book a room in advance if you are going to be there when it's all happening. The Tourist Information Office is at 41 The Quay, Waterford, Tel: (051) 75788.

**Dunmore East**, a little seaside place, is rather like a Devon fishing village with beautiful little headlands made of old red sandstone carved into cliffs and safe bathing beaches. Sea pinks grow along the cliff edges which have some lovely peaceful places to walk. You will meet the colourful fishermen in the bars, though they can be quite clannish. The harbour was designed by Nimmo in 1814, at that time Dunmore was the centre of a thriving herring industry and the Irish terminal for a mail service from England. You can hire a boat to go *sea angling* if you ask in the local hotels, or go *sailing*, contact June Bullock, Dunmore East, Tel:

(051) 83230. Seisiún, the traditional music entertainment is held weekly from June to August in the Haven Hotel. Nearby on the Waterford Harbour is the village of Crooke, roughly opposite and a little further down\is Hook Head, interesting because the two are immortalised in the saying 'by Hook or by Crooke', a phrase first used by sailors.

**Tramore** is the place to go if you want to meet Irish people on holiday rather than fellow foreigners. Its three miles of sand are swept by the gulf stream which makes the sea fun for *bathers,* and *surfers.* Tramore has all the usual amusements of a seaside resort within a 50 acre park. Knockeen Dolmen and the Doneraile Cliffs on the west side of Tramore Bay are smothered in sea pinks and campion. A wooded glen past Doneraile walk leads to Pier Cove. **Eating: Annestown**, nearby, also has a lovely beach and an excellent restaurant. **Annestown House** stands above a strikingly beautiful bay, six miles from Tramore, booking is essential, Tel: (051) 96160. Tramore has a *caravan park* and is well served by buses from Waterford City. The Tourist Information Office is in the Railway Square, Tel: (051) 81572. The shops are closed all day Thursday.

**Portlaw** on the River Clodagh was founded as a model village by a Quaker family who had started up a cotton industry in the 19th century; unfortunately many of the quaint houses have been modernised and become dull in the process. Beside the town is Curaghmore House and gardens, the family home of the Marquis of Waterford. It is open to the public every Thursday afternoon. The Beresfords were noted for their dominance in the Church and Government; one of them was called 'sand martin' because of his skill in picking sinecures and plum jobs for his many friends.

**Dungarvan** is a pleasant seaside resort where the River Colligan broadens into Dungarvan Bay. About five miles south is the famous Irish speaking village of **Ring** where Irish scholars go to study. You might come across the Master McGrath Monument two and a half miles north west of Dungarvan; in case you did not know he is remembered for winning the Waterloo Cup three times, the greyhound is still remembered in ballads and by a brand of superior dog food!

**Ardmore** further west on the coast is set in lovely countryside and has a graceful round tower and a group of early Christian buildings, probably founded by St. Declan in the 5th century. Some say St. Declan was busy converting the pagans to Christianity whilst St. Patrick was still a slave herding cattle. St. Declan's Oratory is typical of the small dark dwellings in which the early fathers used to live; apparently this preference for separate cells grouped together comes from the Coptic Egyptian influence in the Irish Church, along with a rejection of the bodily senses and a deep suspicion of women. St Declan's Oratory was not in fact built until the 9th century, but Irish architecture seems to advanced very slowly. The Cathedral is a mixture of Hiberno-Romanesque from the 12th century and Early English, with a wealth of figure sculpture spread over almost the whole of the west gable. The figures are badly weathered but it is just possible to make out the Judgement of Solomon, Adam and Eve with the Tree and the Serpent, and the adoration of the Magi. About half a mile to the east is Saint Declan's Holy Well and Temple Disert (the secluded Hermitage). Down on the Strand is a crannog, visible only when the tide is out.

**Eating:** BYRON LODGE, Tel: (024) 4157, is a small restaurant specialising in seafood and there is a B* family run hotel. *Fishing*, and *pony trekking* can be arranged, ask at the local hotel.

The road through Clashmore, and Aglish to **Cappoquin** follows the stretches of the Blackwater, which are lined by stately grey houses. **Cappoquin** is at the head of the tidal estuary of the Blackwater River, graceful timbered hills surround it, whilst the southern slopes of the Knockmealdown Mountains rise to the north. This is an excellent place to *fish* for trout or roach, most of the fishing is free, but you should collect a free permit from the local coarse fishing association and if you are after trout, from the local guest houses. Four miles to the north is the Trappist Cistercian Abbey of Mount Melleray, the order has built up an almost self-sufficient community which still keeps the old rule of monastic hospitality, so do not hesitate to accept if they offer you a meal. The village has a very good craftshop.

The road from **Cappoquin** to **Lismore** follows the River Blackwater – flowing smoothly between green fields and trees, overlooked by gracious houses. **Lismore** has one of the nicest castles in Ireland which dates back, in parts, to the original built by King John in 1185. It belonged to Sir Walter Raleigh in 1589 and he sold it to the adventurer Richard Boyle, later the first Earl of Cork, who apparently said, 'I arrived out of England into Ireland, where God guided me hither, bringing with me a taffeta doublet and a pair of velvet breeches, a new suit of laced fustian cutt upon taffeta, a bracelet of gold, a diamond ring, and twenty-seven pounds three shillings in monie in my purse'. His son, the 14th child, is remembered as the Father of Chemistry. Eventually the castle passed through the female line to the Devonshire family. The gardens are open to the public from mid-May to mid-September in the afternoons on weekdays, closed on Mondays; The Castle will soon be opened to the public.

**Lismore** is a place of ancient renown both for its learning and piety. Under St. Colman in the 8th century it won the style of the Luminary of the Western World and men came from all over Europe to study there. The Norsemen, of course, were attracted to it, as bees to honey and looted the town and abbey frequently, but the monastery and abbey were finally destroyed by Raymond le Gros in 1173. The cathedral of Saint Carthach is one of the loveliest in Ireland and approached by a tree lined walk. It dates from medieval times but was restored by the Earl of Cork in 1633 and the graceful limestone spire was added in 1827. The *salmon fishing* on the Blackwater is legendary, and the *coarse fishing* good, you can get a permit from Lismore Castle and from the hotels. The Nire Valley is fantastic for *views, pony trekking* and *walking*, on either side are mountain slopes, clear, tumbling streams and woods. It lies between the Comeragh and Knockmealdown ranges and can be approached from **Clonmel** to **Ballymacarberry** and then back to Clonmel via a mountain road. Free fishing for *brown trout* in the Nire River and lakes and you can hire ponies to go trekking in the mountains from Melody's in **Ballymacarberry**.


## PLACES TO STAY IN COUNTY WATERFORD

**Ardmore**
Mrs Sylvester, Sea Crest, Grange, Nr. Ardmore, Tel: (024) 4171
**Ballymacarberry**
Mrs Ryan, Clonanav Farmhouse, off main Dungarvan-Clonmel Rd, Tel: (052) 3614
**Cappoquin**
Riverview Hs, Cook St, Tel: (058 54073
The Toby Jug Guesthouse, grade B, Tel: (058) 53317
**Dungarvan**
Mrs Kiely, Ballyguiry Farm, Tel: (058) 41194
Mrs Croke, Stella Maris, Youghal Rd, Tel: (058) 41727
The Ryan Family, Ballylemon Lodge, Cappagh, Tel: Cappagh 18
Mrs McHugh, Cielito, The Burgery, Abbeyside, Tel: (058) 42282
**Dunmore East**
The Ocean, grade B* hotel, Tel: (051) 83136
Guesthouse, Corballymore Hs, Tel: (051) 83143
Mrs M Kent, Foxmount Farm, Halfway Hs, Tel: (051) 74308
Mrs Power, Creaden Cottage, Tel: (051) 83191
**Lismore**
Mrs Landers, 2 Park's Rd, Tel: (058) 554033
Youth Hostel, Glenagara.
**Tramore**
Mrs Walsh, Newtown House, Coast Rd, Tel: (051) 81625
**Waterford**
Mrs E Purnell, Blenheim Hs, Blenheim Heights, Tel: (051) 74115 (rooms with bath).
Mrs Ryan Beechwood, 7 Cathedral Square, Tel: (051) 76677
Mrs O'Brien, Annvill, The Orchard, Kingsmeadow, Tel: (051) 73617

**Binge Places**
Ballyrafter Hs, Lismore, Tel: (058) 54002
Ardree, grade A* hotel, Waterford City, Tel: (051) 32111
Granville, grade A hotel, Waterford City, Tel: (051) 55111

# PART VI
# THE PROVINCE OF
# ULSTER

---

## Ulster (Uladh: Land of the Ultonians)

**Ulster** is a proud fighting province, its legendary past tells of fierce heroes and warrior women, the notorious present tells of terrorists and gun men. Some experts on the Irish race maintain that in ancient times the North was full of Picts and the South full of Milesians; we do know that Ulster was the most systematically planted province because of its continued fierce resistance to the English. Thus, the hardy Scots were introduced into the province to provide a loyal garrison. The sign of Ulster is the Red Hand. The symbol is the result of the race for the overlordship of Ulster between the MacDonnells and the De Burghs. The first to reach land would take the prize and as the two contestants struggled through the shallows off the Antrim coast, MacDonnell fearing that De Burgh who led the race would win, cut off his own hand and threw it far onto the strand where it lay covered in red blood. Thus the symbol of this fair land is oddly prophetic of the many bloody struggles for its conquest.

The two great clans of the west were descended from the sons of the great High King of Ireland, Niall of the Nine Hostages. Their names were Conal and Eoghan and they gave their name to districts in west Ulster: Tyrconnell and Tyrone. When Brian Boru instituted surnames in Ireland, their followers took the names O'Donnell and O'Neill respectively, and it was they who rebelled against English rule.

**NORTHERN IRELAND**
Visitors are discouraged by Northern Ireland's bad press thus creating a countryside open to those of a more adventurous spirit. When you cross the border and encounter the security forces you may indeed feel that the

234

subversives are laying seige to the government. The Ulster border has meant much through the ages: Cuchulain, the Hound of Ulster, was perhaps its most famous guard when he defended it against the host of Ireland during the epic battles of the Brown Bull of Cooley (recounted in the Tain). The Northern Ireland you will see today has suffered most in its towns but the countryside is as beautiful, and perhaps more accessible than anywhere else in Ireland because of the development of forest parks and the like. The North is also different because it was industrialized during the 19th century and so endured the more ugly stages of capitalistic development, while Southern Ireland is trying to pull itself out of its agriculturally based economy and build factories now.

Having said all that, the visitor should not ignore Northern Ireland thinking it's a foreign country within Ireland, because it certainly is not. One great plus point for the North is its teeming lakes and rivers which because of 'the troubles' have scarcely been fished for twelve years. *Coarse fishermen* find nothing like it anywhere else in the British Isles and as a tourist all sides welcome you unless you are stupid enough to go into extreme Provo or UVF ghettos and start shooting your mouth off. The vast majority of Northern Irish people are friendly, witty and very kind.

The six counties which make up the North are Antrim, Armagh, Down, Fermanagh, Londonderry, Tyrone. They are also included in the ancient province of Ulster together with Cavan, Monaghan and Donegal.

---

# County Cavan

Cavan like neighbouring Monaghan is full of wooded 'drumlins'. The rivers and streams which broaden into lakes and ponds provide a bewildering choice of angling water, in fact large areas of Cavan appear to have more water than land and you can easily get lost on the small roads and lanes which lead to them, so use a good map. Ordnance survey maps can be acquired from the Tourist Office, Cavan, Townhall St, Tel: (049) 31942 or Belturbet, Tel: (0492) 2207.

Because Cavan offers the fisherman such opportunities I have given a short run down of the various well known areas. For more detail, there is information and lots of maps in *Fishing in Ireland, The Complete Guide* by Dick Warner, Kevin Linnane, and Peter R Brown, published by Appletree Press, Belfast, 1980.

Near **Cavan Town** the Lough Oughter system of small to medium sized lakes is really an off shoot of the River Erne complex. This is a well known *coarse fishing* area. Lough Inchin on the eastern side of the Oughter water system is noted for pike fishing, whilst recently roach have been introduced. The Killykeen Forest Park is a good access point to the

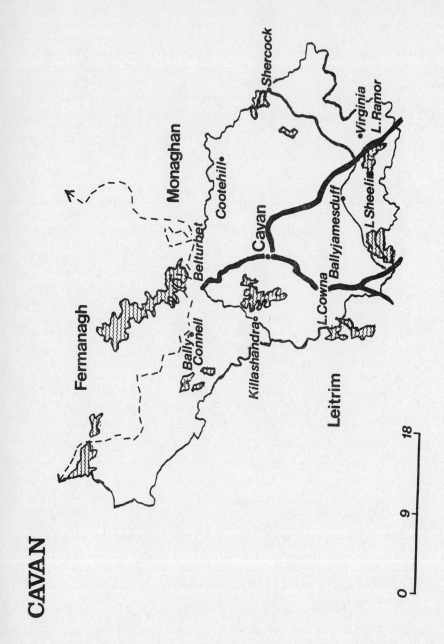

CAVAN

Shercock

Monaghan

Virginia
L. Ramor

Cootehill

Belturbet

Cavan

Ballyjamesduff

L. Sheelin

Fermanagh

Bally's
Connell

Killashandra

L. Cowna

Leitrim

0      9      18

Lough Oughter system as it has many other recreational facilities, *walking, riding, swimming* as well as *coarse fishing.*

To the west, round **Gowna,** there is another complex of water shared by Westmeath. Lough Ramor near the picturesque town of Virginia (an early plantation town as you might guess from the name) is good for trout fishing and coarse fishing. The scenic qualities of this part have made it a favourite spot among amateur *artists.*

Cavan is an undiscovered county to those who are not in the angling league, and this is undeserved. It has its fair share of antiquities, for being in the lakelands there are a number of crannog sites (early lakeland dwellings) like Rann Ford. One of the most curious finds from west Cavan is the three faced Corleck Head, now in the National Museum, Dublin, it is a rare example of a pagan trinity figure. Christianity percolated slowly through this lake maze and even up to the 17th century some recorded devotions to saints have a pagan flavour (the veneration of the carved head of St. Brigid near Urney, Cavan). Cavan is also a border county, one of the three countries excluded from the modern making of Northern Ireland Ulster. In ancient times the counties on the borders of the provinces seem to have shared this modern ambiguity, being feuding areas difficult to hold and conquer.

Cavan (An Cabhan – the Hollow) the county town is an inconspicuous town (though it probably would warrant the description "progressive" from the new houses being built there). Once it was important as an O'Reilly stronghold in the ancient kingdom of East Breffny. Their castle Clough Oughter (pronounced 'ooter') is the best preserved example of an Irish circular tower castle and is situated about three miles outside Cavan near Rann Ford (a good picnic site). There are some worthwhile diversions around Cavan. There is a private Folk Museum called the Pighouse Collection, Tel: Mrs Faris (049) 37248, admission 50p; or you might take the opportunity to buy a bit of Cavan Crystal from the factory shop on the outskirts of town. For those interested in pre-historic sites a few miles out of Cavan on the Cootehill Road (L5) are 'Finn Maccool's Fingers', standing stones within which the Princes of Breffny were crowned. On the Annalee River, there is the small Derragara Museum, which has among its exhibits a full-sized mud and wattle homestead, typical of the rural house/cabin of the 18th century Ireland. **Eating:** Also worth visiting is the DERRAGARA INN, run by Mr and Mrs John Clancy, food is available all day, Tel: Butlersbridge (049) 31003.

Another lakeland town is **Belturbet,** once a thriving depot for the traffic on the Ulster Canal which used to start on the Erne a few miles up. THE SEVEN HORSE SHOES, is an atmospheric inn in the main street (Tel: 0492 2166). This is a good area for *coarse anglers.* Near by, at **Milltown** is a Columban site called Drumlane with the remains of a later church and tower. Going north west you reach **Ballyconnell** one of Cavan's 'tidy towns', set on Woodford River. For a panoramic view of the neighbouring countries take the road to **Glangevlin,** go through the Glan Gap to the summit of the Cuilcagh Mountains. On the way you pass through **Swanlinbar,** once known as the Harrogate of Ireland because of its sulphur baths. **Blacklion**, another small village on the Fermanagh

237

border, has a Giant's Grave within the vicinity. This limestone region is marvellous for pot holers.

The drive round the west of Cavan takes you through the wooded drumlin country with rivers and lakes round every corner.

**Eating: Killeshandra** (Cill na Seanratha – Church of the Old Ring Fort) is another good angling centre, it has a hotel famous for its home cooking, THE LOUGH BAWN HOTEL, Tel: (049) 3442. At Ballyjamesduff you can admire yet another 'tidy town' competition winner. That versatile rhymer Percy French and his 'Come back Paddy Reilly to Ballyjames-duff' gave the town some immortality. THE PERCY FRENCH HOTEL is a comfortable place to stop off for refreshments. Lunch costs about £IR3.50, à la carte from about £IR6. Tel: Ballyjamesduff 24.

The picturesque village of **Virginia** is also in the tidy town league. Lough Ramor, scattered with pretty wooded islands, is close at hand. The charms of this town and area include *golfing* facilities and an excellent hotel, THE PARK HOTEL, Tel: Virginia 235, is good value; lunch costs £IR5 and dinner £IR8 per person. Other expeditions should include a visit to Cuilcagh Lough, where the great Dean Swift is reputed to have composed part of Gulliver's Travels in a house, now lost, called Stella's Bower. On and over the border to Meath are the Loughcrew Hills (about 8 miles south) with a handsome heritage of megaliths. Loughcrew House is the birthplace of one of Ireland's most recently canonized saints, Oliver Plunket.

Turning northwards, the traveller will pass through wooded lake studded country, pretty villages like **Bailieborough,** and **Shercock,** and **Kingscourt**. Vist the forest park of Dun-na-Ri, on the former demesne of the Pratts of Cabra. Cabra Castle is now an expensive hotel, Tel: (042) 67160. Cootehill, named after the founding family who were 17th century planters, is the centre of a poultry business. You will probably be offered Cootehill duck anywhere in Ireland. Outside Cootehill, coming from Shercock, there is a good example of a double-court cairn.

The main Tourist Information centre for this region is in **Mullingar** although there are offices in **Cavan** and **Belturbet,** so for planning ahead Tel: Mullingar (044) 8761/2/3/4 or write to them at Dublin Road. You will get full details of boat hire from the main and subsidiary offices, but here are a few names and addresses just in case.

**Bultersbridge**
Mr V Bartley (for Annagh Lake), Tel: Bulter's Bridge 31009 (five boats).
Mr J Clancy, Derragara Inn, Tel: 31003 (seven boats).
Mrs A M Farrell, Annalee House, Tel: 31007 (five boats).

**Belturbet**
Richard Harris, Coarse Fishing Club, Tel: Belturbet 2160 (five boats).
Mr P Doherty, Book-a-boat, Tel: Belturbet 2147 (four boats).

**Cootehill**
Miss V Greenan, 'Do Come Inn', Lisnalong, Tel: Cootehill 207
Thomas Brady, White Horse Hotel.
Joseph Smyth, River House, Tel: Cootehill 50

**Killeshandra**
G Nicholson, Ardlough House, Tel: 108

**Virginia**
A Arnold and S Reynolds, Park Hotel, Tel: Virginia 2235

Don't forget that personal enquiries are much better than written lists. Many guest houses in the fishing areas (Chambers near Lough Sheelin) and hotels have boats for clients to hire.


## PLACES TO STAY IN COUNTY CAVAN


**Ballyjamesduff**
Mrs N Lynch, Holywell Lodge, Ballyheelan, Tel: (049) 30150. Dinner, boats and boathouse near Lough Sheelin.
**Belturbet**
Mrs A Cassidy, Sugerloaf Hs (on main Cavan/Dublin road), Tel: (0492) 2212
Mrs P Gardner, Omega Restaurant (main Cavan Road), Tel: (0492) 2283
**Butlersbridge**
Mrs P Mundy, Ford Hs, Deredis (4½ miles from Cavan town), Tel: (049) 31427.
**Cavan Town**
Mrs R A King, Brough Hs, Poles, Tel: (049) 39141, B&B £5.50
Mrs K Prior, Glenara, Swellan, Tel: (049) 31136
Mr and Mrs Georgan, Killygowan Hs, Tel: (049) 31906
Farnham Arms, Cavan Town, Tel: (049) 31286
**Cootehill**
Mrs E Smith, Hillview Hs, Corick, Tel: Tullyvin 39. Fishing nearby.
Mrs M McPhillips, Drum Moir Hs, Corick, Tel: Tullyvin 44
Mrs V Greenan, The Beeches, Station Road, Tel: Cootehill 207
Whitehorse, Tel: Cootehill 24. Rooms with bath, expensive.
**Killeshandra**
Mrs G Burns, Tullvista, Corglass, Miltown, Tel: (049) 34119. Near Lough Oughter, boat available.
**Lough Gowna**
Mrs B Hudson, Dernaferst, Tel: Lough Gowna 18. Overlooks the lough.
**Mount Nugent**
The Sheelin Shamrock, Tel: Mount Nugent 13. More expensive, full board.

**Binge places**
The Park, grade A hotel, Virginia, Tel: Virginia 235
The Percy French Arms, grade B*, Ballyjamesduff, Tel: Ballyjamesduff 24.

# County Donegal

Donegal (Dunn na Gall: Fort of the Foreigner) is like a microcosm of Ireland with the Gaeltacht west, its mountains, heathery moors and boglands, home of the dispossessed Celt; and the rich pasturelands of the east, its plantation towns and long settled families originally Scottish or English. Set northwest against the Atlantic, much of its beauty comes from its proximity to the sea; from the sweep of Donegal Bay, the maritime cliffs round Slieve League, the intricate indentations of the coast up to Bloody Foreland, and the northern peninsulas formed by long sea loughs.

Some people say that Donegal is the 26th county in a 25 county state, meaning that there is an individuality and independence up here which Dublin likes to ignore. This Ulster country has the largest number of Irish native speakers of any county in Ireland, though curiously enough, 'official Irish' is based on the Leinster dialect and the Ulster dialect has more in common with Highland Gaelic, than with the southern strain. There are great links with Scotland, many districts of Glasgow are reputed to be like parishes of west Donegal, and you will see many buses on the road going from places like **Annagry** to **Glasgow**.

The politicians from here have a reputation for being independent; Neil Blaney, independent Fianna Fail being the character on which one student of politics based his analysis of the 'Donegal Mafia'. The current baby boom in Ireland is being experienced in this county more than anywhere else, which makes up for the rural depopulation which has scourged the countryside since the famine, although, of course, the new generation are not being brought up on the deserted homesteads in lonely picturesque valleys, but in the numerous new cottages which line the roads and near the factories that the Irish government has enticed in with substantial financial assistance.

The average visitor will not perhaps be as interested in the politics of rural development as the natural beauties: in this county the ancient mountain ranges (older than any others in Ireland), the light which brings alive the subtle greens and browns of the landscape, and the strength of blue in the sky and sea, have many praise singers. Walkers should take note of the excellent guide in the series of Irish Walk Guides by Patrick Simms and Gerard Foley (Gill and Macmillan), £IR1.25. Although there are some exciting walks for the experienced (the area round Poison Glen was used as practice ground by members of one expedition to Everest) there is plenty of unexacting terrain. However, if you are going off on a hike be sure to leave some indication of your route, there are no mountain rescue teams. Details about Donegal's part of the Ulster Way can be obtained from the Planning Department, Donegal County Council, Lifford (Tel: Lifford 5)

**South west Donegal.** Because of the mountains in central Donegal, the weather is often quite different in this quarter. If you come up from Sligo along Donegal Bay, a superb sweep, you will encounter one of Ireland's older seaside resorts, **Bundoran**. There is on the long main street, a typical hodge-podge of hotels, amusements and souvenir shops.

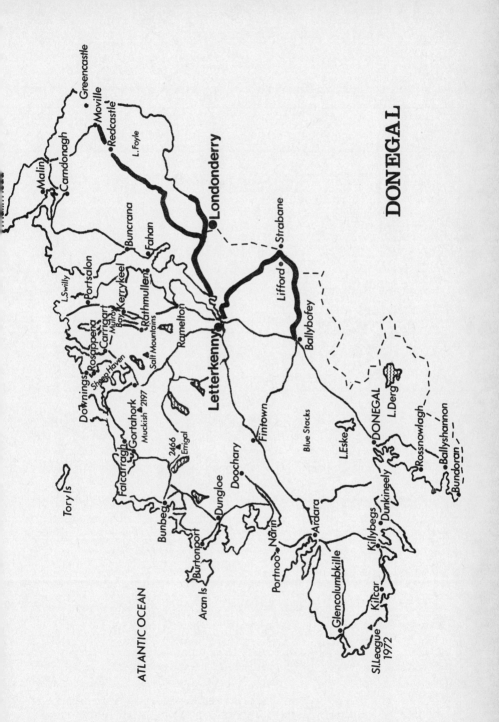

DONEGAL

Greencastle
Moville
Redcastle
Camdonagh
Malin
L. Foyle
Londonderry
Buncrana
Fahan
Strabane
L. Swilly
Portsalon
Kerrykeel
Lifford
Rathmullen
Ballybofey
Carrigart Mulroy Bay
Rosapenna
Ramelton
Downings
Sheep Haven
Salt Mountains
Letterkenny
Gortahork
Muckish ▲ 2197
Fintown
Blue Stacks
DONEGAL
L. Derg
Falcarragh
2466
Errigal
Doochary
L. Eske
Rossnowlagh
Tory Is
Bunbeg
Dungloe
Narin
Ardara
Dunkineely
Ballyshannon
Burtonport
Portnoo
Killybegs
Bundoran
ATLANTIC OCEAN
Aran Is
Glencolumbkille
Kilcar
Sl. League
1972

ATLANTIC OCEAN

241

Nearby are wonderful beaches and one of the best known *golf* courses in Ireland, Christy O'Connor used to be based here. The green fees are quite reasonable and novices can get instruction from Mr Frank McGloin at the Club (Tel: 0722 41302)

**Eating:** Bundoran fish and chips are great, but for other meals you will find the main hotels reliable although prices range greatly. There is much to do in the evenings: *bingo,* though you will be in with the experts at a place like this; *cinema,* the Grand Central shows twice nightly, and *dancing,* not to mention *cabaret* sessions at the hotels in the season. Full details from the Tourist Information Office Tel: Bundoran 41350 open from May to September.

For those who are avoiding populous resorts **Ballyshannon** is ideal. Said to have been founded in BC 1,500 when the Scuthians settled a colony on a little island in the Erne estuary, the town spreads near the river. It has its own poet, the bard of Ballyshannon, William Allingham whose poem

"up the airy mountain, down the rushy glen,
we daren't go a hunting for fear of little men"

must have been chanted by many generations of children.

*Bicycles* can be hired from P B Stephen & Co, Castle Street, though be prepared for energetic riding for you are in drumlin country again. Nearby are the sands of **Rossnowlagh** where you can park a *caravan* or hire one.

**Eating:** There is also the SANDHOUSE HOTEL for good food at reasonable prices (Tel: 072 65343) £IR5 for lunch, £IR8 for dinner. If you are here around the 12th July you may witness the last remaining Orange procession this side of the border from Northern Ireland. Otherwise **Rossnowlagh** is known for its surfing.

At the Franciscan Friary, before you reach the pretty little town of **Ballintra,** you will find the diminutive Donegal Museum which has a few interesting items, including a piece of Muckish Glass, named after the mountain you will see as you go further north. **Donegal** town is the meeting point of roads which travel into the heart of Donegal, to the north and to the west. Situated on the River Eske, with a long history of habitation from its strategic site, it is a crowded busy place even without the tourist buses which tend to congregate near the hotels on the Diamond. A Diamond, a square to most visitors, is an area where fairs and gatherings were held, and in the plantation period it stood in the shadow of the castle so as to guard against the fighting that was the accompanying feature of these occasions. Donegal Castle, once a stronghold of the O'Donnells, the princes of Tyrconnaill, and then taken over by the planter Brookes is naturally near the Diamond. There is also a friary where the history of old Ireland, the Annals of the Four Masters (written by the O'Clerys, historians and tutors to the O'Donnells, in 1623-36), is reputed to have been written.

Nowadays **Donegal** is one of the best places to buy tweed. Magees, an old fashioned department store on the Diamond, has a long established business in tweed manufacture and made its reputation through the handloom weavers of the hill farms round about. Prices are very reasonable (especially if you are changing from sterling) for material, or made up garments and knitwear. If you want to go on a tour of the weaving premises enquire in the shop for the daily tour times.

**Eating:** Of the hotels in the diamond the ABBEY HOTEL (Tel: Donegal 14) is worth visiting for a meal, it also has a self service cafeteria (lunch from about £IR3 on, dinner from £IR6) Cheaper places for snacks include the ERRIGAL GRILL on TirConnaill Street. There is quite a wide choice of pubs, and in the summer you will be able to join in on some music sessions.

Since **Donegal** is the last big town until you get to the east of the country any supplies of fishing tackle and the like should be picked up here. Charles Doherty on the main street is good for fishing tackle, and you can hire *bicycles* from here (Tel: Donegal 119). Donegal town acts as a centre for tours: CIE offer a variety, including the hills of Donegal and the folk village at Glencolumbkille. The Tourist Office in Quay St will give you particulars (Tel: 148). Further inland lies the pilgrim's shrine of Lough Derg. Although most holy tradition in Donegal is associated with St Columkille (Latin, Columba) this is known as St Patrick's Purgatory, and is the scene of one of the most rigorous Christian pilgrimages, between June and August 15. Information can be obtained from the Prior, St Patrick's Purgatory, Lough Derg, **Pettigo.** Closer at hand is the lovely Lough Eske which gives good *fishing* for trout. At the northern end of the Lough, at **Ardnamona,** you will find a collection of rare rhododendrons and you can stay out here in the ARDNAMONA GUESTHOUSE (Tel: Donegal 92).

**Donegal** town is a few miles away from the Gaeltacht which officially begins after **Killybegs**. This is where you can walk into a shop or bar and catch fragments of that old language; for Irish is the oldest recorded Aryan language, it is a strange language, rich, almost soft but shot through with harsher guttural tones; it is like folk music, poignant, moving but not melodious. The spoken English of Gaelic speakers is on the other hand, soft and poetical as though through the translation they have made a second language of it.

Through **Mountcharles,** with its splendid view of Donegal Bay, **Bruckless** and **Dunkineely** (all centres of the now defunct lace industry and still good places to buy hand embroidered linen) the small winding and climbing road leads you to **Killybegs**. In the summer, bordering hedgerows bloom with honeysuckle and fuchsia and as you get further west the sweet acrid peat smell on the damp soft air becomes all pervading. At **Killybegs** you reach an important fishing port; the progressive features of this harbour town are the modernised aluminium and glass shop fronts which are slightly at odds with the old worldliness of the neighbouring villages. There is very good *fishing* here, as you might expect, especially salmon. Contact Mr McBrearty, Church St, about hiring boats. **Killybegs** is also famous for its carpet factory producing Donegal hand tufted carpets. To make an appointment to see the factory ring Mr Campbell at Killybegs 21.

Beyond this town you encounter some of the grandest scenery in Donegal; the great cliffs of Bunglass, Scregeither and Slieve League are amongst the highest in Europe rising to 1,972 feet. If you walk along the cliffs from Bunglass along One Man's Pass, a jaggedy ridge, you will see, on a clear day, fantastic views right down to County Mayo. The determined bird watcher should be able to see puffins and cormorants, and the botanist should be able to find alpine arctic species on the back slopes of Slieve League. The village of **Teelin,** under Slieve League, is popular with students on Irish language courses, whilst **Kilcar** is the site of the Gaelterra Eireann factory of Connemara fabrics and yarns.

**Glencolumbkille** should be visited next. Father McDyer, a remarkable personality, established a rural co-operative here to try and combat the flight of youth from the village through emigration. This town also has a folk village: three cottages representing three different periods of Irish life (open weekdays 10am-6pm). You can *hire a cottage* for £IR90 per week (half that during the winter) which sleeps four to six people. Enquiries should be made in writing to Glencolumbkille Folk Village.

The countryside is full of pre-historic antiquities, dolmens, cairns (including a famous horned cairn called Clochanmore) and ruins of churches connected with St Columkille. On the other side of the mountain, through the spectacular Glengesh Pass, you arrive at **Ardara,** another centre of Donegal hand woven tweed. The Tourist Information Office is situated in Campbell's tweed shop (Tel: Ardara 340). There are several pubs which are famous for their *music* evenings including NANCYS, and PETER OLIVERS.

**Eating:** the NESBITT ARMS provides meals (Tel: Ardara 3 or 51), lunch £IR4.

If you travel a few miles on to the next little peninsula you will come to **Portnoo** and **Narin,** two popular places for holidaymakers from Northern Ireland. At Narin *caravaners* can park or hire caravans. There are some fascinating forts round here. For a good picnic expedition go to Doon Lough (near **Narin**) where there is a massive fort, said to be 2,000 years old, built on an island. At the neck of this peninsula, you go from **Maas** to **Glentie** (Na Gleannta: the valley, from its position at the junction of glens) which is a good place for knitwear. There is a striking Catholic Church designed by the innovative Irish architect, Liam McCormick.

All along the coast you will see mountain ranges broken by long river valleys which reach into the hinterland. Any route along these valleys brings you across the harsh mountainy areas where beauty is bleak and the cost of wresting a living from the poor soil is no longer acceptable. One such town **Fintown,** situated on a lough, has become the centre of controversy because of the uranium deposits in its rocky fields. Exploitation of these rich deposits may bring untold wealth, or untold disaster to the area, depending what side you take on the conservation issue.

There is rather a zigzag road from **Fintown** to **Doochary** called the 'Corkscrew' which brings you into the **Gweebarra Glen.** Northeast of this, between the Derryveagh and Glendowat Mountains, the valley

244

extends into Glenveagh, which is now part of a national park. However you should keep heading out towards the sea on the road to Dungloe (do not pronounce the 'g') if you want to see the 'Rosses'. Although this area is going through a housing boom, it is still one of the most charming routes you can take to the north coast; loughs and loughlets are scattered through hilly country and the beaches are lovely. If you make your way to **Burtonport,** an attractive unspoilt fishing port, you can get out to **Arranmore Island.** Ring Arranmore 5 to find out about boats, and ask the boatman about places to stay on the island.

**Arranmore Island** has the only rainbow trout lake in Ireland, Lough Shure. **Cruit Island** can be reached from the mainland by a connecting bridge, from here you can look out at **Owey Island,** and across at **Gola Island** with their deserted cottages. Despite the difficulties the islanders had to face most of them did not want to leave their homes and many return for the summer months or for *fishing*.

If you do not have time to go island hopping, go for a walk on Gortahork's great strand which curves out into the sea. It nearly locks in shallow Ballyness Bay from the ocean; if you are here in the evenings you can see cattle fording the waters back to the home farms. **Gortahork** (meaning garden of oats) is a small town on one arm of this bay. In July you can go to the **Gortahork** exhibition craft centre, opposite McFadden's Hotel, and buy paintings by the Tory fishermen which have been promoted by the artist Derek Hill, although some of the more famous of the island painters have their sales in Belfast and London.

**Eating:** in **Falcarragh,** you will find many eating places. Gortahork's MCFADDEN'S HOTEL is fairly modest. This is a good centre for *ceili music*. Try St. Finian's Hall, Falcarragh or Gortahork's Colaiste Uladh when there are pupils in the Gaelic colleges (early July to Late August).

Looking inland you can not help but notice the glorious outlines of Errigal (coneshaped), Aghla More and Aghla Beg (a spaced double peak) and the shoulder of Muckish, or pig's back. You can approach these mountains from this angle, or you could take the road from Bunbeg past the secret Dunlewey Lough overlooked by a roofless white church. Hidden behind this is the Poison Glen, so called because the water in the lough is unfit to drink because of certain poisonous plants at the water's edge, or so another story goes, from the name some French travellers gave it having caught some fish there: Poisson Glen.

Climb Errigal and after about a hour's climb you will reach a narrow ridge of 2,400 feet from which you will see Dunlewey Lough on one side and Altan Lough on the other side. Climb Muckish from the Gap end, if you go straight for it from the Falcarragh side you may find yourself going up by the old mine works, for the mountain was worked for its mica to be used in glass making, and this is quite a dangerous, and interesting ascent. The old weaver poets had a good phrase for Muckish like 'an owl turf stack' and so it is, flat topped with its flat outline broken only by the remains of a cross (the real Columban cross is supposed to be at **Ray**). Looking across to Tory, St. Columba is said to have thrown his staff from the top of Muckish and there is a huge hole on Tory where it should have landed after that mammoth sling.

Back to the coast between **Falcarragh** and **Dunfanaghy** is the great granite promontory of Horn Head. From a Falcarragh view point it does indeed look like a horn of rock. You can do a complete circuit taking the little road which leads you past old Hornhead House, which was drowned by sand when the bent grass was cut. The road climbs round the rocky farms giving you dazzling views across Sheephaven Bay to Melmore Head to the east and back towards Bloody Foreland. There is a good walk ahead of you to an old tower, you can peer over the 300 foot cliff heights to see if the puffin population is in residence; there are some caves and blow holes.

**Eating:** HEGARTY'S at Dunfanaghy is a good place to halt for snacks and drinks. You can stay at two old family run hotels: ARNOLD'S, Tel: Dunfanaghy 36208. Meals from £IR4(lunch), £IR6 (for dinner). From here you can go *ponytrekking*, a good way to admire the view, costing about £IR2.25 per hour, £IR3.50 for 2 hours, £IR4 for 3 hours. Between **Dunfanaghy** and Port na Blagh, there are opportunities for *caravaners* to pitch their caravans.

Sheephaven Bay is a complicated indentation with beautiful golden sands and wooded shore. **Marblehill** with its special provision for *caravans* is a favourite place for holiday makers. The mystic poet-politician George Russell used to stay here in Marblehill House. Further on the forest of Ards provides scenic walks and splendid view.

At **Creeslough** you can admire another modern church, its shape is in keeping with the view of Muckish that you have from there, designed by Liam McCormick. Otherwise it's a busy town with good shopping and pubs. On the road to **Carrigart** is one of the most romantic castles in Ireland set on the waters' edge: Doe Castle. This castle was built by the MacSwiney's who came over from Scotland in the 16th century at the invitation of the O'Donnells.

At **Carrigart** you will find some good shops for tweeds and knitwear and now McNutts of Downings have their own shop called 'Nothing but...' which combines the modern and the traditional in a tasteful fashion, you can buy craft goods including wools and rugs, and see a weaver at work.

**Eating:** upstairs you can have a delicious meal or snack in DEBBY AND JAMES' RESTAURANT which is open from morning coffee to about 5pm.

To get onto the Rosguill peninsula you cross a neck of sand similar to the causeway at Hornhead, and arrive at the fishing village of **Downings** which is strung out between the 'holiday makers' zone of **Rosapenna** a long established resort, with a good golf course and harbour. You can sail out to the islands from Downings to Tory or Inishbofin. Enquiries have to be made at Mrs Buchanan, Tel: Downings 48. The tweed making factory of McNutts should be visited, and after that you can make the Atlantic drive circuit. You should follow the dividing of the roads past the Tra na Rossan youth hostel, curiously the only house designed by Edwin Lutyens in Ulster, and then head up to the wilder beaches of **Melmore**. There are a number of *caravan parks* on the peninsula, non registered sites, Rosapenna has official parks. Bookings can be made at the Letterkenny Tourist Information Caravan (Tel: Letterkenny 21160).

Leaving **Carrigart** you can follow the loughside road which will take you down to Mulroy Bay, a narrow necked lough bordered by the Fanad Peninsula on the opposite side and strewn with wooded islands. Behind **Carrigart** rises the Salt Mountain, a little moor bound road crosses this range and comes out near **Cranford**. High in these mountains is the deepest lough in Ireland, Lough Salt. To take advantage of the panorama you should go up to the Lough from the **Letterkenny-Creeslough** road (L76) and look out to the bays from Hornhead to Fanad. If you choose to go by **Mulroy** or are staying in the area you should have a binge at the OLD SCHOOL HOUSE RESTAURANT run by an Australian and his Irish wife. You have to ring before 5pm. Tel: Downings 64. The way is well sign-posted.

Down the road is **Milford**, a pretty town on a hill and near some good *fishing* at Lough Fern.

**Eating:** you can get a good cup of coffee at The Coffee Break plus snacks. It also boasts a good *cinema:* the La Scala. From **Milford** you can explore the Fanad Peninsula on the old road, which takes you past the Knockalla range by **Kerrykeel** and into the hidden reaches of Mulroy by **Tamney**. In this secluded land there survives a very idiosyncratic Gaelic, but it was not untouched by the settlements of the 17th century and even in their isolation the Irish and the Scottish settlers remained distinct. At the farthest north eastern point you can see Fanad Lighthouse which guards the entrance of the Lough Swilly and looks across to the hills of Inishowen.

**Portsalon** is beautifully situated over Ballymastocker Bay, an immense curve of strand, and like all towns on the Swilly it is curiously linked by the water in its landscape to the opposite view on Inishowen rather than separated, it's a little like the Greek idea of the sea being a bridge. Portsalon has an imposing hotel and nearby is the all in one grocery bar run by Rita. You can sit with your drink and watch the small harbour or take in the larger view of the Swilly. High tea and supper is also served. Holiday apartments are available for hire from the hotel in this picturesque harbour.

A terrific coastal drive has just been built with fabulous views over the Knockalla hills. This brings you to **Rathmullen**, nestling in a sheltered plain which borders the Swilly down to **Letterkenny**. It is now time to explain how important a shelter the whole of Lough Swilly has been to all manner of generations. Deep enough to accommodate modern fleets of war, as indeed it did in the First World War, it has also been the departure route for the Gaelic aristocracy, where the earls of Tyrconnaill, and Tyrone took their leave for France in 1607. Lough Swilly has been called the lake of the shadows, an apt enough description, although from the Irish it means Lake of Eyes or Eddies (Loch Suilagh).

**Rathmullen** (Rath Maolan's ringfort) is a charming town with lots of tourist attractions like sandy beaches and hotels and it is unspoiled. There used to be a ferry that operated between **Fahan** and the harbour here which as you will see is quite large.

**Eating:** there are two country house style hotels:

FORT ROYAL where you can get quite reasonably priced meals (Tel: Rathmullen 11) and RATHMULLEN HOUSE. The latter is set in beautiful grounds, has the distinction of the Relais de Campagne award, and is a little more expensive: lunch from £IR4 per head and dinner £IR8 per head. Tel: Rathmullen 4. It is worth every penny. In the town you can get snacks at THE COFFEE HOUSE. Visit the Carmelite Friary built by the MacSwineys, and climb Croghan hill behind.

One of the most lovely routes in Ireland is on the road between **Rathmullen** and its neighbour **Ramelton**. The place name of course translates as Mealtan's Fort, but the town you will see is a relatively unspoiled plantation town built by the Stewart family, one of the so called undertakers of the plantation, meaning that they undertook to supply fighting men and build fortified dwellings to subdue and keep the wild Irish at bay. It developed as a prosperous market town with goods coming up the Lennon estuary from as far away as Tory Island. **Ramelton** was nearly self-sufficient in those 18th century days what with locally made whiskey, linen, leather goods, and other manufactures and the Ramelton merchants built themselves fine houses in the Mall. However **Letterkenny** stole a march on the town fathers when the railway came and now Ramelton is famous for its annual festival in July, and for its thriving bottling industry: today, McDaid's Football Special refreshes the youth of Donegal!

**Eating:** can get a good steak at MIRABEAU'S on the Mall (Tel: Ramelton 130) soon to be challenged by a new restaurant at the end of the Mall run by Debby and James. Patronise some of the bars: the most picturesque are Conway's opposite the Post Office, and the Salmon Inn, across the Bridge. Follow the course of the Lennon up by the mill, and watch the waters race over the weir. The Ramelton pool is famous for salmon and peacocks.

**Letterkenny** must be the most thriving town in Donegal; with its new factories on the outskirts, and new housing enclaves, yet it still manages to maintain its country town aspect, with one, long main street that loops round into the Swilly Valley. You can use this town as a centre for expeditions east and west. Folk music lovers might time their visit for the Letterkenny Folk Festival which hosts *folk dance* and *music groups* from all over Europe in August (second last week). You can hire *bicycles* from the stationary centre in the Port Road. The bus station, at the junction of the Port Road and the Ramelton Road, sees express buses go daily to Dublin, and the CIE and Lough Swilly Bus Company link up the north and the west. The Tourist Information Office on the Derry road is open all year round, and sells a variety of useful publications as well as giving advice and booking your accommodation. Tel: (074) 21160.

**Eating:** *The GOLDEN GRILL*, Ramelton Road, offers some of the highlights of Donegal night life with live music (see the local papers like the *Donegal Democrat* or the *Derry Journal* for details) and dinner. HEGARTY'S HOTEL in the centre is comfortable and old fashioned with substantial meals. Further into the town you can eat at THE MEWS RESTAURANT, just next door to McGinley's new style Irish pub, where all the fashionable people around Letterkenny drink. THE

BALLYRAINE HOTEL is also very popular. Tel: (074) 22700.

If you go through **Letterkenny** up the Swilly Valley you reach the countryside where St Columbkille spent his first years. He was born on a height overlooking the two Gartan loughs, a large cross marks the spot (it is just on the Glenveagh Estate). Gartan Clay (which can only be lifted by a family who claim descent from the followers of Columbkille) has power protective properties; soldiers fighting in the First World War carried it. You should follow the road round the lough; if you take one of the forest trials on the Churchill side a glorious prospect amid the glens awaits you. The long glen which begins at Doochary on the south west coast penetrates this far, parallel to the valley of Gartan. **Glenveagh** (in Irish the valley of the birch) is beautiful and isolated with a fairytale castle figured against the mountains on the loughside. The gardens here have been developed by Mr McIlhenny, a millionaire whose grand-parents came from these parts. They are open in July on Wednesday afternoons and a visit is to be recommended. It would be difficult to find another such garden which combines the exotic and the natural with such ease. Henry McIlhenny gave the wild, heathery acres of Glenveagh to be used as a National Park. Deer roam the glen and peregrine falcons nest in the rocky ledges. Close by at **Churchill**, the artist, Derek Hill has given his house and art possessions to the nation. Very soon, visitors will be able to walk around this plain Georgian house packed with exquisite and curious objets d'art.

On the way back from **Glenveagh** you should pass through **Kilma-crenan** (Church of the son of Neanan) called after one of Saint Columbkille's nephews. There are some ruins of a 15th century friary, but the fame of the place rests on the claim that it was here Columbkille received his education. Near here at Doon Rock about two miles on the road to **Creeslough** the Princes of Tyrconnaill would be inaugurated; at the curious Doon Well, the grateful cured have left tokens of their illness, rags mostly, although there is a story that a visiting film star left her lipstick.

**Eating:** at **Kilmacrenan** you can have a homely meal in DUFFY'S tea rooms, whatever's cooking for the family, for about £IR2.

If you are travelling east from **Letterkenny** bound for the north, you will pass through the more prosperous midlands of Donegal whose centre is **Raphoe,** an ancient town with a venerable old cathedral and a pretty village green. Outside the town the stone circle of Beltany (on the land of one of the guest houses listed) has some mystic alignment. Your fellow passengers on the road will probably be bound for the mart, the key of most Irish farmers' life, and another indication of the importance of **Raphoe.** The main tourist centre for this region is in **Sligo.**

**Inishowen** (Inis Eoghain; Eoghan's Island). This great hand reaches out to the Atlantic between Loughs Swilly and Foyle, a kingdom of its own, and indeed, as its name conveys, it forms a different territory to the rest of Donegal which is part of Tyrconnaill (Land of Connell). An unforgettable sight of this unexplored almost islanded land can be obtained from the Grianin of Aileach (the sun palace) of the O'Neills near **Burt.** After leaving **Letterkenny** you pass through the rolling plains round **Manor** and **Newtowncunningham** to the neck of the peninsula. Turn by an unusually roofed modern Catholic church, another of Liam McCormick's, and climb the mountain road which gives you views onto the Swilly. Why this ancient stone hill fort is not as well known as Tara, considering its spectacular position and its associations must be one of the curious twists in the recording of history. Besides the circular stone fort with its terraces there are three stone and earth ramparts and underneath the hill of Aileach there are said to be underground passages connecting the hill top with Scalp; I have even heard the story that sleeping heroes of the past lie within the hill who will be wakened at Ireland's hour of need. You can understand why this site was chosen for the Grianan or 'weeping place of women', where they and their property were secure against the onslaughts of any enemy. The fort guards all approaches, which is why it affords such good views over the Foyle, and the Swilly.

**Inch Island** signposted off the main **Buncrana/Londonderry** Road is a beautiful, untouched place. Ask for directions to Inch Fort and Brown's Bay and look across the limpid water to **Fahan** or go for a swim. Mr Brown (ask in the only shop on the island)) will hire you a boat or take you out *fishing*. Unfortunately, there is nowhere to stay on **Inch** but **Fahan** is nearby.

Fahan is famous for its St Mura's Cross in the Church of Ireland graveyard. Here, in the rectory, looking across to Inch Top Hill, Mrs Alexander wrote *'There is a green hill far way'*.
**Eating:** it is worth stopping at ST. JOHN'S RESTAURANT. Just about the best restaurant in the north Tel: Fahan 94. Dinner only is served and this not very expensive. **Fahan** also has a very friendly *Yacht Club* and a beautiful beach with lovely views all round which stretches up to **Buncrana,** a rather jaded seaside resort with an excellent shirt factory shop for real bargains. The only snuff factory in Ireland, Grant's, might provide some interesting souvenirs for smokers or sniffers.
**Eating:** places to eat include the LOUGH SWILLY HOTEL. Tel: Buncrana 172, and FOUR LANTERNS FAST FOOD Tel: Buncrana 94 serving hamburger style food. There used to be very good *salmon fishing* on the Cranagh by the simple old Cranagh Castle which offers picnickers good sites. **Buncrana** is the gateway to the Inishowen circuit which you will find distinctly signposted.

This is O'Doherty country and you will find one of their castles near the River Cranagh. You can take the road which leads through the mountains to the spectacular Mamore Gap, and gaze at the return view of the Fanad peninsula. There are plenty of good beaches on the way, such as Linsfort and Dunree, then on the other side of the Gap, past Clonmany and the beaches round Isle of Doagh. This is an unspoiled country, full of fuchsia hedges and little whitewashed cottages. There are some interesting monuments, including the Marigold Stone which has the same ornamentation as St Mura's Cross and at **Carndonagh,** further east, there is one of the most far famed crosses in Ireland, said to be the oldest low relief cross (650 AD). One authority relates the design to the Book of Durrow in Trinity College, Dublin. You should not miss the most northerly village in Ireland, **Malin,** which has a pretty green and a tidy look, as well as the Malin Hotel where you can have a meal, and nearby is the lovely Five Fingers strand and an excellent craft shop.

If you want to see the furthermost tip of Ireland, Malin Head, familiar to all of you who listen in to radio shipping forecasts, you take a road passing extensive sand dunes, then you come to the pebbly coves where you can pick up semi precious stones and make necklaces or bracelets if you are clever enough. From Malin Head you can see lighthouse islands, from here to Glengad Head are cliffs rising to over 800 feet.

**Culdaff** facing towards the Londonderry coastline, is a pleasant resort with a well known singing pub called Bernards. The *fishing* purports to be good round here judging from the number of angling competitions. Further down the coast you come to **Moville,** formerly a point of departure for many emigrants to the New World. Moville to **Muff** was a coastal foothold for many planter residences or castles. Behind them rise rather forbidding mountains, though if you venture on the mountain roads you come across lost clochans, megalithic monuments, and what's more unique you will find yellow raspberries in the hedges lining the lanes.

You can go *horse riding* from Redcastle House, near **Moville** Tel: Moville 73. *Sea angling* can be arranged from Moville, boat hire enquiries to Mr Brian McManus, Anchor Bar, Moville.
**Eating:** eat in **Moville** at McNAMARA'S Tel: Moville 10 or in **Green-castle** at the FORT HOTEL. Down the coast road towards Derry stop off at the Point Inn, **Quigley's Point** and hear some *music,* Tuesday nights are Irish music nights.

# PLACES TO STAY IN COUNTY DONEGAL

**Annagry**
Mrs M Bonner, Bay View, Tel: Annagry 75. Meals available.
**Ardara**
Mrs M Bennett, Bay View Hs, Portnoo Rd, Tel: Ardara 45. Rooms with bath.
Mr & Mrs Molloy, Greenhaven Sea & Mountain View, Portnoo Rd. Rooms with shower.
Nesbitt Arms, Tel: Ardara 3, grade B.
**Arranmore**
Glen, Tel: Arranmore 5, grade C, open in summer months, meals available.
**Ballybofey**
Mrs M C Gallen, Tower Main St, Tel: Ballybofey 290.
**Ballyshannon**
Dorrian's Imperial Hotel, Tel: (072) 65147, grade B.
Royal Millstone, Tel: (072) 65172, grade B.
Mrs K Connolly, Carrickboy Hs, Allingham Rd, Tel: (072) 65278
Mrs M McGee, Killeadan, Bundoran Rd, Tel: (072) 65377. Some rooms

have a shower.
**Bunbeg**
Gweedore Hotel, Tel: Bunbeg 85, grade A.
Seaview, Tel: Bunbeg 18, grade B* (cheaper).
Mrs H McGarvey, Hillcrest Hs, Tel: Bunbeg 154
Mrs S McGarvey, Brookvale Hs, Tel: Bunbeg 65
**Buncrana**
Lough Swilly, Tel: Buncrana 172, grade B, expensive.
Central, Tel: Buncrana 47, grade C, cheaper but less attractive.
Mrs A Diggin, Berwyn, Shore Rd, Tel: Buncrana 318
Mrs M McConigly, Kinvyra St, Oran's Rd, Tel: Buncrana 178
**Bundoran**
Holyrood Tel: (072) 41204, B+, good value for money.
Maghery House, Tel: (072) 41234, B+
*Guesthouses;*
Bayview, Tel: (072) 41296, grade B.
Casa del Monte, Tel:,(072) 41201, grade B.
Mrs N Rinsella, Glena, Tel: (072) 41245, big B&B.
Mrs A McGloin, Stella Maris, East End, Tel: (072) 41201
Mrs C McGloin, Atlantic View, West End, Tel: (072) 41403, rooms with shower.
**Burtonport**
Campbell's Pier House, Tel: Burtonport 17, grade B.
**Carrigart**
Carrigart Hotel, Tel: (074) 21881, reasonably priced.
Mrs B Doherty, Hill Hs, Dumore, Tel: Carrigart 51.
**Clonmany**
Mrs B M Doherty, Swilly View, Claggin, Tel: Clonmany 37
**Culdaff**
McGrory's guesthouse, Tel: Culdaff 4
**Donegal Town**
Abbey Hotel, Tel Donegal 14, B+
National, Tel: Donegal 14, B+
*Guesthouses:*
Atlantic, Tel: Donegal 147, grade B.
Four Masters, Tel: Donegal 205, grade B.
St Ernan's Muckross, out of Donegal Town, Tel: Donegal 65, grade B.
Mrs M McGinty, Ardeevin, Lough Eske, Barnesmore, Tel: Donegal 190
Mrs L Sweeney, Ivy House, Summerhill, Tel: Donegal 171
Mrs D A Kenney, Arranmore Hs, Coast Rd, Tel: Donegal 242
**Dunfanaghy**
Arnold's Hotel, Tel: (074) 36208, B+
Carrig Rua, Tel: (074) 36133 B+
Miss K McGee, Maolfion, Portnablagh, Tel: (074) 36173
Mrs M Ward, Tara Rosa, Rockhill, Portnablagh, Tel: (074) 36126, near Sessagh Lake.
**Dungloe**
Ostan na Rosann, Tel: Dungloe 91, B+, centre for night life in the summer.

Mrs C Ward, Lake & Seaview Hs, Tubberkeen, Tel: Dungloe 54. Boat available.

Mrs V Boyle, The Chalet, Marameelan, Tel: Dungloe 235

**Fahan**

St John's, Tel: Fahan 92. A memorable restaurant. B&B 1982.

**Glencolumbkille**

Mrs J P Byrne, Corner Hs, Casnel, Tel: Glencolumbkille 21

Glenbay guesthouse, Tel: Glencolumbkille 3. Very comfortable.

**Glenties**

Highlands, Tel: Glenties 11, grade B.

The Glenties Hotel, Tel: 71, grade C.

**Gortahork**

McFadden's Tel: Falcarragh 17, grade A.

An Shorlan, guesthouse, Tel: Falcarragh 72, grade B.

**Killybegs**

Mrs B Cahill, Lismolin, Fintra Rd, Tel: Killybegs 35

Mrs B Murrin, Harbour Heights (opposite the RC church), Tel: Killybegs 71.

**Letterkenny**

Ballyraine, Tel: (074) 22700 B*

Gallagher's, Tel: (074) 22570

Mrs M Carrigy, Shalom, Ballyraine, Tel: (074) 21727

Mrs R M Devlin, Riverside Hs, Oldtown Rd, Tel: (074) 22038

**Lifford**

Inter County Hotel, Tel Lifford 153

Mrs E Patterson, The Haw Lodge, The Haw Lifford (on road to Donegal)

**Malin**

Malin Hotel, Tel Malin 6, grade B*.

**Mountcharles**

Coast Road guesthouse, Tel: Mountcharles 18, grade B.

Mrs A Furey, Ashling Hs, Mountcharles.

**Moville**

Foyle Hotrel, Tel: Moville 25

MacNamara's, Tel: Moville 10

New Park House, Tel: Moville 100, a converted country house, grade B.

**Narin/Portnoo**

Lake House, Clooney 23, Portnoo, Tel; Clooney 10, grade B*.

**Port na Blagh**

The Shandon, Tel: (074) 36137, expensive but family hotelish.

The Pier, Tel: (074) 36177

**Raphoe**

The Central, Tel: (074) 45126, grade B.

Mrs R Eaton, The Tops, Tel: (074) 45146, with an incredible stone circle, Beltany, like Stonehenge.

**Rathmullen**

Fort Royal, Tel: Rathmullan 11

Pier Hotel, Tel: Rathmullan 3

Mrs S Deeney, Knockalla, Coast Road, Letherdan, Tel: Rathmullan 30

Mrs N Patton, Creevery House, Longhill, Tel: Rathmullan 29

**Ramelton**
Mrs J H Grier, Drofton Lodge, Augnnish, Tel: Ramelton 58, scenic and cosy.
Mrs F Scott, The Manse, Tel: Ramelton 47, comfortable atmosphere, good company.
**Rossnowlagh**
The Sand House Hotel, Rossnowlagh, Tel: (072) 65343
Mrs R Downey, Sea View, Tel: (072) 65167
**Tamney**
Mrs M Borland, Avalon, Tamney P.O., Fanad Peninsula, Tel: Tamney 31
Mrs S Sweeney, Tamney, Fanad, Tel: Tamney 31
**Binge Places**
Definitely the best place to luxuriate with lovely scenery and in comfort is:
Mrs Scott's Manse, Tel: Ramelton 47, hard to beat, except perhaps in Fanad, at Mrs Borlands, Tamney, otherwise Rathmullen House Hotel, Tel: Rathmullen 4
Redcastle Hotel, Tel: Moville 243
**Youth Hostels**
These are some of the best situated youth hostels in Ireland:
**Carrick** The Red House, Carrick, open all the year.
**Donegal** Ball Hill, Donegal, open all the year.
**Downings** Tra na Rosann, Downings.
**Dungloe** Crohy Head, Dungloe.
**Glenvar** Bunnaton, up the Fanad Peninsula.
**Gweedore** Dunlewey, underneath Errigal Mountain.

# County Monaghan

This pleasant sheltered county is caught at the top between the counties of Armagh and Fermanagh. Throughout this century and especially in the past few years, there has been much unrest along the border area, its reputation has caused the saying –'In Carrickmacross and Crossmaglen there are more rogues than honest men.' Still do not be put off for Monaghan is the ideal place to spend a quiet holiday, especially if you are a *fisherman*. There are no really high hills, just lots of little ones forming gently rolling countryside. To the north lie a small fringe of mountains, the central area is hillocky with fairly rich farming land, in many ways reminiscent of County Down. Set among the hills to the south, at almost every bend of the road, lie small well-wooded lakes and sedgey bog-holes. The little cultivated fields, trim hedges, tiny lakes, the profusion of wild flowers and the hoards of dragonflies, green and red, make it a land of satisfying detail. In contrast to the smallness of scale,

# MONAGHAN

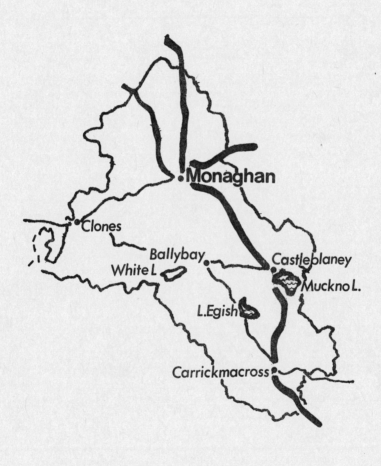

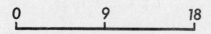

0       9       18

there still remain a few large estates, with their landscaped parks, lakes, formal gardens and age old trees. You get glimpses of these 'big houses' and the forgotten ones which are crumbling into ruins. Copper beech trees seem to have gone wild everywhere in Monaghan, quite a rarity in Ireland. A native of the place swore that this was the last retreat of the Fir Bolgs who were squeezed out of the rest of Ireland by the de Danaan and the Celts. Look out for small, dark, wiry types who look remarkably like leprechauns!

**Monaghan** town is a good place from which to start one's tour of the county. Built on an old monastic site, this market town has some very fine urban architecture, especially round the market square, the diamond. The large market house dates from 1792, there is also a surprising amount of red brick in the smaller streets off the square. It is a very busy prosperous town with lots of shops and a very good restaurant in the square. The rapidly expanding small county museum founded in 1974, won the EEC museum award in 1980. The museum has amongst its treasure the Clogher Cross, a fine example of early Christian metalwork, with its highly decorative detail. There are objects collected from the nearby early lake dwellings, crannogs, including sandals and glass beads. There are also displays dealing with everything from lace-making to railways. In the past, the town prison had been known to hire out its inmates for agricultural labour, and let the pickpockets out to pursue their profession on behalf of the governor! Monaghan town becomes very crowded during the Fiddler of Oriel Festival every year in July which is all about Irish music and dance. The Tourist Information Office is in the courthouse, Tel: (047) 82211 (open during the summer only). *Water skiing* is available nearby on Annaghmakerrig Lake, Tel: Newbliss 32 and *canoes* can be hired from Brendan and Anne Lillis, Tel: (047) 81721. There is *horse riding* at the Castle Leslie Equestrian Centre, Glaslough. Tel: Glaslough 61 or 9.

Not far to the south is Rossmore Park, a beautiful estate, whose grounds are open to the public. This woodland demesne has a lake, *golf course, nature trails* and forest *walks*. Beyond, the roads radiate out across the country. Over to the south-east lies **Castleblaney** on a narrow strip of land at the head of Lough Mukno, the county's largest stretch of water and perhaps the best *coarse fishing* there is, though all the lakes around vie for that description. Founded in the reign of James I, it is now a prosperous town.

Heading southwards, meandering between the hills and fish filled lakes you come down to the town of **Ballybay,** on the shore of Lough Major. It is rather scruffy, despite some fine 18th century buildings set in a particularly beautiful farming area. **Ballybay** was noted for its horse fair which took place beneath the railway bridge, not a terribly bright idea as horses tended to stampede whenever a train passed! Flax growing and tanning used to be very important, but has virtually disappeared. Apart from the excellent *coarse fishing* in the nearby lakes there is good *trout fishing* **on the Dromore River.**

**Carrickmacross** is a market town and famous for its hand-made lace, a cottage industry which was established at the beginning of the century.

The very fine lace, applique work on tulle, is much sought after. Examples can be seen in the little lace museum in the Convent of St. Louis at the top of the main street.

**Eating:** one of the many Georgian houses is the SHIRLEY HOTEL where you can get a friendly cup of tea or a quick meal, or you could try MARKEY'S LE BISTRO, Tel: (042) 61524. Nearby is Mannan Castle, a great hill-top moate and bailey.

Not far from **Carrickmacross,** near the border with County Louth, is the small village of **Innishkeen.** St. Dega founded a monastery here in the 6th century and you can see the remains of the old abbey and round tower (40 foot high) with a raised doorway. The Folk Museum deals with local history, folklife and the old Great Northern Railway which ran through the village. Open on Sundays, May to September 3pm-6pm.

Over to the west there are hundreds of small roads and lanes to explore with lakes caught between, like a spider's web in the morning dew. Quite near the County Cavan border lies the small village of **Rockcorry.** Here too is the Dartry estate with its open parkland, little lakes and much woodland, now all in the care of the Forestry Commission. Nearby lakes with names like Coragh, Avaghon and Drumoona are full of *fish*. Further west is the pretty riverside village of **Newbliss** where you can enquire about *waterskiing* Tel: Newbliss 22 and 5 miles further on, the town of **Clones.** Between the two towns, near **Killeevan,** lies the little country church of **Drumswords.**Dating from 750 AD it has now sadly fallen into disrepair but one window still has the remains of fine basket tracery, indicating that Gothic never really died in Ireland.

**Clones** was once linked to **Monaghan** by the old Ulster railway and Ulster canal, and is still an important agricultural centre. Built on an ancient site, it has some fine remains, many of which have been whisked away to the National Museum, but it still has a rath with three concentric earthworks, an abbey, a well preserved 75 foot round tower and a finely carved early Christian sarcophagus. If you want to visit it the key is available from Pattons pub nearby. Presiding over the triangular market place, perversely called the diamond, stands an ancient much inscribed Cross. There are many fine old houses, particularly, the imposing market house, now the library. Clones is the main centre of traditional handmade crochet lace. *Golf* and *fishing – coarse* and *trout* are available. *Seisiun* and *ceili* happen in the Creighton Hotel on Thursday nights during July and August. The Tourist Office is only open during the summer, Tel: Clones 198.

Only a small part of the county lies to the north of **Monaghan** town. It gently rises up from the flood plain of the Blackwater, to the high moorland of Slieve Beagh. Near the village of **Glaslough,** on the shores of a small grey lake, is the Castle Leslie demesne. It is an Italianate house, full of art treasures though not open to the public. You can go *riding* there at the Castle Leslie Equestrian Centre, Tel: Glaslough 61. To the west of **Glaslough** lies **Emyvale** on the shores of Emy Lough, the sloping fields are white with duck destined to be prepared for deep freezes! The *trout fishing* is reputed to be good.

257

## PLACES TO STAY IN COUNTY MONAGHAN

**Ballybay**
Mrs McNally, Cannon Hill Hs, Knocknamaddy, Tel: Ballybay 114

**Carrickmacross**
Mrs McMahon, Arradale Hs, Corduffkelly, on Kingscourt Rd, Tel: (042) 61941 (farmhouse)
Shirley Arms, Tel: (042) 61209, grade C hotel.

**Clones**
Mrs Smith, Stonebridge Hs, Tel: Clones 242 (farmhouse).

**Glaslough**
Pillar Hs, Tel: Glaslough 25, grade B.

**Newbliss**
Mrs O'Grady, Glynch Hs, on Clones-Newbliss Rd, Tel: Newbliss 45
Mrs Quigley, Ceidin, Lisnagore, Tel: Newbliss 72 (farmhouse).

**Monaghan**
Westenra Arms, Tel: (047) 81517 grade B

---

# County Antrim

The coast has a well deserved reputation for being one of the most lovely and spectacular in Europe. Behind are the well-known glens with their evocative names derived from the Gaelic. Rising up from the coastal shelf land is the moorland plateau with mineral deposits like bauxite (near the almost deserted village of Newtown Crommelin) and coal (near Ballycastle).

The Moyle or North Sea Channel here never offered much difficulty to travellers, either to the shifting Scotti who moved from Ireland to Scotland when the Kings of Dalriada held sway over the Antrim Coast, the Islands and the West of Scotland, or to the MacDonnells, the most famous family along this coastline. Their territory straddled both sides of the Atlantic up to the Elizabethan era. This proximity to Britain has been significant in the history and importance of Antrim. Although thoroughly settled in the Jacobite plantations and full of staunch loyalists who would man Paisley's army given half a chance, there is a Celtic fringe along the coast and in the Glens or Glynns (woods) of Antrim. Many mythical characters of Irish legends are associated with places in Antrim: the poet Ossian, son of mighty Finn MacCool, the sons of Osnach who died for Deirdre's beauty, and the children of Lir, condemned to spend their lives as swans on the waters of the Moyle.

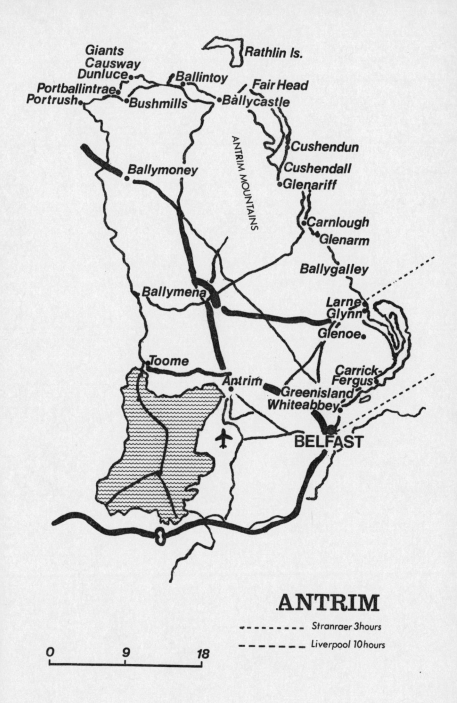

Giants
Causway
Dunluce
Portballintrae
Portrush
Ballintoy
Rathlin Is.
Fair Head
Bushmills
Bàllycastle

ANTRIM MOUNTAINS

Cushendun
Cushendall
Glenariff

Ballymoney

Carnlough
Glenarm

Ballygalley

Ballymena

Larne
Glynn
Glenoe

Toome

Carrick-
Fergus

Antrim
Greenisland
Whiteabbey

BELFAST

# ANTRIM

- - - - - - - Stranraer 3 hours
- - - - - - - Liverpool 10 hours

0        9        18

# Belfast City
(Beal Feirste: Mouth of the Sandy Ford). Population 360,000.

Belfast has one of the most beautiful natural settings of any city. Ringed by hills which are visible from most parts of the town, and hugging the shores of the Lough, it grew from an insignificant town by a river ford into a prosperous commercial centre and port in the 19th century with famous shipyards; the Titanic was architected by the ingenious Ulster men. Now Belfast's unprepossessing appearance is a good illustration of her changing fortunes as her former industries become obsolete. There is also the more macabre impact of the 'troubles' with which Belfast is so much associated: the only people who seem to make much out of the situation are the glass and building merchants and the journalists who make their reputations here.

**Belfast** has only been a city, officially, since 1888. Although industrially it is dying, as the administrative centre of the six counties it acts as the nerve centre for artistic and cultural life. Among the Irish poets known outside the Ulster community Seamus Heaney started writing here when he was at Queen's University in the 60's, and Paul Muldoon lives here. In many ways, Belfast is the centre of the present literary and artistic renaissance in the North. Because it is a 19th century town it lacks the graciousness of Dublin: its city fathers were plutocrats rather than aristocrats, but you will find compensations for northerners are the wittiest people in Ireland and the best hearted; there is less blarney and much humour in the people you meet, just as much charm and a better memory for their friends and promises.

On the whole northerners are aware and proud of their heritage, and the conservation of monuments is much better organised here through the pressure group Ulster Architectural Heritage Society, and the National Trust. Of course there are dangerous areas. Visitors should exercise a certain amount of caution; do not go walking around at night, stick to the centre and the university area unless you are spoiling for a fight; do not make expeditions in to the 'ghetto' areas, into the pubs or (illegal) drinking clubs, remember which area is what, Shankill is Protestant and Loyalist, Falls is Catholic and Republican. Do not photograph soldiers or you may find yourself in trouble.

Although many of the splendours of Belfast date from its period of mercantile importance there was a great quickening of spirit in the 18th century. United Irishman, Henry Joy McCracken, whose family first published the *Belfast Newsletter* in 1737 the longest running morning paper in Great Britain, was a son of the city. Other 18th century personalities include William Drennan who coined the phrase 'the Emerald Isle' and founded the Royal Academical Institution, a distinguished looking building designed by Sir John Soane at the end of Victoria Street. The City Hall in Donegall Square was built in 1896-1906, a grand composition with a central dome and corner towers borrowed from Wren's St. Paul's Cathedral, which make it a good land mark. The Grand Opera House, Great Victoria Street, designed by Frank Matcham, is the last old-style theatre in Ulster and boasts some very fantastical decoration. You should not miss an opportunity to hear real opera here, and there is a programme of other entertainment such as ballet and plays, which you can check up in the local papers: the *Newsletter*, *Belfast Telegraph*, and *Irish News* or Tel: Belfast 49129. Booking Office 41919.

Away from the centre which is also the oldest part of Belfast, you come to the Tudor style Queen's University in red brick which is next door to the Botanic Gardens. Beside pleasant gardens, notice the Palm House, which like the Grand Opera House is being restored. The celebrated Richard Turner was responsible for this glass house, sections of which comprise the earliest surviving cast-iron and curvilinear glass architecture in the world. The Ulster Museum is also well worth seeing. It has a wide variety of collections; of special interest are the treasures from the wreck of the Spanish Armada vessel the *Girona* including some real gold bullion. The Irish antiquities as you would imagine, are strong. There is also an outstanding modern art collection with a good representation of Irish artists like Sir James Lavery, whose wife was the Irish colleen on the old Irish pound notes. Refreshments are available; the museum is open Monday to Saturday 10am–5pm, Sunday 2pm–5pm.

Few people would realise how many *parks* there are in and around Belfast. In south Belfast, upper Malone area, you have Barnett's Park, formerly the headquarters for the National Trust in Northern Ireland. Nearby is the Dixon Park where rose fanciers will get a chance to view the Belfast International Rose Trials. Near Newtownbreda you have Belvoir Park; apparently the young Arthur Wellesley, the late Duke of Wellington spent holidays here with his mother's family. Follow the River Lagan which winds through these pastures and you will come to the picturesque Shaw's Bridge. Continuing up the Malone Road those of you interested in Neolithic sites should visit the Giant's Ring, near Ballylesson, a spectacular earthworks with a dolmen in the centre known as Druid's dolmen. The farmers here used to stage horse races in this huge circle. On the northern side of the city, on the Antrim Road, the baronial style Belfast Castle appears somewhat unexpectedly from the wooded slopes of the Cave Hill. The grounds are open to the public, and you climb up to MacArt's Fort where the United Irishmen, Wolfe Tone and his followers took their oaths of fidelity in 1798. The visitor is not advised to go rambling about on the neighbouring hills and through the glens (Divis Hill, Black Mountain) without some one from that part of the world as you might stumble across dangerous secrets. Also on the Antrim Road, further up, are the Bellevue Zoological Gardens.

There are several interesting places within easy reach of Belfast which are worth a visit. On the southern shores of Belfast following the dual carriage road that takes you past the huge cranes (among the world's largest) of the shipyards and the aircraft works at Sydenham you arrive at the wooded suburb of Cultra. Here in a parkland of over a 100 acres The Ulster Folk and Transport Museum provides a unique opportunity for visitors to explore the past of the province. It is an open-air museum with representative buildings of rural Ulster: a linen scutch mill, a blacksmith's forge, a spade mill and farm houses of different regional styles. These are all furnished appropriately, real fires burn in the grates and the visitor is able to immerse himself in the atmosphere of Ulster's agricultural communities. Those of you interested in the history of every day objects: kitchen equipment, furniture, patchwork and agricultural equipment (remember Ferguson invented the tractor in Belfast) will find this a rich store house. For those early vehicle enthusiasts amongst you, an instructive collection of carriages and railway engines will be found across the Belfast-Bangor road. Opening times May to September: Monday to Saturday 11am–7pm. Sunday 2pm–7pm. Between October and April the museum closes at 5pm. Admission charges, adults 30p, children 10p. Teashop. Folklore enthusiasts should look out for the 'Journal of Ulster Folklife' produced by the museum. To get there by bus: Ulsterbus route 1: Belfast-Bangor goes to and from Oxford St, Bus Station. **Holywood**, now a continuation of pleasant suburbia, is built around a Franciscan Friary, the ruins of which are visible in the High Street.

**Eating:** there are a number of pubs where you can get food: THE SCHOONER INN, 30 Main St, Tel: Holywood 5880, WHOLE FOOD RESTAURANT, and THE COFFEE POT in Church St. Further on this road **Crawfordsburn** has a picturesque Inn, Tel: Helen's Bay 853255. If you're willing to splash out, two places worth going to are: the CARRIAGE RESTAURANT Tel: Helen's Bay 852841 and THE LONG SHOT, 8 Church St, Tel: Holywood 2120. This is an attractive area, with Crawfordsburn Park near by for seaside strolls.

**EATING OUT IN BELFAST** can be fun. Belfast is not renowned for its cuisine, but the gastronome need fear no dreadful upsets, and might relish perhaps a little adventure. Do not overlook the ubiquitious bakery: northern Irish bread and cake shops, and home bakeries' are in a class of their own. They are nearly as prevalent in small towns here as in Scotland. Potato bread is a speciality; try it with apple filling, as especially good combination.

Pub food is becoming more common; the traditional bar existed solely for drinking. Patronise pubs in the city centre or around the university area only or else you may find yourself paying contributions to some paramilitary outfit. For atmosphere, the CROWN SALOON BAR on Victoria Street, a National Trust Monument, offers pub lunches in an authentic boothed bar. Next door at ROBINSON'S BAR you can get oysters and Guinness for lunch. KELLY'S BAR, (Bank St, behind Bank buildings now Primark stores) dates from the 18th century and is more attractive than most bars. It is open for pub lunches, and up to 6 pm on Saturdays.

For sandwiches HUNGRY JACK'S, Wellington Place offers value for money (£1 upwards). There's a whole food bakery on Great Victoria St, called SASSAFRAS where you can get snacks (no sitting down). There is a whole food restaurant called the OPEN COLLEGE RAINBOW CAFE, near the Technical College in College Square East. For delicious unhealthy fried meals you can try the chain of cafes, called NUMBER 6 and NUMBER 7. PICCOLO'S in Wellington St, offers American style hamburger food. Rosemary Street has a number of restaurants, the best is DELANY'S open for morning coffee till 5pm (dishes from £1.20).

In Botanic Avenue there are a number of reasonably priced snack rooms. Round the University you will find some night time eating (the centre is pretty dead). Chinese restaurants are the most common: the best are the REGENT PALACE, and GREEN GARDEN TAKE AWAY in Botanic Avenue and in University Road, there is the UNIVERSITY EVERGREEN.

THE TERRACE RESTAURANT in Stanmillis Road open on Friday and Saturday evenings, and for weekday lunches, bring your own wine and enjoy the good food. Round Botanic Gardens near the museum, there are a number of snackeries; there is also a memorable Egyptian take-away called the SPHINX in Stranmillis Road.

CIRO'S in Great Victoria Street is an authentic Italian restaurant with a colourful proprietor whose paintings decorate the spaces saved from the fishing net decorations. Its mediterranean ambience attracts all sorts, including stray journalists who are tired of keeping their ears to the ground in the trouble spots. Bring your own bottle for lunch or dinner, try tasty and inexpensive à la carte dishes.

THE EUROPA, just down the street is a survivor. Bombed about 30 times (conservative estimate) it still continues to provide quite a sophisticated venue for Belfast business men and visiting journalists; the salad bar goes under exciting name of Whip and Saddle! Dishes from £1.90) while the CARRIAGE RESTAURANT is more a coffee snack bar. Upstairs you can pretend you are anywhere in the world but Belfast in the LOUNGE BAR. The LINEN HALL, a pub in Linen Hall St has a good atmosphere, serves salads, hot food and jazz on Saturdays. ZERO VEGETARIAN RESTAURANT is very scrummy, you find it at 2 University Road, Tel: Belfast 42338.

**BELFAST HAS MANY ENTERTAINMENTS**, besides the *Grand Opera House*, which puts on shows as well as opera, (Booking Office, Tel: Belfast 419191) there is the *Lyric Players Theatre* which operates under the aegis of the Arts Council (Box Office, Tel: Belfast 660081). There is also the *Arts Theatre,* Tel: Belfast 24936. In the summer the Ulster Orchestra plays a series of subscription concerts in the Ulster Hall, Bedford Street, Tel: Belfast 21341.

You can hear some good Irish traditional music in Belfast, the best is supposed to be in the Republican areas but you are not likely to be able to go to the Falls Festival unless you have friends there. Tamer but safer are pubs near the University. During term time the *Queen's Folk Music Society*, 29 University Square, put on fortnightly sessions, check at the Union across from the square for the actual days. Rock, Punk or New Wave music concerts are poster advertised, and sometimes take place in the Ulster Hall. The best source of information for these events are local papers.

The Arts Council for Northern Ireland issues 'current awareness' publications like 'Artslink' and 'What's on in Northern Ireland' which have listing of cultural and recreational events throughout the province.

The Arts Council gallery is worth visiting for information, and for the shows usually Irish and Ulster artists. Bedford House, Bedford Street, Tel: Belfast 44222.

**TRAVELLING FROM BELFAST:** Donegall Square is the central departure point for most city bus services. Information on routes can be got from the Citybus Coach Station, Tel: Belfast 46485 or from the Tourist Information Centre, 50 High Street, Tel: Belfast 46609 and Belfast City Hall, Donegall Square, Tel: Belfast 20202 ext 216. The fares are flat rate in 1981, 45p.

For Ulsterbus departure points, Oxford Street Coach Station services: Antrim, Down, Londonderry (East), and the Cookstown area, Tel: Belfast 46485.

Great Victoria Street Station (entrance Glengall St) services: Armagh, Tyrone, Londonderry, Fermanagh and west Down, and the Republic of Ireland.

Railway stations operated by Northern Ireland Railways, Tel: Belfast 30310/35282 consist of the new Belfast Central (East Bridge Station) for Dublin, Co. Down, Antrim and Londonderry.

Botanic Avenue station is a subsidiary of Central Station. York Road station caters for Larne (and the Stranraer & Cairnryan Boats) **Shipping services:** P&O Irish Sea Services operate the Belfast/Liverpool crossing (which may be cut this autumn) from Donegall Quay, 94 High Street, Tel: Belfast 23636; British Rail Sealink services (the Larne-Stranraer ferry) has offices at 24 Donegall Place, Tel: Belfast 27525.

**Useful addresses**
Youth Hostel Association, 93 Dublin Road, Tel: Belfast 24733.
AA, 108-110 Great Victoria Street, Tel: Belfast 26242. Breakdown service; Belfast 44538.
RAC, 65 Chichester St, Tel: Belfast 33944. Rescue service, Tel: Belfast 30919.
Hospitals: Belfast City Hospital, Lisburn Rd, Tel: Belfast 29241.
Royal Victoria, Grosvenor Road, Tel: Belfast 42614.

**PLACES TO STAY IN BELFAST** Dialling Code 0232

There are a number of hotels, most are very expensive (£25 per night upwards) so only for expense account visitors, these are listed at the end under 'binge places'.
**Grade B Guesthouses** are your best bet, expecially those around the University area.
Mrs Thomasina Lowry, Westwood, 85 Eglantine Avenue, Tel: Belfast 668554.
Mrs S J Moore, Botanic Lodge, Botanic Avenue, Tel: Belfast 27682.
Miss M McBride, Beechdene, 71 Botanic Avenue, Tel: Belfast 41684.
Further out: E & M Hughes, 37 Rossmore Avenue, Ormeau Rd, Tel: Belfast 643924.
R & E Johnston, Dunmore Guest Hs, 294 Antrim Rd, Tel: Belfast 749499.

You can get meals at all these, either lunch, high tea or dinner or just the evening meals. All have bathrooms available for use on payment of an extra charge.

**B&B Accommodation**

University Area: Mrs Pearl Blakely, Pearl Court Hs, 11 Malone Rd, Tel: Belfast 666145. A lot of double rooms, so cheaper for two.

Nan Campbell, Camera Hs, 44 Wellington Park, Tel: Belfast 660026/667856, fairly pricey but a good area. Lots of single rooms.

Mrs S Kelly, 155 University St, Tel: Belfast 29854. Very cheap.

During the summer months when students are not in residence contact The Queen's University, University Road, Tel: Belfast 45133 where you can get a room for around £3, but no breakfast.

There are two YWCA's: Wellesley Hs, 3/5 Malone Rd, Tel: Belfast 668347.

Queen Mary's Hall, 70 Fitzwilliam St, Tel: Belfast 40439.

**Binge Places**

Europa Hotel, Great Victoria, Tel: Belfast 45161. £25 B&B. Lots of bathrooms. Lots of family rooms (200) so it could be very cheap if you shared. Choice of restaurants, and a chic lounge. You even get a certificate for 'bravery' after staying a night in Central Belfast.

Wellington Park Hotel, Tel: Belfast 661232. £29 for a double room. A la carte meals. Music in the evenings.

Further out: Beechlawn, Dunmurry Lane, Tel: Belfast 612974

Glenmachen Tower Hotel, Holywood, Tel: Belfast 63441. Not so many rooms but attractive surroundings in the Holywood hills.

If you start off from **Belfast** (the county town of Antrim) for the **Antrim Coast** take the loughside road passing the industrial districts and comfortable suburbs of **Whitebbey** and **Greenisland** to the oldest town of Northern Ireland, **Carrickfergus**. It takes its name from one of the Dalriadic Kings, Fergus, who foundered off this point on one of his journeys between Antrim and Scotland. The Kings of Scotland were descended from this line, and therefore, the Kings and Queens of England. He is said to have brought his coronation stone from Ireland to Scone, certainly the rock, now in Westminster Abbey, of red sandstone embedded with pebbles, is like rock found along the Antrim coast.

**Carrickfergus Castle** is the most prominent sight in the town, a massive Anglo-Norman Tower built by John de Courcey in the years after 1180. It has been militarily occupied for $7\frac{1}{2}$ centuries, but since 1928 it has been a museum, with an impressive array of weaponry and armour on display, plus the history of such Irish regiments as the Inniskilling Dragoons. Beside this splendid fortification lies the grand new promenade, the largest of its kind in the six counties, and a harbour. **Carrickfergus** has an old parish church (Coll) founded by St. Nicholas in 1185, and rebuilt in 1614. Louis MacNeice, whose father before he became Bishop, was rector here, wrote charmingly of the skewed alignment of the aisle.

'A church in the form of a cross but denoting
The list of Christ on the cross in the angle of the nave.'

**Eating:** at DOBBIN'S INN you can have some refreshment, lunch or high tea, and admire the 17th century massive fireplace. (6/8 High St. Tel: 63905). There are a number of fried food places, good for take aways: like the FISH AND CHICKEN BAR at 28 West St. (Tel: 62500).

On your way out of **Carrickfergus** you pass **Kilroot**. At **Whitehead,** early locomotive enthusiasts can indulge in train rides on early vehicles. You can go up the coast as far as **Portrush** on the Portrush Flyer from York St. (Details: Mr A K Love, 12 The Close, Marino Holywood, Co. Down. s.a.e.). At Whitehead there are excursions on vintage trains every Sunday in July. August and September. The road to **Larne** takes you along by the lough which is almost land locked by Island Magee, a small peninsula with popular beaches.

Before you get to Larne you will pass one of the glens that break through the Antrim plateau, Glenoe, with four waterfalls. It is now under National Trust care. The little village of **Glynn** is actually on the shore of Larne Lough, and was the setting for a film called the 'Luck of the Irish'. Although there are some hideous buildings and unecological views produced by the industrial sites round Larne, this is an important port and the gateway to the Antrim Coast proper so you can not very well avoid it. There are railway services at regular intervals to and from York St. Station in Belfast. These connect with the sailing times of the boats between **Larne,** and **Stranraer** and **Cairnryan.** It's the shortest sea crossing from Ireland to Scotland taking only 70 minutes once you are in open sea.

**Eating:** You can get a good meal at the LAHARNA HOTEL, Main St, Tel:2311/2 and there are a number of take-aways in the vicinity.

If you want to get to Island Magee you can get on a ferry they leave half hourly between 7am-9pm, which takes you to **Ballylumford.** On a promontory south of the harbour you can see Olderfleet Castle, a corruption of the Viking name Ulfrecksfiord. Round here so many middle Stone-Age artefacts have been found that the term Larnian is often used to describe the Mesolithic culture of Ireland. You may not be surprised perhaps to learn that the discovery of so many early sites in the Black North (ie in 'protestant' areas like **Larne,** or **Mountsandel,** near **Coleraine**) has given rise to an interesting theory of history, whereby the central argument rests on anthropological differences between the two warring factions of the north east: the aboriginal Protestants, (heirs of the Dalriadic kingdom who came back from Scotland to claim Meland) and the Celtic Catholic invaders. Another rather incredible figure of Larne's more recent past was the romantic novelist Amanda McKitterick Ros, who was wife of the station master here. 'Delina Delaney' and 'Poems of Puncture' were among her better known works; the young Aldous Huxley and his mates formed a reading circle to admire their awfulness.

Beyond **Larne** you have some of the most marvellous maritime scenery to be seen this side of the Atlantic. Armed with some geological knowledge you may see for yourself the formation of the earth's outer crust, for this coastline has been compared to a pictorial textbook of the process.

Basically, archaen schists (over 300 million years old) formed the first crust over the once molten earth, and these schists are covered by layers from later eras, the latest of which is lava, or basalt (the largest lava field in the British Isles was formed 50-70 million years ago). The red sandstone, formed from the sands of a desert existing 190-150 million years ago (Triassic) was succeeded by a sea which formed the lias clays; then in another era, when the land was again invaded by the sea, chalk was formed by the minute plankton in the water giving rise to the white cliffs on the coast (120-170 million years old). Finally there came the volcanic period. During the Ice Ages, the Glens of Antrim were formed by the movement of glaciers which cut through the moorland which includes the Star Bog above **Larne,** and the Garron Plateau. These are remote, uninhabited except by sheep.

The coast road links each of the nine glens, from south to north they are: **Glenarm, Glencloy, Glenariff, Glenballyeamon, Glenaan, Glencorp, Glendun, Glenshesk** and **Glentaisie.**

From **Larne** you follow a road which goes beneath cliffs and passes through the Black Cave tunnel. At **Ballygally** there is a very Scottish style castle, now a hotel (Tel: B'g 212). A couple of miles inland you can get a panorama of the Scottish coast with the 'bee hive' outline of Ailsa Craig from the Sallagh Braes. At **Glenarm** (Glen of the army) you can visit one of the oldest of the glen villages dating from King John's time. The castle here belongs to the MacDonnells who are descended from Queen Elizabeth's great enemy Sorley Boy. If you go into Glenarm Forest you can look back at this turreted castle which reminds many of the Tower of London. The street are old and attractively named, and those who are looking for *folk music* may find it here.

This part of the coast is full of chalk and limestone, **Glenarm** exports it from the little harbour, and there used to be quarries at **Carnlough** which is the town at the foot of **Glencloy** (glen of the hedges). This area has been long inhabited and farmed, with drystone walls enclosing the land. Although **Carnlough** attracts local holidaymakers because of its sandy beach, solitude can be found on Garron Moor, and in the other little glens. On your way round the Garron Point to Red Bay you will notice a change in the geology from limestone to the Triassic sandstone exposed on the shore.

All along this coast road you will find breathtaking sea views and if you want to explore there are odd little hamlets, deserted or forgotten; this road was built to ease the hardships of the glens' people, but it also gave them a route out resulting in a much diminished population. **Glenariff** (Ploughman's Glen) is the largest and most popular of the glens with its waterfalls, Ess na Larach, rendered as Tears of the Mountain and Ess na Crub, Fall of the Hoof. With names like these you can understand how easy it was for poets to praise these valleys; Moira O'Neill is one of the 'landscape rhymers'. **Waterfoot** at the foot of the Glenariff River is where the Glen of Antrim Feis is held every July, so if you want to see some Irish dancing and hear some music try and be there. In the glen you will see steep climbing mountains and a green narrowing valley floor which gives some aptness to Thackerary's description: 'Switzerland in miniature'. This is perfect ground for nature rambles with lovely wild flowers, and the moorland of Glenariff Forest Park.

Along the east flank of the valley you can see the remains of a narrow gauge railway which a century ago transported iron. On the west side, at the Alpinesque cliffs of **Lurigethan** you can look for the mound of Dunclana-Mourna, home of Finn MacCool and his son, the poet Ossian. The warrior Finn was leader of a mighty band called the Fianna; he was renowned for his wisdom (gained through eating the Salmon of Knowledge), for his shining beauty (Finn means fair) and his bravery. His deeds were recounted in the legends and epics of Ireland and Scotland. Finn is the giant of the Causeway, he took up a sod of land to throw at another giant, leaving Lough Neagh and forming the Isle of Man.

**Eating:** try the GLENARIFF FOREST PARK CAFE for snacks. Open from May to September. Continuing on the coast road we get to **Cushendall,** called the capital of the glens. It lies at the foot of the Glenballyeamon (Edwardstown glen) a lonesome glen, and the two glens, Glenaan and Glencorp (meaning glen of the Colt's Foot, or Rush Lights, and glen of the Slaughter respectively). The town owes much to Francis Turly who built the Sandstone Curfew Tower; he also deflected the course of the river Dall (said to take its name from a victim of the warrior poet Ossian).

**Eating:** You could try the THORNLEA HOTEL, Coast Road (Tel: 223/403) for a meal.

Those who want to honour the legends should go to Ossian's grave, it is a Megalithic tomb and stone circle at the top of a lane in Glenaan, about 2 miles west of Cushendall. This Celtic Orpheus was entranced by a vision of the golden haired Niamh, and followed her to her father's kingdom of Tir na Og. He returned to find his companions dead and St. Patrick preaching. He died unconverted for the clerks (priests) music was not sweet to him after Finn's. Further up the road is Beagh's Forest which stands in splendid open country from where you can look back at the mountains Trostan and Slemish where St. Patrick spent many lonely hours in his youth watching sheep.

The road through **Glencorp** will take you past the fairies hill of Tiveragh, a rounded volcanic plug. In the past precautions were taken to prevent the rifling and swapping activities of the fairy legions. At **Cushendun** you reach a 'protected village'. The village and its beach are in the care of the National Trust. Clough Williams-Ellis designed the Cornish style cottages and there are *caravan* and *camping* facilities tucked away. Within the hidden glen of Glendun (Brown glen) and its wood, Draigagh, there is a mass rock carved with a crucifixion scene, supposedly brought over from Iona. The poet John Masefield, whose wife came from here wrote, 'In the curlew calling time of Irish dusk'. Perhaps he was thinking of this glen which is full of wildlife and flowers.

You have not finished with the glens yet, but you have some wonderful views from the headlands coming up. Go by **Tor Head**, it means traversing a twisty road through Culraney townland, which remained an enclave of Scots Gaelic speakers until about 60 years ago. Here you can look to the Mull of Kintyre, only about 15 miles away. You can understand why this part of Ireland felt nearer to Scotland than any other kingdom. From here to Fair Head is Murlough Bay where the Kings of Dalriada had their summer residence. Here you can see the archaen Schists which formed the very first layer of the crust covering the molten mass which was to be terra firma. This bay is in the care of the National Trust; the best way to reach it is from Ballylucan. At Fair Head, reached from **Ballyvoy,** you can look down from the highest cliffs in the north east, but still more impressive is the heather covered top with its three lakes, one even has an ancient lake dwelling or Crannog, where you may see the odd wild goat.

Fair Head gives you a good view of **Rathlin Island,** called Raghery by people hereabouts. The story goes that Finn MacCool's mother was on her way to get some whiskey for him in Scotland, and she took a stepping stone to throw in her way across the Moyle, this was **Rathlin.** This 'L' shaped island lies about 8 miles from Ballycastle, and 14 miles from the Mull of Kintyre rising with white cliffs from the sea. It is populated by families who retained their Scots Gaelic longer than any other community. It has a fascinating history, mostly full of battles and competition for its strategic position. But it was a good hideout for Robert the Bruce: he had to take refuge in one of the caves (underneath the East lighthouse) and there he saw the persevering spider that inspired the saying 'If at first you do not succeed, try, try again'. You may have to be persistent to get out to **Rathlin,** for boats leave from Ballycastle on a journey that takes about 50 minutes, but you may get held up on the island if there is a storm in the sound, Tel: Ballycastle 62024/62225. There is a camping site near the Inn but other accommodation is limited so you must make arrangements beforehand.

Ballycastle is one of my favourite resort towns. Although it's fairly lively with lawn tennis courts in the old harbour, golf and other amusements near by, this is the landscape for the two saddest stories of Ireland. Round the waters of this part of the Antrim coast the Children of Lir were said to have spent some of their years of imprisonment in the swan form their wicked stepmother condemned them to. At the east end of the Ballycastle sands is a rock called Carrig-Usnach where the ill-fated Deirdre landed with her lover and his two brothers, the sons of Usnach, at the treacherous invitation of King Conor who, desiring her beauty, had lured them back from Scotland.

**Ballycastle** is divided by the market end and the harbour end. The diamond market place is the site of the Ould Lammas Fair held at the end of August. Visitors from the Scottish islands such as Islay travel over for this ancient, famous fair. There is a rhyme that goes:

'Did you treat your Mary-Ann
To dulse and yellow man
At the Ould Lammas Fair in Ballycastle-O?'

Ballycastle Museum, in Castle Street, is worth a visit, it is open during the holiday season. **Ballycastle** was a stronghold of the Macdonnells; at Bonamargy Friary, east of the town the great coffins of some of these redoubtable chiefs lie in the vault. The other family associated with the town was the Boyd family who developed the coal mines; the entrances to these may be seen if you go across the golf course to the foot of Fair Head. The Corrymeela Community House is also along here (Corrymeela means hill of harmony in Irish) this place is an interdenominational conference and holiday centre.

**Ballycastle** is a splendid touring centre. The other glens which make the quorum of nine Antrim Glens can be visited from here. Glenshesk (the sedgy glen) is well wooded lying east of the Knocklayde. Breen Wood, at the head of the Glen, is a nature reserve with very old oaks who probably witnessed the fights between the O'Neills and MacDonnells for mastery of the area. On the other side of the Hill of Knocklayde lies the last glen, called after Taisia, a princess of Rathlin, she seems to have been something of a warrior winning a great battle on this broad glen which now carries the main road from Ballycastle to Armoy. Another expedition to be made from the town is to Kinbane Head, stronghold of Colla MacDonnell, Sorley Boy's brother. Now it stands as picturesque ruins on its narrow white promontory reached from the road going to the Giant's Causeway.

A better known tourist attraction is the swinging **Carrick-a-rede** rope bridge north of **Ballycastle,** and about a mile on from Kinbane head. It used to be a real dare to cross on this apparently slight causeway to the rock on which there is a salmon fishery house. You can look across to a bird sanctuary on Sheep Island, but this is only one aspect of the views which are tremendous at any point here. One of the prettiest towns on the coast is **Ballintoy:** if you catch it on a good day it looks like a Mediterranean fishing village with its white church and buildings. The harbour is reached by a precipitous little road. You can walk from here to Whitepark Bay, a great curve of bay with sand dunes which is a National Trust property. In under the cliffs is the little hamlet of **Portbraddan** with a tiny church dedicated to St.Gobhan (patron saint of builders). You should take your time here, beachcombers can find fossils, flower enthusiasts can examine the dunes, there is even evidence of Stone Age settlement at the east end for any amateur archaeologist.

**Eating:** for those wanting refreshment before setting out on these excursions on what is called the causeway coast, **Ballycastle** provides some ports of call: open only in the summer months is the MOYLE CAFE, North St, (Tel: 62602) and the GINGHAM ROOMS, at 41 St.Ann St, (Tel: 62515). Near the harbour there are fish and chip bars, plus the usual sort of candyfloss and icecream stalls you get with dodgems. County Antrim is very well endowed with home bakeries, and the potato bread round Ballycastle is quite a speciality. Also sold here is the dulse and honeyman of the fair rhyme: dulse being dried seaweed, salt and chewy; and honeyman being one of the most delicious confections you can imagine (a bit like the inside of Crunchy bars). As in most fishermen's towns the pubs are good and friendly. Note that you can stop off at Ballintoy Harbour for snacks at ROARK'S KITCHEN (down at the harbour) Tel: Ballycastle 62225; it is open 7 days a week June to August, and at weekends in April, May and September.

Next on the horizon, after Whitepark Bay are the unique cliffs and basalt columns of the **Giant's Causeway**. You can walk to the Giant's Causeway from Dunseverick Castle. Once it was a main terminal for travellers from Tara and an embarkation point for Scotland. Now it is a lofty ruin along a cliff top path. From here you will find yourself gazing down at the strangeness of the petrified hexagons. The castle can also be approached by the National Trust entrance with its information on the history of the cooling lava. It is an extraordinary sight, you can not really describe it as beautiful; if you were shown a picture of it and did not know it was a natural phenomenon, you might term it surreal.

The formations of the basalt columns which disappear into the sea and come out at **Staffa Island** (with the same legendary figure attached, Finn MacCool or Fingall) have different nicknames. The Causeway is one part, there is also the Giant's Organ (the tallest columns are arranged like organ pipes) others are the Honeycomb, the Wishing Chair, and some more esoteric shapes which you need the National Trust booklet to identify. On the western side a huge sea tunnel called the Portcoon Cave casts up strange glimmery reflections from the sea. You can walk along another coastal path to **Portballintrae**, a picturesque fishing village, past a huge strand with strong Atlantic rollers (though be careful of the undertow) called Runkerry. A Spanish galleon, the **Girona,** was sunk off the Giant's Causeway, it contained the most valuable cargo yet found. You can see the recovered treasures in the Ulster Museum, Belfast.

**Bushmills** which lies inland from **Portballintrae** is famous for its whiskey distillery which claims to be the oldest in the world. Whiskey coming from the word: Usquebaugh, uisce beatha or sweet water is one word that the English have taken from the Irish. Before whiskey became a genteel drink, the best Coleraine was admitted to be a connoisseur's drink. Peter the Great in 1697 on his study tour of Europe was amongst many to appreciate the northern Irish liquor. Bushmills distillery can be visited by appointment Tel: Bushmills 31521. Tourist information can be obtained in the Antrim Arms Hotel from Mr. Verner.
**Eating:** Try the COFFEE SHOP, Main St, The Square for snacks; for lunch try the OLDE MILL, Lower Main St, it also does high teas. Tel: 31291.

If you like adventure stories of the old fashioned historic variety read one of George Birmingham's (say Northern Iron). He used to live round here and incorporates scenes from Irish life on this part of the coast and elsewhere in the north very happily. Incidentally many of Charles Lever's novels are set round here; his books are more thrilling, on the lines of a Denis Wheatley.

From the quiet little town of Bushmills you can move onto North Ireland's biggest seaside resort **Portrush.** Before you reach this mecca of amusements and fish and chips visit Dunluce Castle, (sometimes translated as Mermaid's Fort) whose bold ruins keep watch over the magnificent coastline. Its long romantic history is available through perusal of a leaflet available at the entrance. Anyone approaching it along the shore (you can scramble from the White Rocks, a range of chalk cliffs accessible from the main road) may see the rare meadow cranesbill flower called the flower of Dunluce. **Portrush** is on a promontory jutting out into the Atlantic. It has a small harbour which is popular with yachtsmen sailing in the west and from here you can take boat cruises to see the Skerries (where the great auk, now extinct, used to nest) and the Causeway Coast. Although it is crowded in the summer it is a friendly place. You will find the Victorian/Edwardian main buildings have their own contribution to make to the unique flavour of a northern coastal resort.

**Eating:** Although there are lots of milk bars and fish and chips you can taste the exotic in DIONYSIUS GREEK TAVERNA, 53 Eglinton St, (Tel: Portrush 823855) and the CHINA HOUSE next door. Go to the Main St for burger/fried food.

As you set off from the coast through mid Antrim via **Ballymena** you will be passing through the richest farmland in the North. The farmers here are among the most progressive and hardworking in Ireland. If you are there during the summer you will see the Loyalist flag, with a white background and red hand on a red cross, fluttering from many a household. You might take a detour to Northern Ireland's only *Safari Park* at **Benvarden Dervock,** north of **Ballymoney.** There is a snackbar called 'TREK OUT' open May to September. Another spot worth stopping at is the little Moravian settlement of Gracehill just outside Ballymena where you can see some of the communal buildings dating from the 18th century around the green. When you make your way down to **Antrim** and Lough Neagh you will see the distinctive shape of Slemish Mountain (east of Ballymena) where St. Patrick spent his youth after capture by Irish pirates.

**Antrim** town stands a little way back from Lough Neagh, the largest stretch of inland water in the British Isles. The town has an old nucleus with a 9th century round tower in almost perfect condition on Steeple Rd (north of the centre) but it is being encircled with new housing and shopping centres. Antrim Castle gateway introduces the park into the town which is a splendid asset, with, it is said, Le Notre gardens. At **Sixmilewater** you can go on a cruise of Lough Neagh (details from the Antrim Forum Tel: Antrim 4131) they go daily from the Marina, May to September.

Another way to see the Lough is on the Shane's Castle Railway: this is at **Randalstown,** a few miles away and is Ireland's only working narrow gauge railway. It operates mainly during July and August, for the particulars ring the manager of Shanes Castle Railway, Tel: Antrim 3380. Lough Neagh is surrounded by flat marshy land so you do not get a good view of it from the road. However it is famous for the eels who spawn in the Sargasso sea and swim across the Atlantic and, struggle up the Bann in springtime, all 20 million of them (though now as many as possible are captured at Coleraine and brought to Lough Neagh in tankers). The eels take about 12 years to mature, and the main fishery is at **Toomebridge,** a very large cooperative managed by local fishermen and farmers. The Lough is home for many birds and plants. It also has many legends attached to it. It takes its name from the horse god Eochu, Lord of the underworld beneath the waters of the Lough.


## PLACES TO STAY IN COUNTY ANTRIM

**Antrim Town**
The Deer Park Hotel, 71 Dublin Rd, Tel: Antrim 2480/2449. Good facilities though expensive.
Mrs W L Mackey, Killside, Killealy, Tel: Antrim 3228
**Armoy**
see Ballymoney
**Ballycastle**
Antrim Arms Hotel, Castle St, Tel: Ballycastle 62204. An old fashioned hotel in the Centre.
Marcus Jameson, Guesthouse, grade B, Hilsea, Quay Hill, Tel: B'castle 62365. Comfortable and friendly, near the harbour.
Mrs Lilian Patrick, Atlantic Guesthouse, The Promenade, Tel: Ballycastle 62412
Mrs K Delargy, Fair Head View, 26 North St, Tel: Ballycastle 62822
Mrs E Simpson, 29 Castle St, Tel: Ballycastle 622976
near by: Mrs E Black, 46 Torr Rd, Twenty Acres, Ballyvoy, Tel: B'castle 62629 (near Murlough Bay)
Mrs Hannah M Smyth, Gortconney Hs, 52 Whitepark Rd, Tel: Ballycastle 62283
**Bushmills**
Mrs Dorothy Taggart, Montalto Gueshouse, 5 Craigboney Rd, Tel: Bushmills 31257
Mrs C Verner, Antrim Arms, 25 Main St, Tel: Bushmills 31343
Mrs E M Dunlop, 36 Castlecatt Rd, Ballyness East, Tel: Bushmills 31252
**Ballygally**
Halfway Hotel, Coast Rd, Tel: Ballygally 265
Ballygally Castle Hotel, Tel: B'gally 212. Cheaper.
Mrs A McKee, The Church Farm, Cairncastle, Tel: B'gally 480
**Ballymena**
The Adair Arms Hotel, Ballymoney Rd, Tel: (0266) 3674. More expensive hotel where you can see affluent farmers.
Leighinmohr House Hotel, Leighinmohr Avenue, Tel: (0266) 2313. Cheaper.
Mr Crowther, The Clarance Guesthouse, Lower Mill St, Tel: 0266 6671
Mrs M Dinsmore, Milltown Farm, Drones Rd, Clucrum, Tel: Loughgiel 233
**Ballymoney**
Mrs E W Hammond, Cooleen, 15 Coleraine Rd, Tel: Ballymoney 63037
Mrs RJ Boyce, Brynhedd, 122 Newbridge Rd, Tel: B'money 63097
In the country Mrs S Gilmour, Enagh Farm, Tel: Ballymoney 63169
**Carrickfergus**
Dobbins Inn Hotel, High St, Tel: C'fergus 63905
Mrs Jean Kernohan, Marathon Guesthouse, 3 Upper Station Rd, Greenisland, Tel: Whiteabbey 62475

**Cushendall**
Thornlea Hotel, Tel: Cushendall 223
Mrs M Martin, Tros Ben Villa, 8 Coast Rd, Tel: Cushendall 741
**Cushendun**
The Bay Hotel, Strandview Park, Tel: Cushendun 267
Glens of Antrim Guesthouse, 16 Strandview Park, Tel: Cushendun 222
**Giant's Causeway**
The Causeway Hotel, Tel: Bushmills 31226
Mrs Frances Lynch, Carnside Hs, 23 Causeway Coast, Tel: Bushmills 31337
**Glenarm**
Drum na greagh Hotel, Coast Rd, Tel: Glenarm 336/7
Mrs M McAllister, Dunluce, Cloney, Tel: Glenarm 279
**Glenariff**
Mrs S E McAlister, 245 Garron Rd, Tel: Cushendall 439
**Glencloy:**
The Londonderry Arms, Tel: Carnlough 85255 an old fashioned hotel
Mrs M Aiken, Bethany, 5 Bay Rd, Tel: Carnlough 85667
**Islandmagee**
Farmhouse Myrtle Montgomery, Roydene, 337 Middle Rd, Tel: Islandmagee 225
**Larne**
Less expensive hotels are:
Curran Court Hotel, Curran Rd, Tel: Larne 5505
Laharna Hotel, Main St, Tel: Larne 2311
Miss A Graham, Manor Guesthouse, Olderfleet Rd, Tel: Larne 3305
Mary McKane, Seaview Guesthouse, Tel: Larne 2438
In Curran Road there are a number of B&Bs:
M Dempsey, 100 Curran Rd, Tel: Larne 2106
Anna M Gillespie, 58 Curran Rd, Tel: Larne 77613
Elizabeth Burke, Greenmount, 231 Old Glenarm Rd, Tel: Larne 3555
**Rathlin Island**
Dominic and Kay McCurdy, Rathlin Guesthouse, Tel: 71217
**Portglenone**
Misses E & J Lowrie, Bannside Farmhouse, 268 Gortgole Rd, Tel: Portglenone 821262. Home baking, good for the airport.
**Whitehead**
There are two hotels:
The Dolphin Hotel, Marine Parade, Tel: W'head 72481
Royal George Hotel, Edward Rd, Tel: W'head 2476 (cheaper)
Mrs J Craig, 90 Hillhead Rd, Tel: Ballycarry 2769.
**Youth Hostels**
Ballygally
Moneyvart, Cushendall
Ballycastle

# County Armagh

The smallest county in Ulster, Armagh's scenery is nevertheless varied from the gentle southern drumlins, and wild open moorland, to the grander mountains and rocky glens further east. An intricate network of dry stone walls gather what fertility may be had into fields with barely enough room for a cow to turn in. As you travel north towards the reclaimed wetlands on the shore of Lough Neagh, the orchards and dairy pastures become more extensive and are dotted with small lakes and the rivers that once turned the wheels of the flax mills.

Just north of the centre lies the ancient capital of Ulster and the ecclesiastical capital of Ireland since the days of St. Patrick. The **City of Armagh,** now sprawled over seven hills used to be the centre of learning and tranquillity when Rome was in ruins and London glowed with endless fires started by the Barbarians. Today, there is little to show of the ancient city; its appearance is distinctly Georgian especially in the Mall. A visit to the county museum beside the Mall helps to fill in the city's background. Here, a 17th century painting shows the old wide streets, space for markets and the prominence of the early hill-top Cathedral of St Patrick. There is also a wide range of regional exhibits, a local natural history section and an art gallery.

The two cathedral churches are unmistakeable features of the city's skyline. The church of Ireland Cathedral has grown from a medieval core. A tablet in the west wall claims to mark the grave of King Brian Boru who shattered the Vikings at Clontarf in 1014, though not before they had sacked Armagh in their usual destructive style. Notice the carved medieval stone heads high up on the cathedral's exterior and the mysterious statues in the chapel. The surrounding streets run true to the rings of the Celtic rath in which St. Patrick directed, so it is said by a flight of angels, built his church. Across the valley are the twin spires of the Catholic Cathedral of St. Patrick; it is a complete contrast with its profusion of magnificent internal gilding, marbles, mosaics and stained glass. The building was finished in 1873, the passing of the years marked by a collection of cardinal's red hats suspended in the Lady Chapel! Another feature of 18th century **Armagh** is the observatory, close to the more recent planetarium and Hall of Astronomy. **Armagh** has got the most advanced facilities for astronomical studies in the British Isles. Travellers come for miles to explore the Hole-in-the Wall Antique shop tucked away off Market Street and reviving cups of tea can be had at several points throughout the city. THE ARCHWAY at the Gaol end of the Mall specialises in gooey cakes and good value lunches.

Heading out on the much improved Newry Road you pass the village of **Markethill** on the right and Gosford Castle – a huge early 19th century mock-Norman castle on the left. These magnificent grounds are now open to the public and owned by the Forestry Commission. The walled cherry garden, the arboretum, nature trails and forest parks, with good facilities for picnicing and *camping* make it an enjoyable place to while away some time. Further south and keeping to the more attractive minor

# ARMAGH

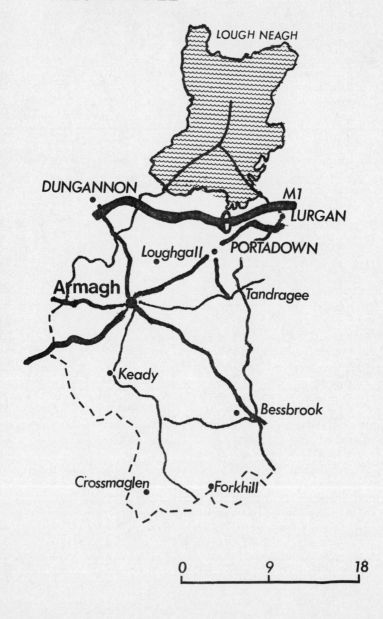

LOUGH NEAGH

DUNGANNON

M1

LURGAN

Loughgall

PORTADOWN

Armagh

Tandragee

Keady

Bessbrook

Crossmaglen

Forkhill

0        9        18

roads, you come across the village of **Bessbrook.** It is a model linen manufacturing town, neatly laid out in the 19th century by a Quaker; it still has neither pub nor pawn house. The design of the model town of Bournville near Birmingham is based entirely on Bessbrook. Remains of the huge old mill, dams, weirs and sluices stand deserted and nearby the impressive cut stone Craigmore viaduct still carries the main line to Dublin. Just outside **Bessbrook** is Derrymore House, a small thatched manor house set in parkland; built in 1776, it was witness to the signing of the Act of Union in 1801 and is now in the care of the National Trust.

Already the land is poorer, the fields smaller, the hedges higher and the roads have more of a twist in them. Soon the hills of south Armagh appear in the distance dominated by the peak of Slieve Gullion. This rugged group of hills is steeped in history and legend. Described as the mountains of mystery, the average tourist never hears of them which is a loss to them as the whole region has magnificent scenery, beautiful lakes, streams and unspoilt little villages. However the present borderland reputation cannot be ignored , but with a little care and thought you can enjoy exploring this delightfully unkempt area, so different from the tamer country in the north. Caught between Camlough Mountain and Slieve Gullion lies the beautiful ribbon like Lough Cam. The surrounding hedges and shorelines are the home of many flowers and birds and there is good *fishing.*

If you have time, it is worth going further southwest towards **Monaghan** to visit the town of **Crossmaglen,** with its staggeringly large market square, the largest in Europe. It is the centre of a recently revived cottage industry – lacemaking. Again there are earthen works to explore: a superb example of a treble ringed fort, remains of stone cairns, and a crannog on Lough Ross. There is good *fishing* in some of the lakes. You are now actually following the old coach road from **Dublin** to **Armagh** itself the ancient link between Emain Macha and Tara. At Dorsey there is the largest entrenched enclosure of its kind in Ireland; constructed a a defensive outpost for Emain Macha, this huge earthwork encloses over 300 acres and lies astride the route. Some of the earth ramparts still remain.

From the other side of the Lough, the road climbs up through the trees to the extensive, recently developed Slieve Gullion National Park. The park caters for the *camper* and there are forest trails to follow. From the top of the mountain wonderful panoramic views of the encircling mountains, that make up the ring of Gullion, and the distant hills of Belfast and Dublin spread before you. Slieve Gullion, in Gaelic mountain of Chullain, is often shrouded in mist, and according to local folklore this eerie mountain is magical. Chullain was a chief who owned a fierce watchdog which was slain by a boy of 15 – the young hero was afterwards called Cuchullain 'the hound of Chullain'. On the southern slopes there is an ancient church dating back to 450 AD, a Holy Well and a prehistoric passage grave. **Jonesborough** is famous for the huge open air market held every Sunday. Here too is one of the earliest datable Christian monuments in Ireland, the inscribed Kilnasaggart Pillar Stone, about $1\frac{1}{2}$ miles south of **Jonesborough.**

Crossing through a multipatchwork of little fields, boggy hollows and forest patches you come to **Glenhu,** long associated with such Ulster heroes as Cuchullain. Both the villages of **Forkhill,** with its trout stream, and **Mullaghbane,** with its tiny museum furnished as a south Armagh farmhouse, are picturesquely situated in their own valleys between the hills. Everywhere there are the trace of early man in the burial cairns, the stones, the cashels and the raths.

Leaving behind the mountains of south Armagh, you enter the attractive upland country know as the Fews. The isolated village of **Newtownhamilton** was founded in 1770, but the neighbourhood is associated with the legendary story of Lir, for it was here that King Lir had his palace. Do not go straight back to Armagh but branch off to the west and climb Carrigatuke Hill. This is yet another place associated with St Patrick. From the top an outstanding view of the area as far as Meath and even Roscommon lies before you. This small area across and down to the border is a miniature 'lake district' with lots of little irregular lakes caught between tiny hills, vestiges of glacial movement and deposition. Many of the lakes are studded with islands. Lake Tullnawood is particularly picturesque and there are stone walks, car parks and picnic places. At **Carnagh** there is a forest park with planned walks through the natural woods and around the lake. There is also a caravan site situated on high ground. Just north of the bootshaped Clay Lake is the small market town of **Keady**. It was once a very important linen centre, hence the number of derelict watermills in the district. Nearby at **Nassagh Glen** there is a mill and a huge viaduct that spans the wide valley. Under the viaduct's arches you could have a picnic among wild flowers, rose briars and red berried rowan. From here it is only a short distance back to the city of **Armagh**.

To the west of the city, beyond the little hilltop village of **Killylea,** lies the pretty village of **Tynan**. In the middle of the main street stands a fine sculptured stone cross, over 13 feet high and dating from the 10th century. There are other ancient crosses in the nearby extensive demesne of Tynan Abbey which was recently burnt down by the IRA. East of Armagh city is Clare Glen, one of the prettiest in the country. A fine trout stream winds under old bridges and past a now silent mill. There are lovely *walks* around here and it is around such country lanes as these that you might come across a game which the Armagh people share with Cork called 'bullets' or road bowls. It is played with balls made of iron which are thrown along a winding road, the aim is to cover several miles in the fewest shots; little children are set up further along the road to warn motorists of the possible danger they might be driving into. Flax milling has ceased but milling still thrives in nearby **Tandragee,** a pretty well kept town with brightly painted houses, it is a considerable age and was founded by the O'Hanlons in 332 AD. The present castle, on the site of a much earlier one is barely more than a century old and now houses the factory of Ulster's foremost crisp, Tayto! Excellent *fishing* is available on the nearby Cusger River.

To the north east is the industrial part of County Armagh with the old linen towns of **Portadown** and **Lurgan** and the new town of **Craigavon.**

Though lacking in beauty they do benefit from their proximity to Lough Neagh and the River Bann with man-made lakes, *boating ponds* and a *dry ski slope*. Near **Portadown** a network of little roads runs through a charming district covered with fruit trees and bushes, and in May and June the gentle little hills are a mass of pink and white apple and damson flowers. You might time your visit to coincide with the Apple Blossom Festival. The orchards here were a part of the old Irish agricultural economy long before the English settlers came here, though many of the fruit farmers are descended from Kent and Somerset families, well used to growing fruit. The tear drop drumlin country is intersected by trout filled lakes and streams, high hedges and twisting lanes. In **Richill**, the fine Jacobean manor with its curling Dutch gables is worth visiting.

The village of **Kilmore** has probably the oldest 'church' in Ireland, in the heart of the present little parish church stands the lower half of a round tower dating from the first half of the 3rd century. Right in the centre of this fertile district is the quaint village of **Loughgall,** which is strung out along the main road, many of its little houses painted in the soft shades of blossom and their gardens bursting with colour. The little museum contains mementos commemorating the founding of the Orange Order here in 1795.

**Eating:** THE BRAMLEY APPLE RESTAURANT, Main Street, Tel: Loughgall 318. Not far away is Ardress House, a 17th century manor much altered and now Georgian in character. Its elegant drawing room has one of the most beautiful decorative plasterwork ceilings in Ireland. The work is Adam in style and both the ceiling and the mural medallions have been carefully restored and sympathetically painted. Set in lovely parkland it is now in the care of the National Trust. There is a farmyard display, picnic area, woodland walks and a small formal garden. Open April to the end of September every day except Friday, 2pm-6pm. Nearby at **Derryscollop** there is a lovely little copse on a hill. Here among the tall silver-trunked beeches, you can enjoy the view and thank the lady who, on her death, left it to the public to enjoy.

**Coney Island,** one of the few islands in Lough Neagh, is also a National Trust property. It lies to the north not far from the mouth of the Blackwater and can be reached by boat from **Maghery.** Apart from the excellent *fishing,* this thickly wooded, reedy island is also worth visiting for its huge and varied *bird-life.* St Patrick used the island as a retreat and there is also a rather overgrown Holy Well. Be prepared for the Lough Neagh flies which are food for the pollen, a fish unique to these waters and absolutely delicious fried in butter. The swarms of flies settle everywhere – in your car, your cup of tea, your mouth!

Returning southwards along the Blackwater, which forms the county boundary is The Argory, one of the National Trust's most recent acquisition. Standing in woodland and parkland this rather lovely early 19th century Neo-Classical house overlooks the river. It is of particular interest in that its contents have remained almost completely undisturbed since the turn of the century. It is much more of a home than a museum, full of treasures gathered over the years from all corners of the earth. The large cabinet organ at the top of the grand cantilevered staircase is quite unique. So is the acetylene gas plant which still lights the house; every room has its own ingenious old light-fittings. Outside you can wander through the stable buildings, semi-formal gardens and woodland and river walks. Open April to end of September every day 2pm-6pm, except Friday.

Not far upstream is the village of **Charlemont,** once an important parliamentary borough, with an 18th century cut stone bridge, and ruins of a 17th century fort built by Lord Mountjoy. Still further upstream are **Benburb** and **Blackwatertown;** between these two towns has been an extensive river park created where there is *fishing* and *watersports* for all.

## PLACES TO STAY IN COUNTY ARMAGH

**Armagh**
Mrs Murphy's guesthouse, 63 Drumcairn Rd, Tel: Armagh 525074
Anne Hayes, Hamiltonsbawn Rd, Tel: Armagh 526156
**Bessbrook**
Mrs E Alderdice, 'Tara' Mullaglass, Tel: Bessbrook 570
**Markethill**
Gosford House Hotel, grade B, Tel: 67678. Fairly expensive.
**Killylea**
Mrs D McLoughlin, 'Heimat', Polnagh, Tel: Caledon 661
**Binge Places**
Mr and Mrs Taggart, Kilcreevy, Lislea, Tel: 523226, near Armagh.

# County Down

Sea bordered and close to the larger island, this county has excited the envy and lust of many waves of invaders or plunderers. The most ferocious of these were the Vikings who swept down from the north and despoiled the rich centres of learning that existed on the east coast in the 9th century. Earlier, in the 5th and 6th centuries, the remarkable missionary Patrick spread the word and raised disciples to spread the Christian tradition. There are many places associated with him: Raholp where he landed after his years in France preparing himself, and Saul, where he celebrated thanksgiving for his return. It's a county rich in monuments of antiquity, these have all been surveyed, so it's unique in Ireland for having a full record of its past (Archaeological Survey of Co. Down HMSO 1966). Now it remains, like Antrim, a cornerstone of Ulster, loyal, flying the 'red hand' standard, although, in the mountain areas where there's a different tradition it's a different story.

**The Ards Peninsula,** which runs along the length of the east shore of

# DOWN

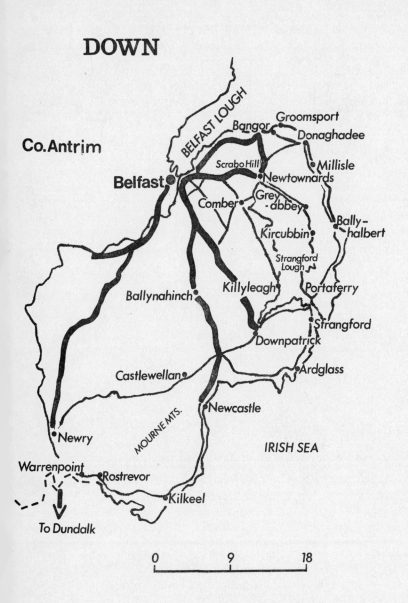

Co. Antrim

BELFAST LOUGH

Bangor
Groomsport
Donaghadee
Scrabo Hill
Millisle
Belfast
Newtownards
Comber
Grey-abbey
Kircubbin
Bally-halbert
Strangford Lough
Ballynahinch
Killyleagh
Portaferry
Strangford
Downpatrick
Castlewellan
Ardglass
Newcastle
MOURNE MTS.
IRISH SEA
Newry
Warrenpoint
Rostrevor
Kilkeel
To Dundalk

0    9    18

Strangford Lough takes its name from the rocky coast (ard-rock). This finger of land curving round the Down mainland contains some of the most charming villages and towns created by the Scottish and English settlers. In between these towns are earlier sites: raths, Holy Wells, and monastic ruins. You are never more than three or four miles from the sea so this is the place for *sea fishing* and *sailing* (from **Donaghadee, Bangor,** and **Groomsport**). Prepare yourself for an exhilarating climate, unusual in Ireland for it is the sunniest, driest and breeziest bit of Ulster. A tour of the Ards is a good way to take in all the beauties. Start from **Bangor,** a seaside resort popular with the Edwardians as you will see from the architecture, but also boasting a rich medieval history. It was a famous centre of learning in the 6th and 7th centuries, and from here Columbanus and Gall set off to found Luxeuil in Burgundy and St.Gall in Switzerland. The plundering Norsemen in the 9th century ravaged the town; all that remains from these times is the tower of the Abbey Church in Bangor opposite the railway station.

**Eating:** Good places for snacks: THE HUMBLE PIE, and B J's. On the oceanside, the HELMSMAN, High Street and the MIDNIGHT LOUNGE.

'Six miles from Bangor to Donaghadee' goes the refrain to an old song; **Donaghadee,** a pretty seaside town with a free harbour and a good number of pubs used to be linked with Portpatrick in Scotland by a regular sailing boat. The poet John Keats stayed at Grace Neill's Bar (on the High Street) and so did Peter the Great of Russia: it is still one of the most attractive pubs in the town. You can go out *stream fishing* in the summer, or at weekends go out to the Copeland Islands, long low islands covered with spring turf and rabbit's trails, enchanting in spring and summer. Enquire for the Simpsons at the harbour for both sorts of expedition.

**Eating:** there are good snackeries tucked away behind the sea front: BOW BELLS in Bow Street, is probably the best. Real homemade icecream is made at the CABIN in New Street.

Following the coast road through **Millisle** down to **Ballyhalbert** you will pass some golden strands, the pebbly beaches are further on at Cloghy Bay. Perhaps you will notice the Scottish influence: snug, unpretentious houses and carefully worked fields. Many of the road names are intriguing, they are taken from the townlands (early units of land holding). The most picturesque town on the Ards is **Portaferry,** situated where the tip of the Ards forms a narrow straits with the mainland of Down. On the water front at one of the Inns you can take your drink out side and look across to Strangford village, in the summer you might be lucky and coincide with some open air music in the evenings.

**Eating:** places to have a meal are the SCOTSMAN (Shore Road Tel: P'Ferry 326) and the PORTAFERRY HOTEL, the Strand (Tel: P'ferry 231).

A ferry runs between **Portaferry** and **Strangford** and the journey (20 mins long) is well worth it for the views up Strangford lough (cost about 80p, 20p per additional passenger). You might be so won over by the charms of this part of the peninsula that artists among you would be interested by the Portaferry School of Landscape Painting open during July (enquiries should be made at the Market House, Portaferry).

On the road which hugs the Strangford Shore you can enjoy the beauty of this nearly land locked water. Scattered with small islands this area is of special interest to naturalists, seven of these islands are operated by the Wildlife Conservation Trust. As you might be able to tell, the name comes from those Viking invaders of Ireland (Strang fiord: Strong ford, from the dangerous tides at the mouth of the Lough) and here in the sheltered bays amidst some of the loveliest scenery the monks built their abbeys. At **Greyabbey**(An Mhainistir Lieath: the grey monastery) you can visit one of the most complete Cistercian abbeys in Ireland. Built in the 12th century by the wife of John de Courcey, Affreca, it represents the new monastic orders introduced to counteract Irish traditions (open April-September 10am-6pm, October-March 10am-4pm). The village has a good supply of antique shops.

**Eating:** you can get a meal or pub grub at the NEW ABBEY ARMS and WILD FOWLER RESTAURANT Tel: G'abbey 260

On the way to **Newtownards,** following the lough, the demesne wall of Mount Stewart, the home of the Londonderry family appears. The house and grounds are now in the hands of the National Trust. Edith, Lady Londonderry (5th Marchioness) one of the foremost political hostesses of her generation, created the gardens over fifty years ago for her children (there are some lovely topiary animals) – and if you ever come across her children's story *The Magic Inkpot*, you will recognise some of the place names from round here. Also in the grounds is the Temple of the Winds inspired by the building in Athens and built in 1780 for picnicking in style. From arcadian pursuits of the 18th century to craft wares of the 20th century, in the Mount Stewart school house you can buy patchworks and hand made cottage furniture.

To complete the tour of the Ards a quick visit to **Newtownards** will be rewarding for the medieval enthusiast as Movilla Abbey built by St.Finian in the 13th century is worth seeing, though it does require a detour to the town's outskirts (road to Millisle) Newtownards has a 17th century market cross and a fine town hall. You won't fail to notice the prominent tower on Scrabo Hill, a memorial to one of the Londonderry Stewarts and a good look out point.

**MID-DOWN** is drumlin country until you reach Slieve Croob, round **Ballynahinch.** Harris, who describes Down in the 18th century, has this rather droll phrase for the country side contours, they are like 'eggs set in salt', cap this with C S Lewis' recipe for his native county – 'earth covered potatoes'!

To explore Mid-Down you might start from **Comber,** a pleasant town with a prominent statue of Robert Gillespie, one of the Ulster's military heroes.

**Eating:** BLADES in High Street, Tel: Comber 877229. Near here, on the road to **Killyleagh** you can visit Nendrum. This is one of the most romantic of the monastic sites founded by a pupil of St. Patrick on **Mahee Island**, it was lost and found again, another missing link in

Strangford's inheritance of abbeys and monasteries. BALLOO HOUSE (Tel: Killinchy 54120) is good for a drink and a bite to eat.

If you go on down this side of **Strangford,** you will cross the River Quoile and arrive at **Downpatrick,** an attractive Georgian town. It is sited at the natural meeting point of several river valleys and so has been occupied for a long time. It has both suffered and benefited from the different waves of settlers and invaders: the missionaries, the monks, the Norsemen, the Normans, the Scots (Army of Edward Bruce). St. Patrick's gravestone may be seen in the Church of Ireland cathedral graveyard (a large bit of granite). Religion and politics are well illustrated by the different episodes of **Downpatrick** history. The Norman John de Courcey established himself here at this centre of St. Patrick's veneration by promoting the Irish saint. He donated some relics of saints Patrick, Columba and Brigid to his Foundation; he also gave the town its name, adding Patrick to Dundalethglas as it was previously called. To the east of the town, some two miles outside, are the Struell Wells. There must have been worshippers at this pagan shrine long before the arrival of St.Patrick, and the waters were long known for their curative properties.

Going towards **Strangford village** you will pass by Castleward. This house's character and aspect is worth a detour. It is a husband and wife compromise expressed in architecture. Built in the 1760's by Bernard Ward, afterwards Lord Bangor, and his wife, Lady Anne, a great heiress, it has a Neo-Classical facade, and a Gothic castellated garden front. The interior echoes this curious divergence of taste: the reception rooms are gracefully classical, following his Lordship, and the library and her Ladyship's rooms are elaborately Neo-Gothic in the Strawberry Hill manner. The property is in the hands of the National Trust, and there are a number of other attractions: a Palladian style temple which overlooks an early 18th century lake, an early tower house and lovely grounds. A goldsmith's studio provides souvenirs for those who are looking for more valuable momentoes than snapshots. The house is open every day in the afternoon 2pm-6pm from April to September. The grounds are open from dawn to dusk all year.

**Strangford village** (which can be reached by a coastal footpath) is a few miles on. This is where you can catch the ferry across to the Ards village of **Portaferry.** No less than five small castles are within reach of Strangford testifying to its strategic importance: Strangford Castle, Old Castle Ward, Audley's Castle, Walshetown and Kilclief and the nicest way to see them is from the Lough, either when the ferry is in midstream or from another boat. More castles can be seen round the fishing village of **Ardglass,** an important port in medieval times and now a centre for herring fishing fleets. There are some very good strands notably Tyrella on the Dundrum Bay.

**SOUTH DOWN** is a mainly mountainous area, and extends across to the south Armagh border, girded to the south and east by a beautiful coastline. The rather splendid fjord-like inlet, Carlingford Lough (a name of Scandinavian origin) cuts through the middle of the upland area. It follows a faultline forming the Gap of the North and this has been the main north-south thoroughfare since ancient times. In this trough, astride the ancient road from **Armagh** to **Tara**, lies the town of **Newry**. Apart from the sheer natural beauty of the whole Newry and Mourne district, there is much to offer the tourist, in particular those with outdoor interests, however varied. There is *walking, rock-climbing, angling, bathing, sailing, camping, ponytrekking, birdwatching, golf* – or maybe just lying on the beach or going for a scenic drive.

Within a 25 mile circle, some 48 peaks rise in a purple mass of rounded summits. The Mourne Mountains do not form a harsh, wild, rugged scenery (Bignian and Bearnagh are the only two with craggy tops) but one that suggest peace and solitude. Few roads cross the Mournes, for this is a *walker's* paradise, endless paths up and down through bracken and heather, peaceful unspoilt lakes and tumbling streams, the wild flowers of moor and heath, birds and birdsong all to be enjoyed under an everchanging sky.

Of the many walks possible, perhaps the loveliest are up to Silent Valley and to Slieve Lough Shanagh from above **Kilkeel,** to the glittering crystals of Diamond Rocks, to the summits above Spelga Dam, and of course Slieve Donard itself where, on a fine clear day, one may see across the water to England. For the benefit of the more hearty, it is worth mentioning the 20 mile boundary wall that links the main peaks. Quite a constructional feat in itself, it is followed by thousands on the Annual Mourne Walk.

Perhaps the best place to start from, when visiting the area, is **Newcastle,** one of Ulster's most attractive and lively seaside resorts, though its popularity has sadly destroyed some of its charm. It has a lovely long sandy beach for *bathing,* and behind it there is the Royal County Down Golf Course, a fine championship course. The Slieve Donard Hotel offers first class accommodation.
**Eating:** both BROOK COTTAGE and ENNISKEEN HOTEL have good restaurants, and there are lots of snack bars.

Near **Newcastle** lies the magnificent forest park of Tollymore, Ulster's first and favourite. It has many lovely, though rather well-trodden, forest trails and *nature walks* on the lower wooded slopes and along the River Shimna. There is *fishing* too, and *pony trekking.* There is an excellent *camp site* plus shop and museum.

Before following the coast round, it is well worth heading northwards to visit one or two places. **Castlewellan,** which appeared on the map as recently as the end of last century, has two large market places, one oval one square. This neatly laidout town is surrounded by well-wooded demesnes, one of which is now a forest park. Renowned for its arboretum and lovely gardens, there are also *forest, trails, pony trekking,* and *fishing.*
**Eating:** try the PHEASANT INN, in Upper Square, Castlewellan for salads and hamburgers.

Due north of **Newcastle,** about two miles away, is Murlough Nature Reserve, where one can explore the sand dunes. Exposed to the wind, the dunes are a wonderfully peaceful haven for waders, waterbirds and shore-birds. Sweet-smelling wild flowers grow unhindered and in the summer delicious wild strawberries lie woven over the sand-dunes. **Dundrum** is not far beyond. On the outskirts of this once flourishing fishing port, now more of a coal quay, are the extensive ruins of a Norman Mote and Bailey Castle, enclosing a magnificent partly-ruined stone castle with circular keep of the tower type. Staircases, parapets, towers and a massive gate-house make this an ideal picnic spot and adventure playground for children.

On the way back to **Newcastle,** keeping half an eye on the road, one can appreciate again the very fine view of the Mournes, with Slieve Donard rising majestically up as the centrepiece. Heading south out of Newcastle, past the old disused swimming pool and the now quiet harbour, one comes to the National Trust Mourne Coastal Path, which runs for four miles from the very popular Bloody Bridge picnic site. A network of by-roads run deep into the foothills behind **Annalong** and **Kilkeel.** Here is the unspoilt, undisturbed Mourne way of life, the thatched cottages, the men and women at work in their pocket-handkerchief fields; the elderly, pipe or knitting in hand, passing the time of day; the children playing. It is not hard to imagine it all in the days before roads were made. Then, the prosperous economy was based on granite quarries and fishing, and the intensively farmed land was enriched from the wrack beds of Killowen, and it has changed little since then.

Back again on the coast road, and round the corner lies the little village of **Annalong,** set against a backcloth of mountains. The little old harbour still flourishes, boats are being repainted, nets repaired, everyone is doing something, no-one hurries. Beach after beach pass below on the left, and one is almost tempted to venture inland again, down some beckoning lane, banked high with fuchsia and honeysuckle. **Kilkeel** is a surprisingly busy prosperous town, home of the coast's main fishing fleet. It is on the site of an ancient rath, and the ruins of a 14th century church still stand in the square. It has a sandy beach, *golf course,* good *bathing* and *angling.* Just to the northeast of the town is a fine dolmen, whose capstone measures over 10 feet by 8 feet. Then the road climbs up and across the Spelga Pass towards **Hilltown.** It has many vantage points for viewing both the mountains and the coastal scenery.

Continuing on round the coast, the land levels out quite a bit. Down to the left lies **Cranfield,** a long strand, very popular for *bathing* and *caravaning.* Already on the horizon one can see Greencastle, the ancient capital of the Kingdom of Mourne, strategically sited at the entrance of Carlingford Lough. The tall, rectangular, turreted keep and some of the out works are all that remain of this impressive 13th century stronghold. From the topmost turret of the castle one can enjoy splendid views across the Lough to the Republic.

The road swings round still more, ever twisting and turning as it makes its way along the indented coast. The houses are larger, their gardens bigger and better kept. Clearly this was, and still is, a prosperous area. Sheltered by high hills and set against a purple and green backcloth of pine forests, the town of **Rostrevor** enjoys a mild and sunny climate, hence the profusion of brightly coloured flowers in the gardens, many of them of Mediterranean origin. It has a lovely long seafront, *sailing clubs,* many hotels and guest houses, superb views across the Lough, but sadly no sandy beach. There is *pony trekking* and *nature walks* in the forest park above the town. A mountain road climbs up northwards, passing the little old church of Kilbrones with its two ancient crosses, and levelling out to follow along the valley of the Bann to emerge at **Hilltown.** The many tumbling little streams, stoney paths and patches of woodland make for excellent picnic sites en route.

Not far on from **Rostrevor** is **Warrenpoint,** – a very lively popular resort. It is more spacious in layout, well planned, with a very big square and a promenade over half a mile long – the town being bounded by the sea on two sides. Prior to the mid-18th century there was nothing there save a rabbit warren, hence its name. The small town museum has items of local historical interest. There is also *golf* and *tennis,* and a passenger ferry across the Lough to Cooley Peninsula. A little to the north, on a spur of rock jutting out into the estuary, lies the square battlemented tower of Narrow Water Castle. Built in the 17th century it is in fact on the site of a much earlier fortification. On the right hand side of the road, through the big gates, there is a well-equipped *caravan* site in the very extensive and rather lovely grounds of Narrow Water House.

From here the road improves dramatically and before long one is in **Newry,** an old and prosperous town sited where St.Patrick planted a yew at the head of the strand, hence its name. It certainly enjoys a strategic site astride both the Clanryne River and what is believed to be the oldest canal constructed in the British Isles. Having been a mercantile town for centuries, the street patterns are inextricably mixed up with the canals and waterways. Ships no longer use the canal, opened in 1741, instead it is stocked with fish. The long prosperity of this old town is clearly reflected in its large and imposing town houses and public buildings, though many are now rather delapidated. St.Patrick's parish church is possibly the earliest Protestant church in Ireland. The 19th century Cathedral of St. Colman boasts some beautiful stained glass windows. The town hall is impressively sited astride the Clanryne River that forms the county boundary. There is much Georgian architecture and shops with small-paned windows and slate-hung gables. Some of **Newry's** oldest houses are to be found in Market Street. Remnants of far earlier centuries are the monastery, the castle and the Cistercian Abbey. Two miles north of the town, near Crown bridge, there is a very fine motte and bailey, giving rise to a crown-shaped mound. And at **Donaghmore** three miles on, in the parish graveyard there is a fine 10th century carved cross on the site of an earlier monastery under which lies a soutterain. *Newry Golf Course* is just south of the town and the best view of Carlingford Lough and **Newry** is to be had from the Flagstaff, a navigational aid high above the County Armagh shore.

Heading from **Newry** back across to **Newcastle** one passes just north of the Mournes. The view across to the mountains is superb, ever-changing, the road is very twisty so it nice to stop and appreciate the many panoramic vantage points. There are two towns worth visiting. The first, **Hilltown,** is the more southerly, and is where the mountain roads from **Kilkeel** and **Rostrevor** converge. It is a small *angling* village located at a crossroads on top of a hill. The views are breath-taking. Just northeast of Cloughmore there is a huge dolmen. Underneath its three massive upright supports and 50 ton granite capstone, there is a double burial chamber. Nearby is the Goward Horned Cairn, made up of three distinct chambers, great fun to explore.

Easily spotted in the distance by its distinctive mushroom-shaped watertower, lies **Rathfriland** – a flourishing market town set high on a hill, commanding wide views of the Mournes and the surrounding countryside. This area from **Loughbrickland** to **Rathfriland** is called Bronte country because here lived the aunts, uncles and, when he was a boy, the father of the novelists Charlotte, Emily and Anne. Anne is supposed to have modelled Heathcliff in 'Wuthering Heights' on her wild great uncle Welsh who travelled to London with a big stick to silence the critics of his nieces' books! The family homestead is at Emdale.


## PLACES TO STAY IN NORTH DOWN AND THE ARDS

**Bangor**
The Winston Hotel, 19 Queen's Hotel Tel: Bangor 4575 (à la carte meals and cheap).
Tedworth Hotel, Lorelie, Princetown Rd, Tel: Bangor 63928 (good value).
Mrs J H Anderson, Beresford Hs, Queen's Parade, Tel: 2143, grade A.
Mr & Mrs Bruce Mulligan, Alpine Hs, 20 Ballyholme Rd, Tel: Bangor 65493
**Grade B**
Miss Annie Eccles, Chatsworth Hs, Princetown Terrace, Tel: Bangor 60248
Mrs Iris Mahaffy, Ennisclare Guesthouse, 9 Princetown Rd, Tel: Bangor 2858
**Ballyhalbert**
Mrs Jean Hall, Camelot, 156 Shore Road, Tel: Ballywalter 321
Mrs V McFerran, Glastry Hs, Tel: Kircubbin 555. Open during summer months.
**Ballywalter**
Evelyn McIvor, Greenlea, 48 Dunover Rd, Tel: Ballywalter 218
Mrs M Hall, Abbey Farm, 17 Ballywalter Rd, Tel: Greyabbey 207
**Ballynahinch**
Mary Rogan, 182 Dunmore Rd, Guiness Tel: B'nahinch 562670
Millbrook Hotel and White Horse Hotel are expensive.
**Comber**
Mrs E Muldoon, The Cottage, 377 Comber Rd, Dundonald, Tel: Comber 878189
**Donaghadee:**
Mount Royal Hotel, Millisle Road, Tel: Donaghadee 882661
Dunallan Hotel, Shore Street, Tel: Donaghadee 883569

**Downpatrick:**
Mrs M E Cotter, 10 Dundrum Rd, Clough, Tel: Seafords 639
Mrs Heather Cowdy, Nutgrove, Annadorn, Tel: Seafords 275
Mrs E M Russell, 27 Claragh Rd, Clough, Tel: Castlewellan 751 (bathroom ensuite).
**Killough:**
Mrs E G McMordie, Ballylig House, 20 Ballylig Rd, Tel: Ardglass 283
**Millisle:**
Dot McCullagh, Emsdale, 120 Mountstewart Rd, Carrowdore, Tel: 661208
**Newtownards:**
Mrs J Bartholomew, Burnside, 28 Ballyblack Rd, Tel: N't'ards 812920
Mrs W M Cochrane 'Ard Cuan', 3 Manse Rd, Tel: N't'ards 812302
Mrs J McKee, Beechill, Loughries, Tel: N't'ards 817526
**Portaferry:**
The Portaferry Hotel, Tel: Portaferry 231. A la carte meals.
J & E O'Hara, Quintin Castle, Tel: Portaferry 467
**Youth Hostel** at Ardglass Minerstown (22 beds).

**PLACES TO STAY IN SOUTH DOWN**

**Castlewellan**
K. Donnelly, 'White Gables', 46 Ballybannon Rd, Castlewellan, Tel: Castlewellan 346
**Hilltown**
John and Elizabeth Quinn, Downshire Arms Inn, Main St, Tel: Rathfriland 30235 grade B.
**Kilkeel**
G McCormick, 'Bridge House', Ballymartin, Tel: 62077
Mrs I Adair, Wyncrest, 30 Main Rd, Ballymartin, Tel: 63012
Mrs Maura Fitzpatrick, Iona Farm House, Tel: 62586
Mrs A Shannon, Murne Abbey, Tel: 62426
**Newcastle**
Dorothy Priestley, Arundel Guesthouse, grade A, 23 Bryansford Rd, Tel: 22232
Mrs Keogh, Savoy Guesthouse, grade B, 20 Downs Rd, Tel: 22513
Mrs J Hart, Ivybank Farm, grade A, Maghera, Tel: 22450
Mrs R Johnston, 23 Causeway Rd, Tel: 23784
Audley Annett, Mourne View Farmhouse, 15 Corrigs Rd, Tel: 22655
**Newry**
Mrs Kelly and Mrs Houldershaw, Mount View House, 12 Mullaghan's Rd.
Mrs O'Hare, The Glebe, 74 Dromintee Rd, Killeavy, Tel: Killeavy 231

# County Fermanagh

This is the lakeland of Ireland, bounded with limestone mountains in the southwest and scattered with drumlins which speckle the lakes with islands. A third of the county is under water: the great lake system of the Erne with its mass of lakelets in the upper Lough and the great boomerang of lower Lough Erne, plus the two Lough MacNeans in their mountain fastness, together with a share of Lough Melvin have discouraged incoming populations, so it's a place of longlasting traditions and folklore. But for those who have the amphibian urge this is a haven of *fishing, boating* and *waterskiing*. Those of a more reflective turn of mind will be fascinated by the pagan idols and christian hermitages.

**Enniskillen:** this town is built on a bridge of land between the Upper and Lower Lough Erne, and at first sight the medieval conglomeration of town and castle makes you think this is a very ancient town. Before the plantation, the Maguires held sway over this lakeland area and used this as a centre for their watery dominions, but its name comes from Cathleen, one of the women warriors of the Fomorian invaders. Her husband, Balor, was head of a pirate gang quartered on the rock island of **Tory,** off the Donegal coast. **Enniskillen** is famous for its home regiments, the air of the Inniskillings became the tune of the Star Spangled Banner so you might say that there is a certain fighting tradition down here. Visit the Castle Keep Museum which is housed in Maguire's Castle a 16th century building, not in the Water Gate which is the fairy tale building with towers and fluttering standards. The museum is one of the nicest and friendliest of local museums, it displays some of the strange head sculptures found in the locality, as well as soldiering relics. Open Monday-Friday 9.30am-4.30pm with a lunch break. Admission adults 20p, children 10p.

You should take a walk through the centre of **Enniskillen,** the winding main street takes on about six names during its course, and you might be impressed enough by the local souvenir, brooches made from fishing flies, to buy one of these unusual ornaments. It's a handy place to buy Belleek china, as the town which produces it sometimes runs low on stocks. **Enniskillen** enjoys an almost legendary status amongst *coarse anglers.* You should get your licence sorted out before you try for some of these champion weight bream, roach or pike. The coarse rod licence costs 50p for a season, or 25p for 15 days; the game road licence costs £2.25 for a season, or 25p for 15 days (includes coarse fishing rights). Youths under 16 need not trouble about licences unless they intend to fish for salmon or sea trout. You are also required to get a *fishing* permit (as well as a licence), ask in a hotel, or post office or at the Tourist Office, Town Hall Tel: Enniskillen (0365) 3110. Most of the fishing waters come under the Department of Agriculture though there are private fishing waters like Lower Lough MacNean, part of the Colebrook River and the Kesh River.

People not afflicted with fishing fever can find other sightseeing compensations. From **Enniskillen** you can visit two of the most attractive Georgian mansions in Ulster. Off the road from Belfast, is the

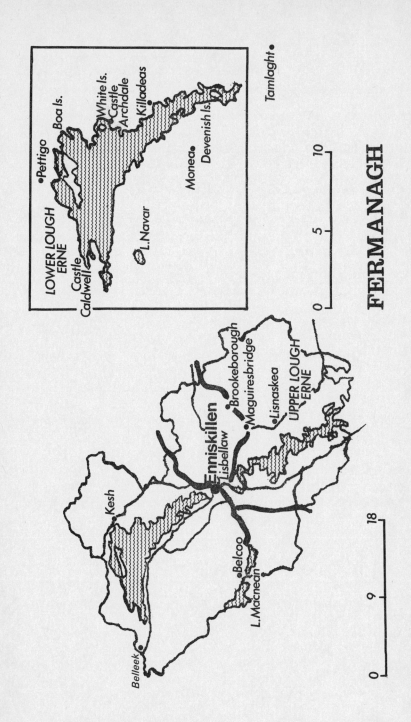

FERMANAGH

LOWER LOUGH ERNE

Castle Caldwell
Pettigo
Boa Is.
White Is.
Castle Archdale
Killadeas
Devenish Is.
Monea
L. Navar
Tamlaght

0    5    10

Kesh
Belleek
Enniskillen
Lisbellaw
Brookeborough
Maguiresbridge
Lisnaskea
Belcoo
L. Macnean
UPPER LOUGH ERNE

0    9    18

assured and beautiful Neo-Classical Castle Coole. Built between 1790-97, with an agreeably simple symmetry, the main block with colonnaded wings was designed by James Wyatt. Inside you can admire 18th century furniture still in the rooms for which it was made. The English plasterer Joseph Ross, who had worked for Adam at Syon and Harewood, made the long journey to supervise the ceilings. The building accounts of the house survive, and since the construction exceeded expected estimates, restraint may have been exercised in the decoration keeping it elegant but simple.

In the parkland surrounding the house there is a lake which has a very long established colony of greylag geese, the saying is that if they leave Castle Coole, so will the Lowry-Corry's, Earls of Belmore, whose seat it is. The National Trust maintain the house which is open April to end of September every day except Friday between 2pm-6pm. Admission 80p. Florence Court, home of the Coles, Earls of Enniskillen, is further away from the town they helped to fortify in the Plantation times. Built in the mid 18th century, it is about eight miles south west on the way to **Swanlinbar.** Sadly this house has suffered fire damage but there is still some fine plasterwork. Very little is known about the builder or architect, so if you want to test your art historical knowledge pay a visit. It is beautifully situated in woodland with views across to the Cuillagh Mountains. Open April to end of September 2pm-6pm. Admission 60p. **Eating:** because **Enniskillen** is in the centre of the development of the Fermanagh lakelands, there is a greater variety of eating places here than elsewhere. For snacks try BLAKE'S of The Hollow, 6 Church St (lunchtime) or HOUSEWIFE'S CHOICE on East Bridge St, which does self service up to 6pm. Pub meals are served at the CROW'S NEST in the High St or at the WATERGATE, Ann St and at MELVIN HOUSE RESTAURANT, in Townhall St (Tel: 22040) which stays open till 10pm (except Mondays) you can get more substantial meals.

**Lower Lough Erne** stretches in a broad arc with a pattern of 97 islands, with **Belleek** at one end and **Enniskillen** at the other. While you can hire your own cruiser from various depots on the lake, there are regular trips from the Round O landing stage *MV Endeavour* (details from Lough Erne Leisure Boating, Queen Elizabeth Road, Enniskillen Tel: Irvinestown 733 and Erne Tours, 24 Willoughby Place, Enniskillen, Tel: Enniskillen 22882.

Details of cruiser hire from bases other than Enniskillen are given below: this is a selection, there are many other companies you can take your choice from:
Aghniver Boat Company (Tel: Kesh 400)
Lakeland Marina, Kesh (Tel: Kesh 414)
Manor House Marine Killadeas (Tel: Irvinestown 561)
Erne Marine, Bellaneck (Tel: Florence Fourt 267)
Belleek Luxury Cruisers (Tel: Belleek 271)

There is nothing nicer than exploring islands, and Lough Erne's scattered islets hold many treasure. You should not miss **Devenish,** there is a public ferry which leaves from **Trory.** On this island St.Molaise founded a monastic community in the 6th or 7th century, probably a more than usually perilous venture in that remote water kingdom where paganism persisted long after Christian practices had taken hold in the more accessible parts. However there is a legend that refutes this, for the prophet Jeremiah is said to have his grave in the waters of Lough Erne. His daughter was married to the son of a High King of Ireland and she bought as her dowry the Stone of Destiny, the same stone that Fergus took to Scotland, the coronation stone of Scone. This story is almost as good as the variation of the Old Testament flood story recounted by the Annalists whereby Beith, Noah's grandson landed in Ireland with a whole arkful of beautiful women which accounts for the comeliness of all Irish women today! Let us return to **Devenish** with its complete round tower, and its elaborately decorated cornice. Another ruin incorporating some outstanding decoration is the 12th century Augustinian Abbey of St Mary. Think of St.Molaise resting from his labours listening spellbound to bird song, which, it was said, was the Holy Spirit communicating. The reverie lasted a hundred years and when he looked around after that interval this abbey had been built.

Another island with more tangible 'supernatural' asociations, is **White Island,** in Castle Archdale Bay north of Enniskillen, famous for its eerie statues. All eight of them are lined up in a row against the wall of a 12th century church. Like many of the sculptures found in Fermanagh and nearby districts there is a pagan quality about these objects. To what time in the distant past are they linked, what was their significance? These are questions which you may ask yourself as the archaeologists do. To me they convey the potency of the sacred/magic object, product of man's striving to harness the forces of the unknown. There are conflicting theories about just what the figures represent, possibly they are of Christian origin employing archaic (pre-Christian) styles, dating between 7th and 10th centuries.

**Boa Island,** joined to the mainland by a bridge at each end, is the largest of the islands. Its name comes from Badhba, war goddess of the Ulster Celts, and there is a tradition that this island remained centre of the Druidic cult long after Christianity had arrived in Ireland. In the old cemetery, Caldragh, at the west end of the island, there is a strange 'Janus' figure with a face on each side. Probably these figures (several have been found, in the Fermanagh area and in Cavan) had some ritual significance; a hollow in the figure's head may have held sacrificial blood. Look for an insignificant signpost on the main road and then climb over a gate, and through a field to this half-forgotton graveyard full of bluebells in spring. The country round the lough is full of the dips and hollows of the glacial drift drumlins. Because of flooding problems in former years you will notice few waterside town settlements although there are plenty of rushes, a very useful source of thatching material.

Leaving **Enniskillen** and following the loughside road you reach St Angelo airport on the Ballinamallard River, where U Boats used to land in the last war. Killadeas was another Druid site which the Culdees or missionary monks took over. The Manor House Hotel (Tel: Irvinestown 561) is a comfortable place to stop off. Near here at **Rossigh** you can *water ski*. During the summer you can arrange to ski Tuesday and

Thursday afternoons as well as weekends. Check at the hotel or in town (Enniskillen Town Hall, or Irvinestown Public Library). Just beyond the lough is Castle Archdale Forest and Country Park which has a very well equipped campsite plus a café and snack bar. From here you overlook **White Island** and **Davy's Island;** it's a good place for setting off by boat to some of the nature reserve islands (boats can be hired from the Manor House Marina). Perhaps the loveliest aspect of this part of the shore are the flowers that decorate the water's edge.

**Irvinestown** is one of the three largest towns in Fermanagh, you can get tourist information at the local library. It is also a good centre for explorations.

**Eating:** try the GOLDEN PHEASANT at Lisnarick (Tel: Irvinestown 205/516/405) for lunches or pub snacks. On the Enniskillen Road, MAHON'S HOUSE is well known for delicious meals. (Tel: Irvinestown 656/657) Another active little town is **Kesh,** centre for Lakeland Marina Ltd, (see under Enniskillen) there is also a *sailing school* should you not trust yourself on the water without tuition. As you might expect there is a boat building industry here; the traditional broad-beamed eel boats are still built for this is a centre, though very subsidiary to Lough Neagh, for eels. From **Kesh** you can make your way to the little island of **Lustybeg** which has holiday chalets for hire; another 'Janus' figure was discovered here. Following the curve of the shoreline, west you reach **Pettigo,** which is split between the North and the South. This was on the pilgrim's route to Lough Derg which lies in Donegal about four miles away.

Castle Caldwell is situated on a wooded peninsula jutting out into the lough, a romantic situation for a romantic and enterprising family. One of them had a barge on which music would be played for his pleasure, unfortunately a fiddler overbalanced on one of these occasions and was drowned. You can see his fiddle-shaped monument with its warning:

On firm land only exercise your skill
There you may play and safely drink your fill.

The Caldwells promoted the original porcelain industry at nearby **Belleek** using clay found on their estate which has a high feldspar content. Now their castle lies in ruins; visitors can wander in their gardens above the shore, admiring the view that made Arthur Young, in 1776, exclaim that it had 'shelter, prospect, wood and water here in perfection'. *Bird watchers* should note that you can use the special wildfowl hides to watch the plentiful ducks, geese and other birds; these grounds also have the largest breeding colony of black scooters in the British Isles.

Further up the River Erne, at **Belleek** you reach another border village. For *anglers* there's a jokey saying that you can hook a salmon in the Republic and land it in Northern Ireland. But it's more famous for its china ware, a distinctive lustreware which is produced as attractive ornaments rather than anything utilitarian. However sometimes you may find that the local shops have sold out, so keep you eyes open. On your way along the southern shore, the road hugs the waterline, for limestone cliffs loom overhead, rising to the height of 2984 feet at Magho.

To visit the forest go inland via **Churchill** or **Derrygonnelly.** From the Lough Navar Forest view point you can see the splendid sight of the lough spread out in front of you, with the hills of Donegal in the distance, and different ranges of Tyrone, Sligo and Leitrim hills in a grand panorama. You will have earned this breathtaking reward after struggling up a steep path starting at Leggs (Shore Road); if you have no intention of climbing take the scenic drive through the forest.

The plateau on the southern shore is covered with forest lands, and behind them are the Cuilcagh Mountains rising to the south. If you stick to the loughside you will pass the plantation Tully Castle, and further inland towards the south, a better preserved castle at **Monea,** both showing the Scottish style favoured by the settler from that country. For more spectacular sights nature has more on her side than architecture, so head towards the mountains in the west. You can take windy confusing roads cross-country from **Monea,** but for a simpler route take **Enniskillen** as starting point.

At **Belcoo** you reach a village lost in the mountains, situated on a narrow strip of land separating the two Lough MacNeans. In this place patterns to the St. Patrick's Well are held on Bilberry Sunday, the traditional date of the Celtic Lughnasa, or festival of fertility, a tradition which surely indicates the chain of pagan and Christian practices which have lingered on here longer than anywhere else.

If you go back by Lower Lough MacNean you will pass by the hanging rock, where you will see the limestone which has endowed this place with characteristic caverns. Marble Arch Cave is the best known among the caves in this area, they stretch in a sort of underground labyrinth through the Cuilcagh Mountains, and some remain to be explored. Do not go *pot-holing* by yourself, apart from anything else streams run into the caverns, you can see this for yourself on Marlbank loop road which takes you round from Florence Court to Lower Lough MacNean where the Sruh Croppa stream disappears into a crevice called the Cat's Hole. The wooded demesne of Florence Court is situated under the steep mountain of Benaughlin; this means in Gaelic peak of the horse and the white limestone showing through the scree at the foot of the eastern cliff did indeed portray the outline of a horse, though it is getting more and more difficult to distinguish. Along the southern shores of Lough Erne you can see one of the best examples of a plantation bawn at **Monea.**

Upper Lough Erne and the maze of waters from the Erne river system provide quite a challenge for the explorer; arm yourself with a good map. This area abridges the less water strewn area of East Fermanagh whose pretty towns you may pass through, some bear names of founder or planter families: **Brookeborough,** near the home of the Brooke family (prominent in Northern Irish affairs) and **Maguiresbridge** called after the reigning chieftains deposed by the planters. This area is supposed to be rich in folk tradition; you might meet someone with the secret of a cure, both for animal and human ailments. If you are interested in the distinctive sculptures you may have seen at the Enniskillen Museum or elsewhere, go and search out Tamlaght Bay near **Lisbellaw** where at Derrybrusk old church you may see some more strange carved heads on a wall. Throughout Fermanagh there is a curious mixture of pagan and Christian motifs in the monuments. Past the old market town of **Lisnaskea,** a town famous for its pubs, you might wet your throat and nibble something at WYVERN'S INN, Main St. At the nearby Aghalurcher churchyard you can see some of the gravestones carved with what seems to be a rather macabre Fermanagh funerary motif: the skull and cross bones, intimations of mortality, I suppose. At **Carrybridge** you can hire *cruisers* or *sailing dinghies* to explore the labyrinthine waters of Upper Lough Erne. See under Enniskillen for other places, and Bellaneck, on the west shore, offers some choice.

**Eating:** You will find at the pretty village of **Bellaneck** a folksy restaurant THE SHEELING Tel: Florence Court 232. Open in the evenings Friday and Saturday.

Islands you should take note of in these upper reaches, going from Enniskillen towards Galloon Bridge at the east end of the lake are: **Cleenish, Inishkeen, Belle Isle** and **Galloon.** There are 54 others and many are inhabited though on an increasingly part time basis. One sad story illustrates the difficulties attendant on an island living even in these easier days: a postman living on **Inishturk Island** was frozen to death when his boat was trapped in ice during the hard winter of 1961. **Cleenish Island** can be reached from **Bellaneck** by a bridge. There are some remarkable carved headstones in the graveyard. Even more interesting is the collection of carved slabs on Inishkeen, accessible by causeway from Killyhevlin. Belle Isle is an inhabited island, which claims to be the spot where the Annals of Ulster were complied in the 15th century by Cathal MacManus, Dean of Lough Erne. **Galloon Island** is large with another ancient graveyard where you may, if you persevere enough, discern the curious carvings on the 9/10th century cross shafts which depict a man hanging upside down; some think this might be Judas Iscariot or else St. Peter.

## PLACES TO STAY IN COUNTY FERMANAGH

**Belcoo**
P & N Catterall, Corralee Lodge, Tel: Belcoo 325, near good fishing.
**Belleek**
Mr & Mrs A E Neal, Shangra La House, Bolusty Beg, Roscor.
**Brookeborough**
For those seeking riding tuition:
Ashbrooke Equestrian School, grade A guesthouse, Tel: B'borough 242, very expensive.
**Castle Archdale** Camping
**Derrylin**
Mount View Hotel, Tel: Derrylin 226/7
**Enniskillen**
There are a number of hotels round about the town, but actually in the town is:
The Ford Lodge Hotel, Forthill St, Tel: Enniskillen 3275, quite good à la

carte meals.

For the rest see Binge Places:

Guesthouses, grade A include:

Mrs Beth Acheson, Erindale Guesthouse, Sligo Rd, Tel: Enniskillen 3279

Mr & Mrs Flood, Will-o-Brook Hs, 8 Willoughby Place, Tel: Enniskillen 22420

Mrs Mary Wilson, Willoughby Hs, Tel: Enniskillen 22882

Outside the town, on the southern shore:

Mrs E L Hassard, Bayview, Tully, Churchill, Tel: Derrygonnelly 250

Mrs E Hoy, Shore Hs, St Catherine's, Blaney, Tel: Derrygonnelly 219

On the northern side of the Lough:

Mrs M Gray, Oghill Farm Hs, Killadeas, Tel: Irvinestown 532

Mrs R M Armstrong, Drogan Farm, Killadeas, Tel: Irvinestown 554

Lilian McKibbin, Broadmeadows Hs, Ardtonagh, Bellaneck, Tel: Florence Ct 395

Mrs M McNulty, Crock Na Crieve, Macken, Tel: Florence Ct 336

**Kesh**

Erne Hotel, Tel: Kesh 275/423, A family type atmosphere.

Mrs K Flack, Ederney Guest Lodge, Ederney, Tel: Kesh 261

Mrs Pearl Graham, Manville Hs, Aughnablaney, Tel: Kesh 668

Mrs A Adams, Glendurragh Hs, Tel: Kesh 349

**Lisnaskea**

The Ortine, Tel: Lisnaskea 21091, more like an inn in the country, the only quite expensive hotel.

Mrs A Crawford, Inishrath Island, Upper Lough Erne, Tel: Lisnaskea 21512 (Telex 748056) Lots of facilities, besides being perfect for fishing, bird watching, expensive.

**Binge Places:**

Killyhevlin Hotel, Dublin Rd, Tel: Enniskillen 3481, numerous rooms ensuite with baths, à la carte meals.

Lakeland Hotel, Bellanaleck Quay, Tel: Florence Court 301, you can hire boats from here.

Manor House Hotel, Killadeas, Tel: Irvinestown 561, for a modest binge, a useful for hiring boats and waterskiing.

---

# County Londonderry

County Londonderry, home of the O'Cahans whose overlords were the O'Neills, was strongly influenced by the arrival of the London Companies who became owners of large areas of Londonderry through grants from James I. The flat plain of the Foyle in the east rises to the hills and mountains, until you reach the sheltered valley of the Bann River which feeds into Lough Neagh.

# LONDONDERRY

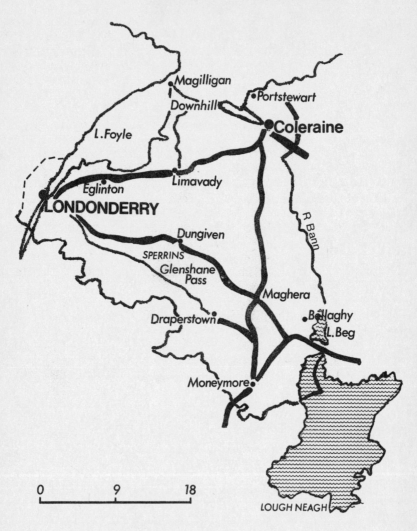

Magilligan

Downhill

Portstewart

L.Foyle

**Coleraine**

Limavady

Eglinton

**LONDONDERRY**

Dungiven

R. Bann

SPERRINS

Glenshane
Pass

Maghera

Draperstown

Ballaghy

L.Beg

Moneymore

0    9    18

LOUGH NEAGH

The road which takes you along the **Foyle Plain** by-passes Eglinton, the site of the airport where the Loganair flights arrive from Glasgow, travels through Ballykelly, where there are remains of the Fishmonger's Company buildings, and through **Limavady.** Limavady is well decorated with loyalist graffitti reminding you of 1690. It was the creation of one Thomas Phillipps who resisted the monopoly and greed of the London Companies in the 17th century. Thomas Connolly, speaker of the Irish House of Commons before the Act of Union, and builder of the beautiful Castletown House near Dublin, was the son of a Limavady blacksmith.

Precious gold representations of a masted boat, collars and a necklace fashioned in the Celtic La Tene style were found at **Brioghter** near the coastal marshes surrounding the estuary of the Roe River. They can be seen in the National Museum, Dublin. Further up the coast, underneath the forest covered Binevenagh Mountain is the triangle of **Magilligan.** Although there is a huge army post here, the strand is better known for its shells, the herbs that grow among the dunes, the birds and for the plagues of rabbits commemorated in a special Magilligan grace. This part of the world has connections with the old Irish music tradition. The last of the old harpers who attended the great Belfast rally in 1792, Denis Hempsey, or O'Hempsey, lived near Magilligan, whilst the musical tradition has found expression in the Londonderry Air.

From **Limavady** you can cut inland through the Roe Valley to **Dungiven** and pass through the Country Park which has caravan and picnic sites, and educative exhibitions at the visitor's centre. There is a cafe open between Easter and September 'THE DOGLEAP CAFE' Tel: Limavady 2074. However, if you want to take advantage of the superb coastline you should go on from **Magilligan** to **Downhill**, and climb up to the pretty resort of **Castlerock**. Try Temple Lounge, 17 Sea Road, for an atmospheric drink. A really worthwhile expedition can be made to the Palace of Downhill, a castle build by the famous Earl-Bishop, Frederick Augustus Hervey, one of the most interesting and enlightened Church of Ireland bishops. It is sited on windswept hill with wonderful views of the Inishowen hills and the Antrim headlands. He was extravagent and well travelled, the Bristol hotels you find all over the Continent take their name from him. He built up a great art collection with the episcopal revenues from his Derry bishopric which was in the 18th century, the second richest in Ireland.

He was a great advocate of toleration, contributing generously to Catholic and Presbyterian churches and their clergy. One of his amusements was party giving: if you go down to the Mussenden Temple, the story of the great race he organised between the Anglican and the Presbyterian ministers before a dinner party is recounted. There was some suspicion that the bishop was more a classicist than a Christian; his temple, on a cliff edge, is modelled on the Roman temple of Vespa, it certainly suggests a certain independent interpretation of religion. The ruins of the palace lie within the boundaries of a farm, but the temple and the little valley beside it are owned by the National Trust, and provide splendid picnic spots.

Eastwards along the coast is **Portstewart**, a seasoned little resort town which is overlooked by the castle-like convent. There are facilities for holiday makers, and its night life is more lively than neighbouring town **Coleraine**. Try the COOKERY NOOK, on the Promenade, Tel: 2905 for snacks and lunches; there are lots of fish and chip places along the harbour or the promenade. Pubs along the sea front are normally set up during the summer season for holiday makers, many of them caravaneers, so you will not miss out on Irish musical evenings. *Big game fishing* also takes off from there. Inland from Portstewart is **Coleraine** (Cuil Rathain: Fern Recess) which is supposed to have been founded by St. Patrick. Most of what you see was developed by the Irish Society. Whiskey from Coleraine was held in high repute though now the laurel has passed to Bushmills, further east.

**Eating:** You can get a meal at BEAU BRUMMEL, Tel: Coleraine 55145 which offers soups and snacks. Further out is LE PETIT JARDIN, 29 New Row, Tel: Portstewart 2373. Hamburger food is served at the BIG O, 11 New Row.

Considering that the New University of Ulster is just down the road the town is pretty quiet. However it is a useful place for connecting the bus and train services. Ulster Bus, Tel: Coleraine 3334. Northern Irish Railway Depot, Tel: Coleraine 2263.

The new University of Ulster is a centre for talks and tours during the summer, Tel: Coleraine 41450. The river Bann, 'fishy and fruitful' to take Spenser's phrase, runs through the town and was the scene of early habitation. At Mountsandel, on Coleraine's outskirts, Mesolithic flints indicate the presence of the earliest settlements in Ireland. If you are in the British Museum in London you will see some of those Bannside antiquities, the most spectacular of which is a huge hoard of Roman coins, evidently seized by Irish pirates, and now returned to England at long last.

You can follow the river through its valley, farmed by the industrious descendants of Scots and English who were tenants of the London Companies. The countryside is very pretty in a cultivated way; at **Aghadowey** you can have a pleasant meal in this quiet countryside at the BROWN TROUT INN, Tel: Mullahmore 209. Before the Bann reaches Lough Neagh it broadens out into Lough Beg with its Church Island, one result of the Earl Bishop Hervey's building ventures. At **Bellaghy** you can see one of the finest bawns or fortified farmhouses in Ulster built for the London Vintner's Company. Try the lovely MANOR HOUSE RESTAURANT for a meal or snack, Tel: Bellaghy 486. At **Magherafelt,** planned by the London Salter's Company near Lough Neagh, you can get the best ice cream in Northern Ireland at AGNEW'S, and a good steak at ARCHER'S RESTAURANT. **Moneymore** further south, is a sister town to **Draperstown**, being developed by the same London Company of Drapers.

A mile outside **Moneymore** is the most attractive of planter residences, **Springhill**, built in the late 17th century with its outbuildings in Dutch style. It is a proper country gentleman's house with soft shadowed interiors, a lovely library and portraits, including one with a following gaze. You can almost imagine you are a guest of the house when you go

there. There is a small costume museum, and other implements are on
show in the outbuildings. The grounds are beautiful, the yew thicket is
said to be a vestige of the ancient forest of Glenankeyne (the neighbouring hamlet of Moneymore means 'the great shrubbery' in Irish) and here
is a herb garden, essential for any household in the 17th and 18th centuries. Springhill is open April to September, every day except Friday,
2pm-6pm. Admission 60p.

**Maghera**, the mountain heartland of the county, is a small busy town
at the foot of the Glenshane Pass, and quite differently laid out to any of
the aforementioned towns. It is said to be the meeting place of the
mountains and plains people rather like **Dungiven** on the other side of
the mountain. At the southeast end of the town there is an 11th century
old church with a lintel decorated with what is perhaps the oldest church
sculpture in Ireland.

Up on the moor, Sperrins sheep farming is practised and the government are planting forests. At the top of the pass between **Maghera**
and **Dungiven** there is an adventure forest. **Eating:** stop off at the
GLENSHANE INN for a pub snack. In **Dungiven**, DAN'S CAFE is a
regular stopping point for buses travelling from Donegal to Glasgow, so
you can be sure the tea will be strong.

Further south (on the Feeny road) you will find Banagher Glen which
has a nature reserve. North of the forest is an old church founded by a St.
Muriedach O'Heney who bequeathed to his descendants the power to be
lucky with the sand from his tomb. Perhaps the poet, Seamus Heaney,
makes occasional pilgrimages here!

On the road from **Dungiven** to **Derry** you pass the Learmount Forest
with its camping and caravanning facilities. Farther on is the Ness
Wood, and the River Burntollet runs through this country. At the bridge
one of the opening conflicts of the present troubles took place on the
occasion of a Civil Rights March, in 1969.

**Londonderry** (Doire: Oak grove) is a symbolic city situated on the
Foyle River. Before the beginning of the present troubles, it was probably
known for the pretty tune the 'Londonderry Air', but now it is known as
one of Northern Ireland's trouble spots. The island of Derry was handed
over by an O'Neill to St. Columbkille who built a monastery on the
oak-crowned hill. He wrote, homesick for this place,

Derry, mine own small oak grove,
Little cell, my home, my love.

St Columbkille never outgrew his love for the city; he would have
sympathised with the emigrant families who left Derry for America
during the 18th and 19th centuries, among them, the forebears of such
famous figures as Davy Crockett and President James K. Polk.

Since the 17th century when Derry aquired its prefix London because
of the position occupied by the London Livery Companies in the building
and development of the city, it has had the epithet, 'the maiden city'. In
the Siege of Londonderry, 1689, the stout Protestant defenders held the
city against James II's supporters, and its great walls were never breached. It survives cut off from its natural hinterland of Donegal; money

from the liberal British purse being poured in an attempt to shorten the memories of gerrymandering electoral boundaries.

For the adventurous a visit to the city is interesting. The old city is bounded by its walls, south of them is the Bogside, not a place for casual visits, and across the Craigavon Bridge is the Waterside. Because of the destruction in the wake of the troubles you can see layers of this old city peeling off; go up Shipquay Street, opposite the red-brick City Hall and you will notice some Georgian houses, some with mediaeval foundations, and at the top of the hill, on the Diamond, excavations are under way to try and uncover the early settlement, possibly the Columban foundation. You should try and visit the Church of Ireland Cathedral, an example of planter's Gothic. The cathedral has a number of exhibits illustrating the spirit of the 17th century siege. The chapter house is open to visitors from 9–3 pm. Outside the city walls is an interesting 18th century chapel called St. Columba's, also called Long Tower Church; it is built on the site of a 12th century monastery called Templemore. The saint is further commemorated in a boy's school of that name. Derry, as it is called by most people, although as you have probably guessed there are some political undercurrents to the form of name adopted, is still a terminal for railway and bus services and is useful for those moving east or west.

Lough Swilly bus company operates services to Donegal from Londonderry, the Ulsterbus depot is beside the Guildhall on Foyle St, Tel: 62261. In Waterside is the new railway station with services to Belfast via the coast and Antrim (connections to the airport). There is a boat train for those going to Larne or Liverpool, Tel: 42228.

**Eating:** Places to eat in this city include ALANA RESTAURANT, 59 Strand Rd, Tel: 62489, where you can get a good fry up; CITY CAFE on Shipquay St serves reliable food till 5pm. For a pint and pub grub try the GRAND CENTRAL, 27 Strand Rd. On the waterside the COFFEE POT, attached to Kelly's supermarket on Spencer Road is a handy place for snacks also 'THE IONA' on Spencer Road is good for a drink. Out on the **Limavady** road out of the city, in CAMPSIE is the WHITE HORSE INN, delicious snacks for north bound travellers, Tel: Campsie 860606. For those with better lined pockets THE EVERGLADES HOTEL on Prehen Road, Tel: Derry 46722 is the nearest thing to the international style you will find in Waterside. Price ranges upwards from £5.

Tourist information, 5 Guildhall St, Tel: Derry 65151, open Monday to Friday 9 am–5.15 pm. For the Derry/Foyle Area: Foyle Tourism Association, 18 Harberton Park, Londonderry. The Bord Fáilte can be found in Austin's Store, The Diamond, Tel: Derry 69501.

## PLACES TO STAY IN COUNTY LONDONDERRY

**Castledawson**
The Swinartons, Moyola Lodge, Tel: Castledawson 224
**Castlerock**
The Golf Hotel, Tel: Castlerock 204, (Modern)
Guesthouses:
Grade A, Mrs Jean Caulfield, Maritima, Main St, Tel: C'rock 388

Mrs Elizabeth Henderson, The Marine Inn, Main St, Tel: C'rock 456
**Coleraine**
Try the guest houses rather than the hotels. If you're there during academic holidays try New University of Ulster, Tel: Coleraine 4141, you can get a room for £4 or so, and it is out of the town.
Mrs G McCallion, 18 Lower Captain St, Tel: Coleraine 2259
Mrs J Stewart, Parkview, 23 Milburn Rd, Tel: Coleraine 2495
Mrd J G Kerr, Rockmount, Ballinrees, 241 Windyhill Rd, Macosquin, Tel: Coleraine 3183
Mrs Margaret Moore, Killeague Hs, Blackhill, Tel: Aghadowey 229
Mrs Sally Neely, Hillview Farm, 40 Gateside Rd, Tel: Coleraine 3992
Mrs M E Smyth, Knowehead Farm, 11 Loguestown Rd, Tel: Coleraine 4695
**Draperstown**
Mrs M B Kelly, Church View, 14 Cavanreagh Rd, Sixtowns, Tel: Draperstown 563
**Dungiven**
Mrs C Buchanan, Mount Prospect, Magheramore, Tel: Dungiven 41262
**Eglinton**
Florence Dinsmore, Carmoney Guest Hs, Tel: Eglinton 810276
Mrs Mary T Feeney, Brisland Hs, 25 Brisland Rd, Tel: Eglinton 810017
**Limavady**
Mrs M Q Currie, Greengables, 61 Church St, Tel: Limavady 2395
Mrs F Sloan, 128 Highlands Rd, Tartnakilly, Tel:Limavady2210. (In the country)
**Maghera**
Mrs P O'Loughlin, Glenburn Hs, Glen, Tel:Maghera 42203
**Magherafelt**
Mr L Donnelly, The Arches Restaurant, 27 Market St, Tel: Magherafelt 32641.
**Magilligan**
Mrs E Craig, Ballycarton Farm, Bellarena, Limavady, Tel: Bellarena (050 475) 216
**Moneymore**
Mrs Rosaleen Hunter, Rosewood, 18 Moneyhaw Rd, Tel: Moneymore 495
**Portstewart**
Sea Splash Hotel, Kincora Terrace, Tel: Portstewart 2688. (One of the more scenically sited)
K M Elgin, Bethesdae Guesthouse, 30 Station Rd, Tel: Portstewart 3347
R & I Bishop, The Links, 103 Strand Rd, Tel: Portstewart 2560
Lily M Hasson, 12 High Rd, Tel: Portstewart 3250
Mrs S E Lobb, Lisnarhin, 6 Victoria Terrace, Tel: Portstewart 3522
Mrs A M Linton, Riverside Farm, Drumslade.
**Londonderry City** International Dialling Code (0504)
There are three hotels:
Everglades Hotel, Prehen Rd, Tel: Derry 46722. Prestigious.
The White Horse Inn, 68 Clooney Rd, which is expanding but is expensive.
The Broomhill House Hotel, Limavady Rd, Tel: Derry 44854. More

moderately priced.
In the city:
Mrs McGinley, Florence Hs, Northland Rd, Tel; Derry 68093
In the country:
Mrs M McKean, Braehead Hs, Braehead Rd, on the way to Letterkenny,
Donegal, Tel: Derry 63195
**Youth hostels**
Learmount Castle, in the Sperrins on the way to Dungiven (50 beds).
Stradreagh, Murder Hole Road, Limavady (20 beds).

---

# County Tyrone

This is the heart of Ulster, the land called after Eoghan (Owen) one of the
sons of High King Niall of the Nine Hostages. It is the least populated of
the six counties, celebrated in many a poignant song by emigrant sons
(some of whom found great fame and fortune in America). A land of
hillside, moorland and good fishing, there is a much quoted tag about
'Tyrone among the bushes, where the Finn and Mourne run'. But the
plantation families have their traditions and big houses here, some of the
loveliest like Caledon are still occupied by their original families, whilst
the most unusual, Killymoon Castle, was saved from ruin by a farmer. It
is an undiscovered county without the romance of Donegal or the
reputation of the Antrim Coast, but it inspires pride and praise from its
native dwellers. Tyrone people are well known for their music and their
talent with language, both the spoken and written word – notice how
many authors come from this part of the world.

**Strabane** (An Srath Ban: The White Holm) is a border town and
almost twin with Lifford across the Foyle (the rivers Mourne and Finn
come together here). Strabane and its environs enjoy a notoriety in EEC
figures, for this area is an unemployment blackspot. However going
through it you are not struck by this sombre thought because it is a
bustling town with friendly people. It was the birthplace of John Dunlap,
one of the printer's of the American Declaration of Independence; you
should try to visit the 18th century printing shop in Main St called
Gray's owned by the National Trust (open April to end of September
except on Thursday and Sunday, 2-6pm) admission 30p. Another Strabane born notable whom I must mention is that curious wit Brian
O'Nolan, alias Flann O'Brien. Friendly pubs to visit include Felix
O'Neill's, Castle Place, and Sean Kelly's, Abercorn Square.

East of **Strabane** you pass into the Tyrone Hills which consist mainly
of the Sperrins range which you will have met in County Londonderry. It

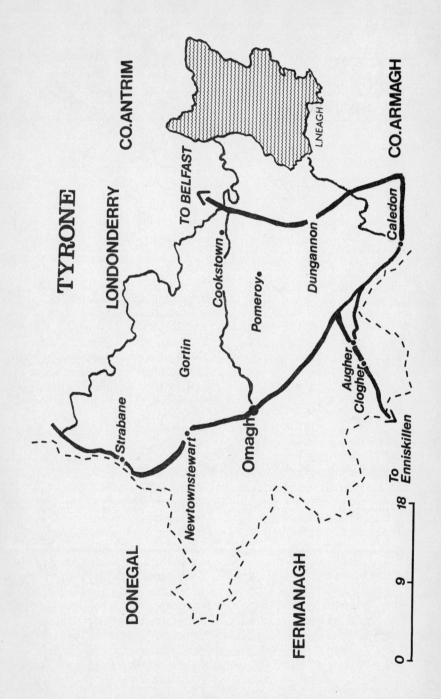

TYRONE

LONDONDERRY

CO.ANTRIM

CO.ARMAGH

DONEGAL

FERMANAGH

TO BELFAST

L.NEAGH

Caledon

Dungannon

Cookstown

Pomeroy

Gortin

Augher
Clogher

Strabane

Newtownstewart

Omagh

To
Enniskillen

0    9    18

305

is perfect walking country full of glens, and mountain passes to **Plumbridge** and beyond at **Gortin.** A couple of miles beyond Strabane on the Plumbridge road at **Dergalt** is the Wilson homestead, maintained by the National Trust. This comparatively humble dwelling, where President Woodrow Wilson's grandfather (among many other children) was reared before he set off for the States to become a newspaper editor, provides a preview for what is available on a grander scale at the Ulster American Folk Park.

The Folk Park is between **Newtownstewart** and **Omagh** and was developed by funds made available by the Mellon family. The idea is to illustrate the conditions of life the emigrants left in Ireland and those they encountered in their new land, by reconstructing the buildings they inhabited. The Irish village has a meeting house, central focus of the Ulster Presbyterian's worship, a forge, a school house and county shop. The New World buildings include log cabins, a clapboard farmhouse and various barns complete with implements. To complete your instruction you can go into the exhibition centre. While you are here look out for the Ulster tartan material, for near here a piece of tartan material was discovered in a bog, with the result that the so called 'Ulster tartan' is full of tanned browns. The Folk Park is open May-August 10.30am-6.30pm. Tea shop 10.30am-4.30pm. Admission adults 20p.

**Omagh,** capital of Tyrone, is separated from the other large town of the county, **Cookstown,** by the Black Bog (accounting for the turfcraft souvenirs you may find as an alternative to the more usual Irish linen hankies or crochet also displayed for your attention). Some people tell you that there is something French about this town, I have not noticed it myself, but it does have a reputation for liveliness. Brian Friel, playwright (his most recent being *Translations*) is a native. Omagh is a good spot for those seeking good *fishing;* those wanting to hear the musical talent should try and time their visit to coincide with the West Tyrone Feis in May.

**Eating:** try some of the outlying areas although you can find some style in Omagh itself in TOP OF THE TOWN RESTAURANT, John Street, (Tel: Omagh 2652). As usual there is no shortage of pubs. Before you get to Omagh on the road from **Newtownstewart** you will find the STRULE TAVERN at Mountjoy (Tel: Newtownstewart 61224) for good pub meals and à la carte. At **Gortin Glen Forest Park,** one of the most attractive and accessible of the increasing number of forests round here, you can have snacks between 1pm-6pm from June to August: Gortin village itself provides some pleasant venues: the GORT INN and PICADOR for pub grub.

**Omagh** is near other forest areas; Seskinore Forest, near Fintona, and Dromore forest, further west, which provides picnic sites, camping and hiking trails. Should you wish to strike across the moor country you can go by **Mountfield** which will take you by the Black Bog; any other little roads you encounter may take you past some of the many antiquities which testify to Bronze or earlier Stone Age inhabitants of this area. **Pomeroy,** high in the mountains, equidistant from **Cookstown** and **Dungannon** there are the remains of seven stone circles. More famous is the Beaghmore Stone Circles outside **Cookstown**, and near **Dunnamore;** these intricate alignments (on a northeast axis) constitute the remarkable architecture of the late Stone Age or early Bronze Age.

Arriving at **Cookstown** you will be impressed by the long wide main street: if you are of a cynical turn of mind you might think it was a good street for leading a charge against insurgents. **Cookstown** has a good nationalist tradition exemplified by the energetic Miss Bernadette Devlin, now McAliskey, as well as a Scottish-Protestant tradition. Bagpipes are made at **Cady,** a couple of miles south of the town.

There are two Nash buildings in the environs of this town: Killymoon Castle an embattlemented towered construction in contrast to the simple parish church at the end of the main street. The conspicuous Puginesque Catholic church, sited on a hill in the middle of town provides a good landmark. The town is situated in the middle of Northern Ireland, near the fertile heartland which traces its course beside the Bann in Londonderry and continues down by Lough Neagh.

**Eating:** You will probably eat Cookstown Bacon in your Ulster frys, the staple house dish of many a bed and breakfast. Other local products include Cookstown cheese. Try POOT'S RESTAURANT, James St. (Tel: Cookstown 62679) for lunches and snacks. For quick foods, CONLON'S CAFE, Burn Rd (Tel: Cookstown 63521) is open till 10pm. You can try your Ulster fry at TULLYLAGAN FILLING STATION, 135 Dungannon Rd, (Tel: 63671) open while the petrol station is, till 9pm.

Places to visit include the loughside Arboe High Cross, a 10th century monument with remarkable sculptured panels which are easily recognisable (many of the other High Crosses you may see are so weathered that you need to concentrate to see the theme properly). On the Lammas fair day many traditional musicians gather, Tyrone fiddle music is apparently in a league of its own. South of **Cookstown** is **Tullahogue** (pronounced Tullyhog) where the O'Neills, great chieftains of Tyrone were inaugurated; when Hugh O'Neill gave in to the British, the Lord Deputy Mountjoy had the throne smashed. At the foot of this hill, in what is now Loughry Agricultural College, is the mansion where Jonathan Swift stayed while writing Gulliver's Travels; the portraits of his two loves, Stella and Vanessa still hang in the house.

**Dungannon,** city on a hill, looks like your average planter town, but it was, in fact the centre for the great O'Neills until the Flight of the Earls deprived the Gaels of their native leaders. It is a quietly prosperous town with a long established textile industry specialising in Moygashel fabrics, and a more recent Tyrone crystal factory. In order to provide for good Protestant education, James I provided Royal Schools as well as charters for land; you may notice one of these with a statue of one of its most famous 'old boys', Major General John Nicholson, whose exploits in India inspired such legendary respect that there was even a sect called 'Nikkul Seyn'. Another Indian connection is the police station which looks a castle with projecting apertures for missile throwing. Apparently it was built according to plans for a fort in the Khyber Pass, because some clerk in Dublin got into a muddle.

**Eating:** if you are looking for liquid refreshment try Scotch St, where there are a number of pubs with food as well; for more regular snack food the Market Square with CASTLE INN and DUNOWEN INN provides a little more choice.

**Tyrone** has its River Blackwater, though it is not in the same league as the Irish Rhine or the other Blackwater which flows through Cork and Waterford. It flows through **Moy** with its 'Italian styled square' created by one of the Charlemonts, and **Caledon,** with its unspoiled Georgian look. Perhaps more intriguing to the traveller is the Clogher Valley which is border country with the Republic and so enjoys that anomalous status of being either frontier outpost or lost territory. This place evidently has a long history of habitation, the villages are ancient and there are other antiquities stretching back to the lost lakeland kingdoms.

Near **Augher,** in the Knockmany Forest, look for the Knockmany Chambered Cairn said to be the burial place of Queen Baine, Queen of Oriel, a 6th century kingdom whose centre was Clogher. The remarkable thing about this grave is its incised decoration, in patterns of concentric circles, zig-zags and other Boyne valley styles. This county besides being a fisherman's haunt is well forested. Old estates like Favour Royal and Fardross gave their names to these new public domains. Someone who recorded the end of an era was a governess called Miss Shaw whose photographs are incorporated in an anthology called 'Faces of the Past' by B M Walker. Another documentor on earlier ways was the prolific William Carleton (1794-1869) the Irish Dickens, who was born at **Springtown** (just outside Augher) who made no bones about the hardships of peasant life, paying tribute to some of the great spirits who existed unsung in rural isolation.

**Augher** and **Clogher** are within striking distance, though the latter has more weight being an ancient ecclesiastical centre giving its name to a diocese said to have been founded by St Patrick. In St MacCartan's Cathedral there is a curious stone 'the Clogh-oir' or gold stone, perhaps it was originally a gold covered idol standing in the porch. Behind this now nominal Christian centre is the Rathmore hill fort, whose presence records past kings of Oriel, and which has been supplying evidence about Iron Age Irishmen. That cryptic genius, Swift, is supposed to have married his Stella (Esther Johnson) near here, there is even an old lime in the old Deanery garden under which the ceremony is supposed to have taken place.

**Eating:** in **Clogher** you can get hamburger and chips in various combinations at CORRAL CAFE, in the Main St, open till 11.30pm. **Augher** has the QUEEN ANYA STEAK HOUSE, Main St, the COPPER INN, Moore St which is open till 7pm weekdays, and later at weekends. For the local speciality, Augher cheese try ROSAMUND'S COFFEE SHOPPE, Station House.

**Fivemiletown** takes its name from its distance from other villages like **Clogher, Brookeborough,** and **Tempo** (Irish measurement 2,240 yards rather than 1,760 yards). It has two quiet hotels which are very convenient for *anglers*, the traveller can eat at the FOURWAYS INN and the VALLEY HOTEL, both in Main St (Tel: Fivemiletown 260 and 505 respectively).

## PLACES TO STAY IN COUNTY TYRONE

**Aughnacloy**
Mrs Kathleen Hillen, 48 Moore St, Tel: Aughnacloy 266
**Cookstown**
Mrs A S Warnock, The Piper's Cave, 38 Cade Rd, Tel: Cookstown 63615, grade A meals available, near fishing.
Mrs W J Crooks, Otter Lodge, 26 Dungannon Rd, Tel: Cooktown 62317, grade B.
H J Quinn, Central Inn, 27 William St, Tel: Cookstown 62255
**Dungannon**
Mrs B McGahan, Greenacres Guesthouse, Drumaspil Rd, Killyman, Tel: Dungannon 23478, grade A.
In the country:
Miss M J Currie, Farm House, Cohannon, Tel: Dungannon 23156
Mrs M Mackin, Ardbrin, 114 Eglish Rd, Tel: Benburb 689
**Newtownstewart:**
Mrs M E Coulter, Strule Haven, 37 Moyle Rd, Tel: N't'stewart 61450
New County Inn, Main St, Tel: N't'stewart 425, meals available.
In the country:
Mrs Hilary Hamilton, Russ Hill Hs, Crosh, 29 Plumbridge Rd, Tel: N't'stewart 61404
**Omagh:**
Royal Arms Hotel, High St, Tel: Omagh 3262 (It has many credits and it has reasonably priced B&B.)
The Silverbirch Hotel, on the Gortin Rd, Tel: Omagh 2520 (à la carte meals).
Knock-Na Moe Castle Hotel, Tel: Omagh 3131/2 (is grander and more expensive).
In the country round about:
Frances Reid, Greenmount Lodge, Tel: Fintona 325, meals available, near the forest parks.
Mr & Mrs D Burns, Mountjoy Forest Farm, Tel: Omagh 2651
Mrs Armour McFarland, Hillcrest Farm, Lislap, Tel: Gortin 284
**Strabane:**
Near by:
Mrs E C Bruce, Glebe Hs, Tel: Bready 395
Mrs D McGinley, 21 Curley Hill Rd, B&B
Miare MacMenamin, 'Teach Mhuire', 89 Main St.
**Youth Hostels** Gortin (38 beds)

# THE COUNTIES OF IRELAND

Northern Ireland Boundary

# Suggested Reading on Ireland

## ARCHAEOLOGY, ARCHITECTURE AND ART

*Antiquities of the Irish Countryside* by S.P O'Riordain (Methuen)

*Churches and Abbeys of Ireland* by de Breffny and Mott (Thames and Hudson)

*Houses of Ireland* by de Breffny and Folliott (Thames and Hudson)

*Georgian Dublin* by Desmond Guinness (Batsford)

*Castles of Ireland* by de Breffny and Mott (Thames and Hudson)

*Irish Art and Architecture* by P. Harbison, H. Potterton and J. Sheehy (Thames and Hudson)

*Discovery of Ireland's Past* by J. Sheehy (Thames and Hudson)

*Boyne Valley Vision* by M. Brennan (Dolmen)

*Early Christian Irish Art* by Francoise Henry (Mercier)

*John Butler Yeats and the Irish Renaissance* by White (Dolmen)

*Early Irish Art* by Maire de Paor (Aspects of Ireland Series)


## GUIDES AND TOPOGRAPHICAL

*AA Guide Book of Ireland* (Hutchinson)

*Ireland Guide* (Bord Failte Eireann)

*Guide to the National Monuments of Ireland* by Peter Harbison (Gill and MacMillan)

*Ireland Observed* by M. Craig/Knight of Glin (Mercier Press)

*A Literary Map of Ireland* (Wolfhound)

311

## IRISH WALK GUIDES

*No. 1 South West* by Sean O'Súilleabháin

*No. 2 West* by Tony Whilde

*No. 3 North West* by Patrick Simon and Gerard Foley

*No. 5 East* by D. Herman, Jean Boidell, M. Casey, Eithne Kennedy

*No. 6 South East* by Martindale (Gill and MacMillan)

## MAPS

*Ireland Touring Map* (Bartholomew)

*Historical Map* (Bartholomew)

*Irish Family Names Map* (Johnson and Bacon)

*Ireland Map* by Bord Failte (Ordinance Survey)

## FOLKLORE, MUSIC, TRADITION AND GENEALOGY

*Irish Folk Ways* by E. Estyn Evans (Routledge)

*Proverbs and Sayings of Ireland* by S. Gaffney and S. Cashman (Wolfhound)

*The Irish Song Tradition* by Sean O'Boyle (Gilbert Dalton)

*Folktales of the Irish Countryside* by Danaher (Mercier)

*The Meaning of the Irish Coast* by James O'Connell (Blackstaff)

*Folktales of the Irish Coast* by P. O'Farrell (Mercier)

*Tales from the west of Ireland* by S. Henry (Mercier)

*The Tailor and Ansty* by E. Cross (Mercier)

*Beside the Fire* by Douglas Hyde (Irish Academic Press)

*The Stone of Truth and other Irish Folktales* by Douglas Hyde (Irish Academic Press)

*Irish Popular Superstitions* by William Wilde (Irish Academic Press)

*Short Story* by S. O'Faoláin (Mercier)

*The Northern Fiddler: Music and Musicians of Donegal and Tyrone* by Feldman, Allan and O'Doherty (Blackstaff)

*Love Songs of the Irish* by J.N. Healy (Mercier)

*Percy French and His Songs* by J.N. Healy (Mercier)

*A Book of Slang, Idiom and Wit* by Gerald O'Flaherty (O'Brien)

*Book of Irish Ballads* by D. O'Keeffe/J.N. Healy (Mercier)

## PHOTOGRAPHY

*The Aran Islands* by Leo Daly (Albertine Kennedy)

*Ireland's Eye: The photographs of Robert John Welch* by B.S. Turner and E. Estyn Evans (Blackstaff)

*Faces of Ireland* by B.M. Walker, A. O'Brien and S. McMahon (Appletree)

## HISTORY AND LITERARY HISTORY

*Concise History of Ireland* by M. and C. Cruise O'Brien (Thames and Hudson)

*States of Ireland* by Conor Cruise O'Brien

*The Green Flag* by Robert Kee (Sphere)

*Hidden Ireland* by Daniel Corkery (Gill and MacMillan)

*Town and County under the Georges* by Constancia Maxwell

*A Short History of Ireland* by M. Wallace (David and Charles)

## BIOGRAPHY AND MEMOIRS

*Granuaile: The Life and Times of Grace O'Malley* by Anne Chambers (Wolfhound)

*The Abbey, Ireland's National Theatre 1904-1979* by Hugh Hunt (Gill and McMillan)

*A Self Portrait of the Artist as a Man (Seán O'Casey through his letters)* by David Krause (Dolmen)

*Oliver St John Gogarty, A Biography* by J.S. Lyons (Blackwater Press)

*The Yeats Family and the Pollexfens of Sligo* by William Murphy (Dolmen)

*Letters from the Great Blasket* by E. N. Shúilleabhain (Mercier)

*Early Memories* by John Butler Yeats (Irish Academic Press)

*Synge and The Ireland of His Time* by W. B. Yeats (Irish Academic Press)

All *The Irish Heritage* Series (Eason)

## FICTION

All the plays by J.M. Synge

*Tales of The West of Ireland* by James Berry ed. Horgan, M. Gertrude (Dolmen)

*Elizabeth Bowen's Irish Stories* by Elizabeth Bowen (Poolbeg)

*The Writers, A Sense of Ireland* (ed. Carpenter and Fallon O'Brien)

*Knocknagow, Or the Homes of Tipperary* by C. Kickham (Mercier)

*The Absentee* by Maria Edgeworth

*Guests of the Nation* by Frank O'Connor (Poolbeg)

*Love Poems of the Irish* by S. Lucy (Mercier)

## COOKING AND CRAFTS

*Traditional Irish Recipes* (Appletree Press)

*Irish Country House Cooking* by Rosie Tinne (Gill and MacMillan)

Anything by Theodora Fitzgibbon (look out for her recipes in the Irish Times on Saturdays)

*Crafts of Ireland* by Louise O'Brien (Gilbert Dillon)

*How The Irish Speak English* by P. O'Farrell (Mercier)

# INDEX OF PLACES
## Oula Jones